AFRICA

AFRICA

FOURTH EDITION

EDITED BY

MARIA GROSZ-NGATÉ, JOHN H. HANSON,
PATRICK O'MEARA

Indiana University Press
Bloomington and Indianapolis

This book is a publication of
Indiana University Press
Office of Scholarly Publishing
Herman B Wells Library 350
1320 East 10th Street
Bloomington, Indiana 47405 USA

iupress.indiana.edu
Telephone   800-842-6796
Fax   812-855-7931

♾ The paper used in this publication meets the minimum requirements of the American National Standard for Information Sciences—Permanence of Paper for Printed Library Materials, ANSI Z39.48-1992.

Manufactured in the United States of America

Library of Congress Cataloging-in-Publication Data

Africa (2014)
   Africa / edited by Maria Grosz-Ngaté, John H. Hanson, Patrick O'Meara. — Fourth edition.
      pages cm
   "All chapters are freshly conceptualized and written for this fourth edition, many with an expanded scope or integration of topics from previously separate chapters. Previous editions had bibliographic essays, and in this edition we add a new chapter on the availability of electronic information on the internet in addition to published materials." —Preface.
   Includes bibliographical references and index.
   ISBN 978-0-253-01292-0 (pb : alk. paper) — ISBN 978-0-253-01302-6 (eb)   1. Africa.
I. Grosz-Ngaté, Maria Luise, editor of compilation, author.   II. Hanson, John H., [date] editor of compilation, author.   III. O'Meara, Patrick, editor of compilation.   IV. Title.
   DT3.A23 2014
   960—dc23

                                                                                    2013036589

1 2 3 4 5 19 18 17 16 15 14

Contents

Preface

More than fifteen years have passed since the third edition of *Africa* was published. Much has changed in Africa, in the continent's relations with the world, and in scholarship during the intervening years. Our vision for this edition is to focus on contemporary Africa in all its dynamism and diversity, to emphasize African agency and resourcefulness, and to stress social processes as well as institutions in revealing the ways that African women and men have constructed meaningful individual lives and engaged in collective activities at the local, national, and global levels. Our contributors, as in previous editions, convey ongoing events and discuss theoretical approaches within disciplines that affect understandings of the continent and the ways in which data are analyzed. All chapters are freshly conceptualized and written for this fourth edition, many with an expanded scope or integration of topics from previously separate chapters. Previous editions had bibliographic essays, and in this edition we add a new chapter on the availability of information on the internet in addition to published materials.

In its emphasis on contemporary Africa, this edition seeks to be comprehensive, but it does not attempt to be exhaustive either thematically or geographically. The chapters reflect their authors' interests and regional specializations as well as their lived experiences in different parts of the continent. In keeping with recent developments and student interest, several new chapters were added to cover African cities, film, health and illness, and human rights. We have only one explicitly historical chapter, contemplating the legacies of the past, including the era of European colonialism, for contemporary Africa; other chapters develop the specific historical contexts for their topics. Geography examines not only Africa's physical environments and their use but also how the idea of Africa as a place changed over time. The chapters on politics and development too reflect current scholarly trends to move from the "crisis" lens that dominated discussions for decades to a contemporary emphasis on "renewal" or, at least, tempered hope. The debate about the prospects for democracy continues, but our contributors seek to move beyond a preoccupation with the short-term and formal transitions to electoral democracy to examine the impact of the long-term and informal processes and institutions of democratic governance.

Intrinsic African processes of cultural production remain a focus, but our contributors also recognize the impact of global cultural flows into and out of the continent. These complex interconnections, for example, brought both Christianity and Islam to Africa and continue to influence their development, even as Africans make these religions their own. African musics express the values in and practices of specific local communities, and they also draw on outside influences and flow into the world: the constant circulation of influences has increased in the last decades. Related processes are in evidence in the visual arts. In the scholarship of African literature, more critical attention is being paid now to the politics of local and international publishing and distribution and to multiple readerships in and beyond Africa. Family, kinship, and community remain central to people's lives but are also highly fluid as women and men respond to material realities and engage forces of globalization. A discussion of livelihoods shows the complex strategies African women and men in rural and urban areas develop to make a living and the local, regional, and international networks they draw on.

In conceptualizing and publishing this fourth edition we have benefited from the suggestions and ideas of those who have adopted previous editions of *Africa* and used it in their classes throughout the world. Our Indiana University colleagues and graduate students also shared input from their teaching, and our undergraduates have pushed us to introduce *Africa* to a new generation of students.

The completion of a book of this scope requires not only the cooperation of the individual authors but also the support and assistance of others. We thank all who have contributed: our Indiana University Press editor, Dee Mortensen, and her assistant, Sarah Jacobi, for their patience and readiness to answer our numerous questions along the way; the University of Wisconsin Cartography Lab for producing the maps in the geography chapter; the Indiana University Art Museum and Lilly Library as well as colleagues here and elsewhere who have provided photographs for various chapters; former African Studies master's degree students Casey Bushman and Steffan Horowitz for researching additional photographs; and, finally, Edda Callahan for preparing the manuscript and for staying with us through numerous modifications.

THE EDITORS
Bloomington, IN
January 2013

AFRICA

Introduction

Africa has moved dynamically into the twenty-first century. It has more mobile phone users than the United States, for example, and cables placed along its Atlantic and Indian Ocean coasts recently have expanded broadband internet access. Africa still has some of the poorest countries in the world, but it also has six of the world's ten fastest-growing economies of the past decade. Africans increasingly are city dwellers: nearly 40 percent of Africans live in urban areas now, and projections suggest that figure will increase to 50 percent by 2030. Occasional famines still claim lives, but overall rates of African infant mortality have dropped significantly in the past decade, and even though HIV/AIDS has not been eradicated, new therapies have decreased mortality and national campaigns have contained its expansion. Armed conflicts have not ended everywhere, but perpetrators of war crimes have been sentenced in courts, and more and more Africans vote in meaningful elections that regularly remove entrenched governments peacefully from power. Challenges still exist, and Africans direct their energies to finding solutions to problems: drawing on local knowledge, African entrepreneurs, politicians, artists, religious leaders, healers, and others are contributing to the social, cultural, and political affairs of their nations. This volume introduces students to African social, artistic, and political processes and structures, Africans and their energy, and the continent's challenges and potential.

AFRICA'S DIVERSITY

Africa is vast, with a landmass more than three times the size of the continental United States. As the second-largest continent after Asia, it has dense rain forests and expansive deserts, undulating grasslands and snow-covered mountains, inland lakes, and many other geographical features. Africa is bifurcated by the equator, and most of its land is in the tropics, with only its northern and southern extremes in temperate zones. For millennia Africans have drawn resources from the continent's depths and used them for myriad endeavors: artisans fabricated iron tools and weapons, architects built tall stone structures, and merchants sold gold that not only adorned African bodies but also circulated in medieval European and imperial Chinese markets. During the nineteenth century Africa's economic potential attracted European powers that conquered most of the continent and exported its resources until the end of colonial rule in the second half of the twentieth century. Today the export of commodities continues and has expanded to include not only a greater range of agricultural products but also gemstones, oil, and minerals essential to the manufacture of contemporary digital technologies. Foreign investors have been acquiring land for the production of biofuels and other crops in recent years, a practice that may threaten food security and livelihoods in a number of countries. New industries are also being developed on the continent, and Africans pursue commercial relations with emerging economies such as Brazil, China, and India as well as established European and North American trading partners.

The continent is home to more than a billion Africans speaking one or more of over two thousand languages, nearly a third of the world's tongues. Some are closely related, but most are not and are distinguished by their grammatical structures, words, and consonants, such as the clicks of some southern African languages. Language is one marker of identity in Africa, and ethnicity is another. Their relationship is complex: many African ethnic groups have common historical experiences and share the same language, while others were independent communities with their own languages and developed collective identities only under colonial rule. Some urban Africans identify with the ethnicity of their parents but speak only the urban lingua franca; others identify ethnically with the language they speak even if they are of different parentage. Given the great linguistic and ethnic diversity of Africa, cross-cultural exchanges are the norm and have provided benefits to individuals and groups; ethnic solidarities lead to conflict only in rare and specific circumstances, generally in a context of access to resources. Often media reports highlight social conflicts, use the term "tribe" in reference to opposing groups, and suggest that enmity has endured for centuries. "Tribe," however, conveys otherness and obscures more than it reveals. Those identifying as Hutu or Tutsi in Rwanda, for example, share the same language and much of the same culture. The terms "Hutu" and "Tutsi" express historical categories for occupational and class differences that became codified and the basis for different access to resources in the European colonial era and which subsequently have been politicized by specific actors in the postcolonial era. Understanding conflicts in Africa, and the more ubiquitous instances of constructive social interactions, requires analysis of the ways Africans define social differences in local contexts and deploy social solidarities to meet specific political ends.

Africa currently has fifty-four states. Centralized political power is not novel on the continent: Africans founded polities with a great diversity of political cultures and organizational arrangements from the time of ancient Egypt forward. The era of European conquest established new colonial territories, with only imperial Ethiopia able to prevent colonial occupation with its victory over Italian forces at Adwa in 1896 and Liberia avoiding colonial rule in part through U.S. protection. Elsewhere Africans found themselves in colonial arrangements encompassing numerous ethnic groups with different political traditions but also frequently dividing groups between colonies. European colonial rule did not endure much past the 1960s, but its structures remained influential in the states that emerged after the African struggle for independence: most international boundaries in Africa today follow the lines drawn by European powers. Nigeria, for example, has more than 150 million citizens speaking more than 250 languages, and its primary political divide between north and south echoes the colonial division of the country into two administratively autonomous northern and southern regions. Some states, such as South Sudan, established in 2011, represent the result of a decades-long civil war that finally severed ties between northern and South Sudan. Not all contemporary African politics replays the colonial past, but the legacy of that era is evident in continuing efforts to create a sense of national identity corresponding to current state boundaries.

Some scholars and international policy makers distinguish between northern and sub-Saharan Africa, frequently considering North Africa as part of the Middle East; popular sentiments add to the perception of a continental divide. The Sahara Desert, however, never was a barrier, as ideas, goods, and people have crossed it for millennia. Arabic is the lingua franca in northern Africa, but it also is spoken as a first language south of the Sahara in Mauritania and Sudan. Berber languages similarly are spoken on both sides of the Sahara. Ethnicity shapes the politics of northern African states as much as in those below the Sahara: Algeria, Mali, and Niger have faced Tuareg separatism in their Saharan regions, for example. Other supposed markers of difference also do not justify a continental division. Islam is the dominant religion in northern Africa, but similar majorities of Muslims live in several sub-Saharan states, such as Chad, Mali, Niger, Senegal, and Somalia. Race too is socially constructed and not a basis for dividing the continent into separate entities. Historical connections between some northern African states are clear: the initial Arab conquests swept across the region, Ottoman rule later united the region from Egypt to Algeria (but did not include Morocco), and the region's location along the Mediterranean coast creates opportunities for more intimate exchanges with Europe than are possible for sub-Saharan regions. Recent political protests against entrenched leaders in northern Africa led the media to refer to an "Arab Spring," but close examination of events reveals connections not only across northern Africa to the Middle East but also across the Sahara to Mali, Uganda, and other African states. Relevant regional blocs are discussed as appropriate, but most chapters in this book draw on examples from both sides of the Sahara to illustrate general patterns.

AFRICA AND THE WORLD

Africa is intimately connected to the world through contemporary processes of migration and travel, technological change, and globalization, but it never has been isolated. Africa's eastern and southern regions provide evidence of the earliest biological and cultural transformations in human history in their rock paintings and in archeological excavations of stone tools and bones. After the first humans migrated from Africa to populate other regions of the world, Africans on the continent continued to engage others, exchanging crops, techniques, ideas, and religions with emerging cultural formations in neighboring parts of Asia and Europe. European scientific expeditions in the nineteenth century created an erroneous impression that Africa was only then being "discovered," even though commercial exchanges had defined Europe's relations with Africa for centuries, including the four hundred years of enslavement and slave trading in which more than eleven million Africans were taken forcibly to the Americas. New research on the "Black Atlantic" points to ways that African ideas and practices influenced Europe and America in this era, beyond the significant contributions of slave labor on plantations and other economic enterprises.

Nineteenth-century transformations associated with the rise of industrial economies in Europe and North America shaped Africa's relations with the world for the past two hundred years. At first Europeans took advantage of new innovations in weapons and other technologies to conquer and colonize most of the continent during the late nineteenth century. The era of European colonial rule lasted less than a century, but it shaped African states of the independence era and structured economic relations. In the postcolonial era some dimensions of continuing relations between European powers and their former colonies have been characterized as "neocolonial"; the period of Cold War politics and economic policies dictated by the World Bank and the International Monetary Fund similarly confined the options African states had for independent action. The last two decades, however, have witnessed growing autonomy through a revitalized continent-wide political institution (the African Union), regional economic and political groupings, and increasing economic power through relations with new trading partners in the emerging economies of Asia and Latin America. Africa is poised to define its role in twenty-first-century world affairs in ways that break from the patterns of the past two hundred years.

Some assume that Africa's global connections first brought education to Africa through schools established by missionaries and colonial governments, but this conception is a narrow understanding of education that ignores the institutions Africans had developed to transmit knowledge, to form moral individuals capable of taking their places in society, and to produce new knowledge. Initiations and storytelling were pervasive, and apprenticeships transmitted technical knowledge to specialists. With the spread of Islam came additional educational institutions at diverse levels and a new script that some Africans used to write in their own languages. These institutions continue to exist alongside or in combination with schools that missionaries, colonial administrations, and postcolonial governments established. The number of languages spoken on the continent poses a challenge for formal education in these latter institutions, as does the availability of resources. In spite of these difficulties, African states have educated citizens who create new knowledge and train future generations, their universities have produced doctors, lawyers, and other professionals, and their policies have encouraged entrepreneurship and the creation of new businesses.

The flourishing cultural production that has characterized Africa in the past continues and innovatively draws on the global circulation of ideas, images, and people. Visual artists, writers, filmmakers, and musicians take advantage of contemporary technologies to experiment with new forms of expression, collaborate across national and regional boundaries, and reach new publics on and off the continent. Scholars too have developed new synergies through continental networks to advance the production of knowledge and enhance its impact. Many diasporan intellectuals actively work with colleagues and institutions on the continent and influence scholarship at home. Engagement with the world is not confined to acclaimed cultural and intellectual producers or to those who migrate to distant lands. Africans in all walks of life who remain on the continent are tuned in to what happens beyond their communities through the media, the internet, and trade networks, and they draw on these creatively to help solve problems of daily life and deal with adversity. They also participate in the world through the imagination and through the use of foreign products that connect them symbolically with the wider world.

Not surprisingly, modernity defines Africa as much as it does other world areas. Africans embrace key markers of modernity, such as organizational rationalization and democratic participation in many areas of life, and they also reflect on their place in the world through art, literature, religion, and other cultural expressions. Outsiders often sharply distinguish between "tradition" and "modernity," but in relation to Africa these labels can obscure complex negotiations in unfolding African cultural processes. "Tradition," for example, can imply, as does "tribe," stasis and rigid continuity, whereas African cultural production has always involved aspects of continuity and change, expertise and experimentation, adaptation and innovation. Understanding modernity requires examining the ways Africans reflect on their communities, conceptualize and evaluate social change, and define their worlds in both local and global terms.

USING THIS TEXTBOOK

Africa's diversity, its involvement with the world, and its experiences with modernity are three of the many themes discussed in the chapters that follow. *Africa* is an introductory text that seeks to avoid academic arguments in favor of clear statements about major issues. The suggested readings at the end of each chapter allow students to explore specialized approaches and detailed arguments. The chapters are not grouped into related clusters because ideas and themes cross the chapters. Geography is first because an appreciation of Africa's physical diversity is important; history and social relations follow to offer perspectives about Africa's past dynamism and contemporary complexity, essential for understanding subsequent chapters. We leave it to instructors to adapt the book to their syllabus—for example, moving from geography and history to livelihoods and urbanization, politics and development, religion and health, or the arts. Chapter 15, "Print and Electronic Resources," provides suggestions for further research to help keep abreast of continuing developments and new trends in Africa.

1 Africa
A Geographic Frame

James Delehanty

Africa is a continent, the second-largest after Asia. It contains fifty-four countries, several of them vast. Each of Africa's biggest countries—Algeria, Congo, and Sudan—is about three times the size of Texas, four times that of France. Africa could hold 14 Greenlands, 20 Alaskas, 71 Californias, or 125 Britains. Newcomers to the study of Africa often are surprised by the simple matter of the continent's great size. No wonder so much else about Africa is vague to outsiders.

This chapter introduces Africa from the perspective of geography, an integrative discipline rooted in the ancient need to describe the qualities of places near or distant. The chapter begins by examining how the world's understanding of Africa has developed over time. Throughout history, outsiders have held a greater number of erroneous geographic ideas about Africa than true ones. The misunderstandings generated by these false ideas have been unhelpful and occasionally disastrous. After this survey of geographic ideas, the chapter settles into a general preference for what is true, probing, in turn, Africa's physical landscapes, its climates, its bioregions, and the way that Africans over time have used and shaped their environments. A final section outlines the difficulties Africa has confronted and the betterment Africans anticipate as they integrate ever more fully and fairly with emerging global systems.

Knowledge of geography is a frame for deeper inquiry in all fields because the qualities of place shape every human endeavor. Anyone striving to understand the challenges and potentialities that citizens of African countries have to work with in their struggle to obtain for themselves and their families the security and prosperity that is their birthright would do well to reflect regularly on Africa's geography. A map, especially one's own emerging mental map of Africa, is an excellent organizing tool. It structures information according to the fundamentally interesting question "Where?" It is a solid place to start any journey, including one's personal passage toward a more nuanced understanding of Africa.

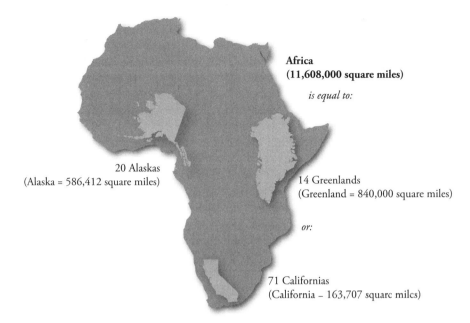

**Africa
(11,608,000 square miles)**

is equal to:

20 Alaskas
(Alaska = 586,412 square miles)

14 Greenlands
(Greenland = 840,000 square miles)

or:

71 Californias
(California – 163,707 square miles)

Map 1.1. The Size of Africa.

THE IDEA OF AFRICA

Places are ideas. Consider, for example, that most significant of places, home. Every home is a physical entity—it exists concretely—but the meaning of home, its reality, is all tied up in the experiences and emotions of the people who live in that place or otherwise know it. Or consider Pittsburgh. Pittsburgh is a particular collection of buildings, roadways, rivers, people, and a great deal else occupying a defined portion of western Pennsylvania, but it also is an idea. More correctly, it is a set of ideas, because each of us has a different sense of Pittsburgh based on our views of cities in general and whatever memories and associations, accurate and false, Pittsburgh as place or word conjures in our minds when we encounter it. So too Africa. Though without doubt a continent, Africa, like all continents, also is a complex of ideas that have flowed through the human imagination, accurately and fancifully, generously and carelessly, over a great span of time, giving rise to many meanings and actions, some grounded in truth and noble, others based in error and unfortunate.

If Africa is a continent but also a product of the human imagination, the first question that must be asked is when it originated. Physical Africa, the continental landmass, is easy to date. Any basic geology text will describe how Africa took shape after the breakup and drifting apart of the pieces of the supercontinent Pangaea about

180 million years ago. As for the idea of Africa, it is somewhat more recent. The idea of Africa came into being over the last two thousand years, and it did so largely in Europe. The fact that the idea of Africa developed mostly in Europe goes a long way toward explaining how Africa is conceived worldwide, even now.

This claim—that Europeans were largely responsible for the idea of Africa—is easy to substantiate and does not discredit Africa and its people. Europeans invented America too, just as Chinese invented Taiwan and Arabs the Maghreb. All through world history, at scales ranging from the continent to the community, outsiders have given identities to places. A common way this happens is by first naming. There were no Native Americans, only hundreds of distinct peoples such as the Ojibwa of the Great Lakes and the Navajo of the western desert, until Europeans crossed the Atlantic five hundred years ago and announced the existence of a continent to be called America. Another way outsiders give identity to place is by inspiring or provoking, sometimes by threat or aggression, unity and regional loyalty where none existed before. There was no Germany until Bismarck, around 1870, convinced the German-speaking principalities of central Europe that they were one and that joining Prussia to form an entity called Germany would be in the interest of all.

Even though few early Africans knew the bounds of the continent or could imagine Africa as a whole (the same can be said of early people on all of the continents), there were exceptions. One interesting case comes down to us from the Greek historian Herodotus, who in the fifth century BCE (Before the Common Era) wrote a brief but tantalizing report of a sea journey by Phoenicians, organized by King Necho II of Egypt, around the landmass we call Africa (which Herodotus called Libya), undertaken about two hundred years before Herodotus's time. While

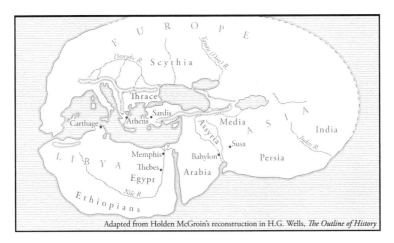

Map 1.2. The World According to Herodotus (ca, 450 BCE).

An African Circumnavigation of Africa 2,700 Years Ago

Here is the entirety of Herodotus's account of an African circumnavigation reported to have occurred two hundred years before his time. The charming anecdote at the end, noting the strange position of the sun, inspires confidence in the story's factuality because, unknown to Herodotus, sailors heading west at the latitude of southernmost "Libya" would see the sun on the starboard (right) side of the ship (i.e., in the northern sky) all day long, just as in Europe and most of North America the sun's daily passage from east to west occurs entirely in the southern sky.

> Libya is washed on all sides by the sea except where it joins Asia, as was first demonstrated, so far as our knowledge goes, by the Egyptian king Necho, who, after calling off the construction of the canal between the Nile and the Arabian gulf, sent out a fleet manned by a Phoenician crew with orders to sail west about and return to Egypt and the Mediterranean by way of the Straits of Gibraltar. The Phoenicians sailed from the Arabian gulf into the southern ocean, and every autumn put in at some convenient spot on the Libyan coast, sowed a patch of ground, and waited for next year's harvest. Then, having got in their grain, they put to sea again, and after two full years rounded the Pillars of Heracles in the course of the third, and returned to Egypt. These men made a statement which I do not myself believe, though others may, to the effect that as they sailed on a westerly course round the southern end of Libya, they had the sun on their right—to northward of them. This is how Libya was first discovered by sea.
>
> —Herodotus, *The Histories* 4.42 (ca. 425 BCE)
> *Translated by Aubrey de Selincourt*

no other evidence of this expedition survives, it is pleasant and plausible to believe that it occurred. If it did, then at least one small group of Africans, probably a few Phoenician adventurers from Egypt, learned of the entirety of the African landmass as long as twenty-seven hundred years ago. This knowledge appears to have died with them. It did not lead to any mapping or broad understanding within Africa of the continent's extent. Even Herodotus knew next to nothing about what those sailors saw; he only reported the legend of their trip.

European ideas about Africa began to take shape during the period of classical antiquity. The ancient Greeks and Romans had a great deal of solid knowledge about the nearer parts of Africa. After the Roman defeat of Carthage (in present-day Tunisia) during the Punic Wars of the second century BCE, the Roman Empire expanded to encompass much of the continent's northern reaches. The cultural and economic ties between Rome and its African provinces were strong. Northern Africa quickly became known as the granary of the empire. The word "Africa" dates from this era. It possibly comes from "Afer," which in the Phoenician language was the name for the region around Carthage. According to this theory, Roman geographers, needing a word for the landmass to the south, borrowed "Afer," Latinized it, and broadened its application to the entire continent south of the Mediterranean (much as Herodotus had used "Libya" in the same way, for the same purpose, a few hundred years before).

Commerce has linked Africa with the rest of the world for the last two thousand years. Never was Africa entirely isolated from the main currents of global interaction and trade. Roman coins and artifacts from the second and third centuries of the Common Era (CE) have been unearthed in lands south of the Sahara, evidence that Africa's great desert was traversed occasionally in early days. Sailors and settlers from Borneo and Sumatra, in present-day Indonesia, traveled to Africa beginning about 350 BCE. Their descendants and language dominate Madagascar today, and the crops that these settlers carried from Southeast Asia, such as plantain, became dietary staples all across continental Africa. As early as the seventh century CE, Persian and Arab traders established outposts up and down Africa's Indian Ocean coast, drawing commerce from the interior, linking producers in eastern and central Africa through trade with the Middle East and the wider world. There are clear records by the fourteenth century of voyages by imperial Chinese trading vessels carrying silk, porcelain, and other goods from the ports of Asia to the East African coast. The Christian kingdom of Ethiopia exchanged emissaries with the courts of Europe, including the Vatican, in the fifteenth century. And many Africans traveled great distances within the continent and beyond. A good example is Abu Abdullah Muhammad Ibn Battuta, commonly known as Ibn Battuta, a fourteenth-century Moroccan adventurer who voyaged all across the northern third of Africa and eventually as far as China and Southeast Asia, reporting his discoveries in Arabic manuscripts read throughout the Muslim world.

These contacts of non-Africans with Africa, and the rich descriptions of portions of Africa provided to the world by outsiders and African writers such as Ibn Battuta, were elements of a partial geography of Africa. Yet an accurate cartography—a map of the continent's position, size, and proportions—awaited the voyages of European seafarers during the fifteenth and sixteenth centuries and their transmittal of information to European mapmakers capable of accurately rendering Africa's outline. In other words, despite early knowledge of many parts of Africa in many lands, including Europe, China, and the Middle East, and of course among every African who ever lived, the definition of Africa as a whole, its description as a geographic totality, fell to Europeans. And this made all the difference. Europe was poised in 1500 to rise to global dominance. The accurate and inaccurate ideas that Europeans began attaching to their categorical creation, Africa, spread around the world with European power.

What of these ideas? What did Africa come to mean in the European imagination? Portrayals of Africa and Africans in the literature and art of Europe before 1500 or so, though hardly widespread, were largely benign. That is, until about five hundred

---

An African Description of the Nile in 1326

Ibn Battuta, a fourteenth-century Moroccan adventurer, is the most celebrated and widely read African traveler of all time. He wrote in Arabic, at
great length, of his travels in Africa and all over the known world.

> The Egyptian Nile surpasses all rivers of the earth in sweetness of taste,
> length of course, and utility. No other river in the world can show such a
> continuous series of towns and villages along its banks, or a basin so in-
> tensely cultivated. Its course is from South to North, contrary to all the other
> great rivers. One extraordinary thing about it is that it begins to rise in the
> extreme hot weather at the time when rivers generally diminish and dry up,
> and begins to subside just when rivers begin to increase and overflow. The
> river Indus resembles it in this feature. The Nile is one of the five great riv-
> ers of the world. . . . All these will be mentioned in their proper places, if
> God will. Some distance below Cairo the Nile divides into three streams,
> none of which can be crossed except by boat, winter or summer. The inhab-
> itants of every township have canals led off the Nile; these are filled when
> the river is in flood and carry the water over the fields.

> —From Abu Abdullah Muhammad Ibn Battuta,
> *Travels in Asia and Africa 1325–1354*
>
> *Translated and edited by H. A. R. Gibb*
> *(London: Broadway House, 1929)*

---

years ago European intellectuals appear to have known little about Africans (only a
few people from Africa would appear now and then in the cities of Europe), and less
still about Africa as a continent, but when they did consider Africa and Africans it
was with a rough sort of equality. This is not to say that Europeans harbored no fantastic ideas about Africa, but their fantasies were not very much different from those
constructed about many unknown lands: rumors of dragons, giants, astonishing creatures, and strange physical and cultural variations of the human family populating
regions that were unbearably hot and forbidding. These were ancient motifs, long
ascribed in many cultures to unfamiliar places. But Africa in Renaissance Europe
was not deemed particularly backward, primitive, or frightful. In paintings Africans
usually were depicted as simply another shade of human being. They were sometimes a point of interest in a picture, but no malign attention was drawn to them.
Physical exaggerations or contortions were not seen. Nor in European writing of this
time do we see much overt anti-African racism, only the kinds of physical and cultural speculations that were applied to unfamiliar people from all unexplored or unknown areas.

   Living standards in Europe and Africa five hundred years ago were little different. On both continents nearly everyone lived off the land, most in agriculture. Diet
was unvaried. Hunger was common. Life span was short. Almost no one on either

continent was well educated. Why should Europeans have considered Africans, five hundred years ago, to be in any manner inferior? There was no material reason for Europeans to stigmatize Africa and Africans in particular at this time, and generally they did not.

This changed. Increasingly in written descriptions and paintings from Europe in the sixteenth and seventeenth centuries, Africans took on qualities that are familiar to us now. Africans came to be defined by Europeans as poor, uneducated, technologically unsophisticated, underdeveloped, and non-Christian.

Why did this happen? Why, about five hundred years ago, did Africa in the European mind go from being a somewhat mysterious but not fundamentally different assortment of peoples and cultures to being the anti-Europe, the antithesis of everything that made Europe great?

One reason was that standards of living, technology, education, and knowledge were rising in Europe, lifting many people (though far from all) above the levels of basic subsistence that had long been their lot. People living in vibrant economies often lose interest in the rest of the world except to the extent that it can supply what they desire. Certainly Europe's economic progress is part of the story. But the main reason for Europe's emerging negative view of Africa was the development of the trans-Atlantic slave trade, which started in a major way in the 1500s and rose to its height over the next two hundred years.

This is not the place to dwell at length on the slave trade, but this much must be said: from the 1500s to the 1800s, European slave traders transported millions of Africans from the shores of the continent to work in European colonies in the New World. Slavery was an ancient and nearly universal human institution long before the beginning of the trans-Atlantic slave trade, but the world had never seen anything like this, with so many millions of people pulled from their homeland in a sustained and organized fashion and sent to the far ends of the earth purely for the economic advantage of well-off Europeans. How could this commerce possibly be justified morally and psychologically? Europeans did so by convincing themselves that Africa was populated by people who did not warrant the concern one might have for others.

As the slave trade ratcheted up, the idea spread quickly around Europe that Africans were not part of our common humanity. Did everyone in Europe during the period of the slave trade think about or firmly believe these ideas? Certainly not. Africa and Africans were quite tangential to the lives of most Europeans. But to the extent that Europeans thought at all about Africa and Africans in early modern times, racist assumptions of African inferiority became the default. Much later, in the nineteenth century, these theories of racial inferiority were elaborated and developed into a pseudoscience, but the roots of anti-African racism are here, in the rise of the slave trade in early modern Europe and the need in Europe and eventually the Americas for a moral and psychological crutch to support it. The trade endured for more than three hundred years. Ideas of inferiority, once embedded, lasted longer than that.

A whole set of negative qualities began to be attributed to Africa and Africans to set them apart from Europeans. These qualities were oppositional: if we are white, they are black; if we are good, they are bad; if we are Christian, they must be immoral; if we are sophisticated, they must be primitive; if we are enterprising, they must be lazy; if we are cerebral, they must be physical; if we are moral, they must be licentious; if we are orderly, they must be chaotic; if we are a people capable of self-governance, they must need our help. We live with this legacy. About the realities of Africa—as opposed to the imagined qualities of Africa's people, land, economies, and political geography—the West knew little until the twentieth century.

What about African ideas of Africa? When did Africans discover and begin to form thoughts about the continent? This is not an absurd question. As noted already, the geographic category of "Africa" arose in Europe, and almost no one anywhere, including Africa, had any knowledge of the extent of the African landmass until the fifteenth century. Thus there is a history of African ideas of Africa, just as there is a history of Western ones. It starts with the slave trade.

Throughout the slave trade period and continuing after it ended, a trans-Atlantic discourse linked intellectuals in Africa to communities of African descent in the Americas. In these communities—in North America, South America, and the Caribbean—a continental perspective on Africa developed early because slaves and their descendants needed a unitary sense of Africa, a conception of Africa as a whole, for their identity and their dignity. After all, people from many corners of Africa were enslaved but as the years passed most knowledge of a family's precise roots in Africa was lost. Adult captives who survived the trans-Atlantic journey certainly knew from where in Africa they had been taken, and sometimes this knowledge persisted through a few generations, passed down from parents to children, often as a scrap of information, perhaps just a word for some now unknown village or kingdom. But even these tidbits tended naturally to fade over time. Eventually most people in the New World whose forebears had been transported as slaves knew nothing whatsoever of the origins in Africa of their various ancestors. They knew not whether they were descended from Hausa, Wolof, Yoruba, or Ewe people (or from what mix of different African ethnicities), but they did know that their people had come from Africa. It was in this context of definitional necessity, largely in the Americas after the sixteenth century, that people first began to conceive of themselves as being of essentially *African* origin and to think of the totality of Africa as a place, their ancestral home.

This continental understanding spread around communities of African descent all over the Atlantic world, and soon (because the Atlantic was an information highway, not a barrier) it became part of the thinking of traders, scholars, political leaders, and other cosmopolitans in Africa itself. The idea of the African continent as a generalizable place, a place inhabited by black people sharing many commonalities (not least the racism and bondage imposed on them for centuries by Europeans), people united in their history with slaves and the descendants of slaves in the Americas, came to be called, in the nineteenth century, Pan-Africanism.

Pan-Africanism still has wide ideological currency today. It is the idea that there is an essential unity to all of Africa, a unity of race, a unity forged through the experience of racism, enslavement, and nineteenth- and twentieth-century European colonialism, a unity that binds all Africans and people of African descent around the world in a community of shared history, oppression, and liberation challenge. This discourse of Pan-Africanism shaped nineteenth-, twentieth-, and even twenty-first-century ideas within Africa about the relevance of the continent as a category of experience. Without pan-Africanism people in Africa might not have come so readily to identify themselves as, yes, Igbo, Kikuyu, or Hausa, and, yes, Nigerian, Kenyan, or Congolese, but also as *African*. All of this is to say that Africa may have been a European categorical creation, but people in Africa had a greater incentive than anyone else to take a continental view, and by the nineteenth century many Africans, especially the educated elite, did just this, largely in opposition to Europe.

So places are ideas, continents are inventions, and Africa is what people have imagined it to be. History shows again and again that what people think about a place, true or not, matters more to the actions they take than does any combination of uncontestable facts. Yet factual knowledge, including accurate geographic information about a place, generally produces better results.

THE PHYSICAL LANDSCAPE

About Africa's physical landscapes only a little needs to be said. While the continent presents many spectacular features and splendid views, it is not, on the whole, a land of sharp transitions. A driving trip of several days in most parts of Africa impresses the traveler as would a similar trip in west Texas or Saskatchewan: the scale of the land is immense, but the landscape variations are subtle.

The major exception to Africa's general landscape regularity is the mountainous east and south. Some geographers helpfully distinguish between "high Africa," extending from Ethiopia all the way south along Africa's eastern side to the Cape of Good Hope, and "low Africa," the vast rolling plain encompassing nearly all of the rest of the continent. Africa's highest peaks—Mt. Kilimanjaro and Mt. Kenya— are in high Africa. Patterns of human livelihood in the east and south always have been strongly influenced by the height of land and the productive volcanic soils found there. The mountainousness and ancient volcanism of the east are closely related to the other prominent landscape feature of this part of Africa: rift valleys. From the Red Sea through central Ethiopia, Kenya, and into Tanzania, Malawi, and Mozambique, great fissures in the earth form long, steep-sided north-south valleys, some partly filled by waters of great lakes, all resulting from the same tectonic processes that have, over eons, thrown up the adjacent highlands.

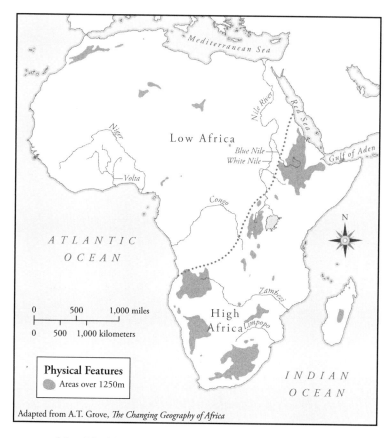

Map 1.3. High Africa, Low Africa, and the Major Rivers.

Even low Africa has some mountains, including the Atlas range of the far north-west, and Mt. Cameroon, one of Africa's highest peaks, only a short distance from the Atlantic Ocean, in the country that bears its name. In general, though, low Africa is flat to undulating. Here are most of Africa's immense rain forests, its expansive savannas, and its greatest desert.

African soils are varied, but in general their productivity suffers from the continent's tropical position and from the absence of vast alluvial plains such as those of India, Bangladesh, and China. On other continents, where rivers rise in nutrient-rich uplands such as the Andes, the Himalayas, or the Tibetan Plateau and then cross gently sloping land to the sea, they deposit their sediments on ever-expanding alluvial plains, building up soils of great depth and fertility. With partial exceptions in Egypt, Nigeria, and Mozambique, Africa has none of this. Its great rivers—the Nile, the Volta, the Niger, the Congo, the Limpopo, and the Zambezi—rise in nutrient-

Figure 1.1. Near the Ahaggar mountains of southern Algeria.
Jeanne Tabachnick.

poor zones and thus carry relatively unproductive sediment, or flow so circuitously to the sea that much of what they do carry is deposited in dry inland regions un- suited to agriculture, or fall so steeply to the sea from the African plateau that their riches are washed to the depths (see map 1.3). As a result, Africa lacks great ex- panses of deep, river-deposited soils that give advantages to other lands, such as eastern China, Bangladesh, and the Indus Valley of India and Pakistan.

Fertile deltas aside, tropical regions generally contain poor soils. Africa, the most tropical of continents, bears a particular burden in this regard. In Africa's humid tropics, where it is hot year-round and moisture is abundant, thriving soil microor- ganisms quickly break down organic matter such as dying plants and fallen leaves and branches. Nutrients liberated by this rapid decomposition cycle without delay from the ground up through the vascular systems of trees and other long-lived plants, and there they stay—as leaves, bark, and wood—until released again to the ground by death. In other words, nutrients in humid tropical systems are plentiful but fixed in the forest canopy, not in the soil, where most agricultural crops can use them. The challenge to farmers in these systems is to get nutrients from the canopy into the earth, where their crops can benefit from them.

Large parts of Africa are tropical but seasonally dry, and here the soil challenge is different. Soil development in the drier tropics is hampered by a lack of organic

Figure 1.2. Rainforest near Mounana, Gabon.

matter (because year-round high heat and moisture deficits during a long dry season limit plant growth) and by the baking and chemical hardening of ground that occur in the seasonal absence of rain under relentless sun.

Africa does have zones of excellent soils, such as the slopes of ancient volcanoes near the rift valleys of East Africa, and nowhere is the soil situation impossible. Africans have made their living from agriculture for a very long time, longer than people have done in parts of Europe. Soil quality is a particular challenge to African food producers, but the continent's soils are by no means an insurmountable obstacle to food security and prosperity. Africa's physical endowment is more than sufficient for all Africans to thrive.

CLIMATE AND BIOGEOGRAPHY

Africa is incomprehensible without a basic understanding of climate and the patterns of life that variability in temperature and rainfall yield. Temperature is straightforward. The equator bisects Africa, and equatorial regions receive relatively direct as opposed to relatively indirect solar radiation during most of the year; thus most of Africa experiences high year-round heat.

There are exceptions to this general rule. In Africa north of the Sahara, the narrow strip of land bordering the Mediterranean Sea, temperatures are similar to those in

Mediterranean Europe: high heat during much of the year but cooler weather from December until March. Likewise, much of southernmost Africa—the Republic of South Africa and adjacent countries—experiences a distinct cool season, but with opposite polarity: here it is cool from June until September. Some snow occurs at high elevations every year in Africa's far south, just as it does in the Atlas Mountains of the north.

A third exception to the general rule of high year-round heat is in highland areas anywhere. In high Africa—from Ethiopia through Kenya and Tanzania all the way south to the Cape—altitudes greater than 1,500 meters (5,000 ft.) above sea level are common. At this elevation, even in the tropics, air temperature is likely to be cool some of the time. The high slopes of Mt. Kilimanjaro, Africa's highest mountain, are glaciated, as are those of Mt. Kenya (though global warming is rapidly diminishing these and all other tropical glaciers). Average temperatures on these peaks are close to freezing. People do not live on the heights of Africa's great mountains, but they do live in Nairobi, 1,600 meters (5,300 ft.) above sea level. In Nairobi, as in many parts of high Africa, daytime temperatures during some months hover around 20°C (68°F), far from hot.

A final exception is in desert regions. Here there are great diurnal fluctuations in temperature: high heat during the day but great cooling at night. Nighttime temperatures in Africa's deserts frequently drop to 10°C (50°F) or lower.

Precipitation in Africa is much more varied than temperature. It is also more complicated and more important to understanding the realities of African life. Variability of rainfall across territory and over the course of every calendar year largely explains patterns of plant and animal types and abundance and the ecological situations that have conditioned the diversity of Africa's human cultural forms.

The processes responsible for rainfall patterns in Africa are complex in detail but simple to understand in a three-part model:

1. *Equatorial low pressure.* Along the equator, where the daytime sun is directly overhead (or nearly so), solar radiation passes through a minimum of filtering atmosphere. Intense radiation striking the earth's surface generates a great deal of heat. The highest heat of all is along the equatorial belts of continents because the sun heats absorptive land more readily than reflective seas. Because hot air rises, all across equatorial Africa air warming near the earth's surface rises into the atmosphere. To take its place, air masses rush toward the equator from the north and south, including moist air masses from over the Atlantic and Indian Oceans. These inrushing air masses also heat up and rise, becoming part of an equatorial low pressure vortex. This hot, moist air rising along the equator cools as it rises. As air cools, its capacity to hold moisture declines, and so it rains. For these reasons, equatorial Africa, except for portions of the mountainous east, is rainy nearly year-round.

2. *Subtropical high pressure.* Air rising at the equator and cooling in the atmosphere must flow somewhere. It does flow—at high elevation—toward the north

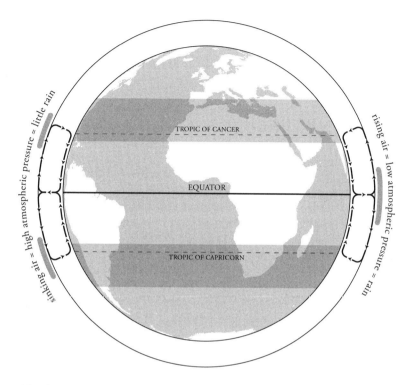

This diagram depicts how atmospheric circulation would influence rainfall levels in different parts of Africa if the sun were always overhead at the equator. But in fact, because the earth is tilted in its angle toward the sun (see below), the belts depicted here—along the equator and near the Tropics of Cancer and Capricorn—shift north and south with the seasons.

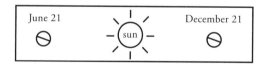

Map 1.4. Generalized Atmospheric Circulation in the Tropics:
The Conditions That Bring Rain.

and south. This poleward-streaming air in the upper atmosphere begins to sink back toward earth at 20–40 degrees north latitude and 20–40 degrees south latitude (map 1.4). As it sinks toward the earth's surface, which is heated by the sun, this air warms. As air warms, it can hold more moisture. Rain is highly unlikely under these conditions. So in two belts influenced by this sinking air (in other words, by subtropical high pressure)—north of about 20° north latitude and south of about 20° south latitude—Africa is dry.

3. *Seasonality.* If parts 1 and 2 provided a fully accurate account, they would describe a straightforward pattern of rainfall in Africa: heavy rains in an equatorial band about 1,000 kilometers (600 miles) wide, declining rain toward the north and south, and eventually, at roughly 20°–30° north and south latitude, no rain at all. However, parts 1 and 2 neglect a major complication: that the earth revolves around the sun at an angle. Only in March and September is the sun directly overhead at the equator. On June 21 it is overhead at the Tropic of Cancer and on December 21 at the Tropic of Capricorn (see the bottom of map 1.4). Thus, the low pressure belt described in part 1 as "equatorial" in fact shifts north of the equator in summer and south in winter. The two belts of subtropical high pressure shift with it. Consequently, much of Africa experiences extreme rainfall seasonality: high rainfall when the belt of low pressure centered on the equator moves seasonally in, and almost no chance of rain when it shifts out and is replaced by high pressure. The movement north and south from equatorial Africa of this rain-bearing belt of low pressure (sometimes called the "inter-tropical convergence zone," or ITCZ) is somewhat variable from year to year but predictable in broad outline. It moves northward with the sun in the months around June and southward with the sun in the months around December. The rainy season is longest, and annual rainfall totals are highest, in areas that are under its influence for most of the year. The rainy season is shortest, and rainfall totals lowest, in areas it reaches only briefly.

Map 1.5 shows average annual rainfall totals in Africa. Though there are a few anomalous regions (notably in the east, where other processes serve as complicating factors), the model outlined above explains the map's patterns well. Where low pressure conditions prevail for most of the year, rainfall totals are high. Where the ITCZ reaches only briefly, totals are low. Northern Nigeria, for instance, receives only about 600 mm (24 in.) of rain per year because low pressure conditions bringing rain last only from about May through September. During the rest of the year, high pressure prevails and there is rarely a cloud in the sky.

Also delineated on map 1.5 are basic climate zones. In tropical Africa (which is the entire continent except the far north and far south) there are four important zones:

- *Humid tropical Africa.* Rain occurs nearly year-round. If there is a dry season, it lasts only a month or two. The average annual rainfall total is greater than 2,000 mm (roughly 80 in.).
- *Sub-humid tropical Africa.* The rainy season lasts six to ten months; 1,000–2,000 mm (40–80 in.) of rain falls in an average year.
- *Semi-arid tropical Africa.* There is a distinct rainy season, but it lasts less than six months, in some areas as few as two or three months. Average rainfall totals are between 200 and 1,000 mm (8–40 in.).
- *Arid tropical (or dry) Africa.* There is little to no rainy season. In the driest parts of the arid tropics, years may pass without appreciable rain. The annual average rainfall total is less than 200 mm (8 in.).

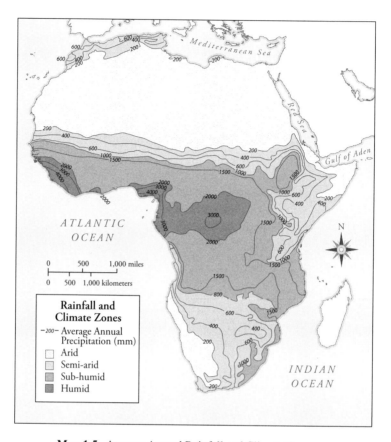

Map 1.5. Average Annual Rainfall and Climate Zones.

Map 1.6 is a map of Africa's principal biomes, or biological regions. The biomes are defined by the putative natural vegetation that would occur in the absence of agriculture and other human modifications (although, as we will see in the next section, on human use and transformation of the environment, this distinction is problematic). The close correspondence between rainfall shown in map 1.5 and vegetation shown in map 1.6 is unsurprising. Africa's humid tropical lands support rain forest. The arid tropics are desert. Between the extremes of rain forest and desert we see gradations of Africa's most characteristic biome, tropical savanna.

A savanna is a grassland studded with trees, but not all tropical savannas are alike. The savannas of sub-humid areas often are labeled "woodland savanna." Here the trees may grow quite large and are relatively closely spaced, though not so dense that they impede the growth of grasses underneath. The savannas of semi-arid Africa are often called "shrub savanna." In these zones the trees are generally

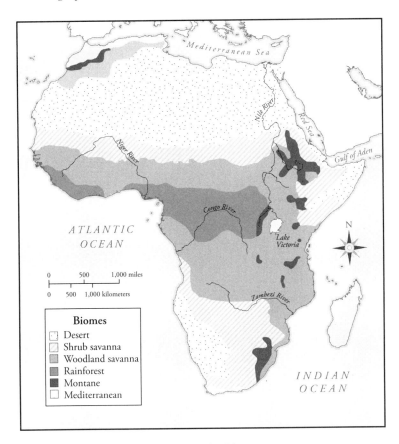

Map 1.6. Major Biomes.

smaller and more widely spaced; grasses predominate, though they typically die back during the long dry season.

As map 1.6 shows, savannas cover large parts of Africa. They encompass much of the continent's best agricultural land and many of its most populated areas. In a great many African societies, therefore, people have learned to calibrate food production calendars and myriad other aspects of cultural life to the rainfall seasonality so characteristic of tropical savanna regions—regular cycles of plenitude and parching—much as people in temperate regions such as Europe and North America adjust their production calendars and other aspects of their lives to the temperature seasonality of winter and summer.

Some of Africa's biomes have common English names. The central African rain forest is usually called just that, but by common convention we give formal names to deserts. The main deserts of Africa are the Sahara, the Kalahari, and the

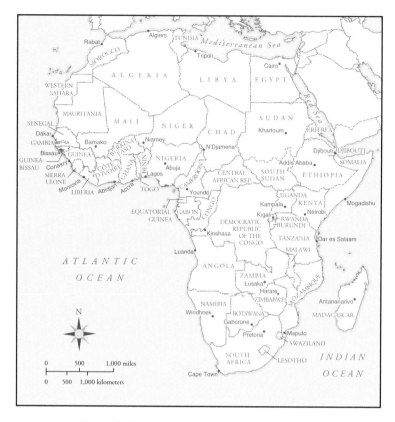

Map 1.7. Countries of Africa and Selected Cities.

Namib. Only one of Africa's savanna belts has a formal name, the Sahel, the dry, shrub savanna just south of the Sahara. This name comes from the Arabic word for "margin" or "shore," in this case the southern margin of the Sahara. Countries that encompass large parts of this biome sometimes are called the Sahelian countries: Senegal, Mauritania, Mali, Burkina Faso, Niger, Chad, and Sudan.

HUMAN USE AND TRANSFORMATION
OF AFRICAN ENVIRONMENTS

It is tempting to divide the history of Africa into three grand epochs—precolonial, colonial, and postcolonial—and to generalize about the human use and transformation of nature in each. This temptation should be resisted. The three-period view of African history, though common, is absurd. The colonial period refers to the years when most of Africa was occupied and controlled by several European powers, the 1880s until the 1970s, a span of ninety years. The postcolonial period

Figure 1.3. In the Sahara of southern Algeria.
Jeanne Tabachnick.

encompasses the few decades since then. And the first period, the precolonial period, covers two hundred thousand or more years stretching back into the primeval past, to the time when *Homo sapiens* first appeared on the planet. This is like dividing the calendar year into three parts, December 31, December 30, and pre–December 30: the periods wildly lack analytic equivalence and contort our thinking about Africa by tacitly suggesting that before colonialism not much happened. True, some of the first period could easily be labeled "prehistoric" instead of "precolonial," but relabeling does not solve the problem, and in any case there is no general agreement about where on Africa's timeline prehistoric gives way to precolonial.

Human history in Africa is almost incomprehensibly long. We now know for certain from genetic as well as archeological evidence that our species evolved in Africa between 150,000 and 250,000 years ago from earlier primate species that no longer exist, and that for most of this immense expanse of time humanity lived only in Africa. People did not push permanently out of Africa until a migration event about sixty thousand years ago, after which our species spread worldwide. We are all African by origin.

Because people have lived in Africa for so long, the concept of "natural environment" is a particular problem there. More than anywhere else, people and nature in Africa have co-evolved. Through millennia, through climate shifts that have shuffled the biomes, people have been adjusting to different African environments, molding them, living, working, taking from the earth, burning, cutting, hunting, planting, nurturing, and destroying; all environments in Africa are natural only in the sense that people are a part of nature. The major biomes of today's Africa are real, but many of their qualities come from a quarter of a million years of human use.

Foraging

Our first impacts on nature in Africa were as hunter-gatherers. For most of human history the only economic activity was hunting and gathering, also known as foraging. It prevailed in all biomes, from deep forest to desert, and it persisted into the present century, though barely. Forager population densities were always low. People lived in small mobile bands, moving across the landscape to take advantage of game and desired wild plants where they were abundant, abandoning areas where resources had been temporarily depleted. Despite being sparse on the land, our African foraging ancestors were entirely capable of altering plant and animal communities. Rarely if ever did they live in benign equilibrium with the rest of nature. They burned grasslands and forests to drive game. They used poisons to take fish. They extirpated unwanted plant and animal species from their territories while intentionally promoting and protecting desirable ones. No people, not even hunter-gatherers, leave the earth entirely as they found it.

The decline of hunting and gathering as a subsistence strategy was long and gradual, beginning with the arrival of agriculture in parts of Africa about seven thousand years ago. Even as recently as three thousand years ago foraging may have supported the majority of Africans, but this way of life continued to decline to the point that it is inconsequential now. A very few societies dependent on hunting and gathering survived to the turn of the twenty-first century, many of them supplementing their foraging by trading with nearby farmers and herders, but in Africa today hunting and gathering are little different than in most of the rest of the world, including Europe and North America: an occasional pursuit enjoyed by a small number of mainly rural people who have other primary occupations, or the specialized craft of a few individuals or families living in communities whose economies are diverse.

Herding

Pastoral herding and agriculture arrived or were independently invented in the northern third of Africa about seven thousand years ago (i.e., about 5000 BCE). From the north these two economies spread across the continent, diffusing especially rapidly after about 1000 BCE. Herding economies are based on the tending of domesticated animals, in Africa mainly cattle, camels, goats, and sheep. Herding is most common in the savanna zones because cattle and sheep require grass for grazing, while camels and goats require low trees and shrubs for browsing. Any temptation by herders to move into forest regions was (and is) checked by poor ecological fit: the absence of grasses and shrubs and the presence of trypanosomiasis, a fatal livestock disease spread by the tsetse fly, endemic in Africa's wetter areas.

Like foragers, Africa's herding peoples always have lived in low concentrations; their economy cannot support high population densities. Yet they occupied (and still do occupy, for this way of life, though rapidly declining, is still with us) vast tracts of Africa's shrub and woodland savanna. Here they move cyclically over the course of the year, knowing where in each season to obtain water and forage for their livestock, and where to trade animal products with farmers for grain.

Pastoral herders have modified Africa's savanna landscapes by intentionally and unintentionally altering the mix of plant species in a region, sometimes following practices that conserve and encourage the growth of grasses and shrubs that their livestock prefer and at other times (especially during drought years) overusing and thus diminishing them. Drought is a particular threat to herders because so much of their land is semi-arid and prone to periods of low rain. Herders usually respond to drought by concentrating their animals for longer than normal periods near the most dependable streams, ponds, and wells. These emergency concentrations may lead to overgrazing and soil disturbance in prime pastures, an example of the many ways that even low-technology economies sometimes have unintended impacts on their sustaining environment.

Agriculture

For several thousand years crop agriculture has been rural Africa's most important mode of production by far. First about seven thousand years ago in the savannas of the northern part of the continent, then during the last two or three millennia in the rain forest and the savannas of the south, most African societies gradually coalesced around farming.

Agriculture spread gradually across the continent, but it did so decisively, for it gave those who adopted it a great advantage: numbers. With a dependable food supply—far more dependable than their foraging ancestors could manage—farming peoples were able to establish permanent, sometimes very large villages on lands that under foraging or herding could support only diffuse roaming bands. Agriculture took hold especially well and led to the highest population increases where soils were relatively productive, including on most of Africa's savannas. The main crops and thus the staple foods developed by savanna farmers were grains: mainly millet, sorghum, and (after the 1500s) maize. It is logical that grains came to dominate savanna agriculture, for all the major grains were developed from graminoids, wild grasses. Grain crops thrive in grassland environments. There was a cost to the agricultural transformation of much of savanna Africa, of course: a decline in diversity as a few crop species covered more and more land that formerly had been home to multitudes of grasses and other plant types. However, nowhere is savanna Africa farmed with anything approaching the intensity of agricultural regions in North America and Europe. Africa has nothing like Illinois's or Iowa's vast acreages of monocropped corn. Patchworks of savanna and farmland remain the norm.

Just as grains dominate savanna agriculture, tree crops and root crops have long predominated in the rain forest zone, especially plantain, yams of many kinds, and (after the 1500s) cassava. Unlike on the savannas, rain forest agriculture generally cannot support high population densities. Soils are infertile, so the land must lie idle between cropping cycles. Typically it idles long enough for the forest to regenerate, often thirty or forty years. Under this system, large tracts of land are needed to feed small numbers of rain forest farmers because at any given time most of the land is regenerating forest, not fields. A map of Africa's human population density at any time in the last several thousand years shows high concentrations of people in the most agriculturally productive savanna zones, as well as in some coastal areas where fishing and trade have supported development, but lower densities in the forested humid tropics (and also of course in the deserts).

Colonialism transformed African agriculture substantially during the nineteenth and twentieth centuries by superimposing on local food production and trade networks an export-oriented agricultural economy that answered to the demands of Europe and the rest of the industrializing world, forcing African producers to add export crops such as cocoa, coffee, tea, peanuts, tobacco, cotton, sisal, rubber, and palm oil to the foodstuffs they had been long accustomed to producing. The next

Figure 1.4. Cassava field in a tree savanna field, Angola.

section of this chapter, about Africa in global systems, outlines some of the implications of these changes.

In Africa today a smaller portion of the population is producing food because more and more rural people are moving to the cities and staying. In general, African farmers are keeping pace with the increased food demand of a growing population while also, in many areas, continuing to produce for export, though in some countries, inevitably, there are food shortfalls, especially during periods of drought or political unrest. While urban Africans depend to a considerable degree on the agricultural labors of their counterparts in the villages, they also partake in a globalized food economy and global regimes of taste, just as residents of Europe, Asia, and the Americas do. They eagerly consume not only the products of African agriculture but also imported staples and delicacies. Supermarkets and even outdoor markets in Africa's great cities feature quantities of foods produced in their hinterlands, but also rice from China, pasta from Italy, condiments from France, and sweets from England. This is to say that Africans are no different from consumers anywhere else in their eagerness to sample diverse foods and enjoy the taste and prestige of products imported from other lands.

Yet all over the world, including Africa, it is most economical and ecologically sound to obtain the largest proportion of food from local sources, and thus urban food cultures in Africa strongly reflect the productive capacities of the different African regions. Nearly everywhere in Africa people are fond of porridges made from local starchy staple crops. Residents of East African cities such as Nairobi and Dar es Salaam and southern African cities such as Johannesburg, Harare, and Lusaka still enjoy as a primary food, respectively, *ugali* and *mielie-meal*, porridges made from the maize that farmers in these regions prefer to grow. The *fufu* much prized in the cities of southern Nigeria, Benin, Togo, and Ghana comes from locally produced and milled cassava and yams; the *tuwo* of northern Nigeria and Niger from millet or sorghum; the *matoke* of Uganda, Tanzania, Rwanda, and eastern Congo from local bananas and plantains.

AFRICA IN GLOBAL SYSTEMS

Over the last several centuries humankind has remade the world as we have grown dramatically in number and come to dominate the planet. The twentieth- and twenty-first-century transformation of landscape in Africa has been substantial, not only because the number of Africans has increased but also because extractive and manufacturing economies have arisen alongside agriculture to meet external demand and to support the complex and enriched lives that people worldwide—Africans are no exception—now expect. The look of Africa remains essentially African, of course, but as mines, factories, cities, roads, and all the accoutrements of the contemporary global system have arrived in Africa, the look and feel of some African places have come to resemble those of cities and industrialized landscapes everywhere. Meanwhile, despite the beginnings of an industrial transformation, many Africans have found it hard to achieve the material comfort that people everywhere seek for themselves and their children. They find it difficult largely because most of the continent entered the industrial and postindustrial age from a position of extreme disadvantage during the nineteenth and twentieth centuries under European colonialism and in its aftermath.

Colonialism arguably brought certain foundations for economic growth to Africa—ports, roadways, schools, clinics, and the like—but it did so not with the viability of an independent Africa in mind but rather to support forms of organized resource extraction that often amounted to outright plunder. New crops introduced or promoted in the nineteenth and twentieth centuries because of demand in Europe drove African farmers to try to farm more intensively and to cultivate more and more land, some of it marginal and risky for agriculture. But rapid intensification and expansion led to soil fertility decline because the fertilizers necessary for sustained intensification were unavailable and fallowing land—letting it regenerate by leaving it idle for a while—became an impossible luxury, as farmers needed all available land every year.

New export crops had the potential to generate wealth in rural Africa, and wealth allows people to afford environmental conservation measures and smart rather than willy-nilly resource exploitation. However, when an agricultural transformation is organized so that the lion's share of its proceeds flows immediately out of the producing region (in the African case, to Europe) and is unavailable for locals to invest in the betterment of their own land and society, a dynamic of decline sets in. Not only Africa's people but also Africa's resource base and natural beauty have suffered the depredations of a colonially transformed rural economy set up in the nineteenth and twentieth centuries to drain the countryside of its natural endowment—forest products, diamonds, copper, gold, ivory, skins, cotton, cocoa, oils, coffee, tea, tobacco, peanuts, vegetables, flowers—while leaving producers and the local region with just enough to keep them producing for another year.

Colonial governments largely took rural people for granted as producers of exportable primary products, neglecting rural development except for token or inadequate efforts here and there. Perversely, Africa's independent, postcolonial governments mostly did the same (though this has begun to change). Neglect of rural development is one reason—though hardly the only one—that Africans now are streaming to the cities.

Cities in Africa long predate colonialism, but the continent's great metropolises—Cairo, Lagos, Kinshasa, Johannesburg, Khartoum, Abidjan, Accra, Nairobi, Kano, and others (see map 1.7)—became vast during the twentieth century and are experiencing explosive growth during the twenty-first. From all corners of rural Africa people are converging on cosmopolitan but often desperately poor cities, cauldrons of exciting cultural change and personal transformation where visions of a new Africa and new ways of being African are emerging but where lack of jobs, space, water, opportunity, health, and wealth threaten constantly to bring the whole enterprise down. Into the mining districts of South Africa, into the oil fields of Nigeria and other countries, and into the slums of great cities all over the continent pour greater and greater numbers of men, women, and children, seeking the betterment that all people want for themselves and their families; while they find vibrancy, excitement, change, and opportunity, they also encounter a more frenzied form of the poverty that they had hoped to leave behind in the countryside.

As cities and the medium-density periurban hinterlands that surround them claim more and more of Africa's people, they are becoming the Africa that matters most to Africans. Therefore they should matter most to outsiders who are serious about Africa. That these areas be safely habitable and that they be zones of opportunity and wealth creation, not despair, is Africa's great twenty-first-century challenge. The benefits of vibrant cities can ripple out across the land. If Africans can transform their cities into zones of opportunity, the cities will generate wealth, which can be invested—by Africans—to preserve nature and encourage sustainable production in the rural areas that fewer Africans are electing to call home.

Africa's cities tie the fifty-four countries of the continent more and more to global systems, flows, tastes, and preferences. Globalization is no threat to Africa; it is Africa's hope. Linkages—connections—are the world's future, and Africans know this and will not be left behind. Connectivity, networking, and community are core African values, glorious ones, deeply rooted in the psyches and societies of nearly all African people. As success in the world increasingly depends on communications, links, networks, and community, Africans calculate that despite the adversity that the continent so obviously faces, their time in an age of global commonweal is somehow coming.

All images are courtesy of University of Wisconsin–Madison, African Studies Program.

All maps are courtesy of University of Wisconsin Cartography Lab.

SUGGESTIONS FOR FURTHER READING

Goudie, Andrew. 2006. *The Human Impact on the Natural Environment: Past, Present, and Future.* 6th ed. Oxford: Blackwell Publishing.
McCann, James. 1999. *Green Land, Brown Land, Black Land: An Environmental History of Africa, 1800–1990.* Portsmouth, NH: Heinemann.
Nederveen Pieterse, Jan. 1992. *White on Black: Images of Africa and Blacks in Western Popular Culture.* New Haven, CT: Yale University Press.
Stock, Robert. 2004. *Africa South of the Sahara: A Geographical Interpretation.* 2nd ed. New York: Guilford Press.
Vansina, Jan. 1990. *Paths in the Rainforests: Toward a History of Political Tradition in Equatorial Africa.* Madison: University of Wisconsin Press.

2 Legacies of the Past
Themes in African History

John Akare Aden and John H. Hanson

Africa and its peoples have a long and distinguished history. The earliest evidence for humankind is found on the continent, and some of the first successful efforts to domesticate plants and produce metals involved African pioneers and innovators. Africans constructed complex societies, some with elaborate political hierarchies and others with dynamic governance systems without titular authorities such as kings and queens. Extensive commercial networks connected local producers in diverse environmental niches with regional markets, and these networks in turn were connected to transcontinental trade networks funneling goods to Asia, Europe, and the Americas. The trans-Atlantic slave trade did not bring European colonization to Africa; only centuries later, when Europeans had more powerful weapons and mechanized transportation, could they invade the continent. Colonial rule ended quickly, however, leaving the current configuration of more than fifty independent states.

Historians have debated whether the European colonial period was a transformative era or merely an interlude in the continent's history. Colonial rule introduced new and enduring political boundaries and unleashed powerful economic forces that remain influential to this day, but it also was uneven in its impact and ambiguous in its transformations. Africans appropriated new ideas, but they continued to draw from the deep wells of local cultural resources. Colonial rule never was so draconian that it prevented Africans from trying to shape their own history, but African efforts were constrained. Formal educational opportunities brought new languages and topics to African students, but indigenous knowledge and the social apprenticeships associated with its transmission remained vital.

Some arguing for colonialism's transformative power would go so far as to suggest that Africa's history only began with the arrival of Europeans. In the early 1960s the British historian Hugh Trevor-Roper noted that "perhaps in future there will be some [African] history to teach. But, at present, there is none. There is only the history of Europeans in Africa. The rest is darkness . . . and darkness is not a subject of history."[1] Trevor-Roper's views are based on assumptions about limited African capacity that unfortunately had dominated European understandings for several generations. His scholarly discipline was only just beginning to recognize African history as a field of inquiry, even though Africans, African Americans, and others had been writing histories of the continent for centuries. It took African independence for the field of African history to flower fully as a recognized scholarly activity in Europe and North America, and in the half century since independence, historians of Africa have produced significant work and made the field a vital arena of inquiry.

This chapter cannot review all aspects of Africa's history, nor can it convey all the developments of the last hundred years. It discusses several themes, suggesting along the way why some argue that the colonial era was an interlude and why others view it as transformative. It begins with themes related to Africa's history before European colonial rule and then examines the European colonial conquest and its aftermath. Some themes are elaborated for the contemporary era in other chapters, and this chapter provides historical background for the more focused discussions to come. Each region has its own distinctive history, and inquisitive students will want to learn more about the African past on their own.

MIGRATION AND CULTURAL EXCHANGES
IN AFRICAN HISTORY

Africans have always been on the move. Out-migration from Africa is the most probable explanation for the peopling of the world, and migration also occurred internally. The earliest movements are impossible to reconstruct, but Africa's linguistic diversity provides a key to uncovering some of this past. Africans currently speak more than two thousand distinct languages, but each language falls into one of four large language families that initially developed separately for millennia: Afro-Asiatic, Khoisan, Niger-Congo, and Nilo-Saharan. Languages in the same family share some vocabulary and certain grammatical features, and each language develops on its own terms, often as a dialect of an existing language before transformations create a new language. Archeological and botanical analyses suggest that the initial linguistic diversity reflects different choices about the transition from gathering and hunting to food production: speakers of the Khoisan languages retained the earliest human lifestyle in the Kalahari Desert and isolated regions in eastern Africa, whereas populations associated with the other language families shifted to food production with different main crops at various times beginning several thousand years ago. These transitions were complex, and subsequent historical events encouraged further cultural transformations, so the current distribution of languages reflects the outcome of thousands of years of interactions. Africans identify as speakers of specific languages associated with recent ancestors: the origins of Africa's cultural diversity are well beyond human memory and reflected obliquely in its four distinct language families.

Settling the continent was not easy. Europeans in the Age of Exploration imagined Africa as a tropical paradise where its inhabitants lived easily off the land. But the continent actually has poor soils except in a few favored contexts, unpredictable rainfall in regions outside the rain forest, and debilitating diseases that afflict humans and domesticated animals alike. Each region had both obstacles and opportunities for the establishment of food-producing regimes. In eastern Africa, for example, the highlands dotting the arid plains west of the coast offered environments where farming was possible, creating islands of demographic concentration in a region where otherwise herding was more viable. Everywhere the production of metals was essential to the full exploitation of any region, and ironworkers emerged as specialists who awed others with their ability to transform ore into workable metal for tools and weapons. In all contexts there was an emphasis on fertility in the face of ubiquitous diseases and other hardships, and Africans transmitted local knowledge about healing and other activities over the generations. The chapters on health, visual art, and other African cultural expressions reveal contemporary elaborations of these practices.

Cultural interaction and incorporation frequently occurred. The widespread distribution of Bantu-speakers in central, eastern, and southern Africa, for example, involved diverse processes over the millennia. European colonial officials initially spoke of a "Bantu conquest," projecting their own imperial expansion onto others in the past. Later scholars imagined a "Bantu migration" bringing knowledge of ironworking from an initial home in western Africa to sub-equatorial Africa. The archeological evidence for a phased spread of ironworking well over a thousand years ago made the second explanation plausible, but careful analysis uncovers complexities. Instead of Iron Age farmers migrating into unoccupied regions, historians now posit a range of scenarios depending upon the linguistic, archeological, and other evidence: ideas could move without people, for example, or the migrations might only involve small groups of ironworkers. Some of these processes are evident in subsequent historical eras. For instance, in regions of central Africa where western Bantu languages are spoken, patron-client relations involving individuals capable of bringing people under their protection is a dominant pattern of the last several hundred years. These leaders, some still remembered by those whose ancestors were incorporated into their entourages, drew clients through their distribution of material largesse, perceived powers to both protect and heal, and knowledge of the physical environment. In southern Africa, where another branch of the Bantu languages is dominant, a cattle-keeping cultural complex facilitated social incorporation during the past several hundred years: bonds were forged not only in the keeping of cattle and the arrangement of marriages around them, but also through age-grade organizations incorporating young men and women through initiatory rituals. Such processes of incorporation through patron-client relations, age-grade initiations, and other social processes, as well as the literal migrations of peoples, explain the current distribution of Bantu and other languages in Africa.

Interactions occurred across numerous frontiers over the centuries. The Holly-wood image of the American frontier as the product of a linear westward expansion over a short period from settlements in the eastern United States is not especially relevant in the African context, for the African experience occurred over millennia with multiple cultural centers and several frontiers moving in various directions. In eastern Africa, for example, the expansion of the Bantu languages occurred where the Nilo-Saharan languages also were expanding, and both converged in a context where Khoisan and Cushitic languages (the latter a branch of the Afro-Asiatic family) were already established. Analysis of material cultures, word lists, and oral narrations allows historians to reconstruct histories for individual groups. In the Great Lakes region, which is suitable for agriculture, pastoralism, and foraging, cultural interactions over several hundred years between speakers of several different languages created regional social formations in which farmers, herders, and gatherers came to speak the same language. Sometimes groups moved into environmental niches unexploited by others: the Swahili peoples, speakers of a Bantu language, for example, separated from other eastern Bantu-speakers and moved into the coastal regions of East Africa as fisherfolk and farmers more than a thousand years ago and then engaged in international trade. Other population movements are closer in time: the Maasai peoples, speakers of a Nilo-Saharan language, have a long history as a people but came to exercise dominance in the Rift Valley of today's Kenya and Tanzania only in the nineteenth century, as they followed the guidance of religious leaders, expanded into the valley, accumulated cattle, and incorporated others in complex social and commercial relations. The metaphor of the frontier is useful, as it reminds us that African cultures were not isolated into fixed social groupings but were open and dynamic, even if they came into conflict over resources during times of scarcity.

Mobility sometimes led to the founding of towns. Ancient Egypt produced the first African urban centers along the banks of the lower Nile River. Regional trade encouraged the rise of market towns, which later became connected to long-distance exchanges across the Sahara Desert, the Indian Ocean, and the Atlantic Ocean. Timbuktu, the famed West African urban center on the edge of the Sahara, was one of thousands of such commercial towns in African history. Other towns were founded by political elites seeking to project their power spatially and to draw subjects to their courts. These towns impressed the initial European visitors to coastal Africa in the sixteenth and seventeenth centuries. Towns declined when historical circumstances changed. The archeological site known as Igbo-Ukwu in today's southeastern Nigeria, for example, points to the existence over a millennium ago of a political capital where, at the time of its excavation, only villages dotted the same countryside. Europeans sometimes founded new towns in the colonial era, but they also expanded existing towns: in northern Nigeria, Kano pushed beyond its old city walls, and Italians built monumental architecture in the old town of Mogadishu in Somalia. The postcolonial era has been a time of dramatic urbanization. Rural-urban migration and other forms of mobility such as African

Figure 2.1. Court life in the central African town of Loango, as represented in a seventeenth-century European drawing in O. Drapper, *Description de l'afrique,* 1686. *Lilly Library, Indiana University.*

immigration to Abu Dhabi and Guangzhou, London and Paris, and Minneapolis and New York are recent examples of a long-standing practice of African exploration of new horizons.

SOCIAL COMPLEXITY AND POLITICAL CENTRALIZATION IN PRECOLONIAL AFRICA

The United Nations is an international body composed of states, the primary political units of the contemporary world. States also have been used as a marker of human development, as centralized authorities often built monuments and left behind written documents valued by archeologists and historians. However, social complexity and cultural sophistication occur just as often in decentralized formations, even if their members do not build enduring structures or if they prefer oral modes of communication. Anthropologists have revealed how societies govern themselves effectively through elders representing corporate groups, and some archeologists and historians have pursued new methodological angles to uncover the history of decentralized societies, as the previous discussion of migration and cultural exchanges discloses. In this section the focus turns to instances of increasingly centralized African social forms. Precolonial African history long has been the story of African states, and this section does not attempt to summarize that past. Instead, examples are chosen from three regions: the lower Nile River valley, the central plateau of Zimbabwe, and the middle Niger River valley. Just a few decades ago these three examples were contested, denied, or unknown, respectively, so their examination here underscores the importance of recognizing African social complexity in the face of erasure and neglect by previous generations of scholars.

Lower Nile River Valley

The inclusion of ancient Egypt as an African example would have given Hugh Trevor-Roper and numerous others pause. Many divide the history of the African continent at the Sahara, but the history of population movements and the cross-fertilization of ideas belie such facile divisions. The Sahara emerged as the world's largest desert only several thousand years ago, and thereafter it has been regularly traversed by Africans and others carrying new technologies, ideas, faiths, and trade goods. Just six thousand years ago, the Sahara had a large inland sea, and settlements along its shores included those who fished the waters, hunted the nearby fauna, and experimented with the domestication of animals and plants. Surviving Saharan rock paintings illustrate these activities, and recent archeological findings point to the social complexity of the human populations living there. Ecological change as well as global climatic developments contributed to growing aridity in the Sahara, forcing most of the Sahara's populations to migrate to more favorable circumstances elsewhere on the continent. The lower Nile River valley was one of several destinations. The migrants joined other Africans who continued their experimentation with domesticated crops, given new relevance by increasing populations.

Well before the rise of pyramids and other monumental buildings in the lower Nile valley, Africans learned how to manage the annual silting patterns of the Nile River. These populations were the first in Africa to adopt agriculture on a widespread scale. Eventually African elites from settlements in Upper Egypt imposed a centralized state over populations throughout the lower reaches of the Nile valley, sustaining three centuries of pharaonic rule in ancient Egypt. The emergence of centralized rule also occurred upriver in Nubia among groups speaking a different language, revealing that it was not pharaonic exceptionalism but the ability and need to centralize that created the first African states; later the Nubians conquered and ruled ancient Egypt for a brief period. The succession of ancient Egyptian dynasties associated with the Old, Middle, and New Kingdoms oversaw developments in law and governance, health and medicine, the arts, and architecture. Ancient Egypt was a major power, projecting influence upon its neighbors and receiving cultural influences from throughout the region. In religious affairs, ancient Egyptians stressed their indebtedness to the black earth inundating the Nile's banks from its origins in the African interior, and their temple doors opened to the lands of their ancestors, the regions lying toward the headwaters of the Nile.

The place of ancient Egypt in African history has been contested during the recent past. After Napoleon's conquest of Egypt, Egyptology emerged as a distinct scholarly enterprise removed from other historical fields. African and African American scholars questioned this separation: the West African historian Cheikh Anta Diop, for example, wrote several influential books about the African origins of ancient Egypt, and similar views were expressed in African American intellectual circles beginning in the Harlem Renaissance of the 1920s and continuing in more recent works by African American scholars. The latter pushed for a new academic agenda, Afrocentrism, which protested the erasure of ancient Egypt from the dominant representations of Africa and framed African history in its own analytical categories, beginning with ancient Egypt as the first African civilization. This effort drove other debates in American intellectual life, including the argument over whether public schools should embrace multiculturalism; in some important respects, today's school standards are a result of the debate Afrocentrists initiated about the place of ancient Egypt in African history. Some of their conclusions about the past may be contested, but not their essential point: that ancient Egypt was African in origin and represented broader patterns of African history.

After the emergence of the Sahara Desert and the rise and decline of lower Nile valley social formations, northern Africa followed its own regional trajectory. It was the southern shore of an interrelated Mediterranean world, as Ferdinand Braudel imagined in his influential historical works. The rise of Islam also brought the Arab conquest of northern Africa in the seventh century CE, leading to the complex social transformations associated with the adoption of Arabic and the acceptance of Islam as the dominant religion in the region. But Islam equally linked all Muslims to common sacred texts and ritual practices, so northern Africa never was isolated from other African regions, where Islam also expanded gradually as one religion among many. Trade across the Sahara was another factor integrating the region Muslims called the Bilad as-Sudan, "land of the blacks," into complex commercial and diplomatic relations with northern Africa. Much later Arabs also began to migrate to selected sub-Saharan contexts, such as oases in the western Sahara (today's Mauritania) and the middle Nile River valley (today's northern Sudan), stimulating again the process of local adoption of the Arabic language. But Arabization in sub-Saharan Africa did not mean that Nubians forgot the past associated with their ancestors, who with the ancient Egyptians produced impressive societies along the banks of the Nile River. And Gamal Abdul Nasser, Egypt's leader during the 1950s and 1960s, celebrated his country's African heritage as well as its Arab and Muslim cultural ties.

Zimbabwean Plateau

One of southern Africa's states left behind massive stone buildings near the Zimbabwean town of Masvingo. Great Zimbabwe, as this complex has come to be

Figure 2.2. Great Zimbabwe's conical tower, a photograph taken by the colonial expedition seeking evidence for non-African origins of the granite structures and discussed in R. N. Hall, *Great Zimbabwe, Mashonaland, Rhodesia: An Account of Two Years Examination Work in 1902–04 on Behalf of the Government of Rhodesia,* 1907. *Lilly Library, Indiana University.*

known, was the residence of some twenty thousand inhabitants at its apogee in the fourteenth century. Located on a plateau, the complex as well as other structures likely housed elites and laborers responsible for the buildings, which are made of almost a million large granite blocks. Goldworking was a central part of this state's modus vivendi, accomplished by using iron smelting and smithing to extract gold ore from its rocky prison beginning around 1000 CE. Gold was also exported to the coasts via the Swahili trading town of Sofala; ivory and enslaved people were exchanged as well. By the fourteenth century, Great Zimbabwe was fully integrated into the Indian Ocean commercial world (see below), with elites displaying imported Chinese porcelain and local bird sculptures made from soapstone found in the region. In addition, smaller stone structures were built throughout the plateau. By the 1500s, however, Great Zimbabwe's population had migrated: some postulate a massive fire, and others suggest that overpopulation depleted the natural environment around the settlement on the plateau. Whatever the case, the inhabitants of Great Zimbabwe took their prospecting and goldworking technologies with them elsewhere in the region, including the Mutapa state near the Zambezi River. As the Portuguese rounded southern Africa and intervened in the region during the sixteenth century, they traded with the Mutapa state, but it eventually was eclipsed on the plateau by the Torwa and Changamire polities.

When Europeans first arrived in southern Africa as colonial rulers, they assumed that Africans could not have built or even been associated with Great Zimbabwe. In Rhodesia, the territory named after the British entrepreneur Cecil Rhodes, the colonial government's museum authority actively propagated the myth that non-African, white peoples had built Great Zimbabwe, even though evidence produced by professional archeologists and historians pointed to African origins. Leaving behind physical evidence of a major social formation did not prevent the erasure of African involvement in the era of European domination and racism. This denial of ancient African stone-building was reversed only when African nationalists came to power in the 1980s and renamed the nation Zimbabwe after this heritage.

Middle Niger River Valley

The middle Niger River valley was the site of a western African culture that has come into clearer view only recently, with the discovery of new archeological evidence. This culture is not associated with monumental buildings, as are the social formations in the lower Nile valley and on the Zimbabwean plateau. It is tied to social transformations in the fertile inland delta of the Niger River, situated in the heart of contemporary Mali. There, in the years after the desertification of the Sahara, Africans domesticated local grains and developed regional trade across the close succession of environmental zones running north and south from the Sahara Desert to the rain forest. As trade expanded, occupational specialization and urbanization increased. These regional developments are evident in the rise of Jenne-jeno, or "Old Jenne," which had emerged as a thriving town by 400 BCE and expanded until it reached some ten thousand residents during the first millennium CE. Today the archeological site is on an island close to Jenne, the contemporary commercial town and Muslim religious center.

At its genesis and for much of its history, the middle Niger River valley social formation did not reflect the centralization of political authority, witnessed, for instance, by the absence of monumental architecture and elaborate royal burial tombs as in ancient Egypt; instead the local inhabitants embraced social diversity and ethnic accommodation. Today, reciprocal relations among Mali's ethnic groups specializing in farming, herding, and fishing in the middle Niger River valley harken back to enduring values of cultural diversity forged thousands of years ago.

Centralized political formations did eventually develop. Gold had been discovered in the early days of Jenne-jeno and was traded regionally, and the expansion of trans-Saharan trade created incentives for political elites to control access to this luxury commodity. Soninke-speaking political elites founded Wagadu (the state referred to as "Ghana" in Arabic texts by Muslim travelers), the first West African empire to benefit from control of the trans-Saharan gold trade. Ancient Mali rose to prominence in the early thirteenth century and oversaw regional integration over a wide swath of West Africa for three hundred years, transforming control over the gold trade into a mechanism for projecting its political and cultural power regionally. Today the Mande languages are spoken throughout the region, a legacy of ancient Mali, much as the Romance languages of western Europe are a legacy of the ancient Roman Empire. Ancient Mali's origins are celebrated in the orally transmitted Sunjata epic, which is recounted to this day. Sunjata Keita, the "Lion King," reportedly was unable to walk until well past puberty, but rose in a feat of great strength through the assistance of a blacksmith and praise singer. Later in this oral epic, Sunjata battled Sumanguru Kante, a blacksmith, sorcerer, and king. Whatever the meanings of this epic, it codified the social relations forged by the Keita dynasty and other Malian elites. This social system was enduring: even after the fall of ancient Mali as a political formation, its social structure defined group relations until the present in three categories: *horon* (nobles, farmers, and merchants), *nyamakalaw* (artisan groups such as ironworkers, potters, leatherworkers, and bards), and *jonw* (outsiders or "slaves"). While nobles claimed pride of place, artisans stressed that nobles depended upon their services. Slaves were not always bound to a life of menial labor, and some rose to positions of great authority as soldiers. The nonhierarchical ethos of the Jenne-jeno era echoed in these contestations among social groups.

As in the cases of ancient Egypt and Great Zimbabwe, ancient Mali declined as an empire. In the shifting political context and changing commercial relations of fifteenth-century West Africa, the Songhay state took control of much of the trans-Saharan gold trade. The political elites of ancient Mali survived, albeit in a smaller political formation, and members of the Keita family still commanded local respect. The Songhay became an empire but eventually declined as well, in its case due to a combination of factors, including the diversion of the gold trade to coastal forts trading with European merchants in the sixteenth century. This latter development points to other commercial networks shaping African history besides trans-Saharan trade.

INTERNATIONAL COMMERCIAL SYSTEMS IN AFRICAN HISTORY

Globalization refers to the widespread economic integration and increasing cultural and technological flows in today's interconnected world. But economic connections and cultural interactions across vast regions are not unknown in human history. Trans-Saharan trade linked sub-Saharan Africa to Mediterranean and Asian trading networks, and cultural flows such as the Islamic religion circulated along these networks. Other trade networks connected Africa to South Asia and the Americas across the Indian and Atlantic Oceans, respectively.

Africa and the Indian Ocean World

The Indian Ocean was the locus of one of the world's first global economies, a trading system linking eastern Africa with Arabia, southern Asia, and Indonesia. The regularity of the monsoon winds in the Indian Ocean facilitated economic inte-

Figure 2.3. Mombasa, with the castle built by the Portuguese in the late sixteenth century, as represented in a nineteenth-century European drawing in W. F. W. Owen, *Narrative of Voyages to Explore the Shores of Africa, Arabia and Madagascar,* 1833. *Lilly Library, Indiana University.*

gration: the dependable shift between northeasterly and southwesterly winds over the course of the year allowed premodern seafaring vessels to move goods, ideas, technologies, and peoples between the continents. An interconnected zone emerged, most markedly from the tenth to nineteenth centuries, when economic linkages supported a wider array of cultural exchanges. No one power dominated the Indian Ocean world of that era, although Islam was the faith of many of the merchants who moved goods and ideas across the seas. When the first Portuguese ships rounded South Africa's Cape of Good Hope and arrived in the Indian Ocean world in the sixteenth century, they found a thriving economy that they tried to control, but their gunboats only allowed them to seize a few ports, such as Mombasa, and did not alter the fundamental patterns immediately. It was only the rise of an industrializing global economy centered on western Europe that eroded the economic and cultural integration of the Indian Ocean world during the last few centuries.

Coastal eastern Africa was one of several African regions integrated into the larger Indian Ocean world. The Horn of Africa and northern regions of coastal eastern Africa long had been linked to the Red Sea and Mediterranean exchanges: one of the documents describing the earlier commercial system, the *Periplus of the Erythraean Sea,* from the first century CE, mentions eastern African involvement with global markets and international merchants from the Mediterranean and western Asia. The expansion of Islam further integrated global trade beginning in the eighth century CE. This trade had its extensions into the broader Indian Ocean world, as dramatically demonstrated by the early fifteenth-century expedition of Zheng He, a Chinese admiral who made a trip to eastern Africa and returned with a live giraffe as a gift for the Ming emperor. The more common exchanges involved African resources, such as gold, ivory, aromatic substances, and timber, for Asian textiles, ceramics, and luxury goods. Seafaring vessels known as dhows, wooden ships with lateen sails, moved between eastern Africa, Arabia, and India, as the monsoon winds allowed travel between these points easily in one trading season.

Africans involved in these Indian Ocean exchanges include the Swahili peoples. They occupied the ecological niche of mangrove coastal forests and coral reefs, which abutted arid desert in the northern regions of eastern Africa and provided the basis for thriving commercial towns along the coast from southern Somalia to northern Mozambique. They spoke a Bantu language, to which were added words from other African languages as well as from Arabic. The Swahili peoples began converting to Islam beginning in the ninth century, and Islam eventually came to be associated intimately with Swahili culture. Exchanges with Muslims across the Indian Ocean occurred, with Arab scholars from neighboring Oman and Yemen frequently visiting the Swahili coast and sometimes settling there, with their descendants becoming Swahili themselves over the generations. Swahili families maintain traditions of origins from elsewhere as well, with some claiming Shungwaya origins, rumored to be in the East African hinterland, and others asserting more distant connections to Shiraz, a Persian trading port. Whatever the historicity of these claims, the social formation along the eastern African coast was African in its origins even as it constructed a cosmopolitan identity.

Various polities emerged to control the trade along the eastern African coast. The Swahili peoples constructed city-states, and they competed with one another for influence in overseas trade; local histories recount these rivalries and the rise and fall of local dynasties. The northern city-states had the initial advantages because of their closer proximity to Asian trading partners, but Kilwa, on Tanzania's central coast, emerged as the most powerful city-state of the fourteenth century as a result of its involvement in the gold trade associated with Great Zimbabwe. The Portuguese used their ship-based cannon to seize control of coastal trade, especially the lucrative export of gold in the sixteenth century. With the decline of Portuguese influence, the Swahili city-states fell under the domination of another regional power, Oman, which used divide-and-conquer strategies to win over some city-states, defeat others, and construct a commercial empire based on the island of Zanzibar, which for centuries was a center of clove production. During the Omani era, clove production dramatically expanded and trade with the interior increased significantly, as the former pattern of waiting for interior merchants coming to the coast was replaced with caravans embarking from the coast. These caravans were armed, and their traders disrupted the lives of humans and animals alike in their search for ivory and slaves to transport to the coast. The ivory went to support the demand for billiard balls, gun handles, and letter openers for the middle classes of Europe, and the slaves often remained behind to work on clove plantations owned by Omani and Swahili elites. Some slaves worked as porters, and with less-wealthy Swahili merchants they strove to extricate themselves from an elaborate system of credit bankrolled by Omani political elites, South Asian financiers, and wealthier Swahili merchants. It was a dynamic era of social transformation, with interior cultures influencing the coast as much as Omani culture did. This cultural dynamism, however, could not prevent the region's subordination to European economic powers, which first traded along the coast and then used treaty relations to assert colonial control in the late nineteenth century.

Africa and the Atlantic World

The Atlantic world emerged as a commercial system centuries after the rise of the Indian Ocean system. It emerged in the aftermath of European voyages of exploration linking Europe with western Africa and the Americas. In contrast to the Indian Ocean world, the Atlantic world was not based on environmental forces such as monsoon winds that facilitated exchanges. In fact, the Atlantic's ocean currents and prevailing winds long limited contact between Europe and both the Americas and sub-Saharan Africa. Once Iberians adapted lateen sails and other technological advances to their sturdy oceangoing vessels, regular contact between the continents was possible, and soon other western European powers followed the Portuguese and Spanish in sailing the shores of the Atlantic. These activities facilitated a series of exchanges across the Atlantic world. One was the movement of plants, animals, and diseases. Crops from the Americas, such as corn and squash, soon were cultivated in Europe and Africa, and European and African foodstuffs and animals were imported to the Americas. Diseases also crossed the ocean, and in the Americas and southern Africa the arrival of European diseases unfortunately led to deaths among Amerindian and African populations without natural immunities. Another dimension of the Atlantic world was the trans-Atlantic slave trade. Western Europeans, who had colonized the Americas and the southernmost point of Africa, organized the largest forced migration in world history through the importation of Africans to the Americas as slave labor. The plantation systems created in the Americas were novel social institutions: in addition to innovations in capitalism underlying their formation, the plantations relied on the knowledge of tropical farming that Africans carried to the Americas. The African contributions to the emerging Atlantic world were innumerable but only recently have historians appreciated their role.

Scholars have debated many aspects of the trans-Atlantic slave trade. One issue concerns African participation in the processes of enslavement, slave trading, and slave holding. Before direct contact with Europeans, West Africans most certainly practiced slavery, but they integrated slaves into social formations with different operating principles and certainly not on the scale that would occur on plantations in the Americas. African war captives found themselves serving political elites, and sometimes rising to positions of influence; indebtedness could see a person volunteer for or be forced into domestic or agricultural service until such time as those financial obligations had been paid off; and Africans convicted of crimes might be punished with servitude to individuals or corporate groups. Slaves were integrated into African communities as domestic servants, farmhands working alongside their patrons, assistants to artisans, petty traders in commercial firms, and professional soldiers and even governors for political elites. In African contexts, over time slaves usually gained more and more rights and privileges; for example, children of enslaved individuals usually took the names of their parents, could not be sold to others, and were entitled to inheritance shares. The gendered nature of servitude also differed in western Atlantic and African contexts, as African men were sold disproportionately into trans-Atlantic networks. Slave trading also was practiced, with slaves sold both internally and across the Indian Ocean and the Sahara Desert for thousands of years. Even though the trans-Atlantic slave trade built on these foundations, it established other precedents and took millions of Africans to plantation servitude within a span of only several hundred years. The social processes unleashed by the trans-Atlantic trade altered the African continent in significant ways.

The plantation system in the Americas was a particularly rigorous labor regime. It emerged out of a historical context, with origins in the Levant, elaboration in the Mediterranean, and exportation and further elaboration in the Americas, where it was tied to emerging forms of capitalism. In North and South America it organized mass labor for the most efficient production of crops such as sugar, which fetched high prices in the expanding Atlantic economy. By the end of the sixteenth century, demand for sugar propelled the slave mode of production throughout the entire western tropical Atlantic basin, especially in the Caribbean and Brazil. Sugar could be sold as it was or made into hard spirits such as rum, the production of which relied on additional slave labor. The emergence of privateers and pirates is a lasting legacy to the ascendancy of the sugar and alcohol economies of the Caribbean. Exported sugar and rum went to Europe and Africa to be traded for other goods. In Africa, however, the voracious demand for enslaved Africans—high mortality rates meant that plantations required a constant resupply of slave labor—drove the commercial exchanges. African elites served as willing providers as they pursued financial and technological opportunities to unseat old and new rivals. Careful study of slave shippers' cargo logs led historians to the figure of approximately twelve million African arrivals in the Americas during the era of the plantation economy; unknown are the numbers of Africans who died during the Middle Passage or in slave raids in Africa.

As demand for slaves to work in the Americas rose, African societies were transformed. Among African slave traders, the previous system of exchanging persons eroded and captives were treated as commodities. African traders sometimes organized raiding parties to obtain persons for exchange with Europeans, in return receiving weaponry, glass beads, metal, and other goods. Warfare increased over time as well, as African political elites found a market for war captives. Regulatory spiritual systems intended to mete out justice in local contexts were contorted by this demand: condemned persons now could be sold to Europeans. Given the preference for men in the external trade, female captives often remained in Africa as dependents of political elites and merchants. Oral traditions, at least the ones controlled by male agency, changed to reflect these transformations, projecting back into the past narratives of male dominance in many societies where women's historical roles had been far greater.

Overall, the level of social subordination increased as larger numbers of disenfranchised people became dependent upon others for safety. Ultimately the era of the trans-Atlantic slave trade allowed some Africans to grow wealthy, primarily coastal traders and African political authorities who fought wars in the interior and sold captives at the coast. Not all societies experienced the same repercussions: some were not very involved, while others lost substantial numbers of adult men and women with considerable expertise and knowledge. Some, such as stretches of coast spanning present-day Liberia and Sierra Leone, received influxes of formerly enslaved people liberated by British naval efforts, creating new, creolized societies rich with tensions sparked by the arrival of these outsiders. Abolitionist efforts in the nineteenth century led to further transformations, as Europeans, including the British, reversed course and no longer purchased slaves, introducing the era of "legitimate commerce" in the nineteenth century. The historical forces leading to wars and enslavement in Africa were not halted, and captives entered regional slave markets and remained in Africa, producing cash crops for sale as "legitimate" goods in global markets. Africa now exported not slaves but peanuts and palm kernels, the extracted oils of which lubricated machines in the factories of the early Industrial Revolution.

During the trans-Atlantic slave trade Europeans negotiated with African elites for the right to build and reside in forts and other coastal enclaves. For years Europeans remained content to stay on the coast and engage in commerce with Africans who traveled to them. During the course of the nineteenth century, however, Europeans began to project their power into the interior. This was the era of travelers and explorers who, among other things, sought to "discover" the sources of the Nile and Niger Rivers; their publications in geographical journals supported those interested in expanding "legitimate commerce" and also sparked new interest by European powers. Commerce remained an activity that brought benefits to all parties, and Europeans made contacts with a plethora of local authorities further and further in the interior, offering treaties of trade and protection. These were but the first steps in a process that culminated in European colonial rule in Africa.

EUROPEAN COLONIAL RULE AND ITS AFTERMATH

Some scholars speak of the "scramble" for Africa when describing the processes that brought European colonial control over most of the African continent in the nineteenth century. From the European perspective, it was a flurry of activity, especially during the last two decades of the nineteenth century, when the pace of intervention accelerated in sub-Saharan Africa. Seven European powers, led by Britain, France, and Germany and including Italy, Portugal, Spain, and the Belgian monarch Leopold II, carved up the continent. These powers engaged in diplomacy among themselves to set terms for dividing the continent into "spheres of influence" before they moved to extend effective occupation through force into those spheres. Historians of European imperialism debate the salience of economic, military, and diplomatic factors in the conquest of Africa. Those who argue for the pressing need of capitalist enterprises to invest abroad overstate their case, but the economic potential of African territories certainly drove the expansion, as did diplomatic rivalries, the desire of European military leaders to make a name for themselves, and local crises which that led some powers to intervene. What emerges from the debate is that the era might best be understood from the European perspective as a series of regional inventions, each with specific economic and political causes, made possible by changes in the technological and military capacities of European powers and the growing racism of the time, which allowed them to justify their actions as a "civilizing mission," complete with social Darwinist and pseudo-scientific justifications.

Africans were not mere bystanders to this event. Although African political leaders were not invited to the 1884–85 Berlin conference where the "rules" of the partition were established, they engaged in efforts to negotiate with agents of European powers who offered them commercial relations and "protection." When Europeans moved to occupy the continent, some African leaders resisted militarily, whereas others tried to obtain favorable positions in the new colonial administration. Some have sought to cast Africans as either "resisters" or "collaborators," but these binary terms obscure the complexities of the times, when Africans adopted diverse and changing strategies to protect their interests in the face of European occupation of the continent. Some who interacted with Europeans also did so to derive benefits for their communities: a pan-African sense of a common front did not emerge, although a dense network of allegiances did arise among some African communities as European power touched more and more people and African political, economic, and social institutions. In the end, except in the case of the Ethiopian defeat of the Italians at Adwa in 1896, resistance did not prevent colonial occupation. But the era of resistance underscores African agency in the face of forceful European assertions. Clearly the term "scramble" does not capture fully this violent era of European conquest.

European Colonial Rule in Africa

European colonial rule had many dimensions, and the following thematic analysis can only begin to discuss the impact of the era for Africa and its peoples. The first point to acknowledge is that the partition of Africa left a clear legacy to contemporary Africa: the current political borders of African nation-states largely adopt the ad hoc imperial geography of the "scramble." Colonial boundaries were altered slightly after World War I as responsibility for the former German colonies in western, southern, and eastern Africa was given to the war's victors, Britain and France, who often incorporated the territories into existing colonies. Boundaries changed again slightly after World War II: the most notable example was the integration of the former Italian colony of Eritrea into Ethiopia, which had suffered an Italian invasion in the 1930s and gained liberation with Eritrea as a new province in the 1950s. This case perhaps illustrates the durability of colonial boundaries: in the 1990s Eritrean liberation forces won the right to form an independent Eritrean state, the boundaries of which followed the former colonial borders with Ethiopia. It is not arbitrary lines across African soils that make boundaries endure, however; the political, economic, social, and other transformations that occurred within those colonial territories continue to influence the present.

Once European powers divided and conquered Africa, they had to rule over its inhabitants. Force and the threat of its use remained a major component of colonial rule for decades, as small numbers of European officials claimed authority over large territories with restive populations speaking languages they did not know. Europeans also turned to Africans to assist them in ruling the continent. Leaders who had signed treaties were one group securing subordinate roles in the colonial administrative hierarchy, but in contexts without such authorities or where leaders had resisted, Europeans recruited others, often adventurers willing to fill these roles. Historians discuss the administrative styles of the European powers, emphasizing, for example, British "indirect rule" and the maintenance of African cultures as opposed to French emphasis on the "assimilation" of French culture by a few Africans and "direct rule" imposed on the masses. Such differences are evident in some cases, but the Great Depression led most powers to reduce expenses and rule indirectly through African intermediaries. Current research is focusing on these chiefs, clerks, translators, tax collectors, and police officers, revealing how they actively shaped colonial rule: European superiors relied on their knowledge to make decisions and then turned to them to implement colonial policies. Recently some historians have argued that African chiefs recognized by the British did not preserve long-standing cultural practices but "invented" traditions to bolster their standing. While there were limits to this kind of invention, it is not surprising that African cultures remained vibrantly dynamic even in the colonial period. The larger point is that a few Africans had greater access to power and influence than others, and analyses of how these African actors turned colonial rule to their advantage in particular contexts is the key to understanding the long-term legacy of European rule in any given former colonial territory.

European officials used their resources and power to set the economic orientation of colonial Africa, although Africans still exercised agency and influenced outcomes in some cases. Colonial administrations favored expanded international trade and built coastal seaports and a network of railroads and later motor routes that facilitated the export of cash crops and mineral wealth from Africa in exchange for consumer goods from Europe. Securing labor was another issue. Forced labor was an option, which resulted in brutal practices by the concessionary companies in the first years of the Congo Free State. Even though these abuses were halted in the early twentieth century, authoritarian labor regimes remained important there and in other colonies where forced labor was employed. Another option was to impose new currencies and demand payment of taxes in cash, thereby forcing Africans to work for European firms or produce and sell cash crops. These taxation policies generated a workforce for the capital-intensive mineral extraction operations established by European firms in southern and central Africa. It also encouraged Africans to produce on their own initiative cash crops, such as cocoa, coffee, and peanuts, for sale in western Africa and selected regions of eastern, central, and southern Africa. African producers also sometimes thwarted colonial designs to establish European plantations; for example, Africans responded with alacrity to the completion of the railhead from coastal Kenya to Uganda by producing large quantities of cotton, which undercut colonial plans to have European settlers produce this crop. Even when European colonists arrived in other contexts, Africans still outproduced settler farmers, at least until colonial laws favored the Europeans, with the result that they ended up working on settler farms. This development illuminates the political economy of the colonial era: where Europeans settled in large numbers, such as the mineral-rich territories of central and southern Africa and the mosquito-free highlands of eastern Africa, settler interests trumped those of the African inhabitants of the territory. Even in western Africa, where cash crop

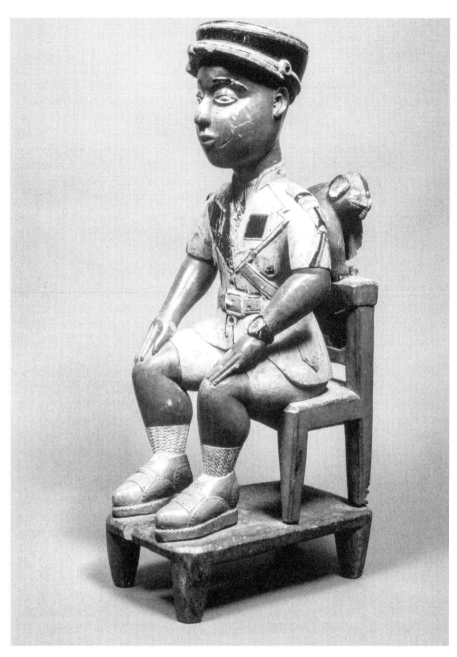

Figure 2.4. Police officer in the French colony of Côte d'Ivoire, as represented by a twentieth-century African carving. Courtesy of Indiana University Art Museum. *Collection of Rita and John Grunwald.*

production was in African hands and few European settlers lived, colonial policies worked to give advantages to the European firms that dominated the lucrative export sector. Many African-owned businesses folded as discriminatory practices pursued by banks, companies, goods transporters, and others increasingly made it difficult for Africans to compete effectively.

Colonial rule encouraged Africans to obtain formal education in European languages and to follow European curricula. One might imagine that this effort would have been central to the era, given the "civilizing mission" espoused during the European partition of Africa. But colonial administrations devoted few resources to provide education to Africans. Mass education never was a goal: they founded schools for sons of chiefs and others whom they wanted to recruit into the colonial administration, and they relied on Christian missionaries to provide education to others. Some Africans saw the value of education in European languages and seized on these opportunities. Historical research on colonial encounters reveals the complexity of the cultural transformations: educated Africans were "middle figures" with knowledge of multiple cultures who acted on their own visions of the future. They reconfigured European ideas to fit local circumstances, and they added indigenous knowledge and values to the equation. These Africans helped expand Christianity in Africa, for example, working as catechists and translating the message of the church into culturally understandable terms, as the chapter on religion discusses at greater length. Some Africans attended institutions of higher learning in Europe and the United States, and in these contexts they made connections, became aware of and elaborated upon the idea of Pan-Africanism, and developed their own ideas about political change on the continent. These and other educated Africans burst onto the political scene in the late colonial era, as they came to demand greater participation in political life and articulated African understandings of nationalism.

Independence and Postcolonial Africa

The decades after World War II were a time of political change for the continent. African nationalists and others pushed for and won independence. There were other changes as well. For example, European powers embarked on economic development schemes that sought to increase African production to benefit metropolitan nations devastated by the war. When finally forced to decolonize, European sought to devolve power to African elites whom they hoped would continue to value these economic ties, a relationship some derided as "neocolonialism." Even if African political elites cut ties with the former colonial powers and embarked on new policies, they often pursued schemes to increase production and thus continued the development policies of the late colonial era.

European powers had hoped to keep their colonies for longer than they did, but forces from within and without pushed change. The new Cold War powers, the United States and the Soviet Union, put pressure on Europeans to decolonize Africa, with immediate results seen in the former Italian possessions of Eritrea, Libya, and Somalia and in northern Africa, where the French granted independence to Morocco and Tunisia. Elsewhere, internal pressure was needed. African workers made clear their displeasure with conditions in a series of uncoordinated labor actions in ports and key economic domains during the late 1940s; African soldiers who had served in European armies during the war added their voices, plus detailed knowledge of European weapons and military tactics, to the civil discontent. Pressing forward too were educated elites who organized political movements to call for self-government. African lawyers and other professionals long had petitioned colonial governments for local involvement in political affairs, but the postwar era brought a new generation of more aggressive leaders, who constructed mass-based movements to apply pressure on colonial powers.

The decolonization process followed its own logic in each territory, but general patterns emerged. Europeans moved to devolve power more quickly in western Africa, where European settler interests did not complicate the transition. There the British and French pursued different strategies and handed over power in the 1950s and early 1960s. The French allowed a gradually widening franchise to vote for representatives to the metropolitan legislative body, and these African representatives pushed for greater changes, such as the elimination of forced labor and ultimately the devolution of power to locally elected leaders. The British also increased the franchise, but for elections to existing legislative councils in the colonies, long with only token African members, to transition initially to African control of internal affairs and eventually full independence. These patterns were evident in eastern Africa too in areas where settlers were not a dominant force, as in Tanganyika and Uganda, which gained independence in the early 1960s. Where European settlers did constitute a potent force, conflicts erupted as African initiatives for peaceful change were rebuffed and gave way to armed efforts. Uprisings such as Mau Mau in Kenya helped convince the British to devolve power, but outright wars were required in some contexts. In Algeria several years of fighting and, by some estimates, millions of North African casualties finally forced the French to end their rule, for example, and in the Portuguese colonies decades of struggle by African liberation forces against an intransigent regime finally led to decolonization after a coup in Lisbon in 1975.

European settlers in South Africa held out the longest. South Africa gained formal independence in 1910, when the British recognized the Union of South Africa, but devolved power resided with the European settler community: for the majority of South Africans the twentieth century was an era of struggle against European domination. Africans, Asians, and those of multiethnic heritage had limited rights, and the 1948 South African elections reduced them further. The victorious National Party, dominated by Dutch-speaking settlers calling themselves Afrikaners, imposed a policy of apartheid, or racial segregation. Apartheid reinforced segregation in everyday life, even though Europeans still depended upon African labor in the gold and diamond mines and in other industries as well as in their homes as domestic servants. Apartheid policies also aimed to create "Bantustans," independent states in marginal areas where ethnically segregated Africans could rule but would still supply labor to a South Africa where they had no rights. The majority of South Africans protested apartheid policies, with the African National Congress (ANC) taking a leading role in organizing peaceful demonstrations in the 1950s and 1960s and then in waging a guerrilla war with its armed wing in the 1970s and 1980s. In this era, South Africans drew upon the example and support of African Americans who waged their own civil rights struggle in the United States, as well as Africans who formed a bloc of frontline states opposed to apartheid. For years the apartheid state's security apparatus brutally suppressed dissent, but the impasse was broken when Nelson Mandela, an ANC member imprisoned for three decades and a symbol for those pushing for political change, was released from prison. Mandela helped negotiate broadly based elections in 1994, which the ANC won with huge majorities. This political history parallels experiences in African colonial contexts and is perhaps best understood within the same analytical frame.

With this last political change, contemporary Africa now can be called postcolonial, as Africans control the state apparatus in more than fifty independent states. Terms such as "neocolonialism," however, suggest that political liberation did not necessarily produce fundamental change: Africa's position in the global economy was structured by the rise of industrial Europe and the colonial intervention, two historical legacies that did not change with political independence. Still, globalization, a concept contested by scholars and business leaders alike, offers both challenges and opportunities for the continent. For example, the rise of China and its rapid economic growth are unleashing powerful currents throughout the continent, providing new trading partners and investors but also sometimes strengthening established political elites, as the chapter on development elaborates. Marking out distinct eras in domains besides the political also is not easy: the end of colonial rule did not immediately change the rhythms of daily life for most Africans. Independence nonetheless allowed for the imagining of new possibilities, and the last decades have witnessed changes in all areas, as the other chapters in this volume discuss at length.

Was the colonial era transformative or an interlude in a longer history? The boundaries of contemporary African states as well as the circumstances surrounding the European devolution of power to African elites set the parameters and shaped political life for at least several decades thereafter. Connections to the global economy forged during colonial rule also structured local economies no matter what policies African leaders pursued after independence. One most certainly can argue that in these two domains the colonial era was influential, but it will be necessary to wait a few more decades to see whether this legacy is enduring. In cultural domains, the colonial heritage is more difficult to tease out from ongoing African initiatives. One may point to the endurance of European languages on the continent, but much of African life is conducted in local languages. Regarding explicit

European (or other non-African) influences in art, literature, religion, and other expressive domains, Africans were attracted by new ideas and practices, but they continued to draw upon local and regional cultural resources of longer standing. Africans appropriated and transformed new ideas, but they also preserved and elaborated on older ones. Dynamism and innovation are constant processes in African history, from the first transitions to food production through the peopling of the continent, the formation of states, the construction of long-distance commercial networks, and the present. Colonial domination stifled some of these expressions, but it did not destroy African culture or the vitality of African cultural production. Africans are as creative today as they were in the past, building nation-states, developing economies, and producing works of art, literature, music and other cultural expressions.

NOTE

1. Hugh Trevor-Roper, "The Rise of Christian Europe," *The Listener* LXX (November 28, 1963): 5.

SUGGESTIONS FOR FURTHER READING

African Cultural Heritage Sites and Landscapes. Aluka (Ithaka Harbors, Inc.). Available at www.aluka.org/page/content/heritage.jsp.

The African Diaspora in the Indian Ocean World: Essays. Schomburg Center for Research in Black Culture, New York Public Library. Available at http://exhibitions.nypl.org/africans indianocean/essays.php.

Akyeampong, Emmanuel, and Henry Louis Gates Jr., eds. 2011. *Dictionary of African Biography.* Oxford: Oxford University Press.

Allman, Jean, Susan Geiger, and Nakanyike Musisi, eds. 2002. *Women in African Colonial Histories.* Bloomington: Indiana University Press.

Boahen, A. Adu. 1989. *African Perspectives on Colonialism.* Baltimore: Johns Hopkins University Press.

Casely-Hayford, Gus. 2012. *Lost Kingdoms of Africa: Discovering Africa's Hidden Treasures.* New York: Random House.

Cooper, Frederick. 2002. *Africa since 1940: The Past of the Present.* Cambridge: Cambridge University Press.

Freund, Bill. 2007. *The African City: A History.* Cambridge: Cambridge University Press.

Getz, Trevor, and Liz Clarke. 2012. *Abina and the Important Men: A Graphic History.* New York: Oxford University Press.

Gomez, Michael. 2004. *Reversing Sail: A History of the African Diaspora.* New York: Cambridge University Press.

Herbert, Eugenia, and Candice Goucher. *The Blooms of Banjeli: Technology and Gender in West African Ironmaking—Study Guide.* Documentary Educational Resources. Available at http://der.org/resources/study-guides/blooms-of-banjeli.pdf.

Keim, Curtis. 2013. *Mistaking Africa: Curiosities and Inventions of the American Mind.* 3rd ed. Boulder, CO: Westview Press.

Phillipson, David. 2005. *African Archaeology.* 3rd ed. New York: Cambridge University Press.

White, Luise, Stephan Miescher, and David William Cohen, eds. 2001. *African Words, African Voices: Critical Practices in Oral History.* Bloomington: Indiana University Press.

Worger, William, Nancy Clark, and Ed Alpers, eds. 2010. *Africa and the West: A Documentary History,* volume 1, *1441–1905,* and volume 2, *From Colonialism to Independence.* 2nd ed. Oxford: Oxford University Press.

3 Social Relations
Family, Kinship, and Community

Maria Grosz-Ngaté

News accounts of violent conflict in Africa frequently make reference to "tribe" and "tribalism" as potent ingredients of discord. The use of "tribe" in the African context is a legacy of colonialism and the research of early anthropologists. Anthropologists wanted to know how African societies without centralized leadership maintained order and stability, while colonial officials demarcated African societies for the purpose of rule, ignoring complexities, interactions between groups, and the fluidity of boundaries. The persistent characterization of African populations as "tribes" gives the appearance of timelessness and glosses over the different forms of political organization that existed in the past. It implicitly suggests that tribe (or ethnic group) is the primary source of identity and mode of sociopolitical organization on the continent. It also obscures the existence of more important forms of identification, relatedness, and belonging that may play a role in, counteract, or facilitate the resolution of conflict. Like people in other parts of the world, Africans are enmeshed in a range of institutions and identify with multiple collectivities. An individual may be a mother, wife, sister, and daughter; a cultivator, cloth dyer, or teacher; a member of an age group, a participant in a local or national women's association, and a member of an ethnic group as well as a citizen of a nation-state. These social positions and identities overlap and cross-cut each other; which of them takes precedence at any given time depends on the context.

This chapter focuses on social relations as lived and constructed through kinship, marriage, and forms of association beyond the family. It illuminates the diverse ways in which individuals negotiate these institutions and the changes taking place as a result of the day-to-day actions of African women and men in the context of historical, political, and economic processes that impinge on their lives. Social relations are dynamic and change is not new; yet transformations are often subtle before they become visible or acknowledged as a result of an event that brings them to the fore. Africans may highlight continuity when asked about specific practices. At the same time, older people contending that young people act very differently than they themselves once did often ignore the variability that already existed during their own youth.

FORMS AND MEANINGS OF KINSHIP

Drawing on Western models of economic transition, twentieth-century moderniza-tion theorists assumed that the importance of kinship bonds would diminish once African economies developed and state institutions created a social safety net. Yet kinship has not lost its salience as a moral order that structures relationships and guides people's actions as they meet the challenges of contemporary life. Anthro-pologists have used the concept of "kinship" to understand who gets counted as "family" in different African societies.[1] They identified kinship, that is, relation-ships constructed through descent (a concept overlapping with what Americans usually call "blood relations") and marriage, as the primary organizing principle. In classifying societies according to the ways in which they formed kin groups, they found that unilineal descent groups prevailed across the continent: a majority of African societies were patrilineal, tracing descent only through the father, and a significant number were matrilineal, reckoning descent through the mother. The de-scent system of the Tuareg, living in Algeria, Burkina Faso, Libya, Mali, and Niger, seems to have shifted from matrilineal to patrilineal in the process of Islamization, although higher-status groups within society appear to have retained more matrilin-eal elements than lower-status groups. Some populations, such as the Beng people of Côte d'Ivoire or the San of southern Africa, have a double descent system, tracing ancestral ties through both the father and the mother. The latter differs from the ways in which Euro-Americans view connections between ancestors and descen-dants in that individuals belong simultaneously to two separately constituted de-scent groups. Among the San peoples, membership in both the mother's and father's descent groups conferred rights to the plants and animals of the territory associated with each group. In Beng society, each kin group is important in different contexts. Agricultural land, for example, is inherited through the matriline, while funerary rites are carried out by members of the patriline.

Kin groups tracing descent to a common ancestor often constituted lineages that acted like corporate groups. Clans encompassed groups that also claimed descent from a common ancestor but not all of the genealogical connections were known. Some populations were organized into lineages and clans, some had one but not the other, and the most decentralized had neither. In some places, lineages became identified with particular territories, mostly when land became scarce. Lineages and clans continue to structure identities and solidarities in Libya and Somalia, but their sociopolitical importance has changed in many other locales. Social status became more important than lineage or ethnicity after centuries of intermarriage between indigenous Berbers and migrant Arabs of the West African Sahara, blur-ring genealogical and cultural distinctions. In Morocco, individual achievements such as wealth or high levels of education now often outweigh descent from an important family. Descent remains important among rural Tuareg of northern Niger but is downplayed in urban areas in the interest of struggles for cultural autonomy.

In matrilineal and patrilineal societies children belong to the mother's or to the father's lineage, respectively, and authority over them is vested in the senior men of these lineages (i.e., maternal uncles vs. fathers). Relations with male kin of the other parent, like relations with sisters, are typically characterized by affection and can be drawn on for support when a child or youth has difficulties within the natal family. The definition of "family" is broader than in Euro-American societies since a greater range of individuals are considered siblings. Who counts as a sibling depends on the descent system. In patrilineal societies, the children of brothers call each other brother and sister; they also refer to their father's brothers as "father" but differentiate between a father's elder and younger brothers. Terms for brother and sister too generally reflect the age hierarchy; that is, someone is always referred to as "elder brother/sister" or "younger brother/sister." Children of the same father but of different mothers are considered brothers and sisters, although their relationship may be fraught with tension and rivalries. Adoption is not a common practice and may even be discouraged because an adoptive child is of different "blood." Fostering, however, is very common. It entails the relocation of children from their natal homes to homes where they are raised and cared for and does not occur only in the event of a crisis such as the death of parents or the mother of an infant: childless women often become "mothers" by raising the child of a brother or sister; and aunts, uncles, or significantly older siblings take in youths who attend secondary school or university in the city. Non-kin foster parents are usually wealthier individuals. In all of these circumstances, parents do not lose legal rights over the children.

Patrilineal and matrilineal societies exhibit considerable variability in residence patterns, claims to authority, and individuals' access to resources. Anthropologists who conducted research in Africa during the 1930s and 1940s focused on kinship in order to elucidate social organization. This led them to emphasize structures, rules, and norms. Although their studies became classics in the development of anthropological thinking about kinship, they made kinship systems appear more timeless and rigid than they are in practice. They did not consider how kinship structures might have been altered by the slave trade or how colonial policies were affecting practices such as inheritance. They also did not take into account the incorporation of individuals or social groups who were not born into the lineage or marry into it. Historians of Africa have demonstrated that kin groups in both sedentary and pastoral societies often expanded by integrating conquered people, slaves, or refugees from conflict or other calamities, while others contracted as a result of famine, disease, or slave raiding. To better capture social dynamism, anthropologists now pay attention to the ways in which individuals and social groups interpret and use rules, construct relatedness through everyday practices, and modify kinship practices over time as political and economic circumstances change.

CONSTRUCTING RELATIONSHIPS THROUGH MARRIAGE

Marriage in many societies is the primary means for expanding kinship relations and reproducing descent groups. Although birth rates across Africa have declined in recent decades and couples increasingly limit the number of children, having children remains an important goal of marriage for the group and for individual men and women. Children may provide social security in old age; they also affirm the social personhood of adult women and men and ensure a form of immortality. Dying without having had at least one child means that one's name and one's influence in the world are not extended. Marriage is also used strategically to develop alliances, especially among those of high social standing, much as European royalty or powerful families elsewhere in the world have done.

Among late twentieth-century patrilineal Bamana people of central Mali, male household heads were obligated to identify suitable spouses for marriageable men in order of seniority. They took into account existing relationships between their own family and those with women of marriageable age, families' social standing, and the character of a potential bride, and sent an intermediary to a woman's kin to express their interest in her and seek their consent to a marriage. Forging connections between kin groups through marriage is valued as a means of developing solidarity within and across villages. Affinal (in-law) relations are transformed into consanguineal (blood) relations over generations when repeated marriages take place between two kin groups. Marriages between cross-cousins—children of a brother and sister in the first or subsequent generations—were preferred because they perpetuated already established ties. They were also thought to be more stable because a bride would be among relatives and family members could intervene to help resolve conflicts, if necessary. These practices connected families and villages across the generations so that, for example, a woman's daughter would be married to the son of one of her male relatives. Elders did not have to respect the age hierarchy when it came to marrying a second wife because it was recognized that some men's personal characteristics made them more attractive as spouses. A family could, for example, propose a young girl as a future bride for one of the young men to reinforce a relationship between the two kin groups.

Intrinsic to the emphasis on the family over the individual was the assumption that the couple would develop affection for each other as they lived together. In the past, the couple was informed only after the arrangement had been concluded. This changed in the second half of the twentieth century, when elders increasingly relied on money earned by young men on labor migration for the payment of taxes and bridewealth (that is, the transfer of goods and services from the groom's family to the bride's family) and for the purchase of agricultural equipment. Through their ability to earn cash, junior men gained greater autonomy within the household. One of the results was that their elders would ask a junior man if he wanted to marry a particular woman before concluding a marriage agreement. Their earning capacity also allowed junior men to ask their seniors to find a

Figure 3.1. Couple during wedding celebrations in a village of Segou region, Mali. *Maria Grosz-Ngaté.*

second wife for them or to initiate negotiations for a woman they had met and wished to marry.

Young women did not receive the same opportunity to express their opinion, even after they began earning money in cash-cropping areas or in the city during the 1970s in order to buy some of the goods they would bring into their marital home. Their mothers sometimes intervened if they objected to the choice, but they often did not prevail. Mothers could, however, delay the wedding a year or more by contending that they needed more time to complete the daughter's trousseau. Occasionally, young women who strongly objected to a proposed marriage refused to return home from working in the city; others ran away after they were married. These actions put them at odds with their male kin and subjected their mothers to criticism.

The preference for marrying people from within a known social network extends well beyond Bamana villages to other African societies and to contexts where marriageable men and women have greater freedom in choosing a spouse. Among the San peoples of southern Africa appropriate marriage or sexual partners are individuals whose grandparents or great-grandparents were siblings. Consanguinity and affinity overlap, and affines can be recategorized as kin. While this may seem

Figure 3.2. Maasai women watching the bride enter in Kajiado district, Kenya. *Jennie Demille.*

highly restrictive to outsiders, it actually allows for considerable flexibility, as San individuals draw on a range of available options to develop and manage a social network that provides support in times of need. A preference for marriage within a (usually extensive) network of relationships does not mean that people marry only within their own social group. In societies where clans were historically important, marriage between members of the same clan was often expressly forbidden. People also marry across ethnic boundaries. This is not a recent or primarily urban phenomenon but extends to populations in rural areas; for example, Maasai pastoralists of north-central Tanzania intermarried with Arusha cultivators to expand their productive strategies, especially during times when drought or disease decimated their herds. The fact that marriage in many societies is often used strategically to strengthen and cement ties based on material interests does not mean that marital relationships in Africa are, or have been, devoid of emotional attachment and passion.

The stability of marriages has varied across space and over time, regardless of whether they are monogamous or polygynous. In some societies (for example, the Hausa of Maradi in Niger, the Mbororo Fulani of Cameroon, or the (!Kung San of the Kalahari), divorce and remarriage have been common. The incidence of divorce has been low in others not only because divorce spells a rupture in relationships between the two families but also because it may lead to disputes over the repayment of bridewealth, especially when the portion to be repaid has already been consumed by the wife's family. Women in patrilineal societies may themselves be reluctant to leave their husbands because they cannot take their children with them. Many women seek a divorce only when conflict is extreme; women in urban southwestern Nigeria, for example, generally do so only if they want to remarry. However, a growing number of women across the continent do not remarry after divorce or widowhood if they have a measure of financial autonomy due to success in trade or other professions.

Prompted by a widespread interest in romantic love on the part of African youths, scholars have begun to explore discourses, sentiments, and practices of love, and the ways in which Africans engage and remake ideals of intimacy from elsewhere over time. They are finding that young people have long used claims of intimate passion to set themselves apart from their parents' generation and that those who defended it in their youth often questioned it as a sound basis for marriage once they grew older. Today's youths debate the romantic love depicted in Latin American television serials, South Asian films, Nigerian videos, and local popular print media, and many embrace it, along with monogamy, as an ideal basis for marriage and as a way of being modern. Young women associate notions of romantic love with companionate marriage, greater support from husbands, and independence from kin. Yet students or urban migrants who wish to marry partners with whom they have developed affective relationships usually inform their parents and elders, who then enter into dialogue, carry out the appropriate rituals, take charge of any gift transfers, and make practical arrangements. Desires to marry for love and to achieve the lifestyle associated with it frequently come up against harsh economic realities. As African economies have declined, an ever greater number of men have to delay marriage because they do not earn enough to provide for the housing and other basic needs of a young family, especially in urban areas. They are therefore prevented from becoming social adults, since marriage is generally considered a passage to adulthood. Under these conditions, men may express their love as well as their masculinity by providing support and gifts to one or more girlfriends. Some women avoid marriage (or remarriage following divorce) and engage in a sexual relationship in exchange for financial support unless they are able to sustain themselves economically.

Christian missionaries in Africa have held up ideals of romantic love and companionate marriage since at least the nineteenth century as part of their efforts to establish monogamy and eradicate polygyny, that is, the practice whereby a man has more than one wife. They perceived African marriages as loveless and duty-bound and led a constant battle to have converts adhere to the exclusive relationship of monogamy. Churches, especially the Pentecostal churches that have expanded rapidly in recent years in many parts of the continent, also promote the monogamous nuclear family and the concentration of resources on this smaller unit, emphasizing the "family" of church members over the extended family, which they assume to be "traditional." Islam allows a man to have up to four wives as long as he is able to provide for each of them equally, yet many Muslims have only one wife. Polygyny is not confined to the rural areas or to those without formal schooling, but it is far from universal even in societies where it is legal. Outsiders frequently consider polygyny as quintessentially African. Yet not all men support polygyny nor do all women reject it, even as African feminists speak out against it. Africans who defend it often cite "tradition" in making their argument and ignore its connection to social status, even in the past.

THE MATERIALITY OF MARRIAGE AND SOCIAL ATTACHMENT

Weddings are among the most important social events in many African societies. They make social ties visible and reaffirm them through acts of reciprocity. The celebration of weddings in the West African Sahel reflects changes as a result of conversion to Islam during the twentieth century as well as increased access to money and material goods. Ritual proceedings vary between rural and urban areas and between ethnic groups, but here as elsewhere in Africa weddings celebrate the alliance not just of two individuals but of two kin groups. While kinship is central to the wedding ceremonies in which I participated in villages of the Segou region in Mali, non-kin relationships and solidarity are equally in evidence: the bridegroom and bride are both assisted by their age-mates, the groom's family is helped by other village households to ensure that there is enough food for the guests, the male elder in the groom's family gets small contributions from other elders, and the relationships that the groom has forged throughout the province are demonstrated by the monetary contributions he receives from other men. Men's ability to establish networks of mutual giving has increased significantly as a result of the cash they earn on labor migration.

Weddings are preceded by ritualized communication and exchanges between the families of the bride and groom, even if the relationship was initiated by the couple rather than by family elders. Gifts in patrilineal societies flow in both directions, but the more substantial prestations move from the groom's family to the bride's, often over a period of years. Although they consist of different categories of gifts, anthropologists refer to them collectively as "bridewealth." Some are made only once, while others occur throughout the period of engagement. Their composition has changed over time in relation to socioeconomic changes. Annual prestations consisted of agricultural products, including millet grain and beer, when Bamana of Mali made a living primarily by agriculture. Millet beer was replaced by grain or money as people became Muslims, and millet grain gradually gave way to money and cloth as young men increasingly migrated to the cities to earn extra income. The annual payments are stipulated by the bride's family at the time the marriage arrangement is agreed on. In pastoral and other societies where animal husbandry plays an important role, marriage relationships are constructed through the transfer of cows, sheep, goats, or camels. Bridewealth may continue to be reckoned in cows or sheep even if it takes the form of cash, and the marriage of a son could be tied to the receipt of bridewealth for a daughter.

Marriage in some societies is delayed when payments are not made. In others the status of a marriage, and the children born of it, may be ambiguous if the wedding takes place before all of the gifts have been transferred or are not completed after the wedding. Incomplete payment or nonpayment of bridewealth may lead to disputes when a deceased woman's relatives claim her body for burial, contesting the right of her husband's people to bury her. This is the case even in settings where there has been a widespread decline in the payment of bridewealth, mostly for economic reasons, but where expectations and demands for it still persist. Among the urban poor, couples often simply live together under "customary law," although what constitutes "custom" and its attendant rights and obligations are continually redefined. In predominantly Muslim Mali, the parents of a young couple often have a religious ceremony performed to give a cohabiting couple social legitimacy. A religious marriage is also considered to be more flexible and easier to dissolve than a marriage with bridewealth and/or a civil ceremony conducted before a representative of the state.

The early missionaries to Africa who encountered bridewealth saw in it merely the purchase of a woman and referred to these prestations as "brideprice." Anthropologists attempted to correct this misperception by highlighting the rights in the productive and reproductive capacity of a woman that the groom's family acquired through these payments. They pointed out that the payment of bridewealth gave the prospective husband and his family rights to a woman's labor and allowed them to claim the children born of the marriage; that is, children belonged to the father's family even if the couple later divorced. Subsequent research led to a more nuanced understanding: the transfer of bridewealth not only compensates for the "loss" of a woman but also establishes her and her family's "worth," expresses social difference, and constitutes not only a marital relationship but also kin and affines. Contributing animals to the bridewealth cattle where these form the medium of payment is a tangible way of affirming one's belonging and position within the kin group. Patrilineal kin were implicated in the agricultural products given by Bamana to a bride's family in the past because they collectively cultivated and harvested the crops. Similarly, members of the bride's kin group were reaffirmed in their position when they received grain or shared in the consumption of millet beer. With the insertion of money into the exchange, the involvement of family members is diminished because the bridegroom can earn the bridewealth on his own by working in the city. Whereas a payment of millet or animals could be forgiven during periods of severe drought, monetary payments are expected regardless of economic circumstances. Money is not redistributed in the bride's family but goes to the father, who gives a portion of it to the bride's mother so that she can buy household goods for her daughter; cloth is given to the mother on behalf of the bride. The development of cash economies over the course of the twentieth century and the increasing availability of consumer goods have led to the gradual commodification as well as inflation of bridewealth payments.

The increase in bridewealth is tied to expectations of what a bride should bring into the marriage. The kind and number of cooking utensils, bowls, cloth, household furnishings, and jewelry considered essential to a trousseau have increased over time and are subject to fashionable trends. Young women set themselves apart from their mothers' generation through the content of their trousseau and also compete with one another, especially in polygynous families. More important, jewelry, cloth, and household items enhance a bride's stature and become the basis for her future home as well as a hedge against hard times. A portion of the cloth and bowls a bride brings with her is redistributed among female kin of the groom at the wedding; the groom and his father also receive some garments. The bride's mother is responsible for accumulating these goods through her own and her daughter's income-generating activities, the bridegroom's gifts, and her relationships with female relatives and other women. A woman who contributes a piece of cloth or an item of houseware when the daughter of a female relative or friend gets married creates an obligation on the part of the recipient. Through these gifts and exchanges women define themselves as valuable social beings. Social relationships between women are created and reaffirmed through contributions to the trousseau just as relationships are expressed and affirmed in the assembling and redistribution of bridewealth.

The range, quality, and quantity of gifts expected of prospective husbands, especially those who migrate overseas, have increased most notably in urban areas. Writing about Senegal, Beth Buggenhagen has shown that bridewealth has become a means of obtaining valued consumer goods and of meeting material needs for the families of prospective brides since neoliberal strategies to downsize the state and restructure African economies have jeopardized their livelihoods. Mothers and female relatives of a bride take on an ever greater role in the process, at the expense of senior men, when they make specific requests for gifts and take charge of their distribution. They use the money, cloth, or other gifts received for themselves and their

Figure 3.3. Bamana women sorting the cloth for a bride's trousseau, Segou region, Mali.
Maria Grosz-Ngaté.

home as well as to strengthen family ties and build their social networks. The money they invest in a rotating credit association will provide them with capital when it is their turn to receive the accumulated funds. Yet the heightened importance of bride-wealth frequently subordinates young women's own wishes to the interests of their senior matrikin and puts considerable pressure on junior men. The upsurge in young people's professed desire to marry for love may be a response to these predicaments and a way of resisting the commodification of marriage; at the same time, youths who embrace the ideals of romantic love also express their sentiments through gifts.

Men have complained for some time that demands on them make it difficult to marry and that women are frivolous in the way they spend money. But the escalation of bridewealth and wedding goods has also been denounced by Pentecostalist Christians and reformist Muslim groups. In Niger, for example, the Izala movement decreed that bridewealth should be restricted to a modest sum and encouraged women to reduce their acquisition of material goods. The governments of Niger and of neighboring countries as well as local communities have at different times set limits on bridewealth payments. These have met with variable success, since agreements could be broken or legislation was not enforced. Moreover, a limit on a cash payment can be easily circumvented because bridewealth consists of a series of gifts rather than a lump sum of cash.

Figure 3.4. Carrying gifts into a bride's new home, Dakar, Senegal.
Beth Buggenhagen.

In societies reckoning descent matrilineally or bilaterally, bridegrooms frequently worked for their future wives' families for a period of time. Among the San peoples of southern Africa, for example, a new husband would come to live and work with his wife's family until several children had been born. He demonstrated his commitment to the group by offering his wife's kin an animal he had hunted or obtained by working at a cattle post or in the mines. During this period the couple periodically visited his descent group and participated in productive activities in order to retain his entitlements to the land occupied by his own group. The converse took place if the family planned to reside with the husband's people after brideservice ended. Such visiting maintained not only social relations but also the children's rights to the land. Some African societies practiced neither brideservice nor the exchange of substantial bridewealth. Among the Asante of Ghana, for example, where marriage did not confer rights to the wife's labor or the children she bore, family elders only poured a libation to mark the alliance between kin groups.

Across the African continent, intimate attachment is expressed through gifts that the groom makes to the prospective bride. Gift giving also continues after marriage: husbands are expected to offer their wives clothing, especially in advance of important holidays; among pastoralists, at the birth of their children women receive animals that are theirs to dispose of as they see fit. Gifts and other forms of material support signify emotional commitment and are evidence of caring, especially under conditions of economic hardship. Affection and economic interests are therefore intertwined rather than opposed, as Western ideology suggests.

Although the sociality and gift exchanges related to marriage play a crucial role in the affirmation of kinship, they are not the only means of expressing social attachment. Other life cycle events such as name-giving ceremonies and funerals may be equally or more important. In the cities of Mali and Senegal, male relatives and friends come together for the name-giving ceremony and offer cash to the father of the baby, while women gather around the mother with gifts of cloth. These presents create obligations much like at weddings. Social attachment and belonging are also made manifest when urban residents or overseas migrants build a home in their village of origin. Urban Nigerians, like North Africans working in France, construct often elaborate homes to establish a presence in their natal villages and demonstrate their success. They may never return on a permanent basis, but the house allows them to maintain connections by having family members live in it and by involving other villagers in the maintenance of the home.

In parts of Kenya and Uganda where patrilineal kin loyalties and territorial attachment have become closely intertwined, the presence of a grave allows descendants of a common ancestor to lay claim to a particular piece of land. Where one is buried therefore becomes highly significant and potentially contentious. Even in places where the identification with land is less tight, burial in one's home village can be important for establishing the identity of the deceased and for situating the living. Funerals and postburial rites themselves link household, family, and the wider community. They create, reaffirm, or reconfigure solidarities and social differences by drawing attention to who is helping or declining to help with expenditures, especially in settings where funerals are lavish events that require substantial resources. New communication technologies allow those in charge to mobilize social networks that stretch across national and international borders. Governments, religious figures, and development experts often criticize large funerary expenditures as drawing money away from productive investment, mostly with little result. However, organizing an expensive celebration for reasons of status and prestige does not mean that family members do not engage in serious debates over it. How rituals of death are conducted varies widely across the continent and is influenced by religious change. They have been the social rituals par excellence among the Asante of Ghana. Elsewhere, elaborate ceremonies are more recent developments, although people may contend they are a tradition. In yet other contexts, burials of women and men who had numerous children and grandchildren had been lively celebrations of life before conversion to Islam but became more austere afterward.

Figure 3.5. Asante funeral in Ghana: sisters sit in the front row on the
ground while the wife sits in the second row.
Gracia Clark.

DOMESTIC ARRANGEMENTS AND FAMILY DYNAMICS

The dominant ideal of the family in the United States is a husband, wife, and children
who reside together in a household, conceived as a physical space such as a house
or an apartment. They own common property, pool income, and share resources.
This ideal elides "family" and "household." It has persisted in spite of changes in
family structure and household composition. In Africa, families have historically
not constituted domestic units that sleep under one roof, pool resources, and make
collective decisions concerning their use. Although the term "household" is widely
used in the literature on Africa, its meaning in a given context needs to be defined
rather than assumed. Kinship principles underlie inheritance and property rights as
well as relations between members, but their interpretation is shaped by political
and economic circumstances, ideologies disseminated through education and the
media, religious affiliation, and state policies. Christianity was closely bound up with
European legal codes that were introduced during the colonial period and frequently
strengthened patriarchal authority. The influence of Islam has already been noted
with respect to polygyny, but it has also affected relations between spouses and
claims to inheritance in areas where it is widely practiced. Family law, known as
code de la famille, seeks to regulate power and authority within the family in countries

formerly governed by France. Recent legislative efforts to amend the law in countries such as Mali and Senegal in order to strengthen women's position were drawn out and did not bring the results hoped for by feminists due to contestations by Muslim groups.

Depending on their position, age, and gender, family members have different rights and obligations. They negotiate access to material, social, and symbolic resources with each other. In addition, individuals have different abilities, aspirations, and personalities that may be in tension. Regardless of family form, mothers occupy a central place in the household and are held responsible for their children's behavior and success in life. Children are linked to their mothers by strong affective bonds and continue to seek them out throughout life, particularly in polygynous families. Conjugal rights and obligations constitute an arena of gendered negotiation, and expectations of what a husband and wife should contribute, do, or be are tied up with changing notions of responsibility. Husband and wife are not expected to be everything to the other spouse, and same-gender relationships remain important after marriage. Women continue to cooperate and socialize extensively with other women within and beyond the family and build social networks; men do the same.

Figure 3.6. A mother and her daughters taking morning chai in the kitchen of a Maasai homestead *(boma),* Kajiado district, Kenya.
Nicholas G. Demille.

Figure 3.7. Women chefs in Marrakech, Morocco.
Corbis.

Although household provisioning is bound up with masculinity in urban and rural areas regardless of what "provisioning" encompasses (for example housing, food staples, school fees, cultivable land for a wife), women increasingly take on roles formerly ascribed to men. In urban Morocco, women in civil service and commercial occupations now often support the family and become the centers of patronage networks, providing resources and helping to navigate the bureaucracy. The shift in women's economic roles extends to the noneconomic domain and may lead to contestations over authority by husbands and other male kin.

Women-headed households have increased across the continent in rural and urban areas. In South Africa, Kenya, and Uganda, child-headed households have also increased. Some children who have lost one or both parents to AIDS and have no grandparents able to care for them prefer to live on their own rather than moving to the home of a relative whose resources are already stretched. So-called child-headed households may involve several children or youths who fend for themselves, an older child in charge of younger siblings, or a youth managing a household with an ailing grandparent.

Among rural Bamana of Mali, as well as in many other societies that trace descent through the paternal line, a family consists of brothers and their wives, married sons, grandchildren, and unmarried sons and daughters. It may be augmented at any given time by short- or long-term visitors, including married daughters and sisters, other relatives, or friends. Historically, families have contracted and new units have emerged when enduring unresolved conflict led to fission and division of the family fields, or when members left the area in response to ecological conditions or new opportunities. The resulting units may be nuclear families. A family cultivates common fields and eats its daily meals in the household of the family elder; the food is prepared collectively by the daughters-in-law. The elder is responsible for family affairs but leaves the management of day-to-day activities to a younger brother or son as he ages; decisions are often made after discussion. Family members belong to different residential units.

Young men construct their own houses once they reach maturity, and these houses become the nucleus of a new household when they get married. Those who marry more than one woman have to provide a house for each wife. While men are considered the owners, each house is effectively the wife's domain; there she lives with her children, prepares an occasional meal, and receives visitors. Women used to work in the family fields but many now are required to do so only during the harvest, giving them more time to engage in activities that generate personal income. Authority among women parallels that among men, but hierarchy is based on the number of years married into the family rather than on age. Living in an extended family brings challenges but also provides mutual support, allows women to share the labor of food preparation, and frees senior women from such duties altogether.

Unmarried Bamana men and women spend parts of the year away earning cash; young married men do so as well but may take their wife (or junior wife) along unless they leave the country. Ideally, a man curtails his time away once he becomes the family elder, but this is impossible if he has no younger brothers or sons able to

Figure 3.8. Women pounding and sifting millet for the family meal, Segou region, Mali.
Maria Grosz-Ngaté.

earn extra income. While men on labor migration are ostensibly subject to the authority of family elders, the lack of local self-sufficiency effectively limits this authority even during periods when they return home. The number of migrants who settle permanently in the city and become heads of new families has increased considerably since the 1990s. Here, as elsewhere, the prescription for sons to reside close to their father after marriage is giving way to economic exigencies.

In southern Ghana, matrilineal Akan couples frequently do not share a residence: about two-thirds of married women live in houses with, or built by, their maternal relatives. Men do the same; if their own family lives far away, they rent a room near their spouse. This pattern has not changed significantly in spite of the fact that Christian churches have tried to promote co-residence and shared budgeting. Domestic units here consist of relatives who trace their descent to a common maternal ancestor as well as of children and adults who are closely or distantly related. The affective and material bonds between husband and wife thus transcend residential boundaries, and the sharing of food by eating together or taking a cooked meal to the nonresident husband becomes a material expression of marriage. Husbands and wives are encouraged to cooperate closely with their respective matrikin, who also provide a social safety net for children when their parents divorce or when fathers cannot meet their financial obligations. Kobena Hanson has argued that an individual's position within the unit is affected by the internal and external economic, social, and symbolic resources she or he can draw on, and which are due in part to the relations she or he has built through gift giving and other contributions. The salience of the extended family among rural and urban Akan has declined, but the nuclear family is not as strictly bounded as among Euro-Americans, so extended family members continue to have rights and obligations.

Changing economic conditions, new production regimes, and urban migration have resulted in more fundamental reconfigurations of rural families in eastern and southern Africa. In South Africa, family unity and mutual support were already undermined in the early twentieth century when black farmers were forced into reserves or tenancy agreements with white farmers. This was exacerbated when those who sought work in the diamond or gold mines were prevented from bringing their families to the mining centers, leading some men to start new families in town. People of the Taita Hills in southeastern Kenya left their homes in search of work earlier and in larger numbers than the Bamana discussed earlier. James H. Smith found that families had contracted to largely nuclear units by the 1990s, with more than 80 percent of households headed by women or by women standing in for men who were away. This reality contrasts with an ideal of patriarchal authority and a conception of the household as an expression of a man's independence from his natal family following the payment of bridewealth. Although supposedly autonomous, many of these households depend on neighbors, kin networks, and even connections with international nongovernmental organizations to sustain themselves. Among the Gikuyu, men with insufficient land moved to the city with their wives and children instead of maintaining two households.

Domestic arrangements in cities vary widely across the economic spectrum. The educated tend to have fewer children and live in households formed around nuclear units, but they also often share their home with an elderly mother, young relatives going to school or university, and one or more domestic servants. They are likely to interact more with members of their social networks than with their neighbors. In middle- and lower-income neighborhoods, homes are subdivided into apartments that are occupied either by members of an extended family or by multiple unrelated nuclear families, some of whom may be recent migrants to the city. Individual rooms are also rented to single individuals, generally men, or to a group of male migrants. Renters may be regarded and treat each other like family, except when conflicts arise. Many household tasks are performed outside, extending the often tight space of the home and leading to increased sociability. Households are lively social sites where neighbors and friends come and go; people of varying ages also socialize in front of the home. Urban residents differ in the extent to which they maintain ties with their rural relatives. Some visit regularly and offer support, while others reduce contact even if they have sufficient resources.

Domestic units in the growing informal settlements of Africa's burgeoning cities are subject to frequent dissolution and re-formation because poverty and illness prevent residents from conforming to ideals of who should live together. According to Fiona Ross, many residents of a shantytown in the Western Cape of South Africa had to reconfigure their households and formalize previously fluid relationships in order to qualify for a new housing development intended as a model community. The pressures toward social conformity and the legal and aesthetic constraints that came with the new formal housing gave rise to an imagined norm of living in nuclear families and to tensions if residents did not abide by it. Previous ways of relying on reciprocity and sharing networks also gave way to new modes of association.

Many African families have become transnational in recent decades, with individual members dispersed between the home country and other African countries, the Middle East, Europe, North America, or Asia. This development is due as much to the pursuit of new opportunities such as work or education as to forced movement prompted by civil conflict. Long-distance migration was once largely a male phenomenon but now includes women who move on their own, not just as a spouse. Among the educated and professional classes, women may study or work in another country while the husband remains at home. Movement between the host and home countries is limited by financial and legal constraints for those at the lower end of the economic spectrum, but they too remain connected by telephone, the internet, photos, videos of family ceremonies, gifts, and remittances. While their remittances help to support those at home, as discussed in the chapter on livelihoods, they also alter family dynamics. Junior men often send remittances to their mothers to help cover daily living expenses, leading to a shift in the gender balance of power within the senior generation. Wives who cannot accompany their husbands for economic or legal reasons may also depend on their mothers-in-law for a portion of the remittances. Separate remittances can give rise to tensions, as each woman may suspect that the other has received a larger share. Migrant couples who raise families overseas have to balance conflicting demands on their resources as they try to make a home, educate their children, and remit money to elderly parents and others in need. They endeavor to send their children home for extended stays with relatives or during school vacations to strengthen ties and teach them their cultural values. Some couples are compelled to leave older children with grandparents or other kin. These children may feel materially and emotionally neglected, especially if other children are born in the host country. The separation may also cause tensions between siblings. Although transnational families have become part of the social landscape for Africans across the economic spectrum, research on many facets of this phenomenon has only just begun.

Kin abroad and at home are a resource. Kin relationships, even distant, come with the expectation to aid in ways small and large. This ranges from hosting a kinsperson or co-villager coming to town for medical treatment to lending money, even if it is unlikely that the borrower will be able to repay it, and helping to establish a small business. Those who have achieved a modicum of economic success and/or high levels of schooling are under particular pressure not only to assist materially but also to facilitate opportunities by using their connections. Assistance within the family can generate a form of patron-client relations since those who have been helped often reciprocate by carrying out domestic or other tasks for the giver. Aiding kin can lead to tensions between spouses when one party is perceived as favoring kin over the immediate family. Individual aspirations and a changing notion of family coupled with economic uncertainty are leading to more instances where elderly parents, relatives, and widows are not cared for. The HIV/AIDS pandemic has also strained familial harmony and kinship relations, so now church congregations often care for sick members who have no other support, or put pressure on members to fulfill their familial obligations. Failure to assist kin may make individuals subject to witchcraft accusations. Conversely, those experiencing misfortune frequently attribute it to witchcraft carried out by jealous kin or to the curse of a parent who has been neglected.

INTERGENERATIONAL RELATIONS

Respect for age has been a constant across the diversity of African societies. Children are socialized to show respect for parents and older kin, and anyone younger is traditionally expected to defer to persons belonging to an older cohort. Children, youths, and young adults could be asked to carry out tasks for anyone who is senior to them. While older unrelated persons are still regularly addressed as "mother" or "father," deference to older kin and non-kin is diminishing.

Displacements caused by civil war and the use of child soldiers have destabilized families, including previously accepted forms of patriarchal authority. The child-headed households that emerged in the context of the AIDS pandemic are another dramatic manifestation of changing family dynamics. Beyond such major disruptions, intergenerational relations are undergoing new transformations as families and governments become incapable of ensuring basic economic security, neoliberal economic strategies undermine collective solidarities, the expansion of Western-style education alters aspirations, and global media purvey fantasies of consumption.

The decline in the authority of male elders as young men provide much-needed cash dates back decades and has been mentioned in relation to migration. A more recent development is the loss of parental authority when new economic opportunities make it possible for children and youths to provide for themselves and even for their families. Charles Piot has seen northern Togolese youths point to "human rights" to back up their refusal to work in the fields or their decision to seek work in Nigeria against the wishes of their parents. David Kyaddondo has highlighted how children in eastern Uganda are becoming more autonomous vis-à-vis their parents due to their involvement in the emergent local rice economy. Previously expected to help with various activities and take on growing responsibilities, their ability to earn and control money is changing the relationship with their parents. Their relationships with other adults are also altered as they deploy individual agency in obtaining work and speak more authoritatively in their interactions with them. Although elders welcome children's economic contributions, they are also concerned about the loss of respect and the reversal of roles. This development is giving rise to a moral debate about intergenerational relations. In a township of the Western Cape in South Africa, male and female youths are redefining their social personhood and standing within the community by drawing on global youth culture. Together with socioeconomic changes, this is eroding the central position adult women long held within the household and the community.

"Sugar daddies," wealthy men who provide young women with material and symbolic advantages in exchange for sex, have been a part of the urban landscape for some time. This phenomenon has expanded to include tourists and expatriate professionals. By entering into such sexual relationships in the short or long term, young women obtain money and sought-after commodities that they cannot get from their parents or from boyfriends of their own social class. Some are even able to start a business. While this flouts moral standards and accepted modes of achieving adult status, it allows them to become patrons to their kin and their fiancés, altering intergenerational and gender relations.

NON-KIN FORMS OF COMMUNITY

Kinship and the family often serve as models for other kinds of social relations, and the kinship idiom can be used to mediate new forms of community and membership, from urban associations to citizenship. Schoolmates forge bonds as though they were kin and draw on these connections as they move through life. Friends can also become fictive kin and be treated like siblings or cousins, and friends of senior relatives may be addressed as "uncle" or "aunt." Among the Mande peoples of West Africa, ritualized joking between different clans and ethnic groups establish relatedness between strangers and promote social harmony.

African women and men have been enmeshed in non-kin relations ranging from close friendships to various kinds of associations as far back as there is evidence of social life. Male and female circumcision, where one or both were practiced, made age-mates out of cohorts of individual participants. The bonds created as they underwent the process and associated rituals crosscut kin ties and social status and lasted a lifetime. Male age-mates played important roles in social life because they generally remained in the same locale after marriage. The creation of the Segou Bamana state (today's Mali) during the eighteenth century is attributed to an age group that rebelled against the elders, and the precolonial Zulu state (in what is today South Africa) relied on male age-grades in building its military regiments. Junior age-grades were often called upon to work in the fields or carry out community projects. The importance of age-grades has been attenuated since boys are now usually circumcised in clinics and because related rituals have been modified significantly or eliminated altogether due to conversion to Christianity or Islam and to schooling. However, they may still put on masquerades during certain times of the year.

In East African pastoralist societies, age-grades were a highly developed social institution consisting of a hierarchy of grades that structured men's experience of the life cycle and shaped their masculinity. Men's roles, rights, and responsibilities changed as they moved through the stages of uncircumcised, circumcised, and various levels of elders; women were central to the rites that marked the different stages. In Kenya and Tanzania the age-grade system began to be transformed as a result of colonial policies, a process that intensified in recent decades when the tourist industry commodified the "warrior" grade and made the Maasai "warrior" emblematic of pastoralist masculinity.

Among the Mande language groups of West Africa, initiation societies created special bonds among men and, in some areas, women. Scholars have also called them "secret societies" because initiates gained esoteric knowledge over time and their activities were kept secret from outsiders. The Sande and Poro of Liberia and Sierra Leone were powerful women's and men's associations respectively; the Komo was an equally powerful men's society in the savanna region further north. Bound up with indigenous religious practices, these societies declined dramatically once members became Muslims or Christians. The masks and other objects associated with these societies can now be found in museums and are discussed in the chapter on art. By contrast, Mande hunters' associations remain active, although they too entail esoteric knowledge and require initiation. Their members distinguish themselves from commercial hunters through their strict code of conduct and their intimate knowledge of flora and fauna. Hunters' associations observe an age hierarchy based on time of initiation, but social status is immaterial. Hunters' music has become highly popular, and the associations themselves have been taking on new roles in new contexts: they have acted as security patrols to protect communities against crime, served as guards in national parks, and participated in and fought against insurgencies. Their leaders forge connections between associations across national borders.

In many areas of the continent, artisans have constituted a separate social category. They were members of kin groups just like their pastoralist or cultivator neighbors but were linked by virtue of their profession. Like people of servile status, they were also often connected with particular families. Which kinds of artisans were set apart in this way has varied widely but generally included blacksmiths. The West African Sahel and savanna region is well known for its highly developed system of occupational groups encompassing blacksmiths and potters (the latter being the sisters and wives of blacksmiths), bards (also known as griots), leatherworkers, and, among the Fulbe, weavers. They were expected to marry within their category and pass their status on to their children; still, boundaries could be redefined. Their social status was lower than that of farmers or herders. At the same time, they were considered to have special spiritual powers. The smiths in particular were known for their occult and healing powers. The griots remembered the royal genealogies, transmitted family traditions, and sang the praises of those who stood out through their actions. They were both respected and feared because they knew family secrets and could choose what or what not to reveal. They were close to the powerful in society and, along with the blacksmiths, served as mediators, since neither category could accede to political office. Among the Tuareg of the Sahara Desert, smiths did much of the work that among the Mande was done by griots. Blacksmiths and leather-workers practice contemporary forms of their professions, while weaving has declined considerably as a craft. Griots still play a role at social and political events, but they have also been criticized for being co-opted by politicians and wealthy individuals who wish to enhance their status. Some have gained fame on the international music scene or, like other artisans, have moved into altogether different kinds of work depending on their educational achievements. Any member of these groups can now accede to political office, but intermarriage outside their group is not yet universally accepted.

James Ellison's research in southern Ethiopia has shown that craft workers and traders in Konso express their separate social status in a kinship idiom by referring to themselves as the Fulto "family," after their eponymous ancestor. Their membership has expanded in recent years as impoverished farmers have sought entry in search of new economic opportunities and the connections that the far-flung networks of the Fulto "family" can provide. "Family" members assist each other and take part in feasts and public rituals. Farmers' adoption of this new identity (and lower

Figure 3.9. Inside the Fulto house, meat and hide bracelets from a sacrificed animal are divided for distribution in all Konso villages.
James Ellison.

social rank) was facilitated by the neoliberal reforms of the 1990s and their embrace of the free market spirit.

African women and men also form various types of association in the pursuit of common goals. Some of these dissolve once they achieve their objectives; others are permanent features of social life. They include cultural organizations, associations devoted to development, and clubs where friends meet to discuss issues of the day in an informal setting. Even those that are economic in nature (e.g., various kinds of self-help societies, including the rotating credit associations discussed in the chapter on livelihoods and, more recently, community and nongovernmental organizations) offer their members sociability, moral support, and an opportunity to expand personal networks. Associations of urban migrants from the same rural area or, if overseas, from the same ethnic group often sponsor the construction of schools, churches or mosques, or development projects; they also often provide assistance when a member dies and the body has to be repatriated. Women's associations in villages or urban neighborhood and the women's wings of political parties embody their solidarity when they dress in the same cloth on festive occasions. Religion is becoming an increasingly important basis of association, whether in the form of church groups, choirs, study groups, or groups devoted to social and religious matters. The *daairas* so prominent in Senegalese religious and social life have been

Figure 3.10. Women's rotating savings and credit associations meeting donors, Dakar, Senegal.
Beth Buggenhagen.

re-created in the diasporas, including in the United States, where adherents of a Sufi order organize religious rituals, provide mutual support to each other and to new-comers, support religious leaders, and negotiate with local authorities on behalf of the group. Finally, Africans living overseas have taken advantage of the internet to create virtual communities centered on their homelands in which they debate issues of public interest with members abroad and at home.

Given the size of the African continent, it should not be surprising that there are differences in the ways domestic units are established, kin groups are defined, and connections between unrelated individuals are forged. Yet these differences have always been fluid, since population groups have modified cultural ideals and practices when, for example, political or migratory processes led to new interactions with others. More important than the variations in forms of family, marriage, and com-munity within and across nation-states is therefore the tremendous dynamism of African social relations. Change, while not new, seems to have accelerated in the late twentieth and early twenty-first centuries. From Algiers to Cape Town, from Mom-basa to Brazzaville and Dakar, Africans develop new forms of relatedness as they engage processes of globalization in everyday decisions and struggle for better futures. People in all walks of life are reinterpreting ideals and expectations of relat-edness in light of education, religion, images circulating through a variety of media, the growth of market-based economies, and environmental change. Domestic units seem to be contracting, relationships between women and men are being reconfig-ured, and intergenerational relations are being renegotiated. New forms of commu-nity that transcend kinship, patronage, and ethnicity are also emerging. Yet these changes are not unidirectional, nor are they inevitably converging on any singular model. Continental and overseas diasporas are integral to these processes and are challenging preconceived boundaries of "African" social relations.

ACKNOWLEDGMENTS

I thank Gracia Clark and Rosa De Jorio for their comments on a draft of this chapter. Figure 3.10 was first published as figure 6 in *American Ethnologist* 33(4): 679, No-vember 2006, and is reprinted here with the permission of James Ellison and the American Anthropological Association.

NOTE

1. The discussion in this chapter does not highlight the specificities of immigrant popula-tions such as the South Asians of southern and eastern Africa, the Lebanese in Western and Central Africa, the Afrikaners of South Africa, and the British and other Europeans in South Africa and elsewhere on the continent. These generally adapted the social structures of their home countries to their new environment but continued to intermarry primarily with others of their community, often even after they had lived in Africa for generations and no longer had a "home" outside the continent.

SUGGESTIONS FOR FURTHER READING

Buggenhagen, Beth. 2012. *Muslim Families in Global Senegal: Money Takes Care of Shame.* Bloomington: Indiana University Press.

Coe, Cati. 2008. "The Structuring of Feeling in Ghanaian Transnational Families." *City and Society* 20(2): 222–50.

Cole, Jennifer, and Lynn M. Thomas. 2009. *Love in Africa.* Chicago: University of Chicago Press.

Cornwall, Andrea. 2002. "Spending Power: Love, Money, and the Reconfiguration of Gender Relations in Ado-Odo, Southwestern Nigeria." *American Ethnologist* 29(4): 963–80.

Ellison, James. 2009. "Governmentality and the Family: Neoliberal Choices and Emergent Kin Relations in Southern Ethiopia." *American Anthropologist* 111(1): 81–92.

Hanson, Kobena T. 2004. "Rethinking the Akan Household: Acknowledging the Importance of Culturally and Linguistically Meaningful Images." *Africa Today* 51(1): 27–45.

Jindra, Michael, and Joël Noret, eds. 2011. *Funerals in Africa: Explorations of a Social Phenomenon.* New York: Berghahn Books.

Kyaddondo, David. 2008. "Respect and Autonomy: Children's Money in Eastern Uganda." In *Generations in Africa: Connections and Conflicts,* ed. Erdmute Alber, Sjaak van der Geest, and Susan Reynolds Whyte, 27–46. Berlin: LIT Verlag.

Masquelier, Adeline. 2004. "How Is a Girl to Marry without a Bed? Weddings, Wealth, and Women's Value in an Islamic Town of Niger." In *Situating Globality: African Agency in the Appropriation of Global Culture,* ed. Wim van Binsbergen and Rijk van Dijk, 220–53. Leiden: Brill.

Newcomb, Rachel. 2009. *Women of Fes: Ambiguities of Urban Life in Morocco.* Philadelphia: University of Pennsylvania Press.

Rasmussen, Susan. 1997. *The Poetics and Politics of Tuareg Aging: Life Course and Personal Destiny in Niger.* DeKalb: Northern Illinois University Press.

Ross, Fiona C. 2005. "Urban Development and Social Contingency: A Case Study of Urban Relocation in the Western Cape, South Africa." *Africa Today* 51(4): 19–31.

Salo, Elaine. 2005. "Negotiating Gender & Personhood in the New South Africa: Adolescent Women & Gangsters in Manenberg Township on the Cape Flats." In *Limits to Liberation after Apartheid: Citizenship, Governance & Culture,* ed. Steven L. Robbins, 173–89. Oxford: James Currey.

Smith, James Howard. 2008. *Bewitching Development: Witchcraft and the Reinvention of Development in Neoliberal Kenya.* Chicago: University of Chicago Press.

Van Dijk, Diana. 2008. *"Beyond Their Age": Coping of Children and Young People in Child-Headed Households in South Africa.* Leiden: African Studies Centre.

4 Making a Living
African Livelihoods

Gracia Clark and Katherine Wiley

THE MEANING OF LIVELIHOOD

Impressive tenacity and ingenuity enable Africans to survive and even prosper under extremely challenging circumstances. The widespread stereotype of the passive victim crumbles away in the face of Africans' incessant efforts to protect their families' interests and ensure security and progress for the next generation. It is a struggle that some people shirk and that many do not win. Even so, people's agency must be taken seriously. Continuous experimentation and innovation are among the legacies of African societies in every part of the continent, as people make their living often under severe resource constraints and despite external shocks such as the recent spiraling prices of gasoline and corn.

Analyzing the strategies that people employ for preserving and adapting families and communities to these constraints has led researchers to adopt the term "livelihood" to indicate the paid and unpaid activities that together sustain communities and individuals over the long term. Conventional U.S. economic analysis makes a sharp distinction between work and family, confining the economy to the work side, measured primarily in monetary terms as gross domestic product (GDP), the value of goods and services produced in a country in a given year. Even calculations that try to include the production of goods and services that are not part of the official record, such as farming for direct consumption or using unpaid family labor, often disregard the domestic and cultural work that maintain a family's well-being over the long run, from cooking and cleaning to the values and social institutions that keep people working together.

The concept of livelihood does justice to the way most Africans interweave their varying public and domestic areas of responsibility and reflects their realities better than earlier studies that analyzed productive and reproductive activities separately. Productive activities, identified conventionally as those taking place in the farm, market, office, factory, or workshop, are not cleanly detached in practice from those that reproduce the proper relations of family and gender, childbearing and child rearing, and community solidarity. A diverse repertoire of choices of work and family arrangements strengthens the flexibility that best prepares people for an unpredictable future. Out of this repertoire, people strategize collectively and individually to achieve and maintain sustainable economic positions. This chapter examines productive and reproductive activities together, asking how both contribute to people's abilities to get by and lead meaningful lives.

The concept of livelihood proves useful at many levels of analysis, including the individual, household, and extended family or clan as well as local community, economic class, ethnic group, region, nation, and subcontinent. At each level a viable livelihood must be constructed from a multiplicity of different activities that, taken together, provide for material needs. The ever-changing configuration of resources, local cultural practices, and historical experiences sets the parameters for viable agency at each level of analysis. For an obvious example on a national level, countries with petroleum deposits have a valuable resource that others do not, but its impact has differed in Nigeria, Sudan, and Angola, just as it has in Norway, Britain, and the United States. On an individual level, children's likelihood of attending school depends a great deal upon where their parents live and the affordability of school fees. Still, poverty does not automatically exclude young people from receiving an education, since some children of poor parents manage to get their schooling sponsored by relatives, neighbors, or teachers.

Livelihood approaches also recognize that multiple dimensions of disadvantage and privilege (such as race, gender, class, nation, ethnicity, geography, and ecology) interpenetrate within this analysis of human agency and shape people's options and constraints. Barbara Cooper has shown how an elite Hausa woman in Niger faces much stricter norms of seclusion than her lower-class cousin who cannot afford to stay home because her family has no servants to fetch water and shop. Unlike her wealthier cousin, the poor woman can visit the market and the well without censure and work in the fields with her family and neighbors. She has more freedom of movement than her rich cousin, but less financial security and less prestige since her life does not conform to cultural ideals of modesty and restrictions on women's movement. In this case, ethnicity (Hausa), gender (man or woman), class (wealthy or poor), and religion (Islam) all make a big difference to the consequences of the same action (going to market). The parameters operating at a particular level rarely dictate what any one person does; rather, they define a range of options in terms of likely consequences and prerequisites. Even in the most constraining circumstances, such as a refugee camp, there is never only one alternative for any person who is trying to construct a sustainable livelihood out of the locally available options. At the wider levels of the community or the nation, prospects for success may look rosy or bleak, but they are always indeterminate to some degree. Conformity and deviance, risk and precaution generate innumerable contradictory and reinforcing layers that accumulate into history.

SUSTAINABLE VILLAGES IN AFRICA

Research on the farm household pioneered the concept of livelihood, and it remains highly relevant to sub-Saharan Africans, 62 percent of whom lived in rural communities in 2010, according to the World Bank. Although agriculture accounts for over 25 percent of GDP in many African countries, most households and individuals engage in several different kinds of work during a year, a month, or even a day. Nonfarming activities that generate income often prove as vital as agriculture to the viability of a rural community that is facing climate or health challenges. A bad year for one crop is likely to be a good year for something else. The combination of diverse activities can act as a cushion against risk, anticipating circumstances that might cripple one activity while sparing another or even enabling it to expand.

Annual fluctuations in the climate and world market prices mean that few African farm communities can survive on agriculture alone. Rural dwellers supplement their farming by engaging in a range of other activities that are paid in food, cash, or other goods. They may work on other people's farms in exchange for a day's meals or a share of the harvest as well as later assistance on their own fields. Other activities might include collecting wild plants to be used in crafts or for food, making baskets or pottery or metal tools, gathering firewood for sale, and selling food brought in from elsewhere. Widows and orphans without land rights or people without the physical strength or help from family members that is necessary to clear a farm may depend more heavily upon these sources of income.

The example of Niger takes us to one of the poorest countries in the world, ranked second to the bottom on the United Nations' Human Development Index in 2011. The average income in this landlocked, mostly desert nation is less than two dollars a day, challenging rural Zarma villagers such as the four hundred adult residents of Fandou Béri to develop creative strategies of getting by, as Simon Batterbury has shown in his research. They received little outside assistance from the weak state's reduced development programs even though their major crop, wet-season millet, suffered from droughts and inconsistent rainfall. Individuals made strategic choices about diversifying their livelihoods, influenced by their skills, wealth, and access to labor and technology, among other factors.

In the late 1990s, although all Zarma households that were surveyed farmed, only two met their food needs exclusively with their own crops. The rest depended upon an expansive repertoire of activities that included operating small businesses, trading, raising livestock, migrating abroad (often seasonally), working locally for wages, and collecting firewood for sale. Both men and women generated income in these ways, but they often did different kinds of work. Men took care of most agricultural tasks, and it was usually they who migrated to places such as Côte d'Ivoire during the dry season looking for additional work. Women often established small businesses where they sold food items or raised sheep, earning significant income. Age also affected the kinds of work that people did. Older men and women generally had increased flexibility in engaging in different kinds of activities, since they had

Figure 4.1. Farms in rural Tanzania.
Katherine Wiley.

more access to resources such as land and capital. Children contributed to household income by gathering local food items that could be sold in the market, performing small paid tasks such as fetching water, and selling jewelry. Since the form of Islam practiced in Fandou Béri somewhat restricted women's movements, children also assisted their mothers with their work, such as by selling in the market the food that their mothers cooked at home. Despite this wide range of income-generating activities, the village did not seem to be becoming dependent on wage income. People continued to farm, some diversifying their crops to protect against drought and other risks, partly because agriculture was still an important part of Zarma culture.

One of the first principles of sustainable agriculture is diversification. Farmers who plant a variety of crops usually mitigate the risk of catastrophic failure, since setbacks such as drought or locusts would need to affect several crops that have very different requirements for their rainfall needs and varying vulnerability to insects and diseases. Relying on one crop alone neglects this basic hedging measure, as when corn dominates farming in southern Africa. Farmers that have access to plots with varying altitudes or different rainfall patterns can plant diverse crops and place each in the location best suited for it. African farmers also commonly intercrop

Figure 4.2. Women in central Mali winnowing millet and preparing it for transport to the granary.
Maria Grosz-Ngaté.

different species in the same plot—for example, cultivating plantain, a fast-growing tall crop, to protect the tender seedlings of slower-growing cocoa trees that will mature years after the plantain has been harvested. Tropical soils are often thin and easily bake hard in the sun or leach nutrients in the rains, and intercropping protects them by mimicking the cover of natural vegetation. Combining export crops with others that are marketed locally or used for food also reduces the risks that accompany market fluctuations. For example, hybrid corn is sold on the world market because new hybrid seeds and chemical fertilizer must be purchased each year, and because people do not like its taste as much as that of local varieties. Mixed farming also provides more balanced nutrition and spreads out the total harvest period, reducing farmers' storage needs and labor bottlenecks.

Most indigenous farming systems involve long fallow periods when wild plants regenerate on the empty fields. Burning this growth just before planting provides the land with maximum access to the nitrogen and other nutrients that are stored in living biomass. This ash fertilizer lasts for only a few years, so the farmer must continually clear new plots that have rested as much as twenty years in order to obtain high-yield harvests. Several factors can restrict rotation capacity and lead to rapid loss of soil fertility and erosion. When large tracts of land are alienated for commercial plantations or white settlement, the crowding of Africans onto the remaining land prevents long fallowing. Labor migration, especially of young men, can also force family members remaining in villages to select new plots with less than optimal vegetation regrowth because they are easier to clear. Legal prohibitions on the burning of fields can make this activity clandestine, with people carrying it out during the peak of the dry season, when wildfires are easy to blame. Timing it during this period rather than right before the rains reduces the fertilizing effect and increases the risk of actually starting wildfires.

Combining farming with livestock raising or hunting is a common practice across the continent. In Ethiopia, Mursi women farm and men herd cattle. A man might be allotted a plot of his family land only when he marries, and a man who cannot provide land for his wife to farm to feed their family may have trouble remaining married. For the Kenyan Maasai, men herd cattle and women milk them, also preparing dairy products for consumption and to exchange for grain with Kikuyu women. The dramatic Bantu migration of recent millennia spread quickly across southern and eastern Africa largely because the migrants varied the balance between farming and herding to suit the ecology of each location. Most pastoralists further diversify by raising smaller animals such as goats, sheep, and poultry along with cattle.

African societies developed many ingenious and effective ways to coordinate the labor of different family members and divide the workload. Some groups define men's crops and women's crops, meaning that each family should enjoy a variety of produce. For example, in West Africa, yams are commonly a man's crop, because yam fields must be laboriously hoed into mounds before planting. Women plant their soup vegetables on the sides of the mounds, stabilizing them and also weeding both crops at once. Women elsewhere grow swamp rice in the dry season or cassava (introduced from Brazil) on land that is unsuitable for yams or millet. In other societies, particularly in grain-growing areas, men and women complete different tasks on the same crop. Men typically clear and plant the fields, while women weed throughout the growing season. In the Cameroonian grass fields, farming and beer brewing are likened to growing a baby during pregnancy, and so are all naturally assigned to the women's domain. Conversely, the Nigerian Yoruba find it equally natural for men to farm and women to trade. Of course, in many places migration and other social changes have shifted the balance of these historical divisions of labor.

Some regional variations have persisted through centuries of change. In most of West Africa each adult family member is entitled to some independent income, giving all of them an incentive to exert extra effort. In Nigerian Hausa villages, the entire extended family worked on the fields of the compound head and he divided that grain among maternal nuclear groups at harvest. In addition, junior men and women expected to be given additional plots where they could grow food for their private use or crops to sell to earn their own money. Mothers could enlist their young children to help on their private plots, but their offspring would ask for land of their own when they were fully grown. In most of eastern and southern Africa, there was less presumption that women needed an income of their own, especially in patrilineal societies where men paid bridewealth at marriage.

FOOD SECURITY

When drought strikes, the first strategy that people employ is often to expand their normal dry-season activities. In her work, Gracia Clark has discussed how women of Damongo, a savannah town in northern Ghana, explained during the severe drought in 1983 that since their crops had died they had no need to weed them. They abandoned their fields and started gathering shea nuts to make butter and locust tree beans to ferment into bean paste, intensifying this usual dry-season work by camping overnight at more distant groves of trees. Noticing that the cassava crop had survived better than others, some women decided to make money by processing it into gari, a dry toasted product that is popular in boarding schools. Since this is a traditional food in the Volta Region, they approached some local schoolteachers from that area asking them to teach them to make a high-quality product, which they successfully sold to schools, military barracks, and jails. For their own consumption, they preferred porridge made from cassava flour, so they dried the stubs of cassava left after grating gari and then pounded them into flour. These labor-intensive products used high quantities of water and firewood but found a ready market in a year when preferred foodstuffs were scarce and expensive, helping people to avoid outright famine.

In Darfur, a semidesert area in Western Sudan, men and women used similar strategies to combat and survive several famine years in the 1970s. Alexander de Waal conducted research during this period, showing that people began to eat wild grains and berries, even gathering them to sell in the market. In famine years, poorer people who had few or no cattle to sell migrated to towns earlier than they did in normal years to take up familiar urban occupations. Men from wealthier families had more cattle and savings and thus more flexibility in times of famine. Due to their large numbers of cattle, they had to take their herds farther, even in normal years, to find enough grass, so they had the contacts necessary to access ever more distant areas where there was still pasture. Their cash savings also helped them avoid selling cattle. Before leaving with their herds, they left money for household expenses with the women in their families, who could stay in the villages longer than poorer women in times of famine. When funds ran out, they also had to move to nearby towns, where they lacked work skills and the better jobs were already taken.

In areas with a very short farming season, such as the dry lands near the Sahara or Kalahari Deserts, migration of at least some family members as farm laborers to more fertile areas is a necessary part of the annual work cycle. Also common is seasonal migration to nearby towns and cities, where people look for casual work in construction, trade, and services. Young men from northern Ghana travel each dry season to Kumasi to work with secondhand-clothing wholesalers, unloading bales from trucks, carrying them to the transport yard for customers, and bringing them home to peddle in the villages. When the rains start they return to the farms, and the clothing trade slows markedly. Younger men historically dominated these types of migration, but today women also frequently travel away to work in domestic service or carrying loads. Young women from parts of Ghana's Upper East

Figure 4.3. Carrying a mobile lunch to market traders in Ghana.
Gracia Clark.

and West Regions now expect to spend some period of time in southern cities, working as carriers to earn money for the dowries of enamelware pans that their mothers can no longer afford to provide.

When farm villages come under economic pressure, these migration patterns can easily be extended to last for years. The "stranger farmers" of the Gambia peanut fields and the "abusa" cocoa sharecroppers of southern Ghana are two examples where this migration founded whole industries and lasted for years or even generations. The resulting loss of farm labor in the sending areas only compounds the stress on their farming systems, but it also reduces the number of mouths to feed and enables migrants to send money back to their families. Such sustained migration patterns generally have social as well as ecological causes. In West Africa, taxation and mandatory cultivation of export crops under colonial rule created pressure to migrate that was hard to reverse. In southern Africa and Kenya the colonial authorities expropriated the best land for European settlers, partly in order to more easily recruit labor migrants who traveled elsewhere looking for work. The notorious apartheid laws in the white-ruled Republic of South Africa represent an extreme form of British colonial pass laws that compelled workers to leave their families behind throughout the region. Majority rule under Nelson Mandela as president ended this legal framework but left intact the disparities it created in land ownership and wealth distribution; these inequalities continue to create the economic circumstances that force urban migration and disrupt families.

Conditions that interfere with drought-coping strategies, such as pass and property laws and immigration control, can turn a drought into a deadly famine. Even when it does not make farming impossible, violence or political unrest on roads and in the major target cities for migrants can interfere with migration or the marketing of cattle and wild foods. It also can raise the proportion of crops lost in transit and inhibit the flow of food back to deficit areas. In colonial Nyasaland (Malawi), British authorities responded to mounting food shortages by prohibiting the movement of grain between districts. Since the matrilineal men normally migrated to more fortunate areas to sell baskets or work on farms or roads so that they could bring back grain for their wives and children, this prohibition on transporting grain essentially forced them to behave irresponsibly, making many ashamed to return home.

Even development projects can have unintended consequences during drought years. For example, pastoralists in Mali normally take their cattle away from farming areas in the rainy season because grass sprouts in distant dry pastures during this period. However, during severe droughts this does not happen, so herders move into areas that are too swampy in normal times for either farming or pasture. During a drought, these swamps dry out enough for cattle to graze safely. In Mali, irrigation projects in the Niger bend took over much of this marshy land, with serious consequences when drought struck. Pastoralists could not graze their flocks in the irrigated area without severely damaging the canals and ditches, so they faced armed guards when they arrived with their herds.

GIFT EXCHANGES TO BUILD RELATIONSHIPS
AND CREATE PEOPLE

The examples above make it clear that Africans have long participated actively in the local and global market economy, buying and selling goods and labor. Livelihood analysis also recognizes non-market parts of creative strategies for getting by, including taking part in gift exchanges. In these gift economies, the donor is not paid immediately in cash, but rather is given an equivalent or more valuable gift object at some later time. Exchanges like these occur in a variety of contexts, ranging from daily exchanges of beer or small food items in the market to ostentatious displays of expensive objects at life cycle rituals such as weddings and naming ceremonies. Such giving can play an integral part in people's economic repertoires and help them to create relationships, display their own wealth and social status, and access other kinds of economic opportunities.

Working with the Kabre in northern Togo in the 1980s and 1990s, anthropologist Charles Piot noticed that they frequently gave gifts to each other. He was struck by the fact that men used half of the earnings they collected from selling agricultural products to buy beer for other men. They also presented people with beer-making items or sacrificial animals to thank them for assisting with the harvest and gave a third of their crops to the women who helped carry grain in from their fields. People also borrowed land from each other, sometimes even when they had excess land themselves. Often these exchange relationships began small and intensified over time. One Kabre man in his fifties, Karabu, described how he started a relationship by exchanging beer with a man in the market. They escalated their exchanges when the man needed a red chicken for a sacrifice and asked if he could trade a white chicken for Karabu's red one. Later Karabu borrowed one of the man's extra fields, and over the years they continued to loan land to one another. Such exchanges may seem utilitarian in nature because they fill people's material needs, and it is true that this very real economic aspect of exchange can help families to support themselves financially. But Kabre exchanges are more complicated than this because developing ongoing gift exchanges helps people to establish enduring connections.

Exchanges bind all kinds of people together. People may enter into these relationships with their peers or relatives, but they also may occur between people of unequal social status and thus can establish difference. In the past in Mauritania, dependent groups paid tribute to higher-status groups in return for protection. In some cultures, entering into exchange relationships in certain circumstances is expected. For example, in Mauritania in-laws are supposed to give each other particular gifts at holidays and ceremonies. Likewise, many African marriages involve elaborate exchanges of money and goods between the bride and groom's families, often stretched out over a period of years (see chapter 3). Since exchange relationships can be costly, people often strategically select exchange partners, sometimes on the basis of trust and reliability.

If exchanges are ways that people seek financial security and establish relationships, they are also a means through which people constitute and display themselves. Participating in elaborate public exchanges of expensive goods at weddings, for example, can be a way through which they demonstrate their wealth and influence. When the mother of the bride in Niger purchases expensive furniture and household goods for her daughter, it signifies the mother's social status, productive ability, and collective networks, since women often draw upon family members and friends to gather the money needed to purchase these goods. Economics often intertwine with social relationships; for example, in the United States holiday gifts may both serve utilitarian purposes and bind individuals closer together. When your mother buys you jeans that you need, her gift still signifies your relationship. Giving a gift can also be a way of asserting power over another person, since this action leaves the receiver in debt to the giver. By providing his friend with the red rooster that he needed, Karabu obligated him to return the favor in the future. Debts like this can provide people with security in times of need, since they can collect on gifts that they have given in the past. This safety net aspect of exchange can be especially important in societies where weak states cannot provide adequate health care or other welfare services. In such settings, exchange networks provide economic security that people can harness in times of hardship. For example, friends and relatives will give money to help defray the costs of sickness, travel, or ceremonies such as weddings or funerals.

Participating in exchange networks can also create opportunities for making other economic transactions. The household goods that a bride obtains from her mother at the time of her marriage can serve as savings, since they can be converted to cash in times of need. They also provide her with some autonomy, since in many West African cultures women retain these items in case of divorce. In Senegal when women exchange expensive cloth at ceremonies, they mark themselves as wealthy and thus creditworthy, which can help them to harness other cash flows.

Relationships that seem altruistic or ceremonial can become material factors in a crisis. James Ferguson has shown how miners in Zambia earned relatively good wages and usually supported many relatives both in town and in their original villages. Some who had lived in mining towns all their lives never expected to return to their communities of origin and thus neglected to help rural relatives. When copper prices dropped, however, the mines closed, and the miners had to suddenly go back to their villages, where they had to rely on relatives for food, shelter, and farmland, perhaps permanently. This could mean humiliation and destitution for those who had evaded their moral obligations.

Of course, such exchanges can spark conflict and challenges. People may question the expectations of giving, such as in Senegal, where young men have contested the high amounts of bridewealth that elders expect them to pay. Establishing exchange relationships can also be risky since the receiver may not have the funds to return the gift or may simply refuse to do so. Similarly, since exchange partners make claims on people's resources, saving money or investing in productive activities can be challenging. This means that part of economic success often involves being able to hold wealth back for oneself in spite of pressure to give. This can be a difficult balancing act, since not giving enough may stigmatize people as stingy, while being too generous means that they risk losing wealth, since there is no guarantee that it will be returned. Strategies that people employ to keep wealth out of exchange networks include investing in goods such as land, buildings, cattle, cloth, or gold, all of which may not easily be converted into liquid form.

Participating in rotating credit societies also puts money out of reach. Members of these associations contribute a fixed amount of money to them on a daily, weekly, or monthly basis. The whole sum is given to one participant at each meeting; each participant gets a chance to receive the sum in turn. This means that the organizers do not hold money between meetings, which reduces the risk of theft. Participating in these sorts of groups keeps participants' money safe from impulse purchases and makes it unavailable to tempt relatives to request gifts or loans.

GETTING BY IN THE AFRICAN CITY

Cities in Africa, like those elsewhere, attract migrants partly because they offer a wider range of alternatives for earning a living and defining one's identity than villages or small towns. Educational and health facilities are disproportionately concentrated there, along with public and private investments. While the bulk of formal sector employment is also situated in cities, many urban Africans earn their living from work in the informal sector—activities that are often not taxed, regulated, or protected by the government and other institutions, and not factored into countries' GDPs. Although associated with modernity and upward mobility, city life brings actual prosperity and secure livelihood to only a minority of urban residents in most African countries. The comfortable middle-class neighborhoods are dwarfed by large clusters of unplanned, substandard housing that is often illegal or quasi-legal and lacks basic utilities such as water, sanitation, and electricity. Nevertheless, the chance of being one of the lucky few who become financially successful, like the possibility of winning the lottery, exerts a powerful pull upon African populations (see chapter 6). Many parents also feel that relocating their children to cities will provide them with better educational and commercial opportunities. In Ghana, for example, wealthy Asante cocoa farmers built or bought houses in the regional capital, Kumasi. One explained this choice by saying, "I don't want my children to grow up in the village," even though it was too late to send them to school. Older traders, even those who had grown up in a village, showed real horror at the prospect of having to retire there for lack of urban assets. As one put it, "I would die in three days; there is nothing to do there." Africans face both opportunities and challenges that arise from living and working in urban areas.

Yet the separation of livelihoods between rural and urban spaces should not be exaggerated. This is illustrated by Berida Ndambuki, an Akamba woman who shared her life story with historian Claire Robertson. Berida was born in Kenya in

Figure 4.4. A tea stall with modern aspirations.
Gracia Clark.

1936 and grew up in a rural town. After marrying, Berida farmed with her husband, Ndambuki, but money was scarce, partly because he drank so much. Struggling to make ends meet with ten children, Berida decided she had to expand her work repertoire beyond agriculture in the hopes of alleviating her children's poverty. She first began brewing beer in a nearby town, then sold corn flour near Kenya's capital, Nairobi. Finally, she began to sell a variety of foodstuffs from her home region, including corn, beans, millet, and sorghum, in Nairobi itself because they sold for higher prices there.

After moving to the city, Berida helped to found Gikomba market, where traders either owned or rented places to sell dried staple foods, vegetables, used clothing, and other items. Although they struggled with authorities over permits, and police occasionally demolished their market stalls, the traders organized their market well. For example, Berida served on the market committee, which resolved disputes over debts and mediated quarrels between vendors or between vendors and customers. Of course, working in an urban area had its own challenges; Berida lost money through robbery and bad debts.

Berida engaged in several more income-generating activities, including selling cows and bringing products such as cloth from Tanzania and Uganda over the border to resell. Which activity she favored depended on larger economic and ecological conditions. During a drought in the mid-1970s, she bought cows cheaply from Maasai herders who were selling them to buy food for their families. She resold them later at a substantial profit, when the rains came and cattle prices rose.

Berida retained many links with her rural home, often returning there on buying trips or to farm during the rainy season. She became a member of several urban and

Figure 4.5. Members of a garden cooperative at work in Kankossa, Mauritania. *Katherine Wiley.*

rural women's groups that pooled resources to help members save money or pay for their medical bills and children's school fees. In the rural areas these groups also collaborated on activities such as jointly farming land or organizing community work projects to build dams. But her rural home connections also brought conflict with her husband over his inability to provide for their family, as well as frustration that her children did not seem to benefit from the education she had financed. Despite its challenges, Berida viewed her work positively, noting, "When I look back I can see that this work has removed me from a lot of slavery. . . . No matter how small my earnings were I would go and pay [my children's] school fees. I am very grateful for my job. I can help myself and I don't have problems" (Ndambuki and Robertson 2000, 86).

Such relationships have their conflicts, but are nonetheless important to family members at both ends. Urban Ghanaians likewise make an effort to retain close ties with rural relatives by exchanging frequent visits and gifts of farm produce from the village and consumer goods from the city. Older children from rural areas often come to stay with urban relatives to attend secondary schools or provide domestic help. Conversely, urban children may be sent to live in the village to receive better discipline or when trade disruptions create urban food shortages. In many countries, adequate transport enables city dwellers to plant farms in their home villages, working on them during the rainy season and leaving them under the care of village relatives after the harvest. Other city residents continue farming within or just outside of the city itself, and raising chickens and goats is also very common. Cultivating backyard gardens reduces food purchases for middle-income as well as poor families.

In the city, such farming is barely visible. A much larger number of home-based enterprises provide services such as tailoring, hairdressing, and car repair, or produce modest consumer items including cooked food, furniture, and shoes. In middle-income neighborhoods, home businesses such as frozen meat and fish shops or pharmacies can require more capital investment and connections. Trading remains the dominant occupation in most West African cities because of their long commercial history and the lack of mobility controls such as pass laws. In Ghana, the 2010 census revealed that about 80 percent of the urban adult female population works in trade, mostly as market and street traders. They provide most consumer goods for urban residents, and distribute complementary foodstuffs from other ecological zones as well as merchandise from ports and local factories to village residents. Specialist buyers travel to other countries in Africa, Europe, Asia, and the Middle East to purchase all kinds of products, from cell phones and boom boxes to clothing and household goods. Much of this work is not officially recorded by the government and is excluded from calculations of GDP. It still is taxed—for example, when market traders pay stall rents—but often not in the same way.

FORMAL AND INFORMAL WORK

The balance between formal and informal sectors in any particular city depends upon its location and the regulatory climate created by the national government; the boundaries between these sectors can frequently be blurred. Several analysts note that informal connections to the state through corruption or market taxes raise serious doubts about the assumption that informal trade lies outside the state system. These unstable definitions lead some scholars to prefer the distinction between legal and illegal trade or between corporate and noncorporate organizations, instead of that between the formal and informal sectors. While often thought of as an archetype of the informal sector, market trade has long been integrated with the state; colonial authorities actually promoted it in Ghana as a source of tax revenue. It is often legally recognized, although not given the degree of legal protection offered the corporate sector (which is frequently far from absolute). Legal protections for workers generally exempt informal sector workers, although their enforcement in corporate enterprises is also very uneven. These contradictions led the International Labor Organization to refocus its efforts on "decent work," but informality remains the dominant terminology in policy and aid circles.

While Berida's story illustrates the precariousness of informal sector employment, it also shows how such work is monitored and influenced by the state. Informal sector businesses may cultivate relationships with government officials or private factories such as breweries, but they can often draw more safely on unpaid family and apprentice labor. In Kumasi, an association of small-scale bakers, studied by Rudith King, sought formal government recognition as a cooperative for its owner-members but kept its relations with workers outside the purview of the minimum wage legislation. This situation encourages informal workers to start up their own operations as soon as possible and to cultivate personal relationships with suppliers and customers or with kin and neighbors, instead of keeping written accounts and contracts. Today, demolition of the stalls of informal traders in streets and markets is still common in Ghana, with notorious episodes also occurring in Zimbabwe, Tanzania, and in Berida's Kenya; while formal sector shops are also subject to occasional extralegal confiscations, they are rarely destroyed.

The subcontinental pattern of variation in the balance between formal and informal economies again contrasts West Africa to East and southern Africa. In West Africa, the informal sector predominates and shows more continuity with indigenous traditions. In many respects, the informal sector in this part of the continent is better organized and more reliable than the formal sector, not least in its ability to adjust quickly to shifts in climate or political unrest. In eastern and southern Africa, the relative size of white and Asian settlement brought more formal sector development, although management positions were often reserved for whites. The trade in imports and local foods in Zimbabwe at the wholesale level, for example, is organized through

Figure 4.6. The Kumasi yam wholesale yard is big business in Ghana.
Gracia Clark.

formal firms owned by Europeans and Lebanese, while Ghana and Nigeria have big African distributors at much higher levels within the informal sector. Informal trade and enterprises can pay better than many lower-level civil service or factory jobs, although not at the smallest scale. In southern Africa, the predominance of men in mine work tends to raise wages for men in other formal enterprises, while lower-paid farm and factory labor includes both male and female workers.

In South Africa, the informal sector and indeed formal African business development was strictly prohibited for so many decades that its growth was seriously retarded. Even after decades of majority rule, much of the street commerce in this part of the continent is conducted in Asian shops or by immigrants from West and Central Africa. Studies of urban township life show effective organization by Africans in only a few occupations, notably as beer brewers at shebeens (illegal bars) and drivers at taxi stands. In squatter settlements such as Crossroads, studied by Fiona Ross, livelihoods are pieced together through casual work arrangements between neighbors for cash or payment in kind. These networks often center around the few people with formal sector jobs or old-age pensions.

REMITTANCES AS GLOBAL FINANCIAL NETWORKS

While many Africans move to urban areas in their own countries to seek better employment opportunities and higher incomes, others emigrate abroad. According to the International Fund for Agricultural Development (IFAD), more than thirty million Africans live outside of their home countries. While much of this migration is to elsewhere in Africa or to Europe and the Middle East, others travel to the United States. The 2000 U.S. Census documented that 881,300 people living in the United States were born in Africa; today the number is probably closer to one million. Many reside in heavily populated urban areas, such as New York, Washington, DC, Minneapolis, and Atlanta, but increasingly also in smaller cities such as Greensboro, North Carolina, and Columbus, Ohio. Although it is commonly thought that primarily young men emigrate, according to the World Bank 47.2 percent of emigrants from sub-Saharan Africa are now women.

Migrations like this are nothing new; for centuries groups have migrated into, within, and out of Africa. Over the last century, increasing urbanization in Morocco and elsewhere in Africa stimulated internal migration as people moved to cities looking for work. Likewise, international migration was sometimes encouraged by host countries. France actively recruited workers from its former colonies in the 1960s and 1970s, including from Morocco, which had been a French protectorate. Today more stringent migration restrictions mean that many workers are undocumented and that some Africans risk their lives traveling to Europe in precarious wooden boats. While some people emigrate permanently, many live abroad for shorter periods, eventually returning home.

These emigrants can have a dramatic impact on the livelihoods of the people they leave behind, particularly through remittances, the money or goods that they send back to their friends and families. Although people emigrate from all African countries, North Africa receives the bulk of remittances largely because of its geographic proximity to and historical relationship with Europe. According to the IFAD, in 2006 45 percent of remittances to the continent went to this region. For example, the World Bank reports that in 2010 Morocco received the third-highest amount of remittances in Africa (behind Nigeria and Egypt), garnering U.S. $6.4 billion, which accounted for 6.6 percent of the country's GDP. Not surprisingly, these substantial remittances correlated with a large number of migrants. In 2010, more than 9 percent of Morocco's population had emigrated, with the top destination countries being France, Spain, Italy, and Israel. Families that remain behind are often headed by women, who use these remittances in a variety of ways such as by supporting the daily needs of their households and paying for education, health care, and better nutrition.

A study conducted in the Todgha River valley by Hein de Haas in the southern High Atlas Mountains of Morocco analyzed the impact of this migration and the subsequent remittances on the local and regional economies. Receiving remittances, especially from international destinations, had a large impact on households: those that garnered remittances from international migrants had twice the income of those that did not. Households that were associated with international migration also had higher local cash incomes, indicating that members actively expanded their work in the local economy rather than passively depending upon money from abroad. The extra funds could also play an important part in household strategies to diversify livelihoods and could minimize risks in the way that insurance might do elsewhere.

Since accessing formal channels that provide financial services such as loans is often difficult for many Africans, remittances can play an important role in financing small businesses and development projects. For example, beyond employing remittances to support daily household needs, people in the Todgha River valley invested this money in improved agricultural techniques, such as buying water pumps to help with irrigation or purchasing new farmland. Others built houses, which could lead to rental income, or invested in private businesses. While not everyone in the region directly received remittances, an increase in construction projects and rising consumption rates resulted in local job creation, which benefited the region as a whole. Beyond helping families to secure livelihoods, in some cases remittances may have even helped people overcome discrimination. They enabled some people of lower social status to access new kinds of income and power, although they could also lead to new forms of inequality between families who had access to remittances and those who did not. While receiving remittances does not guarantee economic success, it can be a way for African households to diversify their livelihoods and protect themselves against unexpected hardships.

The livelihood approach to understanding how people get by in Africa invites us to acknowledge the complexity of their strategies, the many factors that shape them, and the innovative ways that people operate in the face of great constraints. As this chapter and its examples demonstrate, Africans tap into local, regional, national, and international networks in order to make their livelihoods viable. Factors such as gender, age, ethnicity, and social class also affect their possibilities for action and can both increase and limit opportunities. While their options may be restricted by their larger historical, socioeconomic, and environmental settings, people maneuver within these constraints to generate creative strategies for getting by and for making their lives meaningful. Livelihood approaches assume that constraint and agency are virtually coextensive and constantly interact and respond to each other.

The agency of individuals does not negate the strength of lineage and community solidarity; rather, it is enacted in terms of those social relationships. It is a question not of people rejecting the group but of finding themselves inside the group and expanding their scope within it. Rules of behavior and entitlement to resources may prescribe who does and owns what, but in practice some people always behave badly or cannot fulfill their duties, sometimes precisely because they lack the resources required to do so. Ideal models in any culture, however devoutly followed, are always supplemented by what happens when things do not work as planned. These "plan B" or fallback strategies are also a valuable part of the cultural repertoire. Although they may be rarely used, they must be available when needed because they are essential to long-term survival.

There remains debate over many questions, such as the effect of remittances on the receivers and their regions. While the Moroccan study suggests that this money can have a positive effect on entire regions, others suggest that it can be detrimental. Citing different examples, some development scholars worry that households can become dependent upon remittances, which can be devastating if they cease. While remittances may lead to increased financial security for some families, emigration can also result in "brain drain" as educated Africans move abroad to benefit from higher salaries. Others argue that when migrants return home, as many do, they bring new skills, knowledge, and resources with them. Development analysts do agree that public policies could do more to encourage remittances and better link them with development. This could include lowering fees on money transfers, easing taxes on remittances, and establishing programs whereby people could use access to remittances as collateral for small business loans. Such measures would also enable migrants to remain better connected with their home countries and families, thus increasing the odds that they—and their accompanying skills—will return home.

Africans are carrying out a nonverbal debate complementary to this verbal one, as they imagine and perform a range of strategies reflecting both their material and ideological constraints and the bottomless font of invention arising from their creative capacity. Conformity and deviance, risk and precaution generate innumerable contradictory and reinforcing layers that accumulate into history. Individuals always retain a significant degree of autonomy, and this helps them adapt to the inevitable changes and surprises of life. This room for maneuver constitutes the potential for social change through individual or collective action, but it is also essential for the maintenance of the social order or social reproduction. In human societies, both rules and exceptions need to be present to create the flexibility and adaptability that allow social systems and individuals to survive. Without the ability to constantly adjust to changing circumstances, no social system, oppressive or otherwise, could last for very long. Livelihoods are socially constructed and contested in a never-ending cycle of renewal and destruction that generates both continuity and change.

SUGGESTIONS FOR FURTHER READING

Ardener, Shirley, and Sandra Burman, eds. 1995. *Money Go Rounds: The Importance of Rotating Savings and Credit Associations for Women*. Oxford: Berg.

Batterbury, Simon. 2001. "Landscapes of Diversity: A Local Political Ecology of Livelihood Diversification in South-Western Niger." *Ecumene* 8(4):437–64.

Buggenhagen, Beth Anne. 2012. *Muslim Families in Global Senegal: Money Takes Care of Shame*. Bloomington: Indiana University Press.

Clark, Gracia. 1991. "Food Traders and Food Security in Ghana." In *The Political Economy of African Famine: The Class and Gender Basis of Hunger,* ed. R. E. Downs, D. O. Kerner, and S. P. Reyna, 227–56. London: Gordon and Breach.

Cooper, Barbara M. 1997. *Marriage in Maradi: Gender and Culture in a Hausa Society in Niger, 1900–1989*. Portsmouth, NH: Heinemann.

de Haas, Hein. 2006. "Migration, Remittances and Regional Development in Southern Morocco." *Geoforum* 27:565–80.

de Waal, Alexander. 2005. *Famine That Kills: Darfur, Sudan*. New York: Oxford University Press.

Ferguson, James. 1999. *Expectations of Modernity: Myths and Meanings of Urban Life on the Zambian Copperbelt*. Berkeley: University of California Press.

Hansen, Karen Tranberg, and Mariken Vaa, eds. 2004. *Reconsidering Informality: Perspectives from Urban Africa*. Uppsala: Nordiska Afrikainstitutet.

Horn, Nancy E. 1994. *Cultivating Customers: Market Women in Harare, Zimbabwe*. Boulder, CO: Lynne Rienner.

King, Rudith, and Imoro Braimah. 2010. "Earning Dignity and Recognition through Formalisation: A Study of a Bakers' Association and Its Members in the Informal Sector of Ghana." Unpublished paper.

Ndambuki, Berida, and Claire C. Robertson. 2000. *We Only Come Here to Struggle*. Bloomington: Indiana University Press.

Piot, Charles. 1999. *Remotely Global: Village Modernity in West Africa*. Chicago: University of Chicago Press.

Ross, Fiona C. 1995. *Houses without Doors: Diffusing Domesticity in Die Bos*. Pretoria: Cooperative Research Programme on Marriage and Family Life, Human Sciences Research Council.

Vaughan, Megan. 1987. *The Story of an African Famine: Gender and Famine in Twentieth-Century Malawi*. New York: Cambridge University Press.

5 Religions in Africa

John H. Hanson

Spirit possessions, harvest festivals, and other activities associated with African traditional religions (or religions with African roots) remain vital, but attendance at Christian churches and Muslim mosques in Africa has increased significantly during the last century. From 1900 to 2010 the number of Christians in Africa grew from less than 10 million to 470 million, more than 20 percent of the world Christian community. The number of Muslims in Africa also grew to more than 450 million, over 25 percent of the global Muslim community. This chapter discusses the endurance of religions with African roots and how Africans have accepted, proselytized, and elaborated upon Christianity and Islam during the past two hundred years.

DEFINITIONS AND PERSPECTIVES

Religion refers to ideas and practices concerning societal relations with unseen powers. It is associated with prophecies, moral directives, and explanations of the world, and religious followers forge bonds with others through rituals, experience ecstatic states in trances, and obtain healing and comfort through rituals, supplications, and other activities. The complete range of religious experiences is difficult to study, but scholars can analyze religious ideas and discuss the roles and actions of religious specialists and their followers in specific times and places.

Religions with African roots were the first on the continent and shaped the religious landscape. They often recognize a creator god and accessible spiritual forces that ritual specialists can contact in specific places or call to become manifest in individuals or objects such as masks or statues. Public rituals engage these unseen forces, and private consultations draw on them to provide individual assistance. European colonialism disrupted and sometimes prohibited these religious activities in early twentieth-century Africa, so current expressions are best understood as contemporary constructions evoking local ideas and practices in complex ways.

Christianity and Islam are monotheistic religions based on scriptures. The Bible and Qur'an provide believers with moral guidance as well as a warning that human existence will culminate in an end-of-time when God will judge humans and grant access to heaven only to those deemed worthy. Early Christians established doctrines and ecclesiastical organizations in the Catholic and Orthodox traditions, and Protestant denominations emerged during the European Reformation. Early Muslims never founded overarching religious organizations, and they largely agreed on the primacy of the Qur'an and the Traditions (reports of the Prophet Muhammad's actions and deeds) and a few core rituals, such as daily prayers, as the basis of the faith. Nevertheless, divisions in the Muslim world emerged, for example, between Sunni and Shi'i traditions. Theological and ritual elaboration continues in both Christianity and Islam, as one would expect in religions welcoming new converts.

The term "syncretism" often is used in reference to elaborations of Islam and Christianity in Africa, but the word conveys an inaccurate impression that Africans somehow fall short of ideals when in reality no "pure" form of any religion exists. Christians and Muslims in all times and places put religion to work in their lives by interpreting scriptures and augmenting ritual practices. Historical research reveals, for example, that core elements of Christian worship, such as praise singing and supplication through prayer, have roots in the ancient, pre-Christian Mediterranean world as well as the religious practices of early Christians. African converts to Christianity and Islam similarly reject their previous religions and enrich their new faiths with interpretations and expressions drawing on meaningful local ideas and practices.

RELIGIONS WITH AFRICAN ROOTS

Religions with African roots historically have been the most numerous religions on the continent. Most did not leave behind written records, but scholars have uncovered evidence of their ideas, practices, and influence on social processes in the pre-colonial era. Acknowledgement of a creator god as well as lesser gods and spirits was widespread, but specific understandings and religious practices varied. Spiritual forces often were associated with localities, including hills, rocks, and sacred forests, but spirits also could become manifest in portable objects such as masks and sculptures, as the chapter on visual art in Africa discusses. In some contexts, religious specialists were mediums who could call spirits; in others they were prophets who merely received messages, and in still others they were diviners who could foretell the future. Most societies distinguished between religious specialists working for the common good and those working for private interests and directing unseen forces against others. Sometimes specific roles were reserved for men and others for women, but gender specializations were not uniform across the continent. Religious specialists could be from families with long-standing ties to the community, but they also could be people from outside, whose social and physical distance added to their authority.

The social functions of religions with African roots were multiple. Some rituals healed the ill or cured the infertile, as the chapter on health and healing in Africa discusses. Others had "ordeals" identifying wrongdoers or mass campaigns to identify asocial persons believed to be witches. Still others aimed at rainmaking. Political leadership also had rituals, such as those associated with the installation of new leaders in office or the commemoration of locally significant events. These activities often were conservative, reinforcing certain ideas about proper behavior or merely celebrating community solidarity, but they could produce social change. For example, rainmaking processes allowed for public commentaries on the efficacy of leaders and could inspire political action by encouraging the ouster of a leader perceived not to be fulfilling the common good. In other contexts, where chiefs had installation ceremonies associated with objects such as stools, rituals existed to remove or "destool" a leader. Not all practices perform the same work, but all religious are intertwined in social processes.

Religions with African roots changed over time. The absence of documentary information makes specific changes difficult to reconstruct, but borrowing from other religions is one indicator. For example, Ifa, one of many local religious cults in coastal areas from Ghana to Nigeria, is a form of divination that draws significantly from Islamic practices known as "sand writing"; Ifa's specialists either borrowed the new practice or adapted elements of Islamic sand writing to their own divination practices. Another example of religious change occurred in the herding areas of today's Kenya and Tanzania, where Maasai peoples currently reside. Ritual specialists performed regular initiations of Maasai youths into adulthood, and many Maasai women supplicated Eng'ai, the high god, as part of their daily religious activities. In the nineteenth century new religious roles emerged during a time of expansion as specific Maasai groups claimed more territories and incorporated others into their communities. Integral to this process were prophets, *iloibonok,* who aided particular Maasai groups in claiming territories and asserting authority over others absorbed into growing Maasai communities during these nineteenth-century transformations.

European Colonial Intervention and Consolidation

In some regions religious specialists became involved in armed struggles against European imperialism. One example occurred in today's Tanzania during the colonial consolidation, after the German administration had imposed taxation and began promoting rubber harvesting and cotton cultivation. The trigger was a severe drought in 1905, after which many rural residents rose up against colonial intermediaries and eventually fought German armies. Various groups were involved, but the movement came to be known as Maji-Maji in reference to the potion religious specialists made from water *(maji)* and other items for followers to ingest for protection against German bullets. Kinjikitile Ngwale, the spirit medium who first concocted *maji* protections, and other ritual specialists associated with the movement were captured and killed by Germans as they forcefully put down the

Figure 5.1. Dogon dancer in late twentieth-century Mali.
Corbis.

resistance. Another example occurred in today's Burkina Faso in 1915–17, as local populations took advantage of the First World War to rise up against the French at a time of perceived military weakness. Diverse communities worked together in the effort to organize and fight, drawing on religious specialists controlling a network of local shrines. In this case, Muslims joined non-Muslims in making common cause against an enemy, and both were targeted by the French and died in this failed effort.

The changes of the colonial era influenced local religious practices. European colonial officers encouraged a number of rituals that they assumed consolidated authority for African intermediaries in the colonial administration, but in some cases these ceremonies were "invented traditions" and not linked to a continuous cultural practice. Europeans also actively discouraged or outlawed certain practices deemed controversial or a challenge to their rule, driving them out of public sight. As religious specialists receded from view, many likely modified or truncated their religious practices. For example, specialists who previously had dealt with a broad range of public healing turned merely to infertility in individual cases; the chapter on health and healing reveals the vibrancy of these practices. Some religions with African roots continued, occasionally under the cover of secrecy in the colonial era, and elements of local religious practices remained a resource for contemporary artistic and musical expressions, political ceremonies, and other activities. For example, Dogon communities in contemporary Mali organize dances with masks on a regular basis and invite outsiders to witness some of their rites and ceremonies.

Some religions with African roots were able to expand in the colonial era. For example, in the northeastern region of today's Ghana, a complex of ancestor and earth shrines in the Tong hills was targeted by the British as a source of subversion to their rule. British officials sent a military force, then tried destroying the caves, and finally relocated African populations residing near the complex in an effort to eliminate the shrines. The British relaxed restrictions in the 1920s, and one of these ancestor cults, Tongnaab, thrived in a new network of shrines in southern Ghana, where other ethnic groups turned to it for witch-finding under the name Nana Tonga. As some Africans gained wealth and no longer acknowledged social obligations, accusations of witchcraft increased, and Nana Tonga's reputation for finding witches was enhanced by the local perception that the northern regions were without asocial people due to the efficacy of their gods. Transformations in Tongnaab and Nana Tonga continue to this day, as its network of shrines remains active and tourists from outside Ghana visits the Tong hills.

The colonial era included the appropriation of Christian symbols by religions with African roots. For example, in Gabon beginning in the 1920s, a movement known as Bwiti established a network of chapel houses emphasizing egalitarianism bolstered by rituals and other shared religious experiences. Ancestors figured prominently in Bwiti, as did initiations during which a local hallucinogenic substance was consumed in a ritual involving singing and dance. While a central religious experience in Bwiti was an encounter with Jesus Christ, this figure was not the "son of

God" of Christian teaching but represented as a local healer. Some members of Bwiti had been educated in Christian missionary schools, but neither they nor other followers of Bwiti would claim to be Christians. Bwiti is a religion with African roots that appropriated Christian symbolism to lend it relevance and authority in the changed circumstances of the colonial era. It drew on ideas and practices of deep historical resonance and engaged Christianity's expansion with its complex rituals and symbolism.

Recent Developments

Religions with African roots are diminishing in influence due to the recent expansion of Islam and Christianity in Africa. Evangelical Pentecostal and charismatic churches, for example, often define "traditional" African religious ideas and practices as "evil," and these churches have been successful in eliminating many such expressions in public contexts. The evocative power of these local religions nevertheless remains significant, as the chapters on art and music in Africa discuss. Private consultations with religious specialists also continue, as religions with African roots still offer compelling messages and offer healing and other services to Africans.

Accusations of witchcraft persist in contemporary Africa, raising questions about the relations between these claims and current practices. Note that accusations and actual involvement in the occult are distinct. In some cases there are personal accounts of possession by evil spirits, but these narratives cannot be corroborated and the confession itself often is an aspect of joining a Christian movement or a Pentecostal congregation. More than one person has made sensational claims to have ritually killed someone as part of his or her "evil" past, only to recant when confronted by authorities. Allegations of witchcraft nonetheless are real, as periods of social change often produce outbreaks of widespread public fear and resentment of individuals who do not share social norms with others. Contemporary witch-finding practices often draw on evocative symbols and practices from the past, but one cannot project a continuous tradition of African witchcraft over the centuries. Africa, in other words, may experience periodic waves of witch-finding, but it is not necessarily inhabited by witches.

CHRISTIANITY

Some of the first Christian communities were in northern Africa. Alexandria, in the lower Nile valley, was an early Christian religious center, and other towns to the west were significant, such as Hippo in today's Algeria, where Augustine wrote his influential theological works. Christianity declined in northern Africa as local populations of Copts and Berbers adopted Arabic and converted to Islam in the centuries after the Arab conquests of the seventh century. Several Christian communities remain in northern Africa, such as the Coptic Church in Egypt, but Orthodox Christianity's major African presence is in Ethiopia. Rulers of Axum, a highland Ethiopian state and regional commercial power, converted to Christianity in the fourth century CE. Through the subsequent activities of Christian monks as well as the support of Ethiopian political elites over the centuries, Christianity thrived and expanded in the highlands. Today with some forty million members, the Ethiopian Tewahedo Church, an autonomous branch in the Orthodox Christian tradition, has its own saints and religious festivals, liturgies in Ge'ez (an ancient Semitic language with origins in the highlands), and religious icons.

Nineteenth-Century Missionary Efforts

The nineteenth century brought sustained efforts to expand Christianity in Africa. Europeans had established Catholic missions in previous centuries, after the initial voyages of exploration of the fifteenth century, but success often eluded them, except in contexts such as Kongo, where the king converted and a local Christian community emerged with its own saints. The nineteenth century witnessed an upsurge in missionary activities: Catholics continued their efforts and Protestants increased their involvement, moved in part by religious revivals in late eighteenth-century Europe and North America. This new evangelism combined with long-standing efforts to abolish slave trading in Africa. David Livingstone, a nineteenth-century Scottish missionary and explorer who wrote about his work in Africa, inspired many others to follow his example. Using European coastal trading enclaves as points of access to the continent, Christian missionaries obtained plots of land from African leaders and sought to establish new communities of Christian converts.

Christianity grew most effectively when African converts spread the message. Receptivity to Christianity initially occurred at the top or bottom ranks of African societies. Royalty sometimes converted and encouraged their subjects to follow; literacy and access to commodities, as much as Christian beliefs and rituals, often were the attractions for African elites. Christianity also appealed to the downtrodden, such as in contexts where warfare produced uprooted people seeking new beginnings. Among the most successful nineteenth-century missionaries were recent African converts. Samuel Ajayi Crowther, for example, was enslaved in today's southern Nigeria in 1821, liberated from a slave ship, and released by the British navy at Freetown, Sierra Leone, where he converted to Christianity; Crowther returned to Nigeria to proselytize and rose to the rank of bishop in the growing Anglican community of late nineteenth-century Nigeria. Crowther and other African Christians spoke from individual experiences and articulated the message in local languages. They also persisted in the faith, even after tropical diseases claimed significant numbers of the first European missionaries in Africa. Martyrdom faced some early converts: in Buganda, for example, Christian and Muslims competed for influence at the capital during the late nineteenth century, and a shift in support led to the deaths of several African Catholics, who are remembered to this day in an annual ceremony in Uganda. The nineteenth century did not bring large numbers of Africans into the fold, but it laid the groundwork for Christian expansion in the century that followed.

European Colonial Intervention and Consolidation

The relations between Christianity and European colonial rule in Africa are complex. The colonial "civilizing mission" was close to the Christian vision for Africa, and some European missionaries encouraged African elites to sign treaties and ally with European powers during the late nineteenth century. Missionaries associated with influential congregations in the metropole tended to be favored by colonial officials in Africa—Catholics in French colonies and Protestants in British colonies, for example—although all Christian denominations were present to some degree throughout the continent. Missionary organizations began to mirror the social and racial hierarchies of colonialism, as additional European missionaries arrived and pushed African converts from leadership positions beginning in the late nineteenth century. But some missionaries criticized the abuses of imperial conquest and colonial consolidation. Ironically, European colonial officials supported African political leaders who sustained local religious rituals condemned by the missionaries. In some cases, colonial authorities even prevented Christian missionaries from proselytizing in regions with significant Muslim populations, such as the northern regions of Nigeria.

Colonial rule created fertile ground for conversion to Christianity. European conquests raised questions about the efficacy of religions with African roots, and colonial consolidation encouraged Africans to seize the opportunities associated with Christianity. Missionary schools offered literacy in European languages, a skill that Africans could put to use as clerks in colonial bureaucracies or European firms. As Africans were looking afresh at Christian mission schools, European missionaries were altering strategies and targeting children for conversion: these circumstances meshed and produced a young generation of converts in the early colonial era. Conversions of adults still occurred too. In Rwanda, for example, many tens of thousands of farmers joined the Catholic Church in the 1930s, following the example of elites who had been converted by missionaries during earlier decades. And serendipity could play a role. In the northwestern regions of today's Ghana, conversions of farmers occurred when it rained on a Catholic mission after an Irish missionary promised it would during a local drought; the children of these converts attended missionary schools and became the social base for a dynamic Catholic community in this region.

Some Africans split from mission churches and founded new congregations, usually called African independent churches. Led by African clergy, these churches went by different names but shared many features, such as a more vibrant ritual life and belief in the role of the Holy Spirit acting through living prophets. The Aladura or "praying churches" of Nigeria, for example, formed in the early colonial period out of the Christian prayer circles of missionary school graduates who held administrative jobs in the colonial towns of southern Nigeria. Under the guidance of charismatic African clergy, prayer circles developed into new churches, expanded into rural areas, and added an emphasis on drumming and healing rituals, activities that were

Figure 5.2. African independent church baptism in mid-twentieth-century South Africa. *Corbis.*

prohibited at mission churches at the time. African independent churches in southern Africa, often called Zionist churches, also emphasized the role of African prophets and local symbolism; some of these Zionist congregations became involved in the struggle against the system of racial discrimination known as apartheid.

Scholars often refer to the religious transformations associated with African independent churches as the "Africanization" of Christianity. This term has merit, as it draws attention to ways Africans appropriated the message and reoriented rituals to make them relevant to their lives. But it is misleading to say that African independent churches are more African than churches that did not experience the rupture of separation. On one hand, mission churches eventually engaged in discussions about liturgy and leadership, with internal reform gradually leading to the liberalization of services and liturgies and to the elevation of Africans to leadership positions. Today these former mission churches, often called "mainline" churches, are run by Africans who retain affiliations to the Catholic or Protestant communities of the initial missionaries. On the other hand, emphasis on Africanization obscures the ways that European missionaries were transformed by their experiences in Africa. Recent work reveals how cross-cultural exchanges served to influence European Christian practices in metropolitan contexts during the twentieth century.

African women converted to Christianity in large numbers and became influential members of many congregations during the twentieth century. In Botswana, for example, Christian missionary efforts initially converted the male elite of the Ngwato state in the late nineteenth century, but by the 1920s Tswana women dominated membership and actively promoted social causes such as temperance. Their religious activities were a transformation of expected gender roles in Tswana society, where women had brewed beer and been excluded from the public sphere. Women also played significant roles in congregations that broke from missionary churches. In Kenya, for example, large numbers of women were moved by the preaching of Alfayo Odongo Mango, founder of the Roho Holy Spirit movement, an African independent church. These women preserved Roho beliefs and practices after Mango died in a fire set by the movement's enemies in 1934; their hymns, songs, and ecstatic visions are the core of the Ruwe Holy Ghost Church, the successor to the Roho movement.

Translating the Bible into African languages was critical to the expansion of Christian communities. Some translations were by Europeans knowledgeable in African languages, but most missionaries relied on African converts as their assistants, and in some cases Africans took the lead in translation. In Uganda, for example, Baganda Christian converts took the lead in translating the Bible into Luganda and carried the new translations far and wide in a successful missionary crusade during the early twentieth century. Their translations incorporated local words for "high god" and other religious expressions; more importantly, they allowed local religious ideas and practices to permeate the sacred text of Christianity. Translated Bibles had other influences too. Once a translation of the Bible had been made, that specific dialect of the African language became the standard over time. For example, after African missionaries disseminated a Bible translated into Yoruba in nineteenth-century southern Nigeria, not only did its dialect of Yoruba become the accepted version of that language, but the Bible and local missionary activities contributed to the construction of a wider Yoruba identity that previously had not been acknowledged by speakers of the numerous dialects of this language.

Recent Developments

The most notable Christian development of the past three decades is the phenomenal growth in evangelical Pentecostal and charismatic churches in Africa. The genesis of these churches was in the colonial era, as the Assemblies of God and others founded missions in Africa, but significant expansion occurred in the postcolonial context, often at the expense of African independent and mainline churches. African ministers in Pentecostal and charismatic churches draw on African interpretations of Pentecostal teachings to stress personal deliverance, baptism by the Holy Spirit, speaking in tongues, prayer healing, and exorcism of demonic forces. In addition, they use mass media to present themselves as "modern": their loudly broadcast church services define their presence and preach a "prosperity gospel" linking material and spiritual prosperity to personal intervention by God.

Some congregations actually provide mechanisms for economic advancement, such as loans to poorer members to start businesses, but their interpretation stresses God's intervention to ensure financial success, and the religious leadership often engages in conspicuous consumption of expensive clothing, luxury cars, and up-to-date electronic equipment as representations of God's blessings. Global connections also influence these Pentecostal and charismatic churches, with frequent exchanges of visiting evangelists between Africa and North America.

Some scholars associate the rise of evangelical Pentecostal and charismatic churches with the diminishing economic possibilities in many African nations during the 1970s and 1980s. The promise of God's blessing is alluring at times of widespread financial hardship. Others note that newly wealthy Africans are attracted to an exclusive spiritual community that reduces their need to fulfill kinship obligations to family outside the congregations. Global exchanges also are valued in an increasingly interconnected world. These sociological observations do not diminish the strong sense of religious community among "born-again" individuals attending the Pentecostal and charismatic churches in Africa.

The mainline Christian churches have not remained static. Many congregations have adopted practices associated with Pentecostal and charismatic churches, such as the use of new media and speaking in tongues. The charismatic movement in the Catholic tradition, for example, has emerged with vigor in the African context as well as elsewhere in the world. African Christians are writing theological works that elaborate on the message for a new generation. Some of these African leaders have gained a following outside the continent, especially in Protestant congregations in the United States, where national bodies have adopted controversial positions on contemporary social issues and stirred opposition in some communities. Some understand these contemporary African engagements with scripture as hewing closely to the Bible's textual injunctions, but all interpretations are social constructions and cannot definitively be portrayed as more or less "biblical."

African Christian groups occasionally use violence to advance their cause. Alice Auma, for example, founded an African independent church known as the Holy Spirit Movement in the northern regions of Uganda during the 1980s. Claiming to be a prophet receiving messages from the Holy Spirit, Auma began by casting off witches, but she eventually formed a militia, the Holy Spirit Mobile Force, to defend the Acholi ethnic community from the Ugandan central government during a time of civil disorder. Auma claimed that spreading blessed shea butter on followers would protect them from harm, and she led the Holy Spirit Mobile Force to several victories in 1987. Her forces were defeated, however, by the Ugandan army in 1988 as they marched to the capital, Kampala: Auma fled to Kenya, but Joseph Kony, one of her lieutenants and a former Catholic altar boy who claimed to be possessed by spirits, convinced remnants of Auma's militia and other dissidents to fight an insurgent campaign under his leadership. Kony's movement, the Lord's Resistance Army, abducted children to serve as its soldiers and ordered the murder or mutilation of suspected enemies in the civilian population. After a decade of atrocities, the Lord's

Resistance Army signed a truce with the Ugandan government in 2006, and Kony and his followers withdrew to the eastern regions of the Democratic Republic of Congo, where the Lord's Resistance Army has continued its activities. This movement was the topic of an internet movie, *Kony 2012*, an ahistorical presentation that obscured more than it revealed.

Christianity has a long history in Africa. It began in the early centuries in towns such as Alexandria and Hippo, was sustained in contexts such as Ethiopia, and expanded during the last two hundred years as foreign missionaries and African converts spread the faith and translated the Bible into African languages. African prophets also emerged to form African independent churches inspired by the Bible, and more recently evangelical Pentecostal and charismatic churches stress the active role of the Holy Spirit in Africa. Christianity had wider influences, as mission schools provided education that was not widespread in colonial Africa. Diverse manifestations of Christianity currently exist in Africa, creating opportunities for dialogue and competition between various churches.

ISLAM

Africa was involved in the history of Islam from the time of the Prophet Muhammad, who reportedly sent some members of the early Muslim community to the highlands Ethiopian state of Axum for refuge from Arabian opponents of the faith. Muslims emerged as majority populations north of the Sahara after the Arab Muslim conquests of the seventh century: over several generations local populations of Copts and Berbers gradually adopted Arabic, appropriated Arab identities, and converted to Islam. Muslim merchants crossed the Sahara Desert and the Indian Ocean, converting local residents who in turn proselytized to others. Initial converts in sub-Saharan Africa often were merchants, and the relations between Islam and commerce remained intertwined for centuries. Political elites and others also converted, but this development was limited to the savannas just south of the Sahara and the coastal areas of eastern Africa. Most Muslims in sub-Saharan Africa kept African languages and local identities: societal adoption of Arabic occurred in only a few regions, such as the upper Nile valley of northern Sudan and in the westernmost Sahara (today's Mauritania). Along the eastern African coast, for example, African Muslims speak Kiswahili, a Bantu language with Arabic loan words. Kiswahili-speaking coastal elites, African in origin, converted to Islam beginning in the tenth century CE, and Islamic practices thereafter were influenced by local Muslim scholars as well as Muslim visitors and immigrants from Arabia, the Persian Gulf, and South Asia. Across the continent African Muslims participated in networks carrying people, texts, and ideas in all directions. Ibn Battuta, the fourteenth-century Moroccan Muslim traveler who logged more miles than Marco Polo, was merely the most notable traveler: numerous Africans went on pilgrimages and embarked on long-distance commercial ventures over the centuries.

Revival, Reform, and Empire-Building during the Nineteenth Century

Islamic revival and reform were a major current in the nineteenth century. Muslims in many regions began to question established notions of Islamic religiosity and emphasize the moral example of the Prophet Muhammad and his companions. Some reformers founded new organizations to provide religious education and social services. These ideas and organizational innovations were not accepted by all Muslims, and reformers sometimes disputed among themselves, creating numerous movements that competed for followers.

Sufi orders were on the forefront of Muslim revival and reform in Africa. Sufism is a spiritual discipline in which disciples seek enlightenment through rituals, such as reciting litanies, in hopes of experiencing proximity to God. Reformist Sufi leaders used the organizational structure of orders to create new communities that offered spiritual instruction and assistance in social and economic activities. In the Horn of Africa, for example, Sufi orders integrated people dislocated from the clan-based societies of the region into new settlements offering Islamic education and coordinating farming and trade. Some Somali Sufi orders were exuberant in expression and allowed sensual stimulation through drinking coffee and drumming at devotional activities; others condemned these practices and performed austere rituals in their communities. Sufi orders expanded elsewhere: in northern Africa, where the tradition had a long history and was revitalized in the nineteenth century, and in regions stretching from Senegal to Sudan and along the eastern coast of Africa, where Sufism often was a new religious orientation.

Sufi orders could become involved in political activism. The Arabic word *jihad* means religious effort or struggle, and it can be interpreted as nonviolent religious advocacy or internal spiritual development, but one important interpretation is jihad as armed action in defense of Islam. In the nineteenth century this latter meaning gained currency for some Sufi leaders. For example, Umar Tal, a resident of what today is Senegal and the leader of the Tijaniyya Sufi order in West Africa, called upon his disciples to fight non-Muslim elites in present-day Mali. Umar followed in the steps of an earlier Muslim leader, Uthman dan Fodio, whose call to military jihad in the early nineteenth century led to the creation of an expansive Sokoto Caliphate covering much of today's northern Nigeria. The Muslim states founded by Uthman and Umar fought religious wars against non-Muslims, and captives were enslaved as domestic servants and on large plantations, freeing Muslim elites to pursue religious activities, such as writing Sufi poetry in Arabic and vernacular languages. Nineteenth-century military jihad movements created several states led by Muslim leaders, establishing a legacy that informs political developments to this day in northern Nigeria and elsewhere.

Other Muslims also engaged in empire building during the nineteenth century. Muslim dynasties founded by Muhammad Ali in Cairo and by the Bu Saidi family of Oman in Zanzibar created extensive empires and encouraged commercial adventurers who raided south of Egypt and west of Zanzibar, respectively, in search of ivory and slaves. The slaves worked on plantations in the imperial heartlands, where they produced crops such as cloves for world markets. Sufi orders operated in the margins, often integrating the uprooted into new Muslim communities. In Egypt's northern Sudan territories, for example, Muhammad Ahmad, often referred to as the Mahdi because of his claims to be the "guided one" of Islamic eschatology, rose up and organized an armed movement that defeated Egyptian overrule in the late nineteenth century.

European Colonial Intervention and Consolidation

European powers confronted Muslim political leaders during the late nineteenth-century colonial intervention, co-opting some elites and conquering others. In Egypt Britain maintained the royal dynasty as it established hegemony over the country in the 1880s, but in the Sudan Britain fought against the Mahdi and defeated Abdallah, his successor, who died with approximately twenty thousand Muslims in the 1898 battle against the British at Omdurman. European intervention sometimes led Muslims to wage guerrilla campaigns, such as in Algeria and Somalia, where Sufi leaders mounted a challenge to colonial rule for several decades before Europeans finally defeated them. Some Muslims migrated to Arabia to avoid living under European colonial rule. Still others resigned themselves to colonialism, withdrew from political affairs, and focused on spiritual matters. The responses of Umar Tal's relatives ran the spectrum, from those who fought and died against the French to others who worked with colonial administrations and those, such as Umar's grandnephew Bokar Salif Tal, who devoted himself to expanding Islam through his Sufi teachings among populations Umar had conquered years earlier.

Some Muslim elites maintained close relations with European administrations and shaped the colonial experience. For example, in the former Sokoto Caliphate, Muslims came to an understanding with the British after the sultan fought against the colonial invasion: Britain retained Muslim elites in office and allowed the exercise of Islamic law and other aspects of the previous order but imposed control in some areas, such as abolishing certain kinds of corporal punishment and gradually ending slavery in northern Nigeria. Similar elite accommodation emerged elsewhere, such as between Britain and the Omani elite in Zanzibar. More ambiguous were the relations between the French and Amadu Bamba, a Sufi leader in Senegal. Bamba tried to keep his distance from politics, but his ability to attract disciples, including former slaves, brought French suspicion, two periods of forced exile from Senegal, and house arrest until his death in 1927. Bamba's order, the Muridiyya, eventually gained French acceptance and was able to expand, engaging in cash-cropping for material support while continuing an emphasis on Islamic education.

The number of Muslims in sub-Saharan Africa grew during the European colonial era. Colonial accommodations of Muslim elites created respectability for Islam in some regions, but nothing replaced inspired preaching as the primary way to win new converts. Sufi leaders welcomed newcomers such as former slaves into their orders, offering outsiders access to new communities based on religion and not class or kinship. Sufi leaders composed poetry in vernacular languages, included local cultural expressions such as dancing and drumming at their devotional sessions, and developed organizations that supported the expansion of cash-cropping or commercial activities. They also drew on local expectations that religious leaders could heal the ill, and they provided herbal cures and made amulets from verses of the Qur'an for spiritual protection. Some leaders came from established Muslim scholarly lineages, but Sufism's emphasis on spiritual matters meant that pious disciples could rise quickly, and several leaders came from humble backgrounds. And while Sufi leaders constructed their organizations locally, they had connections with global Sufi networks.

Sufism's expansion included women. Some Sufi leaders educated their sisters, wives, daughters, and other female relatives and inducted them into the orders. These women in turn brought other women into the order through gender-segregated activities in their homes. As women joined the movements, Sufi leaders often allowed mixing of the sexes at public events, such as celebrations of the Prophet Muhammad's birthday and devotional sessions; women usually wore modest clothing styles, taking their cue from local standards for Muslim dress. These gatherings nevertheless attracted criticism from some Muslims, resulting in greater gender segregation over time. In Somalia, for example, the twentieth century saw the rise of women's Sufi events where women recited *sittaat,* hymns invoking notable women from the early history of Islam; the women believed these figures might assist with their fertility or childbirth concerns.

Other Muslims contributed to Islam's expansion in sub-Saharan Africa. In rural areas, former slaves returned to their regions of origin and sometimes carried the faith of their masters with them, refashioning it in new contexts. In towns, Muslim Africans met non-Muslims in their service as police officers or colonial clerks and convinced some to join the faith. Other Muslims founded urban associations to support Arabic-language schools. Muslim missionaries from abroad were active too. For example, the Ahmadiyya Muslim community, founded in the late nineteenth century by the Indian Muslim Ghulam Ahmad, sent a small number of South Asian missionaries to Africa, where they converted Africans and worked with them to found schools and translate the Qur'an into African languages. Muslims usually have not translated the Qur'an, but others followed the Ahmadi example: most notably, the East African scholar Abd Allah Salih al-Farsi translated selected passages of the Qur'an into Kiswahili and added it to his instructional pamphlets in Kiswahili about performing Muslim rituals. The Muslim world in sub-Saharan Africa was alive with efforts to expand the faith and to provide the requisite knowledge for the growing number of new Muslim converts.

In northern Africa European imperialism led to shifts in political consciousness. Secular nationalism was a strong current, but Islam was another. In Egypt, for example, Hassan al-Banna, a schoolteacher, founded the Muslim Brotherhood (al-Ikhwan al-Muslimun) in 1928 to stress conservative Muslim values while providing social welfare through health clinics and social cooperatives. The Muslim Brotherhood opposed British colonial rule, and its military wing engaged in bombings and assassinations in the 1940s, culminating in al-Banna's death in a retaliatory killing and the banning of the movement by the authorities. The Muslim Brotherhood eventually disavowed violence, but its early history influenced one of its members, Sayyid Qutb, to write influential texts about armed Muslim opposition to corrupt rulers that have influenced extremist Islamists to this day.

Recent Developments

Independence brought new challenges to African Muslims. South of the Sahara in particular, Muslims found themselves at a disadvantage vis-à-vis Christians as positions opened in state bureaucracies for individuals literate in European languages adopted as national languages in postcolonial Africa: Christians had access to mission schools to learn European languages, but the colonial state often had not provided an extensive network of Western-style schools in Muslim areas. Postcolonial states also stressed secularism, stirring emotions among some Muslims who perceived these changes as undermining religious autonomy. Recent Muslim calls for greater implementation of sharia in part reflect these changing circumstances. Sharia (the word is often translated as "Islamic law") refers to Muslim legal processes that developed over the centuries. Recent uses of sharia sometimes include instances of turning to Islamic legal manuals produced by classical jurists to apply a rigid code with specific punishments for certain crimes, but the practice of sharia also is nuanced, as it has been for centuries. Muslims acknowledge that the ultimate judge, God, is forgiving, thus allowing for latitude in juridical decisions and punishments.

A new wave of Muslim reformism has swept across postcolonial Africa. Global Muslim influences are evident, such as Salafism, named for a diverse group of Islamic movements that stress the precedents of the *salaf,* Arabic for "ancestors," including the Prophet Muhammad and his initial followers. Emphasis on the example of *salaf* has deep roots in the Muslim world, and many credit the rise of contemporary Salafism to the evangelism of the eighteenth-century Saudi reformer Abd al-Wahhab and the nineteenth-century Muslim scholars Muhammad Abduh, Jamal al-Din Al-Afghani, and Rashid Rida. In its contemporary expressions African Muslim reformers draw on these ideas and also put their own intellectual effort into addressing local problems with a scripturalism that emphasizes knowledge of Arabic and promotes the Qur'an and Traditions as a basis for fostering piety in social life. African Muslim reformers criticize most Sufi leaders, whom the reformers see as fostering unacceptable innovations in religious practice. Reformers argue in vernacular languages for their text-based understandings and adopt new media to communicate with a mass audience, no longer emphasizing the intimate face-to-face encounters of Sufism. In many cases, these reformers founded Arabic-language

Figure 5.3. Mosque association praying for safe travel on the hajj in
early twenty-first-century Senegal.
Beth Buggenhagen.

schools that have adopted an instructional method breaking from the rote memori-
zation found in the established Qur'anic schools run by Sufis and other African
Muslims. Transnational networks provide African reformers with access to resources; Arabic-language schools, in particular, benefit from financial support from
oil-wealthy governments in Arabia and elsewhere, and their top students often gain
fellowships to further their studies abroad. The willingness of some African states
to include Arabic-language schools in the national educational system also ex-
pands opportunities for employment. Educational assistance, however, is merely
one element of support that flows from Arabia and Iran; medical clinics and other
humanitarian assistance are provided as well. Arabian assistance often leads to
greater adherence to Salafist ideas, and Iranian assistance has supported small
Shi'i communities in Africa.

Sufi orders and other Muslim movements that grew in the colonial era have continued to play a role in religious life. While Sufi orders have lost influence in some
regions, they remain vital in others, using new media for proselytizing. In Senegal,
for example, the Muridiyya expanded from its initial base in rural Senegal to add a
presence in Dakar and other Senegalese urban areas. The annual pilgrimage to
Touba, the spiritual center of the Muridiyya movement, remains a focus, and Sufi
leaders regularly tour urban areas, including cities such as New York and Paris where

immigrants have settled and rely on recordings of Sufi litanies and other new media to keep their faith alive. Sufi orders have remained active in eastern Africa as well, such as in Tanzania, where the orders still are the most widespread and popular Muslim organizations. The Ahmadiyya Muslim community's efforts continue in Africa: beginning in the 1970s, the Service to Humanity Scheme has increased access to educational and health services in Africa through development projects funded by donations from Ahmadi Muslims worldwide and led by local Ahmadi members and expatriate Ahmadi volunteers committing themselves to working for a set period in Africa.

In northern Africa the Muslim Brotherhood and other Muslim movements have emerged as major political forces in the aftermath of recent protests that swept entrenched governments from power. The protests began in Tunisia in 2010 after a fruit vendor set himself on fire, provoking mass demonstrations against President Zine El Abidine Ben Ali, who from 1987 oversaw a repressive state apparatus and economic policies that did not benefit the masses. The protests removed Ben Ali from power in January 2011 and sparked other protests in the region. In Egypt, where President Hosni Mubarak also had promoted state repression and economic liberalism, protesters adopted strategies from their Tunisian counterparts, such as using social media to organize nonviolent civil resistance through the occupation of Tahrir Square in Cairo. The Muslim Brotherhood joined the protests and offered support as the movement removed President Mubarak from power in 2011. The transitions in Egypt and Tunisia are not complete: in their immediate aftermath Muslim political parties, the Muslim Brotherhood in Egypt and Ennahda (a political movement inspired by the Muslim Brotherhood) in Tunisia, won elections and assumed the task of governing, but in 2013 military action swept the Muslim Brotherhood from power in Egypt and saw new protests challenging the Ennahda government in Tunisia. In Libya the influence of the Tunisian and Egyptian protests resulted in the ouster of longtime ruler Muammar Qaddafi, but only after the Libyan resistance waged an insurgent military campaign aided by international airpower. The aftermath of the Libyan uprising did not lead to a stable, centralized government: many groups, including those advocating reformist Islam, are competing for influence in the postrevolutionary era.

Militant Muslim movements have emerged in contemporary Africa. The recent events in northern Africa, for example, have triggered an uprising south of the Sahara. As discussed in the chapter on African politics, Tuareg separatist groups in Mali, joined by Tuareg fighters fleeing Libya with arms from Qaddafi's weapons caches, recently waged an insurgent campaign in northern Mali. Ansar Dine, one of the Tuareg insurgent groups, is a Muslim militia that made an alliance with Al-Qaeda in the Islamic Maghreb, an Algerian group now recruiting young Muslim men from across the region to fight in the Mali conflict. In Nigeria, the Muslim group known as Boko Haram embarked a campaign of bombings, initially targeting the police but later attacking United Nations offices and Christian churches; some Nigerian Muslim leaders who condemned Boko Haram's militant tactics have been assassinated by this shadowy group. In Somalia, two decades of civil unrest led to the rise of Al-Shabab, a Somali Muslim militia formed to support the Union of Islamic Courts, a grassroots movement that sought to erode the power of armed Somali clan leaders. When Ethiopia invaded Somalia in 2006 to dislodge the Union of Islamic Courts, Al-Shabab fought the Ethiopians and gained popular support; it took control of much of southern Somalia in 2009 when Ethiopia withdrew its forces. Once in power Al-Shabab rule was strict in its application of a literalist interpretation of the Qur'an, leading quickly to the loss of popular support among Somalis. Its leadership also organized terrorist bombings in Uganda and developed an internet presence advocating global jihad. Omar Hammami, an Alabama native and convert to Islam, for example, migrated to Somali and composed hip-hop lyrics about dying for Al-Shabab's cause. Kenya and Ethiopia invaded Somalia in 2010, and while Al-Shabab lost control in towns, it remains a force in some rural areas: a radical leadership consolidated control, purging members such as Omar Hammami through assassinations, and embarked on acts of terrorism in Somalia's towns and elsewhere, such as the 2013 assault on a Kenyan shopping mall. In contexts outside Al-Shabab control, however, Somali Sufi orders are remerging as influential groups. The activities of Al-Shabab, Boko Haram, and Ansar Dine attract attention as radical groups using force to impose their interpretations of Islam on others, but most African Muslims engage in peaceful religious advocacy and are tolerant of religious pluralism in Africa.

Africa's Muslim communities, long established on the continent, grew in numbers and influence during the past two hundred years. Sufi orders led reformist efforts in the nineteenth century and, after European colonial intervention, turned to expanding the numbers of the faithful through proselytism. These conversions encouraged local engagements with Islam, but homogenizing pressures are mounting as a result of increased interactions between Africa and the rest of the Muslim world. African Muslim reformers resolve tensions between local and global Islamic currents through the adoption of forms of Muslim piety based on readings of the Qur'an and connections to affluent regions of the Muslim world. But Sufism remains significant in some contexts, and other forms of Muslim religious expression continue to be relevant. In northern Africa Muslim movements have benefited from regime change to contest elections and come to political power. In a few contexts, such as Mali and Somalia, radical Muslim movements embracing a militant agenda have arisen, using force to impose an interpretation of Islam not shared by most others.

Religions in Africa are diverse and dynamic. Religions with African roots draw on rich pasts as they respond to contemporary efforts to represent their actions as irrelevant. Christianity's long history in Africa produced numerous congregations of Orthodox, mainline, African independent, and evangelical Pentecostal and charismatic churches. Islam has similar longevity and vitality, with Sufi, reformist, and other Muslim movements defining the contemporary scene. Religions with African roots have spread to diaspora communities in the Americas and elsewhere, and global interactions keep African Muslims and Christians in contact with others in their faiths. Africans will continue to elaborate on religious ideas and practices as they make religion relevant to their lives.

SUGGESTIONS FOR FURTHER READING

Allman, Jean, and John Parker. 2005. *Tongnaab: The History of a West African God.* Bloomington: Indiana University Press.

Bascom, William. 1969. *Ifa Divination: Communication between Gods and Men in West Africa.* Bloomington: Indiana University Press.

Brenner, Louis. 1983. *West African Sufi: The Religious Heritage and Spiritual Search of Cerno Bokar Saalif Taal.* Berkeley: University of California Press.

Falola, Toyin, ed. 2005. *Christianity and Social Change in Africa.* Durham, NC: Carolina Academic Press.

Isichei, Elizabeth. 1995. *A History of Christianity: From Antiquity to the Present.* Grand Rapids, MI: William B. Eerdmans.

Kalu, Ogbu. 2008. *African Pentecostalism: An Introduction.* Oxford: Oxford University Press.

Landau, Paul. 1995. *Realm of the Word: Language, Gender and Christianity in a Southern African Kingdom.* Portsmouth, NH: Heinemann.

Levtzion, Nehemia, and Randall Pouwels, eds. 2000. *The History of Islam in Africa.* Athens: Ohio University Press.

Loimeier, Roman, and Rudiger Seesemann, eds. 2006. *The Global Worlds of the Swahili: Interfaces of Islam, Identity and Space in Nineteenth- and Twentieth-Century East Africa.* Berlin: Lit. Verlag.

Mack, Beverly, and Jean Boyd. 2000. *One Woman's Jihad: Nana Asma'u, Scholar and Scribe.* Bloomington: Indiana University Press.

Mbiti, John. 1969. *African Religions and Philosophy.* New York: Praeger.

Peel, J. D. Y. 2000. *Religious Encounter and the Making of the Yoruba.* Bloomington: Indiana University Press.

Pew Forum on Religion and Public Life. 2012. "Tolerance and Tension: Islam and Christianity in Sub-Saharan Africa." Available at www.pewforum.org/executive-summary-islam-and-christianity-in-sub-saharan-africa.aspx.

Robinson, David. 2004. *Muslim Societies in African History.* New York: Cambridge University Press.

Spear, Thomas, and Isaria Kimambo, eds. 1999. *East African Expressions of Christianity.* Athens: Ohio University Press.

Umar, Muhammad Sani. 2005. *Islam and Colonialism: Intellectual Responses of Muslims of Northern Nigeria to British Colonial Rule.* Leiden: Brill.

6 Urban Africa
Lives and Projects

Karen Tranberg Hansen

In Africa and everywhere else, cities are where the action is. Cities are gateways to the global world, the prime sites for globalization's translation into local understandings and experiences. This urban global exposure demands that scholars of urban life in Africa pay attention to people's engagements with a diverse sweep of processes that range from the economic to the cultural. As they manifest themselves in distinct urban locations, such global exposures resonate in complicated ways with local cultural norms and practices. Focusing on a selection of themes that arise from these processes, this chapter is concerned with spatial transformations (residential space and housing; commercial space and markets), economic shifts (informalization), demographic changes (youth), and cultural issues that play out through consumption. Important themes that fall beyond this chapter's purview revolve around the general environmental and health effects of rapid population growth on urban livelihoods, varying from people's prospects for longevity to the places where they are buried. The chapter also does not deal with cross-border, interregional, and transnational migration processes in which cities are major conduits. The general background is sub-Saharan Africa, with many (but not all) specific examples drawn from southern and eastern Africa.

Today's rapidly growing cities in Africa are part of a long history of distinct urban traditions that in some parts of the continent extend back for more than a thousand years (such as Cairo and Alexandria in Egypt) and in others are the products of colonial rule (such as Nairobi in Kenya and Lusaka in Zambia). There are also new cities created as capitals after independence, such as Abuja in Nigeria. Some urban settlements with precolonial origins have been abandoned or remain very small (for example, Axum in Ethiopia and Timbuktu in Mali). Regardless of these differences, rapid urban growth is a fairly recent phenomenon, largely a twentieth-century process that is obscuring many former distinctions. The period since the 1970s has been a crucial moment for significant changes in urban lives and projects. Taken together, the debt crisis of the 1970s, the International Monetary Fund–

promoted economic restructuring of the 1980s, and more recent programmatic shifts revolving around poverty reduction strategies constitute a global political and economic conjuncture with far-ranging urban effects. These processes have been instrumental in transforming Africa's urban spaces in many ways, including stimulating widespread economic informalization and the growth of informal housing. At the same time, new technologies, especially the rapid adoption of mobile phones, are transforming sociability and economic practices. All of these developments are marked by complicated changes in the political economy of sex, in which economic hardships are unsettling widespread norms of male-female relations. In combination, these processes are bringing about a degree of convergence across much of urban Africa in spite of the historical variations among Africa's cities. In most large towns in Africa today, an obvious example of this convergence is a South African–financed supermarket or mall and one or more Chinese-owned shops.

These are new times in Africa's cities. Scholarship since 2000 has helped to push the study of urban Africa beyond approaches that have restrained us from grappling with the dynamic unfolding of urban lives in their own right. Some of these perspectives have introduced unhelpful distinctions between "world" or "global" cities and "third world" cities. World or global cities, in the view of some scholars, serve as organizing nodes in the global financial system, forming a hierarchical core network and second tier. Privileging global finance capitalism as the engine of growth, this approach to urban dynamics excludes vast areas of the urban world from its scope. It also ignores the productive role of exchange and consumption in the urban economy and their sociocultural imprint on urban space. Recent works have taken the global city approach to task for misconstruing the dynamics of urban Africa and for viewing the continent's cities merely as experiencing a delay in the type of development conventionally associated with the rise of industrial cities in the West. There is an assumption in much of this scholarship that the development path of third world cities will eventually follow that of cities in the West. Having not quite arrived by Western norms, African cities are seen as having "failed."

Such formulaic approaches to world/global cities and third world cities hide Africa's manifold urban dynamics from view. Jennifer Robinson, for one, has pointed to the wide range of contemporary cities in Africa and the very ordinariness of urban life. Rather than privileging specific kinds of cities, she approaches all cities as part of the same field of analysis. Viewing all cities as globally interconnected, she invites scholars of urban life to bring such connections to bear on their analyses.

Interconnections between urban areas across the world mean that cities play important intermediary or brokerage roles. Approaching urban Africa from an angle that encompasses both diversity and ordinariness requires a very inclusive research strategy analyzing the city as a space of interaction that brings together people, things, and ideas from around the country and the wider world. In this very inclusive sense, all cities are global, as Anthony King noted long ago when he claimed that all cities today are world cities. In effect, the overlapping themes of space, the economy, demography, and culture are embedded in locally diverse ways in this general view of an interconnected urban global world.

AN URBAN LEXICON

It is instructive to set out several terms used in the study of urban life. "Urbanization," the process involving the move of ever larger numbers of people from rural to urban locations, should be distinguished from "urbanism," the way of life of the people in cities. This apparently straightforward observation facilitates the exploration of grand processes such as globalization and urbanization from the point of view of the people who are living through them as well as in terms of how they are experiencing their effects and responding to them in their everyday lives. When sociologist Louis Wirth drew this distinction, he saw urbanism as a way of life, as a cultural product of industrialization, the growth of the market economy, and the routinization of modern society. This chapter suggests instead that urbanism as an African way of life today is a product of the distinctive types of economic activity that postcolonialism, and more particularly the political and economic developments of the last decades, has set into motion across Africa. Urbanism has its own spatial, economic, demographic, and cultural features, which display striking contrasts and sharp discontinuities. These do not line up neatly in dichotomous terms but rather crosscut the urban scene, contributing to its vitality and drama. Viewing urbanism in this way makes it possible to explore both the structural constraints that circumscribe people's lives and what they do to navigate and negotiate them.

What about the term "urban"? There is no clear-cut division between cities and towns and no universally adopted definition of urban places; the differences between definitions of "urban" definitions matter mainly to smaller towns and cities that might be classified as either rural or urban (National Research Council 2003: 132–35). For comparative discussions, the United Nations' city-level estimates and projections are useful. Extensive data are presented in the annual *Demographic Yearbook;* a second major source of data is the biennial *World Urbanization Prospects.*

How does this relate to Africa? The world's cities are growing at a tremendous rate. Globally, the level of urbanization is expected to rise from 52 percent in 2011 to 67 percent in 2050 (United Nations 2012: 4), especially in the South, and Africa is urbanizing more rapidly than any other region of the world. According to United Nations figures, 39.6 percent of Africa's population was urban in 2011, and this figure is expected to rise to 47.7 percent in 2030 and 57.7 percent in 2050. Africa's urban population will undergo rapid increase, trebling over the course of the next several decades. In fact, United Nations data indicate that by the middle of the century most of the world's urban population will be concentrated in Africa and Asia (United Nations 2012: 11, 12). This rapid growth is recent, even though Africa has long and varied urban histories that predate the colonial period and were influenced by it in complex ways. Some of this growth is a result of migration from rural areas, and some of it is due to urban population increase. Many African capitals doubled

Figure 6.1. Dar es Salaam skyline.
Katherine Wiley.

in size after independence in the mid-twentieth century, after numerous colonial constraints on urban development (for example, on migration, employment, and housing) were removed. In the 1970s and 1980s, this rapid increase gave way to somewhat slower growth rates along with population shifts from big cities to smaller towns. With the changes that have taken place in the political and economic regimes in many countries since the 1990s, Africa's cities are experiencing massive growth as a result of major transformations on several fronts: demographic, socioeconomic, and political. Africa's relations with the rest of the world have changed as well.

SPATIAL TRANSFORMATIONS

Scholarship on globalization has not, with a few recent exceptions pertaining specifically to South Africa, been concerned with the effects of international development efforts on cities and urban space in the developing world, nor has urban development policy been a part of the globalization curriculum. Leading theorists on globalization have been preoccupied with finance and economic circuits, technology, and all kinds of cultural flows. They have paid little attention to international development cooperation as an important form of globalization and to how this

Figure 6.2. Shopping in Soweto supermarket in South Africa.
Corbis.

process contributes to the reorganization of urban space in the South. In effect, globalization as mediated through international development programs has important implications for urban space. Structural adjustment programs and neoliberal reforms have been transforming urban space by reshaping the distribution and location of economic opportunities within specific cities, between cities in specific regions, and globally. Such policies have major ramifications across urban space, affecting the livelihoods of different population segments in unlike ways, sharpening social and spatial inequalities, and extending them in new ways.

The nature and availability of urban space in many cities in Africa is changing with regard to land, infrastructure, and markets, for example. Foreign investment has resulted in changes in urban spatial layouts and in the location of commercial activities, creating new patterns of physical and market segregation. South African retail capitalists are an important case in point. Since the mid-1990s, they have explored new possibilities for accumulation in the rest of Africa, especially (but not only) through upscale shopping mall developments. Workers at the Lusaka and Maputo locations of Shoprite, a major South African–based multinational that has expanded into Zambia and Mozambique, are implicated in a new politics of scale that asserts claims not only at the local level but also regionally, nationally, and globally, in ways that turn the Shoprite workplace into an important agent of a new regional imagination. These Zambian and Mozambican workers claim inclusion in the company on an equal basis with South African workers, in this way privileging their ties to South Africa through the company. There are other investments in malls at various scales by local firms, including by consortia of naturalized Asians in Lusaka and by Lebanese in Dakar, Senegal, and in warehouse development by businessmen of Lebanese, Portuguese, and South African Indian and Pakistani background in Oshikango, Namibia's rapidly growing entrepot on the border with Angola.

What is perhaps more conspicuous, or at least more controversial, than the post-apartheid South African retail expansion across the continent is the growing Chinese economic involvement in Africa. At issue are not Chinese investments in primary sector commodities such as minerals and agricultural products, in infrastructure such as railways and roads, or even in construction, an area where, in South Africa for example, the Chinese outnumber South Africans. What is at stake, rather, is wholesale and retail commerce carried out both by sizable Chinese investors and by small-scale traders of Chinese background, who have become a common presence in many African cities since the late 1990s.

Because marketing and trade provide a major source of livelihood for a very large proportion of Africa's urban residents, Chinese involvement in urban commerce is causing growing resentment. In the urban small-scale wholesale and retail sector, Chinese-owned and -managed shops that sell low-cost housewares and apparel are pushing a competitive wedge into a commercial sector that in the past was dominated by others. The fact that some Senegalese consumer groups in Dakar praise the Chinese for making affordable everyday commodities available while others criticize them for taking work away from the residents of Dakar captures the ambiguity that is at the core of reactions to the growing presence of the Chinese on Dakar's commercial scene. At the Grand Marché in Lome, Togo, West Africa's chief market for printed textiles, a widespread rumor held that dressing in Chinese-produced fabrics is dangerous. Indeed, when the Chinese-made wrappers of two young women caught fire in 2004, their three-piece outfits "burnt like timber." In Benin, there is a debate about the damage that imitations of high-quality "wax" fabrics, sold cheaply by Chinese enterprises, are causing to the domestic textile sector; at the same time, China holds strong shares in the textile industry, where many domestic plants have collapsed. In northern Namibia, the pioneering Chinese businesses in Oshikango are benefiting from the town's rapid growth as a major trading center for Angola and from customs regulations allowing them to source a variety of goods in transit from China without paying import tariffs. But while they supply affordable goods and create some employment opportunities, the Chinese traders also establish new dependencies rather than responding to local productive concerns.

A highly visible consequence of these commercial developments since the mid-1990s has been the displacement of small-scale trading and service activities from city centers to areas on the periphery in order to free up prime space for shopping malls, upscale stores, hotels, and private housing developments, including gated communities. Because recent investments tend to target upscale consumers, many new market developments charge rental fees that exclude small-scale operators, who then turn to the streets as a location for economic activity. It is not surprising that violent confrontations between urban authorities and street vendors over the use of public space for commerce continue to take place, as does the intermittent removal of these vendors. With new institutional dynamics promoting political decentralization, local authorities in many African cities are caught in a bind regarding the regulation of urban space for residential and commercial activity, including open markets. The ensuing conflicts are fueled by party politics in many cities where space is scarce and vendors are courted as voting blocs in a love-hate relationship that has proved difficult to regulate.

Political-economic reforms promoting foreign investment and privatization have not only affected the place and nature of commercial activity as the construction of malls in urban Africa and spatial marginalization of small-scale trade demonstrate. These reforms are also changing the value of urban land, with adverse effects on the housing market, especially for urban residents with limited means. The legacy of racial segregation of urban residential space persists across much of eastern and southern Africa, with income replacing race as the chief criterion of access today. In most cities, high-income gated communities now lie next to low-income residential settlements. Throughout the southern African region the term "compound" came into use to describe racially segregated housing for Africans, first implemented at the gold and diamond mines in South Africa in the late 1880s. Today more than 75 percent of Lusaka's population, for example, lives in informal or squatter settlements, locally still called "compounds," in the periurban areas, because housing markets have been privatized and no low-cost government-run housing has been constructed since the 1970s. The result is extreme population crowding in the existing settlements and the development of a rental housing market there, including the subletting at exorbitant rents of rooms that are often controlled by absentee landlords, a process that has been widely observed across urban Africa. Many of these residential areas do not have good prospects for the development of services and small-scale manufacturing activities because they have inadequate access to electricity, water, sanitation, and transport, or lack it entirely. For these reasons, home-based enterprises may have better potential in high-income residential areas. Possibilities for periurban expansion are constrained by large-scale business developments including, in Lusaka, the international airport, commercial farms, and cattle ranches that lie just next to low-cost housing areas.

Along with provoking extreme crowding in existing settlements, the privatization of housing markets introduces new disparities. Rental housing that formerly was strictly controlled by government and private employers has given way in many cities to privatization, with such housing units offered for sale to their current tenants. But many tenants have insufficient means to effect the purchase and instead sell their units to better-off people. As a result, midpriced housing areas have begun to be upgraded, while their former tenants have few options besides seeking shelter in already crowded squatter settlements. Because in many cases women have less access to loans than men, gender is critical to this process. So is youth in the sense that young people rarely have the means to obtain housing for themselves and thus are likely to delay establishing households of their own. Widespread youth unemployment and the drop in marriage rates are affecting male-female relations, especially insofar as they involve sex and economic support. This has ramifications for social organization, headship, and power relations on the domestic front, consequences that become evident in social relations and across space.

ECONOMIC TRANSFORMATIONS

Economic liberalization, including the privatization of formerly state-controlled companies, has reduced employment prospects by pruning the ranks of the already employed and constraining new formal job creation in most of Africa's urban areas. As a result, more and more people are pushed into an already crowded informal economy. The structural adjustment programs of the 1980s and neoliberal policies of the 1990s did not by themselves bring about this expansive process of informalization. Rather, such programs and policies added new dynamics to long-standing informal urban processes that vary across the continent but which have been more

Figure 6.3. A busy street corner near the Kumasi Central Market in Ghana.
Gracia Clark.

prominent in West Africa than in eastern and southern Africa. What is more, the latest crop of World Bank–recommended poverty reduction strategies are not tackling the urban challenges caused by the overwhelming lack of jobs, insufficient housing, and declining infrastructure and services. As new waves of informalization entangle urban economies in far-flung commodity circuits that expose them to global market forces, many distinctions in level and intensity of market activity, such as those between West African cities and South African ones, are disappearing. Across urban Africa today, markets and streets provide economic avenues for a growing number of residents.

The new dynamics of the informalization are at first sight demographic, yet they have manifold social and cultural ramifications across urban space. The chief demographic observation is that young people are everywhere in Africa's growing cities, accounting for 60 or even 70 percent of the overall urban population in some places. The next section will attend to definitional questions about youth; here it suffices to note that unlike their parents, who lived through government controls and outright scarcities of basic goods, today's young people have grown up after the shift to liberalized regimes. The global exposure of the young to shopping malls, internet cafés, and media differs radically from that of their parents' generation, as do their personal expectations. The effects are confounding because along with this global exposure, some young people have had limited access to education and services as a result of International Monetary Fund–imposed policies of economic pricing of basic services, changes that were central to the structural adjustment programs of the 1970s and 1980s. Even young people with advanced education cannot expect the types of jobs in government or private firms that their parents took for granted after completing secondary school.

Another important demographic observation revolves around gender and generational dynamics. When we refer to the enormous growth of the informal economy since the 1970s, we gloss over the many inequalities that are embedded within it in terms of activity, location, and organization as well as gender. In addition, age or generation plays a role, although the significance of this for future urban livelihoods has not received the attention it deserves. When the adverse effects of structural adjustment programs on formal employment began to become evident in the 1980s, it was middle-aged women in particular whose informal earnings ensured household survival as husbands and partners were laid off. The shift in the early 1990s toward economic privatization pushed even more adults of both sexes into the informal economy, thus limiting the entry of young people. In urban settings in southern Africa, where the apprenticeship practices for which West Africa is so well known are very limited, many young people ended up on the margins of the informal economy performing low-level jobs with few prospects for upward mobility and the acquisition of higher qualifications that might enable them to improve their economic prospects.

Markets and streets are among the most important sources of non-formal urban employment. Street vending entails more risks and dangers than trade in authorized

Figure 6.4. Demolition of market stalls at Soweto market, Lusaka, 2004.
Post Photo Archives, National Archives of Zambia.

markets, and it is not surprising that many street vendors are young and male. Because urban space is a scarce good, its usage is heavily politicized and filled with tensions. Small-scale entrepreneurs are criticized for transgressing into public space, the more so when they are young and male and regarded as a public health nuisance, suspected of disrupting established business, or considered to be criminals or illegal immigrants. In many of Africa's cities and smaller towns, conflicts over the regulation of informal trade in authorized markets and public space result in intermittent removals of street vendors and clampdowns on markets, targeting non-fee-paying traders. Such clearances tend to have only temporary effects, and new wrangles and clashes continue to arise over space for trading. Vendors return to the streets in new disguises, with new sales strategies, at different times of the day, and in strategic spots. Such events are spectacular enactments of disaffection by a population segment whose livelihoods have been squeezed by the convergence of global and local processes that were highlighted at the beginning of this chapter.

There is a long and well-reported history of market associational activity in West Africa, but it was not until fairly recently that urban scholarship in other parts of Africa began to pay attention to organizational efforts among informal market actors. Because of their love-hate relationship with local governments, many informal economy organizations seek to improve their situation by establishing networks

Figure 6.5. Market stall selling *chitenge* (printed cloth), secondhand shoes,
and sneakers at the COMESA market, Lusaka.
Karen Tranberg Hansen.

or federations locally, as well as national, regional, and international alliances. Combining grassroots initiatives and NGO- and human-rights-inspired rhetoric, such
emergent groups have since the 1990s begun to establish footholds, with varying
degrees of success, in the urban and national arenas from which they were for so
long excluded. For example, in Lusaka's urban regulatory environment, which was
generally extremely hostile toward informal activity, the Cross-Border Traders
Association achieved an almost unbelievable feat by securing prime land in the
heart of the city's center for a market for its vendors.

The Cross-Border Traders Association is one of thirteen informal organizations
that in 2001 formed an umbrella organization, the Alliance for Zambia Informal
Economy Associations (AZIEA), comprising a wide range of associations, including those for task-specific groups such as tinsmiths and carpenters as well as broader
groupings such as the *tuntemba* (makeshift stalls) association. AZIEA seeks to bar-
gain with the government with the goal of turning informal workers into a recognized part of the labor force that enjoys International Labor Organization (ILO) labor
standards. Reaching out beyond Zambia, AZIEA is an affiliate of StreetNet International, a South African–based organization that was inspired by the 1995 formation

of the Self Employed Women's Association and was formally established in Durban, South Africa, in 2002. StreetNet has branches in Africa, Asia, and Latin America. Inspired by a class-based organizational model, StreetNet seeks to create alliances with labor and social movements rather than to focus on the microenterprise sector and the NGO development sector. This organizational model contrasts sharply with the network- and federation-based approaches pursued by informal sector organizations concerned with informal housing, among them the Shack Dwellers Association International.

CITIES OF YOUTH

In today's transformed urban space, young women and men from poor backgrounds have fewer economic options than their parents' generation enjoyed. While the meaning of "youth" depends on context, youth is everywhere defined both in subjective terms by young people themselves and relationally by adults and the surrounding society and its institutions. In a very general way, young people long to experience youth as a distinct outlook on life, a mentality, an experience in its own right, while adults and society define them as dependent and subordinate in a hierarchical and gerontocratic understanding of how society ought to work.

As we have seen, young people in Africa's towns and cities form a large proportion of the overall population; they are everywhere and highly visible in urban public space. In these cities of youth, urban space is charged in different terms by gender. Because young women are more vulnerable than men when moving in public space, they tend to enjoy less freedom of mobility than young men. When young people turn markets and streets into economic avenues, it is young men who dominate the street vending scene, operating as independent actors, whereas young women work as hired hands at market stands and stalls or try their luck at home-based trades. Much of this activity is piecework and highly irregular, with low and uncertain earnings.

Urban-based youth are struggling to become independent in ways that differ by gender and class. Widespread norms of social adulthood attribute household headship to men, but few young men today earn enough to provide shelter and economic support for a family of their own. Young women, for their part, look for husbands who hold regular jobs, are stable (as indicated, for example, by church membership), and can provide for a wife and children. Because mutual gender expectations are not synchronous, sexuality becomes a charged practice on the urban scene. Masculinity is often construed in terms of an aggressive sexuality that is problematic for many young men to enact because they have insufficient means to provide women with material support.

The political economy of intimate relations that is emerging responds, in part, to the broader scope of consumerism and new notions of love. In daily interaction, gift giving is taken as evidence of love. But in the context of increasing urban economic hardships, the distinction between gift and exchange becomes blurred. As a

Figure 6.6. Discotheque in Luanda, Angola.
Corbis.

result, notions about transactional sex have become frequent in research on urban sexual and reproductive behavior. Because young women may have few economic means, transactional sex becomes one route to consumption. Some young women rely on boyfriends and older male partners for basic expenses such as school fees, not to mention money for desirable consumer goods. For example, in Lusaka, young women described their ideal boyfriends as those who have the "four C's": a car, a crib (house), cash, and a cell phone. But there is more to this than gifts and money. While at first sight gift exchanges revolve around sex, they do not preclude affection, support, housing, and other forms of mutual assistance. In fact, in the absence of formal marriage, gifts may signal commitment, trust, and love.

In Africa's rapidly growing cities, young people are everywhere highly visible. Boys and young men crowd markets and streets. They, and increasingly young women, turn vacant spaces into football (known in the United States as soccer) fields, sometimes playing with balls made from scrap. They all use mobile phones as a vehicle for claiming their place in the city. In short, young urban people pursue a greater variety of interaction than their elders ever imagined.

THE CITY, CONSUMPTION, AND NEW FORMS OF SOCIALITY

Taken together, the processes described in previous sections—new investments, informalization, and economic actors—have reshaped urban space in many ways, among them by creating new consumption sites where urban residents pursue their desires and new social sites where communications technology may open up new vistas. It is the simultaneity of these processes that is placing a particular imprint on contemporary urban development. In the colonial past, it was labor migration and urban living that were the key processes to turning Africans into active consumers. At stake historically were both the regulatory side and the supply side, involving markets, shops, and sales techniques, as well as the demand side and specific consumer desires for material goods. But controlled economies in many countries after independence curtailed the scope of consumerism. Yet the political transitions of the 1990s combined with market reforms have made a wide range of affordable goods available to differently positioned consumers. Targeting distinct consumer niches and different urban spaces, boutiques selling imported fashions and market stalls selling imported secondhand clothing today make the latest trends available to all. Indeed, the proliferation of shopping venues in recent years makes consumption a particularly challenging angle through which to delineate changing urban lives in Africa in relationship to globalization.

Commercial vigor, from tiny market stalls and street vendors to upscale malls, is part of the urban dynamism that is central to the productive role consumption plays in the city. This is evident in the types of transformed geographies and spaces for work, shopping, and home life discussed earlier. Shopping malls and stalls in local markets crowded with small-scale entrepreneurs offer major sites for consumption and hanging out. Young people with money to spend can afford to frequent the malls' cinemas and fast-food outlets, whereas those with limited means window-shop and socialize. What all these venues offer is a degree of freedom to watch and interact with peers and others. Privileging actual or vicarious consumption, such sites create a dynamism that translates into freedom and leisure, as illustrated by the following two perspectives: one concerning football, the other revolving around mobile phones.

Although it is a colonial import, football has been infused with cultural notions of solidarity and nationalism that make it Africa's sport par excellence today. With African male football players contracted to major foreign leagues, football is a truly global sport whose local pursuit has wide-open imaginaries. On the post-colonial development agenda, football is a widespread and highly popular pastime in rural and urban areas alike, engaging children and young people through informal matches in the streets and through organized play in clubs, associations, and academies. What is more, football is advocated as a means to encourage young people to focus on self-improvement, education, and physical and social empowerment as well as to promote discipline and responsibility. Young women are also getting involved, especially as international sports leagues, governments, and NGOs, in their concern to stem Zambia's HIV/AIDS pandemic, have turned to football to help challenge inequality and sexism and effect behavioral change.

Football plays a significant role in shaping a distinct urban youth culture that is overwhelmingly male. In effect, the sport is played in deeply divided societies where resources are always insufficient. Although African women's championships for football and other sports (netball, handball, basketball, and track and field) have grown, the immense popularity and social importance of the men's game has made it difficult for a women's football game to develop. In fact, the burdens of household work fall disproportionately on girls and young women, leaving them less time for play and skills development. There is the enduring assumption that women who play football place their reputations at risk by spending too much time exposed to the public gaze. Because of dress and visibility, such young women are perceived to be highly vulnerable, and their presence among men is discouraged. Some parents and guardians are suspicious of young women's socializing and hanging out at sports grounds, readily infusing notions of sexual availability into socialization practices that take place in public space.

Across urban (and increasingly rural) Africa today, mobile phones are becoming a major means of interacting that is qualifying the long-held connection between consumption, class, and income. Unlike football, the mobile phone may be a gender-neutral tool, as there appear to be few differences between women's and men's practices of using mobile phones. This applies both to where and how frequently they use their phones as well as to what they use them for.

Sebastiana Etzo and Guy Collender contend that the use of mobile phones has grown remarkably fast in Africa, with a twelvefold increase in subscribers between 2000 and 2006, making Africa the fastest-growing region of the world in terms of the mobile phone market even if it still is the least penetrated. This is also corroborated by the United Nations Conference on Trade and Development (UNC-TAD 2008: 251). Mobile phone users keep up contacts and establish a wide range of networks and connections in ways that both incorporate local practices of sociality and facilitate new networking and dreams.

The prepaid phone system that has been widely adopted by African mobile phone users suits people with insecure or irregular incomes. Social uses such as chatting and keeping in touch may be driving mobile phone usage among the less well-off, of whom many make use of mobile phones at public access points. Usage practices are influenced by local norms of mutual assistance and supportive behavior. Above all, phones are shared extensively. There is a widespread practice of "beeping," that is, dialing a number but hanging up with the expectation that the person at the other end will phone back, paying for the call. And text messaging (SMS) is an easy and cheap means of communication. Mobile phone calls and SMS messages are important means for announcing urgent matters such as funerals and to draw attention to what is going on in the social scene. Last but not least, mobile phones keep young people, including lovers, in touch privately. Indeed, across class, young people consider mobile phones to be a required accessory for urban life.

In addition to its widespread social uses, the mobile phone has very quickly become a necessary tool in business transactions. Its flexibility and ease works very well for microenterprises and small businesses. Users obtain information concerning prices and availabilities of specific goods that has a practical effect on short-term decision making about where to source and when to supply customers. In some countries, such as Nigeria, Uganda, and Kenya, credit can be accessed by using mobile phones. In short, mobile phones may help to support livelihoods. Their connectivity keeps people in touch and helps them set up new contacts. In Africa's rapidly transitioning economies, people avidly use mobile phones to connect in ways that fit with their backgrounds and means. The contacts and spaces they create in this way enable them not only to keep in touch with family and friends but also to pursue new practices of sociability and association. The result for young urban people is a positive sense of being connected on local terms, of reaching out, and in lifestyle terms of being a part of the global world.

African cities have always been where the action is. But political and economic events of the last three decades have ushered in new times. Focusing on urban engagements across space, the economy, and culture, this chapter has delineated a story of convergence that plays itself out most visibly and dramatically in young people's efforts to claim space and identities as autonomous actors, performing and appropriating new skills, and using new means. This generational difference characterizes their distinct outlook on urban life and may become influential in inciting change.

Africa's cities are cities of youth where consumption and class introduce new dynamics that are complicated by gender. Exchange and consumption deserve recognition for their creative and productive functions instead of being swept aside as parasitic activities, as was the case in approaches that used wage labor as the lens for studying Africa's urban economies. The twenty-first-century urban world is a globalized world in which shifts in the flow of capital, commodities, and labor are redefining the place and role of cities, including in Africa, where built-up land today in many places generates more revenue than agriculture. And because informal work and its organizational resourcefulness—by far the chief source of urban livelihoods across most of the continent—are insufficiently accounted for, the overall economic scope of African urban life continues to be difficult to assess. The same holds for its diversity, vitality, and dynamism because of persisting scholarly preoccupations with widespread problems of urban sustainability. Even then, as has been demonstrated, there is no doubt that these are new times in Africa's cities, whose majority populations, the young, negotiate and navigate complicated constraints on their actions as they enable themselves with diverse means and skills to turn the ordinariness of everyday urban life into strategic resources for tomorrow.

STATISTICS CITED

National Research Council. 2003. *Cities Transformed: Demographic Change and Its Implications in the Developing World.* Washington, DC: National Academies Press.

United Nations Conference on Trade and Development (UNCTAD). 2008. *Information Economy Report 2007–2008: Science and Technology for Development. The New Paradigm of ICT.* New York: United Nations.

United Nations Department of Economic and Social Affairs/Population Division. 2012. *World Urbanization Prospects: The 2011 Revision. Highlights.* New York: United Nations. Available at www.esa.un.org/undp/index.htm.

SUGGESTIONS FOR FURTHER READING

Alden, Chris, D. Large, and R. Soares de Oliviera, eds. 2007. *China Returns to Africa.* London: Hurst.

Anderson, David M., and Richard Rathbone, eds. 2000. *Africa's Urban Past.* Oxford: James Currey.

De Boeck, Filip, and Marie-Françoise Plissard. 2004. *Kinshasa: Tales of the Invisible City.* Tervuren, Belgium: Royal Museum of Central Africa.

Etzo, Sebastiana, and Guy Collender. 2010. "Briefing: The Mobile Phone 'Revolution' in Africa: Rhetoric or Reality?" *African Affairs* 109(437): 659–68.

Hansen, Karen Tranberg. 1997. *Keeping House in Lusaka.* New York: Columbia University Press.

King, Anthony. 1990. *Urbanism, Colonialism and the World-Economy: Cultural and Spatial Foundations of the World Urban System.* London: Routledge.

Larkin, Brian. 2008. *Signal and Noise: Media, Infrastructure, and Urban Culture in Nigeria.* Durham, NC: Duke University Press.

Myers, Garth Andrew. 2003. *Verandahs of Power: Colonialism and Space in Urban Africa.* Syracuse, NY: Syracuse University Press.

Robinson, Jennifer. 2006. *Ordinary Cities: Between Modernity and Development.* London: Routledge.

Wirth, Louis. 1938. "Urbanism as a Way of Life." *American Journal of Sociology* 4: 2–24.

7 Health, Illness, and Healing in African Societies

Tracy J. Luedke

In African societies, as elsewhere in the world, health and illness are experienced both at the level of the individual body and at the level of the social body. Individual suffering often reveals social structures and tensions, for example when a child's illness strains family relationships or when a treatable disease proves fatal among the poorer members of a society; healing practices may also create new kinds of community, as when a doctor and patient form a lasting bond or when the pursuit of health care spawns a social movement. The experiences associated with health, illness, and healing always reflect and affect social relationships, whether they forge, preclude, strengthen, or strain them. This chapter addresses health in sub-Saharan Africa as a product and a project of social contexts ranging in scale from the intimacy of the family to the broad power dynamics of the global political economy.

AFRICAN HEALTH IN GLOBAL CONTEXT

Before turning to questions of well-being and illness in specific cultural contexts, it is important to start by considering the comparative framework of biomedical assessments of the health of the world's populations. In doing so, it becomes clear that the frequency and severity of debilitating illnesses are closely tied to political and economic power dynamics; in short, patterns of poverty are closely associated with patterns of disease. Africa's economic position correlates with its disease profile, which includes a high prevalence of communicable diseases, high maternal mortality and infant and child mortality rates, and notable effects of pandemics. Overall health indicators reveal that health is generally poor on the continent—the average life expectancy in Africa in 2009 was fifty-four years, which makes it the world region with the lowest life expectancy rate (WHO 2011b: 54). According to the World Health Organization (WHO), the leading causes of mortality in Africa (based on 2004 figures) are HIV/AIDS, lower respiratory infections, diarrheal diseases, and malaria, in that order. Communicable diseases are the primary threat to Africans' health, accounting for 70 percent of the causes of death (WHO 2008a: 54).

HIV/AIDS and malaria are significant challenges to well-being on the continent and also illustrate more broadly the ways that patterns of marginalization inform health on a global scale. Sub-Saharan Africa is the region most affected by the global HIV/AIDS pandemic. According to the Joint United Nations Programme on HIV/AIDS (UNAIDS), in the year 2009 a total of 1.8 million people died of HIV/AIDS, 72 percent (1.3 million) of whom were Africans (UNAIDS 2010: 25). AIDS is now the leading cause of death in sub-Saharan Africa. This reflects the fact that in Africa HIV/AIDS is a generalized epidemic that affects the population as a whole (unlike in other regions of the world, where HIV transmission is primarily concentrated among particular subpopulations). There is, however, considerable regional variability in the scale of the disease's effects. Southern Africa (Angola, Botswana, Lesotho, Malawi, Mozambique, Namibia, South Africa, Swaziland, Zambia, and Zimbabwe) is the most heavily affected, accounting for 34 percent of all people living with HIV and 34 percent of all AIDS deaths in 2009, as well as 31 percent of new HIV infections. Four southern African countries have HIV prevalence rates of more than 15 percent (UNAIDS 2010: 23, 28). High rates of HIV/AIDS also increase the incidence of other diseases. For example, tuberculosis, which was previously largely under control, increased in frequency nearly fourfold between 1980 and 2000, as it became a primary opportunistic infection associated with AIDS (WHO 2008b: 52). In Southern Africa, greater than 50 percent of the tuberculosis patients who were tested were found to also be HIV positive (USAID 2011: 3).

Although Western epidemiological and public health approaches to HIV/AIDS have often stressed individual behaviors, much recent social scientific work has emphasized the social, political, and economic structures that influence susceptibility, transmission, and treatment. For example, Meredith Turshen has pointed out that structural adjustment policies exacerbated economic insecurity, increased labor migration, and disrupted family life, all of which furthered the spread of HIV/AIDS. The internal power dynamics within African societies also condition patterns of transmission. According to Anne Akeroyd, gender informs vulnerability to the disease and access to care in contexts where women often have less control over their sexual lives, are dependent on men for access to key resources, and may engage in high-risk activities in order to support themselves and their children. Some 40 percent of all adult women with HIV live in southern Africa (UNAIDS 2010: 28). The dramatic physical and population effects of HIV/AIDS and its connections to sexuality and premature death have made it a stigmatized condition in Africa, as elsewhere, which often means that the physical suffering of the disease is accompanied by the pain of social isolation. These potent social meanings and associations make HIV/AIDS a source of suspicion and a site of blame, as noted by Paul Farmer; local interpretations of and responses to the disease often involve identifying the human agents, whether the "promiscuous" individuals, malevolent sorcerers, or power-hungry Western governments, deemed responsible.

Although it has not received the same level of media coverage as HIV/AIDS, malaria has also had a profound effect on Africans' lives. In 2010, 81 percent of worldwide malaria cases and 91 percent of malaria deaths (596,000) occurred in the African region, with children under five the most heavily affected (WHO 2011c: xiii). Although the immediate cause of malaria is infection with a parasite transmitted by mosquitoes, broader social conditions, including poverty and armed conflict, contribute significantly to the shape and severity of the pandemic. Under conditions of poverty, malaria infection and mortality are more likely due to lack of insecticides and mosquito nets, lack of pharmaceuticals that prevent and treat malaria, and poor-quality housing that does not protect its occupants against mosquitoes. Armed conflict further exacerbates the effects of malaria through forced migration into malarial areas and use of provisional housing by refugees, disruption or destruction of health care systems, alterations in vegetation that encourage the breeding of mosquitoes, and malnutrition and other physical stresses of conflict conditions. Besides poverty increasing the risk of malaria, there is also evidence of the converse relationship, that malaria increases poverty. Paula Brentlinger contends that malaria has a significant effect on human productivity in the most-affected African countries, accounting for a loss of an estimated 1.3 percent of GDP growth per year; it also takes an enormous toll at the household level in terms of time and resources spent caring for the ill. When malaria morbidity and mortality increase owing to parasite resistance to drugs such as chloroquine, treatment programs have had to either turn to more expensive remedies to combat the resistant strains, further exacerbating economic pressures, or leave patients vulnerable with inadequate treatment.

Although both local and international biomedical responses to ill health on the African continent have evolved over time, they remain for the most part inadequate. In the Alma Ata Declaration of 1978, a milestone in public health policy, members of the international community endorsed a strategy of primary health care as the means to "health for all" by the year 2000. In the succeeding decades African governments attempted to institute integrated national health programs; unfortunately, biomedical health care resources still fall far short of Alma Ata goals in the majority of African countries. Factors including weak economies and high levels of external debt have made it difficult for African countries to implement health care programs that might address the significant health challenges described above. High rates of poverty, lack of basic social services such as clean water, instability in food supplies, and the disruptions caused by political conflicts have further undermined both health and health care. African governments' spending on health care remains low, averaging U.S. $137 per capita in 2007 (WHO 2001a: 14).

In the postcolonial period, many African countries implemented multilevel health care systems, in which both decision-making powers and resources are organized hierarchically from the ministry of health and teaching hospitals of the capital city down to provincial-level hospitals, district-level hospitals, and finally rural health clinics and posts. A review of primary health care in Africa found enormous disparities between resources allocated to urban versus rural components of these systems: although rural health clinics, dispensaries, and posts are the primary interface between people and the health care system, serving 80 percent of the population, they receive only 20 percent of the resources allocated to health services (WHO 2008b: 37). These rural health care facilities are therefore often lacking in equipment, supplies, and qualified personnel. The majority of highly trained health practitioners, especially physicians, are located in cities, and many African doctors ultimately move abroad in search of better opportunities. The Alma Ata Declaration also encouraged the utilization of traditional healers and traditional birth attendants as part of national health care programs, but to date such practitioners have for the most part not been successfully integrated into national health care systems. Some African countries have had more success with such an approach, such as Ghana, which recognizes and regulates traditional healers through its ministry of health, but many have found it difficult to bridge the disjunctures between biomedicine and local health practices in illness categories, notions of causation, treatment regimens, and practitioner training. Critics such as Brooke Schoepf question the call to integrate traditional healers into national health care programs, suggesting that the rhetoric of cultural acceptability and cost efficiency masks a lack of will to provide the most current and most effective biomedical treatments to the world's poor.

The public health interventions enacted by international organizations and African governments in response to the most pressing health concerns provide insights into both the enormous challenges these diseases present and the powerful constraints of the political economic context in which they are embedded. Global efforts to address the toll that malaria takes in Africa and elsewhere have been spearheaded by the Roll Back Malaria initiative, established in 1998 through a partnership between WHO, the United Nations Children's Fund (UNICEF), the United Nations Development Program (UNDP), and the World Bank. The primary interventions on which this and other antimalaria programs rely are insecticide-treated bed nets, indoor residual spraying, and treatment with artemisinin-based combination therapies. Although these techniques are effective against malaria and significant progress has been made in some regions, each of these measures also presents notable challenges. Insecticide-treated bed nets tend to be most utilized by the wealthier members of the societies in which they are introduced, especially when they are distributed through social marketing schemes, leaving the poorest and most vulnerable members of society still susceptible, as Paula Brentlinger has argued. Spraying insecticides in and around homes raises logistical and cost questions as well as concerns about potential toxicity. And while artemisinin-based combination therapies are the most effective current antimalarial treatment, given widespread resistance to chloroquine and other monotherapies, they are significantly more expensive than these other drugs and therefore difficult for many African nations to afford.

Yet significant progress has been made in recent years: the percentage of sub-Saharan households that own at least one insecticide-treated bed net increased from 3 percent in 2000 to 50 percent in 2011. Although this is a remarkable increase, it also creates new challenges—the effectiveness of such a treated net is estimated to last for three years, so many of the nets distributed in recent years are now in need of replacement. The number of people protected by indoor residual spraying in the African region increased sevenfold between 2005 and 2010, but this still only amounts to coverage for 11 percent of the population. In terms of diagnosis and treatment, the percentage of suspected malaria cases subjected to parasitological testing has also risen dramatically, yet in many African countries the overall testing rate remains low. However, due to intensive antimalaria campaigns, malaria-specific mortality rates in Africa fell by 33 percent between 2000 and 2010. One of the biggest obstacles to continued success is funding: WHO estimates the resources required to meet disease control and elimination targets at $5 billion per year, but current funding is only $2 billion per year and is expected to decrease in coming years (WHO 2011c: ix).

A number of scholars, such as R. Bayer, have suggested that HIV/AIDS prevention and treatment policies, in Africa and elsewhere, have been less effective than they might have been by virtue of "HIV exceptionalism"—a tendency to stress individual rights and privacies as opposed to addressing HIV/AIDS like any other infectious disease that poses a wide public health threat. Thus HIV testing in African societies has remained relatively low. James Pfeiffer has argued that HIV/AIDS education and prevention strategies in many sub-Saharan African countries have been dominated by social marketing programs in which principles of free market economics are used to promote the distribution and utilization of condoms. Critics of such programs suggest that this approach focuses exclusively on individual behavior change, ignoring the structural determinants of health behaviors, including the economic strains and worsening inequalities that were engendered by structural adjustment policies. The effectiveness of such campaigns is also debated since claimed results often rest on reported behavior collected through surveys, as opposed to any evidence of actual condom use.

Yet there are signs that recent attempts to combat HIV/AIDS are having a positive effect and treatment options for those living with HIV/AIDS have expanded considerably. Between 2001 and 2009, HIV infection rates fell by more than 25 percent in an estimated twenty-two sub-Saharan Africa countries. In southern Africa there were 32 percent fewer children newly infected and 18 percent fewer AIDS-related deaths in 2009 than in 2004. At the end of 2009, 49 percent of adults and children eligible for antiretroviral therapy were receiving it in the region overall (56 percent in eastern and southern Africa and 30 percent in western and central Africa), compared with only 2 percent in 2003 (UNAIDS 2011: 97; UNAIDS 2009: 25). However, the scope of treatment programs varies considerably among countries: by 2010, 93 percent of people in need in Botswana were receiving antiretroviral treatment, whereas in Mozambique, the figure for the same year was 40 percent (UNAIDS 2011: 98).

MEDICAL PLURALISM AND THE QUEST FOR THERAPY

Although there are significant structural constraints on Africans' health, as the above description suggests, it is important to recognize that people are not merely the passive victims of disease. Even in the face of enormous obstacles, the ill actively pursue well-being. This "quest for therapy," as John Janzen has called it, often involves both the sufferer and his or her family and community members and may lead those in search of care and a cure to multiple and varied health practitioners. In much of Africa, the landscape of health resources comprises a multiplicity of practitioners and treatments, including biomedically trained physicians, spirit-possessed mediums, herbalists, diviners, and Christian and Muslim healers, who utilize pharmaceuticals, medicinal plants, and prayer and religious texts to treat their patients. Within this diversity, there is also a great tendency to innovate—new healing techniques, spirits, and medicinal plants are continuously discovered; new ways of combining biomedical and spiritist approaches or of combining pharmaceuticals and herbal medicines are constantly sought out. Indeed, patients appreciate such innovation and are drawn to healers who bring something new or unprecedented to the range of available services. In such a context of medical pluralism, the ill and their associates must choose among an array of possible healers, techniques, and remedies, and research shows that people often opt to utilize multiple healing regimens, whether simultaneously or sequentially. The medical pluralism of Africa is not unique. Indeed, people the world over make use of multiple healing practices. For example, in the United States a patient seeking treatment can visit a physician, a reiki master, a chiropractor, an aromatherapist, a naturopath, or a Chinese medicine specialist, as well as a variety of other medical practitioners. In addition, the U.S. government maintains the National Center for Complementary and Alternative Medicine (NCCAM), a unit of the National Institutes of Health (NIH), to conduct research on these and other healing practices.

The cultural complexity of African healing environments also means that in many African societies there is an active and ongoing debate about the relative efficacy, legitimacy, and appropriate place within national health care plans of various kinds of health practitioners. So-called traditional healers organize themselves into professional associations, incorporate biomedical techniques into their practices, and seek out international validation. Their work has been encouraged, at least discursively, by international health organizations that seek to capitalize on healers as a human resource in contexts where there are very few biomedical health professionals relative to the population. For example, for the African nation of Mozambique, it has been estimated that there is approximately one traditional healer for every two hundred people (Green et al. 1994: 8), whereas the number of biomedical doctors is around five hundred to serve a population of twenty-three million, for a rate of approximately one physician per forty thousand people (WHO 2011b: 120). Comparable numbers exist elsewhere in Africa, and WHO estimates that about 80 percent of Africans make use of traditional healers at one point or another. In light of such figures, in 2007 the World Health Organization's Regional Office for Africa issued a Declaration on Traditional Medicine, pledging to "develop mechanisms for institutionalizing the positive aspects of traditional medicine into health systems and improve collaboration between conventional and traditional health practitioners" (WHO 2007: 3). Yet, as mentioned above, attempts at collaboration are often difficult given the epistemological differences between biomedicine and other varieties of healing, as well as the political complications of the contexts in which these debates are acted out. Thus, questions of health and healing in Africa often intersect with national and international politics regarding the organization and use of health resources, the place of "culture" in state policies, and the relationships between science and religion, the natural and spiritual worlds, and the "traditional" and the "modern."

CASE STUDY: MEDICAL PLURALISM AND RELIGIOUS HEALING IN CENTRAL MOZAMBIQUE

A case study of religious healing in a context of medical pluralism illustrates these and other themes regarding health and healing in sub-Saharan Africa. This case study is based on my field research in central Mozambique, in southeastern Africa. In this region, there are a variety of health resources that local people can and do turn to in response to illness. There are government health clinics or hospitals located in provincial and district capitals, and smaller health posts in rural localities. These clinics are sometimes staffed by physicians but more often are staffed by nurses or medical technicians, who examine patients and write prescriptions that can be filled at on-site pharmacies. When I visited one district capital hospital, I found that patients began to line up early in the morning and often had to wait for hours to be seen by the doctor. Just down the road from this hospital was an outdoor marketplace where a variety of foods and household goods were sold. In addition, it was possible to purchase pharmaceuticals without a prescription, many acquired across the border in Malawi, as well as herbal medicines. There were other less formal clinics scattered across the landscape in the rural areas, which often involved healers working out of their homes. At one clinic that I visited, the practitioner dispensed both herbal medicines and pharmaceuticals. Many patients came to get the penicillin injections this healer became well known for administering. Other healers dispensed exclusively plant-based medicines (constituted primarily of tree roots), drawing on the knowledge they had acquired through an apprenticeship with an older healer or relative. These healers often employed divining instruments that helped them ascertain the nature of their patient's condition and an appropriate treatment for that person. One such healer I visited utilized an animal horn that spun on a handle; the healer posed questions about a patient's health and the horn indicated the answers by pointing in a particular direction. Other healers diagnosed and treated their patients by means of their relationships with spirits. Some of these healers worked with the spirits of deceased ancestors. These family

Figure 7.1. Vendor of traditional medicines, Maputo, Mozambique.
Tracy Luedke.

Figure 7.2. Diviner, Tete province, Mozambique.
Tracy Luedke.

members, some from the distant past, others they had known personally, returned to possess the bodies of their descendants and heal through them. One such healer I met explained that her ancestor had consumed potent medicines during his lifetime that allowed him to come back after death in the form of a lion and to incorporate in her body as a powerful healing spirit. Other healers in the area had relationships with another variety of spirit; these healers were called prophets and were possessed by Christianized spirits with names such as Mary, Joseph, Lazarus, and Job. These healers wore white gowns with crosses sewn on them and utilized Bibles in their healing practices.

Although the nonbiomedical healers working in this area were diverse in their appearances, practices, and sources of knowledge, they sometimes came together under the aegis of the Mozambican national traditional healers' association, AMETRAMO (Associação de Medicina Tradicional de Moçambique). This professional organization first arose in the early 1990s, at an important moment in Mozambique's history. Mozambique was a Portuguese colony and only achieved its independence in 1975 after a protracted armed struggle. After independence the new Mozambican government, led by the political party FRELIMO, which had also led the war for liberation, adopted a socialist platform. Among its policies was a mandate against what it considered to be "backward" cultural practices, including traditional healing. Instead, FRELIMO wanted to create a new, modern society

Figure 7.3. Prophet, Tete province, Mozambique.
Tracy Luedke.

based on the ideas of "scientific socialism." During this era, healers were suppressed and many had to hide their activities.

Unfortunately, shortly after independence from the Portuguese, Mozambique was once again plunged into warfare, this time at the hands of regional political regimes that sought to destabilize the new nation, including the government of Rhodesia (which later became Zimbabwe) and South Africa's apartheid regime. The second war lasted until 1992 and did enormous damage to the country, undermining infrastructures in health, education, and transportation, and causing a great deal of suffering, dislocation, and loss of life. The effects of this warfare also destroyed the possibility of true independence on the part of Mozambique. Instead the country became dependent on foreign aid for survival and was therefore subject to the demands of international lending institutions such as the IMF. Under the conditions of a structural adjustment program instituted in the late 1980s, FRELIMO abandoned its socialist rhetoric and shifted its economic policies toward the free market. Likewise, it relaxed its restrictions on cultural practices including religion and traditional medicine. It was in this context, then, that AMETRAMO was able to claim a space for traditional medical practitioners in public dialogue. AMETRAMO's activity in the region where I conducted fieldwork revealed the ambiguities of its relationship with FRELIMO. AMETRAMO leaders often expressed dismay at what they perceived as a lack of support and respect from the FRELIMO government and particularly from the Ministry of Health; at the same time they frequently claimed to be associated with or even to be part of the government in order to justify their authority over healers and their practices.

PROPHET HEALING

Of the many kinds of healing I encountered during fieldwork, I focused my research on the prophets. My interest in their practices and perspectives was motivated in part by another way that Mozambican political history has informed healing activities in this region. The period of warfare throughout the 1980s and early 1990s in Mozambique was especially brutal, with more than one million people killed and some six million displaced from their homes. In the central province of Tete, many people fled the effects of the war by crossing the borders into the neighboring countries of Malawi, Zambia, and Zimbabwe. Many of the prophets I encountered in northern Tete had lived as refugees in Malawi for as many as ten years. Indeed, it was during their time in Malawi that they had first made contact with the biblical spirits with whom they worked. Before the war and the displacement it caused, I was told, there had been various kinds of healers in northern Tete, but no prophets; when Mozambicans repatriated in the years after the war ended in 1992, they brought home with them what they had encountered on the other side of the border, including their prophet spirits. Thereafter, the number of prophets and the scale of their healing activities continued to grow and created a vibrant social network. The phenomenon of prophet healing in postwar Tete province was thus one of the ways that people responded to the physical and social suffering that the war brought about—prophet healing both treated ailing bodies and engendered new kinds of sociality and community.

The nature of the social relationships that characterize the prophet community are important for understanding the healing they effect. The prophets are a network of healers and patients brought together by suffering and the desire to overcome it. Both the affliction and its treatment are understood to derive from Christianized spirits known as prophets (or *aneneri* in the local language, Chichewa). Prophet spirits come into an individual's life as an illness, especially one with strange or lingering symptoms. It is often after multiple attempts at healing with a variety of practitioners that the afflicted individual makes his or her way to the compound of an established prophet healer, who diagnoses the ailment as a sign of the presence of a spirit. If the patient accepts this diagnosis and the treatments proffered, he or she is brought into a new set of relationships: with the discovering healer, who becomes his or her "mother" and mentor; with other prophets with whom this individual will regularly engage in collective ritual activities; and with the spirit or spirits who have come to inhabit his or her body. Thus the individualized path of a single prophet and her quest for healing is inextricable from the broader processes through which the community of prophets is generated and grows. Becoming a prophet involves both an individual transformation from sufferer to healer and incorporation into a social community.

THE PROPHETS AS *NGOMA*

Although prophet healing is quite new to northern Tete Province, it is also an example of a long-standing cultural institution across Africa that has been referred to in the anthropological literature as "cults of affliction" or *ngoma*. Victor Turner, in his work on religious life and ritual in Zambia, coined the phrase "cults of affliction" to describe social groups that addressed particular ailments. Turner was especially interested in the transformative rituals by which individuals became part of such groups, and he adopted a tripartite model of "rites of passage" (separation, margin, aggregation) to describe the process. He was especially interested in the middle phase, liminality—the "betwixt and between" condition that is symbolically associated with death and decay, on one hand, and with gestation and birth, on the other, and which marks the transition from one status to another. Many local and regional studies provide examples of the kind of African healing cults or communities that Turner describes.

The synthesizing work of John Janzen on comparable groups from across the southern and central regions of Africa, which he refers to as *ngoma,* suggested a broader and deeper framework into which to fit these various examples. Janzen drew on his own research on healing networks in Congo, South Africa, Swaziland, and Tanzania, as well as the evidence of other researchers, to identify the key features and underlying logics of a long-standing regional "ritual therapeutic institution."

Ngoma involves an experience of illness, its identification and labeling by a member of the group, and initiation into the group through a rite of passage. *Ngoma* practitioners often evaluate illness through spirit mediumship and recognize the roles of a diversity of spirits in illness and well-being. The most characteristic element of *ngoma* is the role of the "wounded healer": through their participation in the group, patients are turned into healers, and suffering and alienation are transformed into healing and social integration. Finally, *ngoma* involves ritual activity, especially performance that includes singing, dancing, and drumming. *Ngoma* (the word for "drum" as well as the word for these ritual activities in a number of the languages of the region) is neither religion nor medicine nor politics, but a unique regional institution that recognizes and responds to misfortune in an organized, communal way.

Mozambican prophets exhibit many of these qualities, and their practices resonate strongly with this description. New prophets enter the community through illness and suffering, which leads them to seek the help of a prophet healer and to embark on a path of ritual transformation. Through engaging with the spirits, neophytes become the "wounded healers" who are in turn able to treat others. This ongoing healing work is punctuated by all-night ceremonial events full of dancing, singing, drumming, and spirit possession—expressive gatherings that bring together a larger regional network of prophets, publicly enacting the communal relationships among prophets.

If prophetic healing is a fundamentally social phenomenon, it is worth noting the key relationships at the heart of the prophet community. First is the relationship between host and spirit. Spirits cause illness in their hosts and make many demands on them. Prophets often struggle to meet these demands, which include avoiding certain foods and drinks such as pork and alcohol, buying special clothing for the spirits' "uniforms," constructing hospitals and churches in which the spirits might work, and staging the all-night ceremonies mentioned above. Hanging over these requests is the threat of the new illnesses spirits may inflict if their needs are not met. On the other hand, prophets recognize their spirits as a source of healing sent by God—the spirits, they explained, came to earth with the altruistic goal of helping those who suffer.

An equally important relationship is that between a new prophet and the healer who discovers his or her spirit. The healer who makes this initial discovery is referred to as the person's "mother" *(mayi),* the term used regardless of the gender of the discovering healer, and the newly discovered prophet is referred to as the prophet healer's "child" *(mwana).* A number of studies of healing networks have encountered kin terms, kin-like relationships, and imagery and symbolism associated with reproduction, suggesting that these groups are in some sense "reconstituted families," as shown by Janice Boddy (1994: 416). The use of kin terms among prophets reinforces a sense of the spirit discovery process as a "birth" and a key element in a process of social reproduction.

The "mother" does not teach the newly discovered prophet to heal sick people or to use medicinal plants. All of this knowledge is transmitted directly from spirit to host. But the "mother" does act as a mentor, guiding the newly possessed person in learning to live with the spirit. This includes guidance on the lifestyle changes that the spirit demands as well as assistance with accommodating the physical effects of the spirit's presence, which can be quite violent, especially for inexperienced newcomers. Spiritual "children" are equally important to their "mother." These offspring will now serve their "mother" as a sign of, and active participant in, her work.

While I have been stressing the internal experiences and dynamics of "cults of affliction," it is important to note that these groups are not closed off from the rest of the society. Although there are indeed some social boundaries, such as food taboos followed by prophets that prohibit them from eating at the homes of non-prophets, prophets spend significant time healing members of the broader society who come to their hospitals for consultations and treatments. Some of these patients are neighbors who reside nearby; others have traveled a distance, seeking out particular healers based on word-of-mouth accounts of their prowess. Many of these patients will not themselves become prophets. Although the transformation of a patient into a prophet is the central mechanism by which the prophet community grows, the spirits' primary mandate is to help all those who suffer, and in their day-to-day work in their hospitals, prophet healers receive and treat a variety of ailments.

Figure 7.4. Prophet ceremony, Tete province, Mozambique.
Tracy Luedke.

Figure 7.5. Dancing at a ceremonial gathering of prophets, Tete province, Mozambique. *Tracy Luedke.*

ILLNESS CATEGORIES AND CAUSATIONS

Examining the efforts of prophets to treat the ailments of the broader community reveals the local understandings of illness, diagnosis, and treatment that underlie not only prophet healing but the range of existing therapeutic activities in this region. There were three general categories of illness causation to which healers might attribute patients' conditions: natural, spirit, and witchcraft. "Natural" illnesses were illnesses that "just happened." This was the least elaborated category of causation and seemed to operate as a catchall for those conditions for which no other causation was identified. Spirit illnesses, as described above, were illnesses resulting from the presence of spirits, who afflicted their hosts as a way of demanding their compliance with the spirits' wishes and initiating an ongoing relationship through possession. Witchcraft illnesses were those that resulted from the evil intentions of other people. These were initiated by means of certain medicinal substances and techniques, and, it was said, were usually predicated on envy, often on the part of family members or neighbors. One of the primary local varieties of witchcraft (called *nchesso* in Chichewa) was often referred to as a "traditional land mine"—sorcerers were said to bury medicinal substances in a path or doorway where their intended victim would walk, and treading upon them caused illness or death.

When I asked prophet healers which category of illness causation they received the most, they nearly universally reported that they received more, or even mostly, illnesses resulting from witchcraft. Most healers averred that there were both more illnesses in general and especially more witchcraft-related illnesses in the present than in the past, which they attributed to an increase in envy and hatred stemming from experiences during the war and postwar conflicts over land. Patients themselves explained that they sought out prophet healers for cases of illness in which they suspected witchcraft because they knew that prophets were especially adept at identifying it. Identifying and treating witchcraft-related illnesses was both central to the practices of prophet healing and an important part of how prophets perceived their role.

Prophet healers explained that many conditions could be *either* natural *or* the result of witchcraft, and the cause of any specific illness could be determined only through a spirit consultation, during which the spirit is able to see into the patient's body to determine the nature and cause of illness. This was the case, for example, for malaria *(malungo),* a very common illness in this region and in many other parts of Africa. For natural malaria, healers offered several causes, including unsanitary conditions (lack of cleaning in the home, eating something dirty, badly prepared food, unclean water), mosquitoes (which breed in waste or stagnant water near the home during the rainy season), and exposure to cold temperatures. Malaria provoked by witchcraft was understood to be contracted in the same manner as other witchcraft illnesses, that is, through the use of medicinal substances against the intended victim, and it was considered far more dangerous than natural malaria, leading more rapidly to death. In making these distinctions between witchcraft and natural illnesses, healers were also identifying the separate domains and strengths of traditional medicine versus biomedicine, and the relative social roles of different varieties of healers in a medically plural society. They suggested that witchcraft illnesses could be treated only by traditional healers. If someone suffering from such an illness went to a government clinic and took the prescribed pharmaceuticals, these would at best be ineffective and at worst turn to poison. This was why patients carefully monitored illness symptoms and the effects (or lack thereof) of various treatments received; if they perceived the signs of an "unnatural" illness, it was necessary to visit a traditional healer.

PATIENTS AND PROPHETS: THREE EXAMPLES

The illness histories of patients I met at prophet healers' hospitals as they sought assistance for ongoing health problems trace the routes that particular patients traveled among a variety of healers and treatments, and their responses to the conflicting explanations and variably effective treatments they encountered along the way. The three case studies presented here also demonstrate the ways prophet healing strengthens some relationships and challenges others. The forces of concord and discord are in fact deployed within the same ritual sphere, in this case the weekly spirit consultation session held at the hospital of husband and wife prophet healers Paulo and Mariya.

Patient 1. When we met, Patient 1 had been at the hospital of Paulo and Mariya for three days, trying to resolve an illness that had plagued her for six years with pains in her legs, heart, and stomach. Before arriving at Paulo's she had been to five other traditional healers, all herbalists, all of whom said she had stepped on a "traditional land mine" *(nchesso).* They treated her, but the treatments did not work. She felt better while she was at their hospitals, but as soon as she went home, the illness returned. She had also visited a stall at the market near her home, where she purchased several kinds of pills for pain and stomach upset, but these too were ineffective. In her initial consultation at Paulo and Mariya's, the spirit explained that her illness was the result of witchcraft. Someone had taken a photograph of her and some thread from clothing she had worn and mixed it with dirt from the cemetery and a medicinal substance, and that is how the illness began.

Patient 2. Patient 2 was a nine-month-old child, brought by his young mother. She and the child had been at Paulo and Mariya's hospital for six days. The child had been suffering from fever, cough, and respiratory problems for a week. In response to the illness, the mother had first taken the child to the government clinic, where he was diagnosed with malaria and anemia and given pills and intravenous fluids, which the mother said were chloroquine and penicillin. The child seemed to improve at first, but within a few days the condition worsened to the point that the mother was afraid the child would die. Seeing this, she brought the child to Paulo and Mariya in the middle of the night and a consultation was done, during which the spirit explained that the child had malaria and anemia provoked by witchcraft, and that the child should stay to receive treatment. For the previous six days as a patient at Paulo and Mariya's hospital the child had received plant-based medicines and was now much better.

The mother explained that she knew of Paulo because she lived nearby and had already used his services on a previous occasion. On the previous visit she had brought another one of her children who was sick at the time. That child, in fact, ended up dying at Paulo and Mariya's. She explained that this occurred because she had spent too much time taking the child to other healers first, so by the time she brought the child to Paulo and Mariya's, he was already close to death and finally passed away there. However, she said, she had seen many other patients with serious illnesses leave their hospital cured and so had faith that they could help the child for whom she was currently seeking treatment. She also explained that she decided to come to Paulo and Mariya's because she had tried at the government hospital and it did not work, which led her to suspect that this was the kind of illness that only traditional healers could treat.

Patient 3. Patient 3 was a young man in his late teens. He explained that lightning had struck near him as he sat drinking beer with friends. Soon after the lightning strike he began to feel pains throughout his body, his bones hurt, and he felt twinges in his belly. He had not used any biomedical treatments before arriving at Paulo and Mariya's, because, he said, he perceived that this was an illness sent by an enemy, and he knew it was necessary to go directly to a traditional healer. He thought so because a few days before the lightning strike there had arisen a dispute among several of his family members, and he concluded that the lightning was sent against him as a result of this.

After their initial treatments, patients staying at the hospital of Paulo and Mariya received weekly spirit consultations to monitor their progress. These were typically performed on Saturdays, the primary day on which the healers received and consulted with patients. On one such Saturday, I was able to observe the consultations for the patients described above. On this particular morning, about forty people assembled in Paulo and Mariya's hospital, a large room decorated with banners and crosses in a building that included several smaller rooms where patients stayed. The assembled participants included eight of Paulo and Mariya's spiritual "children" (who occupied one corner and acted as a sort of chorus, accompanying the healers in singing hymns); six new patients anticipating their first consultations; about fifteen returning patients in ongoing treatment, there for a checkup and to renew their medications; and various family members accompanying the ill. Thus within this one ritual space were represented individuals at all stages of incorporation into the social body of the *ngoma*, from lay outsiders (new patients and their families) to long-standing insiders ("children" of the healers who now participated in healing activities). The participants sat along the walls, leaving the center of the room open for the doctors to work from.

Paulo and Mariya stepped into the hospital. Paulo was wearing a long red gown and a floppy orange hat with a cross on it and many brightly colored sashes tied around it and streaming down his back. He carried a Bible and a whisk made of an animal tail. Mariya wore a white smock, white pants, and a white headscarf, all decorated with blue crosses. She held a small mirror in each hand, and there were whistles and crucifixes hanging from her neck. The pair immediately began to sing animatedly, and those assembled joined in.

Paulo dipped at the knees, swaying and spinning as he sang. Mariya began to tremble and shake, jumping and gesticulating. Although she was otherwise quite calm and reserved, with the spirit in her body she became bold and aggressive, talking loudly and directing the proceedings. She led the group in a song, during which she hopped and danced in a lively, jittery way. Mariya began to do consultations for the assembled patients, each patient coming forward to stand when it was his or her turn. After she had performed a series of consultations, Paulo took over and carried out a number of consultations himself, a tag-team arrangement that reflected the rigor of the work: it would have been difficult for one person to sustain the frantic energy and support the draining presence of the spirits for the whole session, which lasted almost four hours.

It was time for the consultation of Patient 1, the young woman who hoped to re-solve her long-term illness. Her mother stood at her side during the consultation. Mariya's spirit spoke, recounting the girl's symptoms and treatments. She went on to say, "These problems aren't natural, and she doesn't have AIDS, as some other people in the area where she lives have said. I can see that you [the mother] and others have thought that this illness is AIDS. If it were AIDS, I would tell you. This illness comes from witchcraft." The person who sent the illness, she explained, was a member of the girl's family on her mother's side. The girl's mother, she said, was considered rich and arrogant by her neighbors and family members, which had encouraged the attack against her daughter. The spirit reassured the girl and her mother that she would be able to cure this condition, that her medicines would cleanse the girl's body and make her well again.

Patient 2, the young woman with a sick infant who had lost another child at Paulo and Mariya's in the past, was the next to be addressed by the spirit. The spirit declared that the child's health problems were a result of witchcraft perpetrated by a group of neighbors intent on killing the child. The spirit explained that this group had fed the child dirt from a cemetery, which brought on the pain and coughing. Mariya assured the mother that the child would recover with her help and encour-aged her also to take medicines to protect her home from further attacks.

Patient 3, the young man who had experienced a lightning strike, stood for his consultation, and his parents stood at his side. Mariya explained that the lightning that struck near the boy had caused his feelings of weakness and mental confusion. She further explained that this lightning was sent by an uncle with whom the parents were involved in a dispute over land. Mariya said she knew that family members of the boy and local community leaders awaited her pronouncements on this case so they would know whom to blame, but she declined to become embroiled in these famil-ial politics. Instead, she declared, she planned to focus on the boy's well-being—he would remain under her care until his health was fully recuperated.

The patients described here, and others like them, were pursuing wellness in a context of great uncertainty. Neither the nature of the illnesses at hand nor which variety of healer or treatment might be effective was known, and the threat of inca-pacitation and death was ever-present. This led the patients to seek out multiple healers and remedies, both formal and informal, biomedical and spirit-based, involv-ing both pharmaceuticals and medicinal plants. These cases reveal the limitations of available health services—the struggles the ill go through in pursuit of wellness and the variable results of their quests. These cases also demonstrate the locally per-ceived insight that illness and healing are political, involving as they do interpersonal power struggles, disputes over resources, manipulation of potent forces, and the forging and breaking of social alliances. Although from a biomedical perspective the notion of witchcraft as an explanation for illness and a basis for treatment may seem erroneous, as an analytical framework, it addresses individual bodily suffer-ing in its sociopolitical context, reminding people that illness and possibilities for overcoming it are more than biological questions.

THE COMPLEX LANDSCAPE OF AFRICAN HEALTH AND HEALING

The profundity of the health needs and the complexity of the medically plural response to suffering in Africa present an important set of challenges. It is crucial that significant health resources be directed toward improving the well-being of Africans, and it is also crucial that the insights of local analyses of health and approaches to healing be recognized. The three examples of patients presented here demonstrate the complicated social field in which illness experiences and responses are embedded: the biomedical disease categories and social threats of HIV/AIDS and malaria appear together with discussions of witchcraft and spirits; chloroquine and penicillin cross paths with locally produced, plant-based medicines; land disputes and intrafamilial tensions intersect with physical pain; the patterns of child mortality that appear in globally circulated public health literatures instantiate in one mother's struggle to keep her child alive. The networks of healers and patients described here as *ngoma* are one significant forum across Africa in which people assess and respond to illness. *Ngoma* exists alongside and intersects with multiple varieties of healers and healing practices, which draw from biomedicine, Christianity and Islam, and possession and divination, and which constantly stretch the boundaries between and around local medical practices with innovative new techniques.

Ngoma healing networks exemplify a fundamental principle of many kinds of African healing: the inherently social nature of health, illness, and healing and the push and pull of forces of cohesion and division within them. Given the broader social circumstances and structural constraints that inform health in sub-Saharan Africa—the stresses on individual and social bodies wrought by poverty, armed conflict, and the power dynamics of the global political economy—such healing activities constitute important interpretations of, and responses to, illness. In addressing the effects of powerful health threats including malaria and HIV/AIDS on local lives, families, and communities, African healers such as the prophets of Mozambique confront and assert analytical and practical agency regarding forces that are in many ways more powerful than themselves. The significant health challenges Africa faces require, and will continue to require, political will, incisive analysis, and creative problem solving at local, national, and global levels.

STATISTICS CITED

UNAIDS. 2009. *AIDS Epidemic Update*. Geneva: UNAIDS and WHO.

———. 2010. *Report on the Global AIDS Epidemic*. Geneva: UNAIDS.

———. 2011. *Global HIV/AIDS Response: Epidemic Update and Health Sector Progress toward Universal Access*. Geneva: WHO.

USAID. 2011. *HIV/AIDS Health Profile, Sub-Saharan Africa*. Available at www.usaid.gov /our_work/global_health/aids.

WHO. 2007. *AfroNews* 8(3): September–December 2007. Brazzaville, Congo: WHO Regional Office for Africa.

———. 2008a. *The Global Burden of Disease (GBD): 2004 Update*. Geneva: WHO.

———. 2008b. *Report on the Review of Primary Health Care in the African Region.* Brazzaville, Congo: WHO Regional Office for Africa.

———. 2011a. *Health Situation Analysis in the African Region: Atlas of Health Statistics 2011.* Geneva: WHO.

———. 2011b. *World Health Statistics 2011.* Geneva: WHO.

———. 2011c. *World Malaria Report 2011.* Geneva: WHO.

SUGGESTIONS FOR FURTHER READING

Akeroyd, Anne. 1996. *Some Gendered and Occupational Aspects of HIV and AIDS in Eastern and Southern Africa: Changes, Continuities, and Issues for Further Consideration at the End of the First Decade.* Occasional Papers, No. 60. Centre of African Studies, Edinburgh University.

Bayer, R. 1991. "Public Health Policy and the AIDS Epidemic: An End to HIV Exceptionalism?" *New England Journal of Medicine* 324: 1500–1504.

Boddy, Janice. 1994. "Spirit Possession Revisited: Beyond Instrumentality." *Annual Review of Anthropology* 23: 407–34.

Brentlinger, Paula E. 2006. "Health, Human Rights, and Malaria Control: Historical Background and Current Challenges." *Health and Human Rights* 9(2): 11–38.

Farmer, Paul. 1992. *AIDS and Accusation: Haiti and the Geography of Blame.* Berkeley: University of California Press.

Green, Edward C., Annemarie Jurg, and Armando Djedje. 1994. "The Snake in the Stomach: Child Diarrhea in Central Mozambique." *Medical Anthropology Quarterly* 8(1): 4–24.

Janzen, John. 1978. *The Quest for Therapy: Medical Pluralism in Lower Zaire.* Berkeley: University of California Press.

———. 1992. *Ngoma: Discourses of Healing in Central and Southern Africa.* Berkeley: University of California Press.

Last, Murray, and G. L. Chavunduka, eds. 1986. *The Professionalization of African Medicine.* Manchester: Manchester University Press.

Pfeiffer, James. 2004. "Condom Social Marketing, Pentecostalism, and Structural Adjustment in Mozambique: A Clash of AIDS Prevention Messages." *Medical Anthropology Quarterly* 18(1): 77–103.

Schoepf, Brooke G. 2001. "International AIDS Research in Anthropology: Taking a Critical Perspective on the Crisis." *Annual Review of Anthropology* 30: 335–61.

Turner, Victor. 1968. *The Drums of Affliction.* Oxford: Clarendon Press.

Turshen, Meredith. 1998. "The Political Ecology of AIDS in Africa." In *The Political Economy of AIDS*, ed. Merrill Singer. Amityville, NY: Baywood.

West, Harry G., and Tracy J. Luedke. 2006. "Healing Divides: Therapeutic Border Work in Southeast Africa." In *Borders and Healers: Brokering Therapeutic Resources in Southeast Africa*, ed. Tracy J. Luedke and Harry G. West. Bloomington: Indiana University Press.

8 Visual Arts in Africa

Patrick McNaughton and Diane Pelrine

African art has been made for many thousands of years, undergoing numerous major and often dramatic changes through the centuries and right up until today. Its forms and materials, meanings and functions have always been tremendously varied, deeply imaginative, and dynamically part of people's individual and social lives. Frequently stunning and formally sophisticated, it has been collected by Westerners for at least half a millennium and in fact profoundly influenced the modern history of European art.

The study of African art has changed drastically over time. For centuries Europeans viewed it as the exotic production of strange societies, which did not warrant much explanation. Not until the twentieth century was it seen to reflect aspects of African social, spiritual, and political organization, although contextual information was minimal. As the twentieth century progressed, and especially since the 1960s, art historians and anthropologists have developed increasingly sophisticated approaches to learning about and understanding African art's subtleties, complexities, and dynamic involvement with society and culture.

To simplify a complex topic, three categories of African art are presented: traditional, popular, and fine or contemporary art.

Traditional art consists of the masks, figures, and other objects made and used in local African contexts involving spiritual practices, initiations, or demonstrations of prestige and status, including leadership activities. Frequently carved of wood, traditional art is intimately bound to the community of which it is a part, both reflecting and shaping beliefs and practices. For most traditional art now in Western museums and collections, the names of the artists have not been preserved, so objects are usually identified with specific ethnic groups—thus, they are referenced as a Dogon figure or a Yoruba mask, to cite two examples.

Popular art constitutes many forms of artistic expression that came into existence with the advent of colonialism. Popular artists may use materials not generally associated with traditional art, such as canvas, cardboard, and plastic-coated wire. Popular art is intended to be seen by anyone; it is not associated with sacred or secret institutions, and it is frequently made to entertain or to advertise.

Contemporary or fine art is art that was made beginning in the twentieth century as a means of personal expression and for aesthetic display. The major difference between fine art and the other categories is that it is not made to be used in localized contexts or as souvenirs, as is traditional and much popular art; instead, artists making contemporary art do so with the intention that it will be displayed *as art* and—most hope—appreciated by a global public. In addition, unlike most traditional and popular art, nearly all examples of fine art can be associated with the names of the male and female artists who created them.

These categories convey the fact that there are differences among the myriad forms of African art and expressive culture. But there is a great deal of formal and conceptual overlap among them, and, in fact, scholars of African art have struggled for decades with how best to differentiate them. We have selected three categories that are widely accepted, but they should not be conceived of as rigid compartments. Instead, they are a framework for beginning to understand and appreciate the diversity that constitutes African art today.

TRADITIONAL ART

To many people, traditional African art consists of masks and figures that come primarily from two large regions: the areas around the Niger and Benue Rivers in West Africa and the Congo River basin in Central Africa. While masks and figures have been (and frequently continue to be) used by many peoples in those regions, they by no means exhaust the diversity and richness of traditional African art, but rather reflect the interest of foreign collectors. Indeed, nonfigural arts are the primary visual art traditions for many African peoples, particularly those of eastern and southern Africa. The Maasai, a pastoral people who live in Kenya and Tanzania, for example, do not make masks or figures for their own use; however, they are known worldwide for their beautiful and innovative beaded jewelry (figure 8.1). In addition to dress and body decoration, nonfigural traditional arts include furniture, such as stools and headrests; other household objects, including ceramic vessels and baskets; and even weapons—objects that Westerners often place in the category of "crafts." These arts are also found in the areas that produce figural sculpture, creating a rich, complex array of visual traditions in many parts of the continent. In fact, for most people, nonfigural arts are far more common and seen far more frequently than masks and figures, which may be viewed only on certain occasions or by particular people.

Traditional African art is most often identified by the ethnic group that made and used it. Throughout much of the scholarly literature and in museum exhibitions, specific styles, or the visual qualities of artworks, are associated with particular ethnic groups. For example, elaborate scarification carved in relief on a figure's face, neck, and torso is one element of the sculptural style that is associated with

Figure 8.1. Maasai woman in Kenya, 1924/1941. *Casimir Zagourski African postcards, 1924–1941 (inclusive).*
Manuscripts & Archives, Yale University.

the Luluwa of Democratic Republic of the Congo (plate 8.1). But many ethnic groups, such as the Igbo in Nigeria and the Bamana in Mali, make art in several styles. In addition, ethnic boundaries are often porous, not only in most cities, which tend to attract people from many areas, but also in the margins of a group's homeland, as well as in many rural regions where spaces are shared by more than one group and a great deal of interaction takes place, from friendships and intermarriage to complementary use of land through farming and grazing and joint business ventures.

In addition, long-distance travel and commerce are an important part of African history, as are expansionistic politics, and the forms, ideas, and functions of art are therefore often highly mobile and interactive. Numerous ethnic groups share many types of art, and often the appearance and functions of specific examples are very similar. Figural sculptures with spiritually charged attachments are a good example. They range from Nigeria and Cameroon across Democratic Republic of the Congo and into Angola to the south and Tanzania to the east (plate 8.2). Huge horizontal masks, found from the coast in Guinea to central Nigeria near Lake Chad, are another excellent example (plate 8.3).

Ownership of traditional artworks can be complex. In some cases, individual ownership is the rule. In Mali, for instance, carved wooden door locks, often sculpted into abstract animals or people, secure people's private rooms. Other objects, though, may be owned by a family or clan. Near the coast of northern Tanzania, Zaramo girls are given small abstract female figures during the period of seclusion that marks their initiation into womanhood (plate 8.4). When not in use, such a figure is kept by a senior woman on the paternal side of the family, who holds it in trust as an important family heirloom. In still other cases, such as the masks worn at performances by Bamana youth associations (plate 8.5), religious or social associations or even entire communities "own" artworks, with priests or leaders in charge of their safekeeping.

Materials and Techniques

Wood is the medium most often associated with traditional African art. The traditional carving tool is the adze, which resembles an axe but with its blade perpendicular to the handle. After carving, some objects are painted. Originally, locally made vegetal and mineral pigments were used. Today, factory-made paints are often preferred for their brilliant color and greater permanence. To Westerners accustomed to art created to be permanent, wood may seem an odd choice of material, given its relatively quick deterioration from climate and insects in most of Africa. With few exceptions, however, objects were not meant to last indefinitely—renewal was both expected and desired.

An equally important material is iron. Among some peoples, such as the Dogon and Bamana, beautiful iron lamps and staffs are testament to blacksmiths' technical skills and aesthetic acumen. More often, however, their products enable other things to be done: fields to be farmed with iron hoes, wood to be carved with iron-bladed adzes. In the hands of master smiths, even these seemingly mundane implements can attain a beauty of form and workmanship that places them above the ordinary.

Traditional African art in clay includes bowls, pots, and other vessels and free-standing figures. Like metal, it is nonperishable, and terra-cotta figures from Nok, Nigeria, are the oldest sculptural tradition known from south of the Sahara (plate 8.6). Most ceramics are more utilitarian vessels, formed by hand, using coil, molding, and slab methods. As plastic and enamel containers have become widely available, pottery making has decreased in some areas, though it still thrives in others and has now become highly desired by collectors.

Cloth is woven from local cotton, wool, and silk, and from imported fibers, such as rayon. In earlier times, barkcloth was made in some areas. Most fabric is strip-woven; that is, strips of cloth, ranging from a few inches to two feet in width, are woven on a loom and then sewn together to make a large rectangle (plate 8.7). Woven patterns, painting, stamping, resist dyeing, embroidery, and appliqué are all used to make African cloth among the most beautiful, complex, and colorful in the world. Factory-made cloth, both imported and manufactured all over the continent, is also popular. Printed images may commemorate special occasions and, particularly in East Africa, often include proverbs, combining verbal and visual arts.

Other materials, such as gold, copper-based alloys, and ivory, are prestige materials: their use generally signifies wealth or importance in the religious or political sphere. This was the case, for instance, in the West African kingdom of Benin, where brass was the prerogative of royalty; altars honoring deceased kings displayed brass sculpture, such as commemorative heads (plate 8.8). In many parts of the continent, elephants were associated with leadership because of their size and strength, making elephant ivory carved into horns, whistles (plate 8.9), jewelry, containers, and charms especially appropriate insignia of political power.

Traditional African sculptors have not used stone extensively, except in about half a dozen areas (in Nigeria, Sierra Leone, Guinea, Democratic Republic of the Congo, Zimbabwe, and Ethiopia). None of those traditions continues to the present day. However, in at least one of these areas, Zimbabwe, stone carving has been successfully revived for the art gallery and tourist markets.

Traditional arts are predominantly three-dimensional, with few examples of painting, drawing, and engraving, which are prominent in the popular and modern/contemporary arts. But painting and engraving on the walls of caves and rock shelters in southern Africa and in what is now the Sahara Desert are the oldest known examples of art in Africa. More recently, the Dogon of Mali paint sacred symbols, encapsulating important aspects of their ethos, on rock, as do Sukuma associations of snake handlers and snakebite curers in Tanzania. Stunning designs are painted on the facades of homes from Burkina Faso to Cameroon and South Africa. Aside from decorating sculpture, however, perhaps the most common use of paint is in decorating the human body, not only for beauty but also to indicate important social and spiritual states and transitions.

Artists

In traditional African art, certain media and techniques are associated with each gender. Metalworking and carving, whether in wood, ivory, or stone, are the domains of men in virtually all societies. One exception is among the Turkana of Kenya, where women make wooden containers that are among the most elegant bowl forms in the world. Pottery is generally considered a woman's art, and in some societies the potters are most likely to be the wives of blacksmiths. Again there are exceptions, such as among certain groups in eastern Nigeria, where women make pots for food and water, while men make anthropomorphic ritual vessels used in divination and healing.

Weaving is practiced by men or women, depending upon the area and, sometimes, the loom type. In parts of West Africa, men weave very long, narrow strips of cloth on horizontal looms, while women in the same areas use broader vertical looms to make wider panels of cloth. Men weave raffia cloth in central Africa, while in Madagascar women are the weavers.

Whatever their gender, people creating traditional art, like artists worldwide, undergo training and are recognized in their chosen fields. This statement belies a common but completely false stereotype about African art: namely, that art was made by anonymous, untutored men and women. This stereotype says much about Western prejudices and misconceptions. First, most traditional African art is anonymous outside the continent only because collectors did not record the artists' names. In most cases within the African setting, the names of artists are well known, whether the objects are ritually oriented or utilitarian. Truly great artists can develop such reputations that people travel great distances to acquire objects made by them. Second, the myth of the untutored artist may fit romantic Western ideas about the "noble savage," but the objects reveal a sophisticated understanding of materials, techniques, and composition. In many cases, training is informal. Elsewhere, training requires formal apprenticeship, sometimes lasting many years. Among the Bamana, for example, blacksmiths are also the woodcarvers, and smithing is a hereditary occupation. By the time a young boy officially begins his apprenticeship, he will already have spent numerous hours at his father's forge, observing and performing small tasks. His formal apprenticeship may last as long as seven or eight years, as he learns first to work the bellows, then to carve wood, and finally to forge iron.

With a few exceptions, most traditional artists create part-time, as ways to supplement a family's income. Of course, famous artists may earn enough money to make it worthwhile for other family members to shoulder additional farming or herding responsibilities, leaving the artists free to devote more time to their art.

Artists often build up stocks of utilitarian objects, which they sell from their homes or take to market, but masks, figures, and the most prestigious utilitarian objects are generally made on individual order. Clients may explain in detail what they want, they may specify the type of object and leave the details up to the artist, or artist and client may negotiate the specifics of a commission.

Traditional Art and History

The older the art, the harder it is to know much about it. This is particularly true for Africa, where many art forms are highly perishable, written documentation is infrequent, and archeology is an expensive undertaking, not always considered as important as a country's other pressing needs. Thus, our knowledge of ancient African art is patchy and incomplete. The evidence we do have from permanent materials, however, suggests rich and varied traditions.

Paintings from a rock shelter known as Apollo 11 in the mountains of the southern Namibian desert are the oldest known artworks from Africa, dating to before 21,000 BCE. Ancient rock paintings and engravings are also found in other parts of southern and eastern Africa, and though determining the age of many remains problematic, evidence suggests millennia-old traditions that in some areas continued well into the time of European contact. Well north, in what is now the central Sahara Desert, rock paintings have been dated using carbon-14 to around 10,000 BCE. Wherever they are located, these paintings and engravings consist of abstract motifs as well as marvelous images of animals and scenes of hunting and spiritual or social activities. Saharan paintings also record the coming of the horse and the camel to the continent, as well as the ancient use of masks. More recent ones in the south depict the use of European firearms. While these paintings and engravings are generally considered to reflect beliefs about the world and cosmos, there is little evidence for definitive explanations of specifics.

Architecture must also be included among the arts for which a long history is evident. Dry stone architecture was found from the first millennium CE at Koumbi Saleh, putative capital of the ancient Ghana Empire, a building tradition that apparently began by the middle of the second millennium BCE in the Dhar Tichitt region of central Mauritania. In southern Africa between 1000 and 1500 CE, the civilization now known as Great Zimbabwe developed complex networks of production and trade, a ruling elite, and a complex and beautifully constructed system of stone block architecture, which was used to create several regional centers. Remains of city and mosque architecture cut from coral masonry blocks and dating from the same time or earlier are also found along the East African Swahili coast. Also from around the same time, or possibly earlier, Ethiopian Christian churches were carved into monolithic rock. Elsewhere, materials that require regular upkeep and refurbishment, such as clay, wood, and thatch, have been the norm, with the result that our understanding of the history of that architecture is limited.

Thanks to historical happenstance and archeology, we know most about the ancient arts of Nigeria. The oldest sculpture yet found from sub-Saharan Africa is clay and dates from between 500 BCE and 500 CE, though it may have begun considerably earlier (plate 8.6). It comes from a Nigerian culture dubbed Nok, after a town where much of it was found. Details, such as the large bundles of beads depicted on male figures, suggest leadership portraiture. The elegant simplicity of Nok figures contrasts sharply with the elaborate metalwork dating to the ninth century CE at the Igbo Ukwu site in southeastern Nigeria. There, large quantities of remarkable cast bronze sculptures were found in shrine and burial contexts. Made by the ancestors of today's Igbo peoples, these pieces include figures of animals and human heads, containers, and replicas of objects such as shells and calabashes. They were associated with a complex, widespread, and powerful spiritual-political organization. Leadership combining political and spiritual capabilities was also important in areas further to the west, in a complex, loose, and constantly competing confederacy of city-states grounded in commerce and expansionistic ambition that emerged as early as the late first millennium BCE. The hub of these polities was Ife, which between the eleventh and fifteenth centuries CE sponsored spectacular leadership arts in clay and brass, including terra-cotta heads, quite possibly portraits of leaders, which are a subtle combination of naturalism and idealized abstraction (plate 8.10). Later, in the same broad area, the kingdom of Benin flourished from the fifteenth century until the British defeated it in 1897. Benin sculpture shows us how rich and multifaceted art in the service of the state can be, with artists working for the king to create shrine objects such as brass heads commemorating deceased kings (plate 8.8) as well as palace furnishings and royal regalia. Much Benin art, pillaged after Britain's attack, was auctioned in Europe, and it played an important role in opening the eyes of Western artists to the power of African creativity.

Findings from other parts of the continent suggest that Nigeria's early arts were not unique. In Mali's Middle Niger region, for example, an iconographically complex array of terra-cotta figures (plate 8.11) came to the attention of the outside world in the mid-twentieth century. Usually dated to the twelfth or thirteenth century, the figures have been looted in large numbers and sold to Europe and North America for half a century, but precious few have been found in systematic archeological excavations, so information about them is extremely limited. Most depict individuals, couples, and snakes, and they may have served on ancestor shrines or as household guardians.

Regular contact with Europeans brought new materials, such as oil paint and chemical dyes, and made others, such as brass and glass beads, more widely available. Changing practices and beliefs led to the creation of new art forms and the elimination of others. In addition, new art markets were created. Afro-Portuguese ivories are a good example. In coastal West Africa, fifteenth-century Portuguese explorers and traders were so taken with the sculpture that they saw in the region of present-day Sierra Leone and Guinea that they commissioned local artists to carve ivory objects, such as spoons, salt cellars (plate 8.12), decorative hunters' horns, and pyxes for export back to Europe. Though European in form, this earliest tourist art is carved in a style that is clearly African.

Traditional Art in Context

Unlike many popular and contemporary arts, traditional arts have been used in specific contexts, from which they derive their importance and meaning. Broadly speaking, they involve spiritual practices, initiations, or demonstrations of prestige and status. Most frequently, a single artwork reaches across at least two of these categories, if not all.

SPIRITUAL PRACTICES

Much traditional African art is intimately connected with what John Hanson calls "religions with African roots" (see chapter 5). Whatever the specifics, most of these locally rooted religions share a belief that deities, spirits, or potent natural forces have the power to affect people, communities, or societies. It is not surprising, then, that practices and rituals, many of which involve masks, figures, and other objects, were developed to encourage these powers to enhance human life.

The Yoruba, who live in Nigeria and the Republic of Benin, have one of Africa's best-known pantheons, which includes hundreds of deities *(orisa)*, and often use artworks in spiritual associations devoted to them. For example, figural staffs or wands are associated with Esu, an *orisa* who is both messenger and trickster, embodying concepts of contrast, provocation, and contradiction (plate 8.13). Esu helps people by carrying their offerings to the other gods; at the same time, he has a provocative nature, causing misfortune and havoc to those who he feels do not make appropriate sacrifices, properly acknowledge his powers, or follow Yoruba moral standards. Sculpture dedicated to him frequently incorporates cowrie shells, which contrast with the darkness of the wood, a visual restatement of the oppositions that are part of the deity's character. Further, as a former medium of exchange, cowries remind viewers of the disagreements that money can engender, as well as the generosity of the devotee.

Artworks relating to ancestor spirits are numerous and well known, providing the opportunity to cherish the memories of beloved relatives while gaining some influence in the spirit realm by showing respect to the deceased who reside there. In Gabon, for example, Kota people both honored their ancestors and appealed for their protection with abstract figures that were set in baskets holding bone relics of a clan's ancestors and placed in a community shrine enclosure (plate 8.14). Also believed to protect the relics, the figures were carved of wood and then covered with copper and brass, which made the sculptures more valuable and more beautiful, thereby pleasing the spirits.

Among the Mende and nearby peoples of coastal Sierra Leone and Liberia, wilderness spirits are represented in the masks of an association called Sande. Members of Sande initiate young girls into adulthood; train them to be good mothers, wives, and citizens; and teach them the intricacies of social and spiritual life. The society also provides older members with an infrastructure of beliefs and activities that connect to aspects of broader community life, offering women significant amounts of power and authority. During association ceremonies, members dance wearing beautiful jet-black helmet masks (plate 8.15) that represent wilderness spirits with whom the individual mask owners have established intimate and beneficial relationships. The masks are considered to be the epitome of beauty, which reflects upon the nature of the spirit and also upon the accomplishment and capacity of the woman who owns the mask.

More generalized forces and energies are also important in local African religions, and artworks often serve as the vehicles for accumulating and activating them. These forces, variously described as the energy that makes the universe possible, the force behind all activities, and the power that allows and constitutes organic life, can only be managed by someone trained to do so: these are the priests, herbal doctors, and divination experts of African societies, as well as the independent sorcerers, who invoke their power to benefit or harm others.

In West Africa, masks are frequently designed to accumulate these powers. Good examples are those belonging to the Mande Kòmò associations (plate 8.3), masks that are believed to have the power to destroy antisocial sorcerers and to protect communities from malevolent wilderness spirits. Mask owners are Kòmò leaders who, like the Mende Sande mask owners, also have close relationships with wilderness spirits. Designed to rest horizontally over a dancer's head, Kòmò masks depict the energies they embody. Their mouths and feathers represent the deep knowledge of the world possessed by hyenas and birds. Their horns suggest wilderness and the raw energies that abound there. The murky coatings of sacrificial materials add power and suggest the ambiguity and indeterminate, secret nature of the energies at work in the mask.

Across Central Africa, figures with all sorts of attachments, such as mirrors, horns, nails, shells, beads, and herbal medicines, also harness power to do the bidding of individuals and groups. Among the people who use them are the Kongo, Bete, Teke, Kuba, and Songye (plate 8.2). The figures vary in size, gesture, and attachments, according to the powers they are supposed to harness and the activities they are supposed to help people undertake. Some cure illnesses, others block misfortune, and still others seek and punish those who commit a crime or try to inflict misfortune on others.

INITIATIONS

In Africa, artworks play important roles in initiations, the ceremonies that mark a change in status, position, or role for an individual or group. In most traditional African societies, nearly every person participates in at least one initiation: that which marks the transition from childhood to adulthood. In the Bissagos Islands, off the coast of Guinea, for example, boys undergo a two-part initiation that includes masquerade. At certain stages, the boys wear masks depicting ferocious and predatory sea creatures (plate 8.16), emphasizing the fact that they are at the height of their physical prowess and strength but as yet do not have the knowledge and wisdom necessary for success as adults in the civilized world. In other parts of Africa, masks are part of ceremonies presenting information boys must acquire to be considered adults, or masks may represent a monster that devours the boys and allows them to be reborn as men. In many places masquerades are part of the celebrations that welcome initiation participants back into their communities as new adults.

Initiations may also mark the acceptance of certain roles or positions within a society, such as when rulers or priests take office. A Kongo chief undergoes an elaborate initiation into office, which includes a period of seclusion and an ordeal intended to ascertain the approval of spiritual forces. Upon successful completion of the ordeal, the chief is given particular objects, including a sword and a staff, as symbols of his leadership. Finally, men and women may be initiated if they choose to join associations or societies that are dedicated to particular causes or ideals. The Bwami association, which most Lega men and women in the eastern Democratic Republic of the Congo joined, is a complex, multilevel institution dedicated to the development of moral behavior. Advancement within the society is based on payments and demonstrations of knowledge appropriate to each rank. An initiate learns the necessary information from a variety of sources, including proverbs, songs, and the manipulation of different objects, both natural and human-made. For some levels, these objects include wooden and ivory figures (plate 8.17) and masks, which become not only educational tools but also emblems of rank and status.

PRESTIGE AND LEADERSHIP

Many traditional arts indicate social, political, or economic status. Frequently known as prestige arts, they are identified by their materials, by the elaboration or decoration of a simpler, more ordinary form, or by the very type or form of the object itself. Objects made from expensive or rare materials that are highly prized, such as gold in Ghana, copper in central Africa, or ivory throughout the continent, are traditionally associated with wealth or position. Intricately woven textiles popularly known as *kente* that include silk (plate 8.7) are more valuable than those woven only from cotton, but because of the complexity of this type of cloth, even a cotton *kente* is more expensive than most other textiles. It is important to note that prestige is not always equated with economic wealth. For instance, traditionally in Maasai society, only a married woman would wear a coiled metal ornament such as the one in the lower left corner of figure 8.1.

An important subgroup of prestige arts consists of objects associated with political leadership: many African art forms proclaim, aggrandize, and enhance the capacities of traditional rulers. The Asante in Ghana provide excellent examples. In addition to the Golden Stool (figure 8.2), which is believed to embody the soul of the Asante confederacy and the right of the *asantehene* (king) to lead it, Asante royal arts today include spectacular arrays of regalia including swords decorated with gold and gold-leaf-embellished staffs that include images associated with proverbs and stories that become royal messages. When notables gather, cloth umbrellas with gold finials protect them from the sun while adding to the visual display. Some state officials wear gold disk pendants that symbolize the purification of the king's soul, while the king himself wears gold jewelry, gold-covered sandals, and *kente* (plate 8.7), cloth that in earlier times was the prerogative of royalty and that remains associated with political leadership, though now it can be worn by anyone who can afford it.

Figure 8.2. The Golden Stool of Asante with its bells, and behind it the stool carriers and guards. 1935.
Basel Mission Archives/Basel Mission Holdings QD-30.004.0002.

All of this splendor asserts that Asante leaders possess the social, economic, and spiritual clout needed to run their state.

POPULAR ART

Popular art is a category that invites debate everywhere, and especially in Africa. It invokes a number of significant issues involving social geography, world history, and artistic training. In fact, its application to African creative expression pulls several scholarly problems into sharp relief.

The category is frequently characterized as restricted to Africa's larger urban centers, with a very brief history that began during the colonial period as a response to the tremendous and fast-paced changes, social, economic, political, and spiritual, that accompanied a newly amplified and highly aggressive Western presence. These changes are understood to have produced an onslaught of new kinds of art, generally grounded in a syncretism combining African and European expressive traditions. This emphasis on change, urbanism, and outside influence is often used to distinguish popular from traditional art, which encourages a basic misunderstanding of the latter.

Many kinds of visual expression can be categorized as popular art. Included are painted signs and decorated walls for businesses, such as restaurants, barber shops, ice cream parlors, and photography shops; bus, taxicab, and truck embellishments in paint and other materials; genre and topical paintings on canvas, hardboard, and various other materials; cartoons, often of a strong sociopolitical bent; cement funerary portrait sculpture; elaborately constructed and painted wooden coffins; wall and table displays of imported enamel crockery; new types of cloth and fashionable clothing ensembles, including the spectacular factory cloth produced all across the continent; and posters announcing events such as movies, political rallies, and health campaigns. Some scholars also include wire and tin toys made by children in this category as well as similar toys made by adults to sell to tourists, and sometimes other forms of tourist art. This fluid and ever-changing cacophony of artistic expression finds parallel zones of creativity in music, dance and masquerade, theater, cinema, radio, television, websites, and blogs.

Problems with the Category

It is easy to see differences between the masks, figures, textiles, and ceramics we have discussed as traditional art and objects generally called popular art. These differences have inspired many observers to characterize the popular arts as largely urban, innovative, and modern responses to colonial and postcolonial life, and "unofficial" in the sense that they are described as not linked to the official ideology of a society or to its well-established traditions of expression. Such assessments are helpful but also simplifications, because many qualities are shared by popular and traditional art. In fact, it is difficult to fit some artworks into either of these categories.

Painted architectural embellishment is a good example. Scattered profusely across urban centers are wall paintings both abstract and figural, often designed to advertise businesses or to attract attention and generate enjoyment. Cartoon characters, spiritual beings such as Mami Wata (a water spirit usually taking the form of a mermaid or a snake charmer that is recognized across much of Africa), airplanes and other vehicles, or stylish abstract patterns are all part of the repertoire. Though it is fair to say that such artworks are more concentrated in urban landscapes, they are not restricted to them, as a zebra-striped restaurant and bar on a rural road northwest of Dar es Salaam indicates (plate 8.18).

A lavish and striking tradition of abstract house painting by women artists is widespread throughout towns in northern Ghana and Burkina Faso. Another can be found in South Africa, practiced by Ndebele women who indicate they developed their tradition from a much older practice by Sotho women that dates back at least five centuries. More recently, Ndebele women were encouraged by their government to create tourist-oriented villages featuring their painting.

In Mali, Dogon people employ a venerable tradition of rock wall painting that features abstract symbols and more figural images, both of which are used to pass information and discussion points from one generation to the next. Similar images, painted or carved in wood pillars that support public meeting areas, have become must-see stops on the trips many European and American tourists take to West Africa. Thus we see in just one kind of example a compromising of the idea that popular painting is urban, only as old as the colonial period, and not associated with official ideologies. We also see that African art designated as popular very often has a crossover relationship with the arts frequently labeled as tourist.

Though change has always been part of Africa's social and visual expression, rapid change is a most salient characteristic of the popular arts. Very dramatic and swift social, economic, spiritual, and political change has been part of African history since the onslaught of colonialism, and part of global history since the industrial revolution. Expressive culture is deeply responsive to the constraints and opportunities contained in change, and so African artistic traditions have transformed and expanded substantially. The same can be said of Western art, which changed dramatically in the twentieth century, in large part from exposure to African and other non-Western artistry.

Thus we often have blurred boundaries between the categories scholars use for African art, which is evident when considering traditional and popular art. Both have been sparked by entrepreneurship, the will and capacity to be creative, innovative, sensitive to opportunity, and imaginative, while staying in touch with the realities of the world and utilizing experience and skill to shape that imagination convincingly. The arts attached to ritual may have changed more slowly than the arts devoted to public entertainment. And the arts viewed as traditional may express innovation in ways different from those viewed as popular. But entrepreneurship has helped shape both categories. Perhaps the most significant difference has been the accelerated rate of dramatic change that began in colonial times and fueled the arts we now call popular.

Popular Artists

A great many men and women creating popular art receive no formal training, teaching themselves by experimenting with materials and techniques. As new expressive traditions develop and become popular, they attract more practitioners, who have the opportunity to learn from already established artists. Often these artists operate workshops where the younger members can gain experience and develop their reputations. Many then establish themselves on their own and even engage in some artistic rivalry with their former teachers and colleagues. As with most traditional art, we do not know the names of many of these artists, but increasingly artists are signing their work, especially in the case of popular painting.

Materials and Techniques

Variety and creativity, frequently born of necessity, characterize the selection of many materials used to create popular arts. Artists have had to be extremely entrepreneurial on this score because supplies are often scarce and expensive.

Painting is perhaps the popular art best known around the world. It has many forms and sources of inspiration. For example, in the Democratic Republic of the Congo, local consumers supported a tradition of genre, religious, and history painting, beginning in the 1950s. Many artists have participated, including such well-known painters as Cheri Samba and Tshibumba Kanda, and the audience for these artworks has expanded greatly to include people from all over the world. Colonialism and its violent aftermath, issues of ethics and spirituality, and often the personal experiences of the artists themselves are presented, along with village scenes, landscapes, and daily activities. In Tanzania, Tingatinga paintings (plate 8.19) have been popular in Dar es Salaam for nearly half a century. The tradition was begun by Eduardo Saidi Tingatinga, but many other artists have since created similar works, which cater especially to tourists and feature colorful, decorative scenes of flowers, animals, and people. Some artists, such as D. B. K. Msagula, paint much more personal visions, often creating vivid portrayals of contemporary social and spiritual ills, sometimes larger than the fit-in-your-suitcase size that characterizes most Tingatinga paintings. In Onitsha, Nigeria, where contemporary music, art, literature and theater combined to create a cauldron of intense creativity in the middle decades of the twentieth century, many painters created both signs and much more personal expressions. One painter, who used the name Middle Art (Augustin Okoye), assisted financially by the European scholar and supporter of Nigerian art Ulli Beier, portrayed the Biafran war. Blurred categories must be mentioned here, because many of these artists participate in contemporary art exhibits and are quite clearly part of the worldwide contemporary art scene.

While some paintings have fixed locations, others move over streets and roadways on buses, minivans, trucks, and cabs, often in combination with written proverbs and statements that cover a range of topics, from religious piety to the derring-do of Africa's professional drivers and road crews. Frequently created by teams, the paintings can be abstract designs or images of famous musicians and movie stars. Sometimes, as in the case of the big buses of Nairobi called *matatu* (plate 8.20), the vehicles are completely rebuilt both inside and out and carry thunderous sound systems and highly theatrical driving crews. This is mobile painting, sculpture, and theater all at once.

Paints of all types are used: oils, acrylics, poster paints, and enamels, the last sometimes preferred because of their natural vibrancy. While Westerners consider canvas as the usual support for portable paintings, its high cost makes it prohibitive for much African popular art. Instead, artists paint on a variety of materials: various kinds of cloth, cardboard, plywood, particleboard, basketry, and glass all become surfaces for popular painting in Africa. In Ghana, flour sacks were used by painters creating posters to advertise films during the 1980s and 1990s (plate 8.21). Artists creating Tingatinga paintings usually use particleboard but may turn to cardboard or burlap if it is not available. During the 1980s, another group of Dar es Salaam painters called Nivada Sign and Arts became quite popular for painting flowers, fruit, and other objects on basketry.

In Senegal, glass painting has become very popular both locally and abroad. Islamic themes have been prevalent since its apparent inception in the late 1800s, but imagery also includes heroes and historical events, and the visualization of stories and proverbs. Here the question of categorization arises again: these fragile artworks are another example of blurred categories. Because some glass painters consider themselves in the fine arts category and the works are often for sale in fine arts galleries around the world, they can also be considered contemporary African art.

Imaginative and innovative uses of materials are even more evident in the creation of objects. A tradition of affordable jewelry in Timbuktu used gold-colored straw instead of metal and beads. Broad, flat winnowing baskets for sale in the Bamako markets are made of packing-strap plastic instead of fiber, while in South Africa colorful telephone-wire baskets of various shapes and sizes are sold in stores and exported abroad. A variety of objects ranging from oil lamps to tourist souvenirs are created from scrap, recycled, and repurposed materials, including metal cans, wire, and worn-out flip-flops.

Steamer trunks are a good example of popular object entrepreneurship. They are made from reclaimed and reworked metal drums and then painted with abstract patterns or depictions of figures such as the mermaid-like water spirit Mami Wata. These trunks enjoy much regional variation in embellishment and can be found as far afield as Mali, Niger, Cameroon, and Sudan. They are often given as gifts to newlyweds and are used all over for storage or even display. They enjoy a history that highlights the entrepreneurial character of much popular African art. Early in the twentieth century, steamer trunks imported from Europe were desirable but extremely expensive. Local innovators taught themselves how to make them at affordable prices, decorated them according to prevailing fashion, and created a land-office business for themselves offering what became a hugely popular item. Much smaller containers made by different artists, in the form of briefcases and purses, also use recycled materials. Some are created from bottle caps assembled on imaginatively constructed frameworks that allow the cases to be semi-transparent, producing a very pop-art feel (plate 8.22). Others are wood covered with flattened cans and replete with interior linings of newspaper comic strips.

Whatever the media, hues are frequently bold and compositions often aim for high contrast between juxtaposed colors, including black and white. Similar uses of color and contrast are seen in wire basketry from southern Africa and house painting from West Africa. They can also be found in textiles, some traditions of basketry, and even painted sculpture and body painting—another example of bridges between categories.

Popular painting styles and aesthetics are noteworthy. Some artists employ an almost cartoon-like technique, outlining figures and objects in black, stacking imagery on top of imagery, or creating checkerboard-style compositions of figures and objects over the whole surface of the work. Often there is no concern for any sense of perspective or three-dimensionality. Other artists create instead a sense of hyperrealism, especially in the heads and faces of people. Still other artists, such as Nigeria's Middle Art, combine these two approaches, adding a lively interest to their works.

Popular Arts in Context

As with traditional arts, context is important to understanding the popular arts—it often sheds rich light on both innovation and continuity. Ghanaian fantasy coffins are a good example. They began with Ata Owoo, who gained local fame in the town of Teshi for designing an eagle-shaped conveyance in which a local chief could ride during processions. Around 1950, another chief commissioned a conveyance in the form of a cocoa pod, an important cash crop in the area and a significant source of wealth. He died before he could use it, however, so Ata Owoo's workshop transformed the vehicle into a coffin, and the fantasy coffin tradition was born.

With Ata Owoo's encouragement, Kane Kwei set up the first shop specializing in fantasy coffins, creating a variety of forms symbolizing success and status: for example, a mother hen for a woman who had successfully reared several children, a giant saw for a skillful carpenter, a Mercedes-Benz for a wealthy businessman, and boats, outboard motors, and various ocean creatures for people who earned a livelihood from the sea. By the time of his death in 1992, Kane Kwei's coffins had been featured in museum exhibitions in Europe and North America, and today several of his former apprentices have their own shops, including his son, Ernest Anang Kwei, whose workshop designed and built the bright pink fish-shaped coffin illustrated here (plate 8.23). Honoring the deceased and celebrating their importance is important in Ghana, and included in more ancient times funerary terracotta figural sculpture. Funerary coffins, with their elaborate, appropriately imaginative shapes and wonderfully bold paint, become part of an elaborate funerary celebration that includes food, music, and dance, and a parade through town on the shoulders of mourners, giving the deceased a final opportunity to say good-bye to favorite places and people before burial.

Fantasy coffins, painted signs, and embellished vehicles impart information, stimulate the imagination, and draw attention to businesses while also amplifying the reputation of the artists, thereby enhancing the artists' business too. This highlights the relationship of popular art to commerce. But it is really just an example of one of art's principal functions, no matter what the category. When well done, art ought to stimulate and influence, and African artists say objects graced with effective adornment are more appealing to potential clients. It is worth noting that aesthetic considerations are often linked both to effectiveness in delivering memorable messages and to success in procuring clientele.

Tourist Art and Toys

Two kinds of visual expression are particularly problematic to categorize: tourist art and toys. Workshops for creating tourist art exist all over Africa. Those in Côte d'Ivoire and Mali are especially known for reproducing traditional art forms—sometimes very beautifully—for shipment to large cities and eventual relocation in living rooms all over the world. Other workshops specialize in creating everything from napkin holders to lyrically styled ebony animals, along with masks and figures that eclectically combine elements from traditional art types all over the continent, often in the same object. It is fascinating to talk to the Western owners of these objects, many of whom are unshakable in their conviction that they possess authentic traditional art. Many middle-class and urban Africans also collect these objects, for a variety of reasons, making them popular at home as well as abroad. There are also beautiful traditions of basketry, some made of fiber, others of beautifully colored wire and even paper, that can be considered to belong to this category.

Toys can be a wonderful form of popular art made by and for kids, or a form of tourist art adults make to sell to foreigners. Airplanes, helicopters, and ground vehicles of all kinds are made of wire, cans, and other scrap materials. In some cases, these too are made in workshop contexts: in Dar es Salaam and nearby towns in 1985, for example, adolescents who possessed the passion, skill, and imagination to create these vehicles often formed their own toy-making workshops, exchanging materials and ideas and helping each other develop their own creativity. Their parents were impressed with and proud of their devotion and ingenuity. The creativity and dedication in this was brought home to us one evening in a Dar es Salaam parking lot when along came a boy pulling a toy truck, the cab of which was hitched to at least ten trailers, all in shiny metal, with lovely little wheels, well-designed axles, and a very long steering column running from inside the cab to the hands of this young entrepreneur. As he drove around the empty parking lot, he was beaming.

Vehicles are not the only things made by young people. In some of the same towns, boys created miniature furniture and decorative bird cages from millet stalks. Dolls are fashioned from wood, clay, cloth, gourds, and even basketry. While these items are not usually made for sale, other very similar objects are. In shops and roadside stands all over the continent there are what we might call toy reproductions—cars, trucks, motorcycles, bicycles, airplanes, helicopters, dolls, and more—made by adults who know that Western visitors have become fascinated with African toys. However they are classified, these expressive objects are also worthy of attention.

FINE OR CONTEMPORARY ART

The second half of the twentieth century saw an explosion of fine art (frequently also called contemporary art) on the continent, and by the end of that century

African artists were being recognized by the international art world, with representation by foreign galleries, invitations to participate in events such as the prestigious Venice Biennale, and artworks made part of the permanent collections of major museums worldwide. In most respects, fine artists in Africa are like artists everywhere: they have had at least some formal training, they work in a variety of media and styles, and few are able to make their living solely from selling their art.

Artists

Many African fine artists today, like artists the world over, are trained in art schools and universities at home and abroad. During the colonial period, formal art programs and schools were incorporated into postsecondary institutions of higher learning in a number of countries, including Ghana, Nigeria, Sudan, and Uganda. For example, one of the most influential, the program at Makerere University in Uganda, became a magnet for art students from all over eastern Africa beginning in 1940. The Margaret Trowell School of Industrial and Fine Arts at Makerere University, named after the Englishwoman who spearheaded its formation, has remained a major center for the study of art, with a curriculum that has expanded from drawing, painting, and sculpture to incorporate graphic design and digital arts. Its graduates, who include Francis Nnaggenda (Ugandan, b. 1936), Sam Ntiro (Tanzanian, 1923–1993), Elimo Njau (Kenyan, b. Tanzania, 1932), and Teresa Musoke (Ugandan, b. 1942), not only have become educators and advocates for the arts but also have gained international recognition for their own sculpture and painting. Since independence, other important schools have also been created, including the Ecole des Arts du Sénégal (now the Ecole Nationale des Beaux Arts), which was established in Dakar by President Léopold Senghor in 1960.

Study abroad has enabled many fine artists to hone their skills, broaden their visions, and participate more easily in the global contemporary arts scene. Not surprisingly, their destinations are most often countries with which their homelands have special political or cultural relationships. Pioneering Senegalese artists Iba N'Diaye (1928–2008) and Papa Ibra Tall (b. 1935), the first instructors at the Ecole des Arts du Sénégal, both were trained in France, for example. During the postcolonial period, destinations also include countries that have developed aid and collaborative programs in Africa. During the 1960s, for instance, with the signing of a cultural cooperation and trade agreement with the Soviet Union by the newly independent Malian government, art students from Mali studied at the Surikov Moscow State Academy Art Institute.

Back on the continent, more informal instruction in the form of workshops, organized during colonialism and later, have also provided training. One of the best-known artists who followed that path is Twins Seven Seven (Nigerian, 1944–2011). An accomplished musician and dancer, he began attending workshops organized by Ulli Beier, a German editor and writer, and his wife, artist Georgina Beier, in Osogbo, Nigeria, in the 1960s. These workshops, part of the Beiers' larger program

Figure 8.3. Twins Seven Seven (Nigerian, 1944–2011). *The Anti-Ghost Bird,*
1960s. Etching on paper. H. 14 7/8 in.
Indiana University Art Museum, gift of Roy and Sophia Sieber.
Photo by Kevin Montague.

of encouraging writers and visual artists and providing outlets for their work, stimulated Twins Seven Seven to try his hand at printmaking and painting; his depictions of the spiritual world and Yoruba folktales are characterized by a lively imagination and a distinctive style. *The Anti-Ghost Bird* (figure 8.3), an etching created during the 1960s, shows the energy and decorative use of line that characterize his work. More recently, in 1998, famed Nigerian printmaker Bruce Onobrakpeya (b. 1932), who has himself attended many workshops, including one in the 1960s at Osogbo, began the annual Harmattan Workshop, short courses in several media, all held during the same period and open to artists of all kinds and skill levels. Artist-organized workshops, frequently financed by outside corporate or nonprofit institutions, have become an important way for artists to interact with each other on both local and international levels.

Not all fine artists enroll in formal schooling or participate in workshops. Some learn how to work in their chosen media through apprenticeship or mentoring, much the same way that many traditional and popular artists do. The internationally recognized Malian photographer Malick Sidibé (b. 1936), for example, known for his images of Bamako youth culture during the 1960s and 1970s, learned his craft through an apprenticeship with a studio photographer. Likewise, Yoruba photographer Tijani Sitou (1932–1999) completed a three-year apprenticeship with a professional photographer in Gao, Mali, before opening his own studio in Mopti, a few hundred miles away, where for nearly thirty years he produced studio portraits that chronicle changing fashions in that city (figure 8.4). In addition, a few artists are self-taught, such as the Congolese artist Bodys Isek Kingelez (b. 1948), whose colorful, fantastic models of buildings and cities have been featured in group and solo exhibitions in Europe and the United States.

While many African fine artists would enjoy the freedom to pursue art exclusively, most, like their counterparts throughout the world, whether university-educated or self-taught, are not able to make their living solely from their art. Many, though, find related employment as art teachers or administrators at schools and universities, as cultural officials, or in other professions that allow them to maintain connections with the art world even if they are not full-time artists. For example, Abdoulaye Konaté (Malian, b. 1953), whose work has been shown both in Africa and abroad (plate 8.24), is currently the director of the Conservatoire des Arts et Métiers Multimédia Balla Fasseké Kouyaté in Bamako.

The relative ease with which people travel today creates questions about exactly what makes someone an *African* artist. A number of students who leave Africa for study remain abroad, appreciating the greater ease with which they can be connected to the global art scene. In addition, of course, as increasing numbers of Africans in all walks of life emigrate or live abroad for extended periods of time for other reasons, their direct contact with the continent becomes limited to vacations or other short trips. The British-Nigerian artist Yinka Shonibare (b. 1962), best known for his tableaus containing headless mannequins dressed in the kind of factory-printed cloth that has been popular in Africa for hundreds of years, is a

Figure 8.4. Tijani Adìgún Sitou (b. Nigeria, active in Mali, 1932–99). *See My Henna* [*Regardez mon henne*], 1983, printed 2006. Ink jet print. 12 by 12 in. *Indiana University Art Museum, gift of the Family of èlHadj Tijani Sitou, © The Family of èlHadj Tijani Sitou.*

good example of the increasingly common ambiguities associated with an "African" label. Born in London to Nigerian parents who had temporarily moved to England in pursuit of additional education, Shonibare and his family returned to Nigeria when he was three. He attended school in Lagos, but the family regularly vacationed in London, and at the age of sixteen he moved back there, first attending boarding school, then art school, where he earned an MFA in 1991. He currently makes London his home. Shonibare's work explores issues of race, class, and African identity and has been shown in exhibitions and museums devoted to Afri-

Plate 8.1. Luluwa peoples, Democratic Republic of the Congo. Standing figure. 19th century. Wood, incrustation. H. 17 in. Indiana University Art Museum, Wielgus Collection. *Photo by Michael Cavanagh and Kevin Montague, © Indiana University Art Museum.*

Plate 8.2. Songye peoples, Democratic Republic of the Congo. Power figure. Wood, iron, horn, cowrie shells, snakeskin, hair, incrustation. H. 12 ½ in. Indiana University Art Museum, Wielgus Collection. *Photo by Michael Cavanagh and Kevin Montague, © Indiana University Art Museum.*

Plate 8.3. Bamana peoples, Mali. Mask for Kòmò Society. Wood, horns, quills, feathers, fiber, animal hair, incrustation. L. 27 in. Indiana University Art Museum.
Photo by Michael Cavanagh and Kevin Montague, © Indiana University Art Museum.

Plate 8.4. Zaramo peoples, Tanzania. Figure. Wood. H. 6 $^{15}/_{16}$ in. Indiana University Art Museum. *Photo by Michael Cavanagh and Kevin Montague,* © *Indiana University Art Museum.*

Plate 8.5. Bamana peoples, Mali. Youth association masquerade. 1978. *Photo by Patrick McNaughton.*

Plate 8.6. Nok culture, Nigeria. Head. Ca. 285 BC– AD 515. Clay. H. 12 ¾ in. AP 1996.04. Kimbell Art Museum, Fort Worth, Texas. *Photo courtesy Kimbell Art Museum.*

Plate 8.7. Asante peoples, Ghana. *Kente* cloth (detail). Cotton, silk. Indiana University Art Museum. *Photo by Michael Cavanagh and Kevin Montague, © Indiana University Art Museum.*

Plate 8.8. Edo peoples, Kingdom of Benin, Nigeria. Commemorative head of a king. 17th century. Brass. H. 11 ½ in. Indiana University Art Museum. *Photo by Michael Cavanagh and Kevin Montague, © Indiana University Art Museum.*

Plate 8.9. Pende peoples, Democratic Republic of the Congo. Whistle. 19th century. Ivory. H. 4 ½ in. Collection of Rita and John Grunwald. *Photo by Michael Cavanagh and Kevin Montague, © Indiana University Art Museum.*

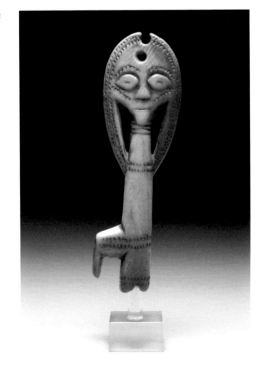

Plate 8.10. Ife, Nigeria. Head, possibly a King. 12th–14th century. Terracotta with residue of red pigment and traces of mica. H. 10 ½ in. AP 1994.04. Kimbell Art Museum, Fort Worth, Texas. *Photo courtesy Kimbell Art Museum.*

Plate 8.11. Jenne culture, Mali. Equestrian figure. 15th–18th century. Clay, pigment. H. 9 ½ in. *Photo by Michael Cavanagh and Kevin Montague,* © *Indiana University Art Museum.*

Plate 8.12. Sapi peoples, Sierra Leone. Afro-Portuguese saltcellar. Ca. 1490–1530. Ivory. H. 12 ³/₁₆ in. Seattle Art Museum, gift of Katherine White and the Boeing Company. *Photo courtesy Seattle Art Museum.*

Plate 8.13. Yoruba peoples, Nigeria. Staff for Esu/Elegba cult. Before 1930s. Wood, leather, cowrie shells, brass, bone, iron. H. 19 ¼ in. Indiana University Art Museum, Wielgus Collection. *Photo by Michael Cavanagh and Kevin Montague, © Indiana University Art Museum.*

Plate 8.14. Kota peoples, Gabon. Reliquary figure. Wood, brass, copper, iron. H. 22 ⅝ in. Collection of Rita and John Grunwald. *Photo by Michael Cavanagh and Kevin Montague, © Indiana University Art Museum.*

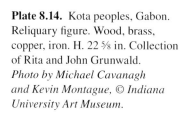

Plate 8.15. Mende peoples. Sierra Leone. Mask for the Sande Society. Wood. H. 15 ⅞ in. Indiana University Art Museum, gift of Toby and Barry Hecht. *Photo by Michael Cavanagh and Kevin Montague, © Indiana University Art Museum.*

Plate 8.16. Bidjogo peoples, Bissagos Islands, Guinea-Bissau. Initiation mask in the form of a shark head. Wood, pigment, fiber. L. 13 in. Indiana University Art Museum. *Photo by Michael Cavanagh and Kevin Montague, © Indiana University Art Museum.*

Plate 8.17. Lega peoples, Democratic Republic of the Congo. Figure for the Bwami Society. Wood, shells, wax or resin. H. 11 ½ in. Indiana University Art Museum, Wielgus Collection. *Photo by Michael Cavanagh and Kevin Montague, © Indiana University Art Museum.*

Plate 8.18.
Restaurant near
Kazimzumbwi,
Tanzania. 1985.
*Photo by Diane
Pelrine.*

Plate 8.19.
Mbwana
(Tanzania).
Tingatinga
painting.
1980s. Paint on
particleboard.
H. 12 in. Private
Collection.
*Photo by Kevin
Montague.*

Plate 8.20. *REVZ*, a painted bus (*matatu*) designed by Hasan Rasta and in use in Nairobi, Kenya, 2004–05. *Photo by Kitty Johnson.*

Plate 8.21. Ghana. Poster for Nigerian film *Cry for Help.* 1980s–'90s. Paint on fabric (disassembled sack for "Pride of the West" flour). H. 63 in. Indiana University Black Film Center/Archive. *Photo by Michael Cavanagh and Kevin Montague.*

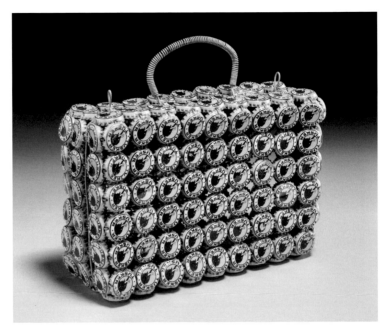

Plate 8.22. Kenya. Briefcase. 1990s. Beer-bottle caps, wire. Private collection. *Photo by Kevin Montague.*

Plate 8.23. Workshop of Ernest Anang Kwei, Teshi, Ghana. Coffin in the form of a fish. 2001. Wood, paint, satin, metal tacks. L. 114 in. Indiana University Art Museum, gift of William and Gayle Cook in honor of Alvin and Phyllis Rutner. *Photo by Michael Cavanagh and Kevin Montague, © Indiana University Art Museum.*

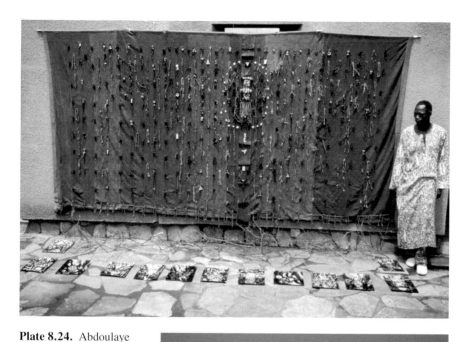

Plate 8.24. Abdoulaye Konaté (Malian, b. 1953) with his *Hommage aux Chasseurs du Mandé* (Tribute to the Hunters of Mande). 1994. Mixed media. W. 122 ¾ in. *Photo © Revue Noire.*

Plate 8.25. Clive Sithole (South African, b. 1971). *Uphiso.* 2007. Clay. H. 17 ½ in. Indiana University Art Museum purchase with funds from the Class of 1949 Endowed Curatorship for the Arts of Africa, Oceania, and the Americas. *Photo by Michael Cavanagh and Kevin Montague, © Indiana University Art Museum.*

Plate 8.26. Kalidou Sy (Senegalese, 1948–2005). *Ci Wara.* 1999.
Acrylic, clay, and metal on canvas. H. 21 in. Eileen Julien Collection.
Photo by Michael Cavanagh and Kevin Montague.

can art, but it has also been included in shows with no Africa connection, such as *Sensation: Young British Artists from the Saatchi Collection,* which toured London and New York at the end of the twentieth century.

Artists living abroad in response to political conditions in their countries of birth also account for a small but significant number. For some of these artists, time living outside Africa may add up to more years than those spent on the continent. For example, Wosene Worke Kosrof (b. 1950) received a BFA from the School of Fine Arts in Addis Ababa in 1972 but left his native Ethiopia in 1978, responding to the repressive and violent situation that enveloped the country following the deposition of Emperor Haile Selassie in a 1974 coup. Earning an MFA from Howard University in 1980, he has remained in the United States, building an international reputation for paintings with elements based on the script used to write Amharic, the national language of Ethiopia.

Fine Arts Materials, Techniques, Subjects, and Styles

The tremendous variety of materials, techniques, subject matter, and styles used today by artists the world over is also represented on the African continent. Certainly powerful and exciting fine art is being created in materials associated with traditional African arts, such as wood, cloth, and clay. South African Clive Sithole (b. 1971), for example, creates ceramics based on traditional Zulu forms, crossing long-standing gender divisions by working with clay, a medium traditionally associated with women. His *Uphiso* (2007, plate 8.25), for example, is based on a form used in the past to transport beer, but the raised images of three cattle circling the vessel and the beautifully mottled surface mark it as a contemporary interpretation.

Other artists have embraced materials and techniques that were brought from abroad, such as printmaking, oil painting on canvas, and photography. In addition, like artists worldwide, some African artists deemphasize the materials and techniques of classic fine arts, instead choosing forms such conceptual, performance, and installation art to express their ideas.

The use of manufactured and natural found materials to create art is worth special note. Though some artists may choose alternative materials because supplies such as oil paints and canvas are expensive and sometimes hard to come by, others purposefully choose to create art by salvaging and recycling used objects and materials. For the painter Kalidou Sy (Senegalese, 1948–2005), for example, the incorporation of found materials, such as the clay and metal fragments that are part of *Ci Wara* (plate 8.26) reflects his belief in the importance of artists interacting with their environments. Similarly, Maurice Mbikayi (b. 1974), a Congolese-born artist who has lived in South Africa since 2004, created his 2010 *Antisocial Network* series by fashioning human skulls from computer keyboard keys and resin to raise questions about the relationship between humans and technology.

No matter what the materials, some African artists believe that the contents, or subjects, of their artworks should show direct connections to their African experiences. This idea was particularly promoted in the early 1960s, when most African nations became independent and when the Négritude movement was particularly strong. It is seen in works of artists such as Papa Ibra Tall of Senegal, who advocated subject matter that was readily identifiable as African in his own paintings as well as in those of his students at the Ecole des Arts du Sénégal. Elsewhere, similar notions are evident in the work of Groupe Bogolan Kasobané, a collective of six artists who began working together in 1978 after studying painting at Mali's Institut National des Arts. They have rejected conventional canvas and commercial oil and acrylic paints, instead looking to locally available materials, particularly the hand-woven cotton and natural dyes used in making Bamana mud-dyed cloth. Unlike that cloth, which is traditionally patterned with nonfigural motifs that can be interpreted only by those familiar with the cloth, the creations of Groupe Bogolan Kasobané depict images that are widely accessible yet also related to West African life and culture.

Another Malian artist, Abdoulaye Konaté (b. 1953), also frequently draws on traditional arts in both subject matter and materials. The red ochre color of his 1994 wall-hanging textile *Hommage aux Chasseurs du Mandé* (Tribute to the Hunters of Mande, plate 8.24) and the small amulet-like additions attached to its surface are clear visual references to traditional Mande hunters' shirts, which are frequently a similar color and covered with animal teeth and claws as well as leather packets containing prayers to ensure the hunter's safety and success. While the large size of Konaté's textile—it is over ten feet wide and more than five feet tall—would not allow anyone to mistake it for clothing, for those familiar with Mande culture its appearance not only instantly evokes hunters' shirts but also calls to mind other aspects of Mande life such as the reddish earth of southern Mali, a rich cluster of ideas and practices associated with hunters and hunting (including special music and oral poetry), and spiritual beliefs and practices. In addition, more generally, *Hommage aux Chasseurs du Mandé* raises questions about the relationship between appearance and reality: while its attachments look like the amulets on the shirts that Mande hunters wear, do they have the same spiritual potency?

While *Hommage aux Chasseurs du Mandé* is clearly rooted in Konaté's Mande heritage and speaks most effectively to those familiar with that culture, some of his other work addresses pan-African and global issues, and in this respect too the artist is typical of his colleagues on the continent. For example, his 2005 *Gris-Gris pour Israël et la Palestine* again refers to the power of amulets or "gris-gris" while, through depictions of the Israeli flag and the Palestinian-Arab head scarf, reflecting on the long-standing conflict in the Middle East that has captured the world's attention.

Exhibitions, Audiences, and Patronage

Most African artists creating fine art have had a difficult time finding audiences and even venues for displaying their work. On the continent, the lack of well-developed gallery systems or other widely accepted means for making work available has made it challenging for artists to publicize, display, and sell their art. Furthermore, the small number of fine arts museums and galleries has meant that exhibitions routinely take place in embassy cultural centers, hotels, and other businesses unrelated to art, or in other impromptu display spaces.

Though beginning in the 1990s there has been a marked increase in the presence of contemporary African art in Western museums, exhibiting outside of Africa has also been challenging. While the major twentieth-century movements in European and American art had their roots in the work of artists who were inspired by traditional African art, such as Pablo Picasso and Henri Matisse, through most of that century African art that showed clear affinities with those movements was frequently labeled as "derivative," a pejorative designation in a sphere where originality is requisite for recognition. During the same period, other work was charged with being too African; frequently these figurative depictions of scenery and daily rural life were considered too parochial to command attention in major Western art centers. The reasons that contemporary African art received little praise—or even acknowledgment—go beyond the actual art, however, and include lingering colonial attitudes, racism, and the structure and business of the American and European museum and gallery systems.

Traditional, popular, and fine arts do not exist in isolation from one another. The popular arts, for example, often apply a population's traditional ideas or activities to a new form of expression, frequently using new materials. Many contemporary artists who show their painting, photographs, sculpture, and mixed media creations in galleries all over the world, often quite divorced from their home communities, nevertheless present imagery that engages and explores the values and concepts their societies hold dear.

Whatever the form and whether visually complex or relatively simple, art is always composed of intricate layers of human imagination and social activity. However it is categorized, African art has as its base shared beliefs about the nature of the world and cosmos, whether those beliefs are shared within a region of the continent, as with most traditional art, or on a global scale.

While Islam, Christianity, colonialism, and participation in global economies and histories have certainly changed much African expressive culture, much traditional art persists, indeed flourishes. Much of it has been transformed by its creators and audiences into new forms, a process that has been going on in Africa for millennia. And much African art has proven profoundly influential elsewhere in the world. It was instrumental in the development of European modern art, and it has been part of the complex historical processes that produced African American folk art and the spiritual arts of numerous places, including Haiti, Cuba, Brazil, parts of Mexico, and parts of New York City, Chicago, Los Angeles, and a host of other Western cities.

Much of the art in all three categories presents a well-developed aesthetic acumen, produced by skilled and thoughtful artists. The range of forms, functions, and programs of symbolism across the continent is astounding, as is the highly innovative use of materials. These features alone make African art worth studying. But just as important for those who seek a rich understanding of the world and the place of people in it, or a broader understanding of the problems all human beings face and the variety of solutions they can use to solve them, the themes and situations the African arts address offer insights into humanity from which everyone can gain.

SUGGESTIONS FOR FURTHER READING

African Arts (Los Angeles). 1967–.
Barber, Karin. 1987. "Popular Arts in Africa." *African Studies Review* 30, no. 3: 1–78.
Enwezor, Okwui, and Chika Okeke-Agulu. 2009. *Contemporary African Art since 1980.* Bologna, Italy: Damiani.
Grove Art Online. www.oxfordartonline.com/public/book/oao_gao.
Kasfir, Sidney Littlefield. 1999. *Contemporary African Art.* London: Thames and Hudson.
McNaughton, Patrick, and Diane Pelrine. 2012. "Art, Art History, and the Study of Africa." In *Oxford Bibliographies in African Studies,* ed. Thomas Spear. New York: Oxford University Press.
Visonà, Monica Blackmun, Robin Poynor, and Herbert M. Cole. 2008. *A History of Art in Africa.* 2nd ed. Upper Saddle River, NJ: Pearson/Prentice Hall.
Willett, Frank. 2002. *African Art.* 3rd ed. London: Thames and Hudson.

9 African Music Flows

Daniel B. Reed and Ruth M. Stone

A man walked down the street in the busy Adjame marketplace in Abidjan, Ivory Coast, in West Africa. Amid the sounds of the street—honking horns, ringing cell phones, goat cries, people's' voices—he heard the latest hit song by reggae singer Tiken Jah Fakoly drifting toward him from a CD seller's stall in the market. The song began with a distinctive slide guitar line, which was a sample from a 1990 recording by Geoffrey Oryema of Uganda in eastern Africa. Anchored by the repeating guitar line, the song developed as a twenty-one-string harp lute, the *kora*, entered along with a drum set and a keyboard. The man hesitated before the CD stand, taking in the song's compelling groove or rhythmic pattern and contemplating the lyrics, which criticize the treatment of young girls in village contexts. Finally, an amplified call to prayer coursed out of loudspeakers, reminding him to continue on toward the mosque for the Friday prayer.

In this scene, ambient street noise was layered with sounds and instruments that reference other parts of Africa and the rest of the world. The reggae music reflected influences from Caribbean Jamaican music as well as African American jazz and rhythm and blues. The slide guitar also derived from African American music practice. But the performer on the slide guitar played music from an East African artist from Uganda. Then the *kora,* which is associated with West African music from the savanna area, was layered with the drum set and keyboard, reflecting influence from popular music of the West. Such layering of disparate kinds of music is typical of the genius in so many music performances in Africa.

Later that week, the same man, who is of Mau ethnicity—one of sixty ethnic groups in Ivory Coast—traveled several hundred kilometers by bus to his natal village in the west of the country to attend his father's funeral. As is typical of a funeral of the Mau people, several musical ensembles played, including a percussion and vocal group that accompanied a masked dancer. Because this genre of mask and music originated among the Mau's southern neighbors, the Dan ethnic group,

Figure 9.1. Performance of stilt mask spirit *(gegblèèn)*, Dan people, Biélé, Côte d'Ivoire, 1997.
Daniel B. Reed.

the vocalists sang Dan songs in the Dan language to honor the Mau man's life. At a key moment, the masked performer sang, *"Ee, ge ya yi kan-bo,"* "(The *ge* spirit has crossed the river)." This song indicated that the spirit *ge* had arrived from the world of the ancestors to bless those in attendance at the funeral. In response to the spirit's call, singers responded, *"Zere ya-ya."* The vocable response, without lexical meaning, nonetheless expressed great sentiment and connection: that the spirit's call has been received. It also illustrated that musical events are frequently peopled not only by those individuals who ordinarily share time and space or contemporaries but by supernatural beings as well. These spirits may be ancestors who lived before and share neither time nor space ordinarily. But in a musical performance moment, time and space may be dissolved as ordinary people and spirits contact each other.

Another instance of such contact with spirits in musical performance took place among Kpelle performers in Liberia when a man playing the *gbegbetele,* or multiple bow lute, called out to his tutelary spirit, the entity who he felt was responsible for making his performance really fine, "Eh Gbono-kpate we" (Eh, Gbono-kpate). Shortly he sang in a high-pitched voice, "Oo," signaling that the tutelary spirit had arrived and was now present at the performance.

These examples not only illustrate the central importance of the spirit world mingling with the everyday world in musical performance in many parts of Africa. They also demonstrate a fundamental structural premise—a call, a response, an exchange that is central to understanding music performance as well as the ways that African musics have developed over time. In the cases above, the call-and-response took place between individuals communicating with each other in a musical event where they are for a time co-present.

Call-and-response is frequently multilayered in performance ensembles. A soloist sings a call and a chorus composed of many singers responds. A master drummer performs a call on his drum, and a dancer responds directly to his invitation. Simultaneously the supporting drums are responding to the master drummer's call. So the call-and-response creates a complex web of relationships between singers and instrumentalists. Sometimes the call-and-response is so close and tight that a side-blown horn might play only one or two notes of the call and another horn may respond with one or two notes. A third and then fourth horn may enter, all fitting in between one another in a carefully calibrated pattern of call-and-response.

Musics in Africa have been characterized by movement and flow—of sound, people, and ideas across time and space. These aspects are clearly evident in the scenes above. Music flowed across boundaries between the worlds of the living and the ancestors along with spirits who are considered participants in music events. And the masked performers routinely borrowed traditions from neighboring ethnic groups, creatively reinterpreting these outside influences. The Mau man himself, like millions of others across the continent, regularly traveled back and forth between city and village, integrating cultural ideas and practice from urban and rural contexts. Meanwhile, like African American hip-hop artists, reggae musician Fakoly

Figure 9.2. Performance of transverse horn *(turu)* ensemble, Kpelle people, Baokwole, Bong country, Liberia.
Indiana University Liberian Collections. Photograph by Quasie T. Vincent.

borrowed and recontextualized a musical motif—the catchy guitar line—originally created by another musician two thousand miles and nearly two decades removed.

Such reformatting of the music is considered both creative and clever and much to be admired. Extraordinary musicians draw upon a wide range of resources to fashion their music and draw from a wide range of materials—often unexpected to those looking for some kind of "pure" African music.

People, ideas, and goods flow throughout, in, and out of Africa, circulating around the globe. This chapter emphasizes an understanding of music within these flows. As if using a computer-based mapping system that allows the user to zoom in and out, the text will shift between viewing Africa from afar—taking in a broad view of geography and interactions linking various parts of the world—and from up close, looking at particular local musical practices. Whether considering broad historical trends or specific contemporary musical ideas and practices, in every case it is evident that music is central to the flow of African life. Music is not a frill but a vital part of human contact and interaction. As one Kpelle ritual specialist put it, if you're upset, you make music to calm down. If you are happy and excited, you make music to arrive at the point of calm. Music becomes a centering point for people as they life their lives.

ZOOM IN: MUSIC IN THE FLOW OF LIFE

African peoples make and listen to musics that are intimately bound to the visual and dramatic arts as well as the larger fabric of daily life. Singing can hardly be conceived without dancing. Instrumental playing gives voice to a material object that is an extension of a person. Singers often enact or dramatize what they are singing, particularly if it is a narrative story.

Performance permeates the life of African communities across the continent. Music, as many Africans view it, is not a thing of beauty to be admired in isolation. Rather it exists only as woven into the larger fabric that also combines games, dance, words, drama, and visual art. As A. M. Ipoku, director of the Ghana Dance Ensemble, noted to ethnomusicologist Barbara Hampton, dance and music should be so closely connected that one "can see the music and hear the dance." Or as a chief in Cameroon expressed to art historian Robert Farris Thompson, "The dancer must listen to the drum. When he is *really* listening, he creates within himself an echo of the drum, then he has started really to dance" (Thompson 1974). And the words that mean "performance" or "event," whether the *pele* of the Kpelle or *lipapali* of the Basotho, are applied not only to music making, dancing, and speaking but also to children's games and sports. Thus, singing and dancing mingle with theater and game and sport, and they are all considered part of the fabric of performance. One sense mingles with another almost invisibly as the visual and auditory and kinesthetic interweave with one another.

In political campaigns singers promote candidates for political office. As Kofi Busia campaigned for the presidency of Ghana, a musical warning was piped from a roving van about the political activities of Kwame Nkrumah, a former leader of the country. Owusu Brempong recalls the song text: "Before it rains, the wind precedes. I told you but you did not listen. Before it rains, the wind precedes. I told you but you did not listen."

Griots, professional praise and criticism singers, on many occasions conveyed messages for their rulers as they have since before the time of Sunjata (1230–1255), the first emperor of Mali.

Performers of *domeisia,* traditional narratives of the Mende people of Sierra Leone, fashioned words, song, and gesture for evening entertainment. Women improvised a comfortable call-and-response pattern as they bent over to hoe the soil for rice planting and sing the songs of work. Elsewhere, a "money bus" driver played a tape in his tape player and the lyrics of Bob Marley and the sounds of reggae rose as the assistant ran along the side of the bus. Gaining speed, he then hopped on board through the open door, jogging a dance to the ambient sound. The members of the East and Central African Apostolic Church of John Maranke invoked the presence of the Holy Spirit with songs. In all of these settings music has been integrated into life, and though diversity throughout Africa is apparent, some common elements penetrate the myriad of details.

A description of an event observed by John Chernoff in northern Ghana shows the interweaving of different media in a single occasion:

> Dagomba funerals are spectacles. The final funeral of an important or well-loved man or woman can draw several thousand people as participants and spectators. Small-scale traders also come to do business, setting up their tables to sell cigarettes, coffee, tea, bread, fruits, and other commodities to the milling crowds. Spread out over a large area, all types of musical groups form their circles. In several large circles, relatives and friends dance to the music of dondons and gongons. The fiddlers are also there. After a session in the late afternoon, people rest and begin reassembling between nine and ten o'clock in the evening. By that time, several Simpa groups have already begun playing. Two or three Atikatika groups also arrive and find their positions, and by eleven o'clock the funeral is in full swing. After midnight more groups come to dance Baamaya or other special dances like Jera or Bila, though the latter are not common. Baamaya dancers dress outlandishly, with bells tied to their feet and waists, wearing headdresses and waving fans. The dance is wonderful and strenuous: while gongons, flutes, and a dondon play the rhythms of Baamaya, the dancers move around their circle, twisting their waists continuously until the funeral closes at dawn.

Some of these same dance genres are also performed in other contexts, such as that of the Ghana Dance Ensemble, which often presents a shortened version of Baamaya on concert stages. Thus, music from one context flows and inflects another context, moving from ritual observance to entertainment, all the while transforming but retaining a core of the original genre.

While the funeral performance described above took place in the 1970s, such traditions persist in the twenty-first century. Funerals became prime sites for political protest during periods of civil unrest. This was the case not only in South Africa during the apartheid era but also in Liberia's civil war, which plagued the country from 1989 to 2003. At the funeral of James Gbarbea in 1989, a former cabinet minister and political leader, who had quarreled with dictator Samuel Doe, a Kpelle choir sang words that they could not speak without being thrown in jail. But in music they had relative immunity to sing:

> Jesus is the big, big, *zoe* [ritual priest].
> We all will go.
> Doe will go.

Thus, political expression that was suppressed in everyday life found a place in ritual music events, particularly funerals, where people's lives were being commemorated. The charged ideas that could not be spoken in public could be sung at funerals. People found considerable solace and community power in being able to express themselves on these musical occasions.

African indigenous religious practice often conceptually links music to other arts and ideas. In performances of *Ge* forest spirits among the Dan of Ivory Coast,

Figure 9.3. St. Peter's Kpelle choir rattle *(kee)* players, Kpelle people, Monrovia, Montserrado county, Liberia.
Indiana University Liberian Collections. Photograph by Quasie T. Vincent.

all elements of the performance—the dancer's mask and costume, dance steps, spoken word such as proverbs, drum rhythms, and song—are conceptually integrated and believed to be the manifestation of *Ge*. What others might hear as "music" is defined simply as the sonic aspect of the presence of spirit.

As is the case for Dan *Ge* performance, music in Africa is often fundamentally tied to particular activities and/or groupings of people. Children perform specific music and dance for their communities at the completion of initiation to mark their passage into adulthood. Women sing songs to the rhythms they create in grinding grain with huge wooden mortars and pestles. In West Africa, Mande hunters, or *donso*, play a hunter's harp lute *(donso ngoni)* and sing songs to encourage their brethren to overcome adversity in the pursuit of game animals. In each of these cases, music is inherent to activities and processes that are part of the flow of life in African communities. Music is so much more than a frivolous expression that can be added on as an extra entertainment. Rather, it is a critical part of the lifeblood of human interaction in African communities, communities that are often under the stress of war and other kinds of duress.

Figure 9.4. Performance of dance mask spirit *(tankoege),* Dan people,
Grand Gbapleu, Côte d'Ivoire, 1997.
Daniel B. Reed.

ZOOM OUT: AFRICA WITHIN CULTURAL FLOWS

Music also exists as a part of a larger world, a world in which people constantly exchange culture via mass media, mass communications, commerce, and increased human mobility. Africans hear music through radio, television, CDs, cassettes, and cellphones, and in urban internet cafés. They quite naturally incorporate these sounds into local music. It is not unusual to find indigenous drums playing with electric guitar and other instruments, amplified electronically, even as songs are sung in indigenous languages. African musics, in turn, are broadcast around the world via these same media. As increasing numbers of Africans immigrate to Europe and North America, they exchange music and other cultural ideas with their new communities, all the while remaining in almost daily contact with their homelands via cell phone and computer messages.

Zeye Tete, a well-known singer from West Africa, received funding from a nongovernmental organization to film a music video of vocal music and dance while she lived in a refugee camp in Côte d'Ivoire during the civil war in neighboring Liberia. She organized some of the young girls in the camp to be a chorus of singers and dancers and accompany her solos as she created a visual as well as sonic spec-

Figure 9.5. Slit-log *(keleng)* ensemble, Kpelle people, Sanoyea, Bong county, Liberia. *Indiana University Liberian Collections. Photograph by Quasie T. Vincent.*

tacle within the camp. When she immigrated to Philadelphia several years later, that video circulated back and forth across the Atlantic among Liberians on the African continent and Liberians residing in the United States, documenting in music the pain of the war as they lived without a home, awaiting the peace and a resolution to their trauma.

Although one cannot deny the dramatic increases in intercultural exchange occurring in the globalized world of the twenty-first century, cultural exchange is nothing new to Africa. In musical and cultural terms, Africa can be understood as a continent, but viewing Africa as a separate space in isolation from its surrounding geographical context paints at best a partial picture. North Africa, for example, is as much a part of the Mediterranean region as it is a part of the African continent, and the horn of Africa is separated from the Arabian Peninsula only by the extremely narrow Red Sea. These geographical realities present themselves clearly in musical instruments, genres of music, ideas about music, and musical aesthetics that are to greater or lesser extents shared across continental boundaries.

How has this happened? In contrast to stereotypes of Africa, precolonial African history was characterized less by peoples living in great isolation and more by a great deal of cultural interchange. Of the many forms of cultural interaction in African history, none has been more important than trade. Trade routes crisscrossed the Sahara, linking sub-Saharan Africa with the Maghreb and points beyond, including Europe and the Middle East. When people exchange goods, they exchange other cultural elements as well, including musical instruments and aesthetics. Pilgrimage has proven to be another prominent promoter of cultural exchange. Muslims from all over Africa traveled north through the Sahara Desert to reach Mecca and Medina, the holy cities in Arabia where they carried out religious rituals that became high points of their lives. As pilgrims from Africa traveled to Arabia, they brought with them musical practices and instruments, which they shared with people along the way. In a reverse way, traders and others from Arabia and northern Africa brought musical instruments and practices to other parts of Africa. The large number of string instruments in the Sahel and Western Sudan regions of West Africa is likely due to that region's long-standing interactions with North Africa, primarily through trade and the spread of Islam. One-stringed fiddles (e.g., Hausa *gorge* or Dagbamba *gondze*) almost certainly were introduced to Sudanic West Africa via contact with Arabic North African traders, educators, and proselytizers of Islam. In such circumstances of cultural exchange, goods and ideas flowed both ways. The three-stringed bass lute *(hajhuj)*, played by Moroccans in *gnawa* spirit possession ceremonies, arrived from the south with slaves brought from West Africa. In the same way, drums from West Africa can be heard playing at night in some towns of western Arabia. Pilgrims left some of these instruments or even settled there permanently, changing the musical landscape of the places they traveled. In the late twentieth century, the *jembe* drum was introduced to Europe and North America primarily by touring African national ensembles, especially Guinea's Les Ballets Africains. Originally from the Mande region near Guinea's border with Mali, this drum eventually spread across the globe, from Japan to Canada to Germany becoming a ubiquitous symbol of Africa.

In other cases, scholars have found it can be difficult to determine the direction of the flow of influence. For instance, though plucked lutes (e.g., the Maninka *koni,* Fulbe *hoddu,* Wolof *xalam,* and Hausa *gurumi*) are played primarily by Muslim peoples in West Africa, these instruments' points of origin have not been definitively proven. Scholars assume that among this same family of instruments can be found the antecedent of the American banjo—an instrument that was created by African Americans.

Even within sub-Saharan Africa itself, single instruments can tell the story of cultural flows and exchange. That the one-stringed fiddle mentioned above can be found in a belt stretching about two thousand miles, from Senegal to Lake Chad, indicates a history of interactions of groups in this region of the continent. Similarly, from the 1920s to the present day, Liberian Kru sailors traveled from port to

Figure 9.6. Bamana musician Almamy Ba playing a four-stringed lute
(bajuru ngoni) at his home, Bamako, Mali.
Daniel B.Reed.

port on the West African coast not only delivering goods but also spreading the guitar and the palm-wine guitar style.

ZOOM IN: MUSICAL INSTRUMENTS AND AESTHETIC PRACTICE

While particular instruments allow us to trace African musical and cultural history, a general consideration of musical instrument types showcases the rich variety of music making in Africa. For Africans, instruments are humanlike, and the sounds of instruments are often considered "voices." In West Africa, for example, different strings of a frame zither serve as different voices: that of the mother for a low-pitched string, and that of the child for a higher-pitched string. Two closely pitched strings may be called brother and sister strings. The Lugbara of Uganda name the five strings of the lyre with status terms for women. Shona musicians in

Zimbabwe told ethnomusicologist Paul Berliner that they name the manuals of the *mbira* as "the old men's voices" for the lowest register, "the young men's voices" for the middle register, and "the women's voices" for the highest register. They go further to describe individual keys: "mad person, put in a stable position, the lion, swaying of a person going into trance, to stir up, big drum, and mortar, with the names showing something about how the key works in the music."

String instruments, with their subtle and often quiet "voices," are often overshadowed in the popular consciousness by the great variety of drums in Africa. But string instruments abound on the continent as well. Perhaps best known is the *kora,* the harp lute that forms the personal extension of the West African *griot,* the itinerant praise-singer, historian, and social commentator of Mali, Senegal, and the Mande region in general. Equally important are the multiple bow lute, frame zither, musical bow, harp, lyre, and lute. The haunting sound of a whispered song of East Africa accompanied by the low, resonant, string-bass-like sounds of the trough zither is hard to forget.

If only drums are taken into account, there are goblet, hourglass, conical, barrel, cylindrical, and frame (tambourine) drums that range from handheld size to large enough to require a stand to support them or several men to carry them in procession. These instruments sound as "voices" of penetrating tone colors and distinct pitches, not simply rhythms. Their character is much more fully developed than is that of drums in the usual Western music conception. The *entenga* tuned drum ensembles of the kings in Uganda, the processional drums carried on horseback in northern Nigeria, the ritual drums laid horizontally on platforms in coastal West Africa, and the hourglass drum of West Africa that plays glides and slides of pitch as the player presses the thongs connecting the heads and tightening the skins with lightning velocity—all these are examples of African drums.

The *mbira,* or *sansa,* as it is known in other areas, with its plucked metal tongues, is a versatile instrument. It is often played at healing events for the Shona of Zimbabwe. In these rituals, musicians gradually build musical intensity and suspense. Finally a medium is chosen by the spirits and becomes possessed.

Rattles of all kinds, both containers and those with a bead network on the outside, join ensembles. Rattles are frequently attached to stringed instruments or drums to make the sound more complex and interesting aesthetically. These attached rattles, often metal discs, may come from found objects such as soft-drink bottle caps.

Clapperless bells struck with a stick are important, often setting the time line of the ensemble. Hollowed-out logs are slit "drums" played alone or in ensemble. The variety of struck, plucked, and shaken instruments stretches the imagination. And because sound is more important than appearance, a struck beer bottle will often replace a struck boat-shaped iron.

Many African peoples associate the sound of the blown instruments, such as flutes, whistles, and horns, with voices of spirits. The spirit of the Kpelle Poro secret society is realized through globe-shaped pottery whistles. Likewise, certain

Dan *ge* spirits can manifest solely in sound produced by blowing through stone whistles and an earthenware pot.

Horns, which often appear in ensembles, are associated with the courts of kings and chiefs. They accompany the ruler and sometimes are played exclusively for his or her entourage. Horns come in many sizes and shapes and are made of wood, cow horn, ivory, or metal. In the Ashanti area of Ghana, local chiefs historically kept short horns, while paramount chiefs were permitted long trumpet ensembles. In more recent times, Africans have extended this historical practice by honoring nation-state leaders with these same ensembles. A Kpelle paramount chief in Liberia

Figure 9.7. Young women dancers emerging from the Sande secret society, Kpelle people, Dige, Bong county, Liberia, 2009.
Indiana University Liberian Collections. Photograph by Quasie T. Vincent.

sent his ensemble of six ivory trumpets trimmed in leopard skin and his trumpeters for the 1976 inauguration of President William Tolbert, to honor the national leader. In 2012 President Ellen Johnson Sirleaf of Liberia had a royal trumpeter assigned to her office who accompanied her on important occasions and signaled her arrival by blowing on a single side-blown ivory horn.

The Babenzele of the forest region of Central Africa play a breathy-sounding flute that leaps from low to high register and back again. The flute players alternate from flute to voice and back to flute. The singing tone is scarcely different to the ear from that of the flute, so similar is the sound they strive to achieve. Other peoples play flutes, singly or in groups. Some famous ensembles include the royal flute and drum players of the country of Benin.

Though instruments of a single kind, such as six side-blown horns or a group of xylophones, may play together in an ensemble, it is much more typical that ensembles consist of a variety of instruments, ranging from drums to horns to struck clapperless bells. Furthermore, these heterogeneous orchestras often perform with one or more singers and dancers in a complex ensemble with different types of participants.

Dancing is ubiquitous in many ensembles and considered a usual part of any performance. In some cases these dancers are specially trained and exhibit extraordinary skill in their movements. One of the places that special dance training takes place for Kpelle children is in the secret society, where they are provided with special instruction, particularly if they show aptitude. On some occasions dancers appear in masked form. On these occasions they represent aspects of the spiritual power and appear with wooden carvings and fabric covering the dancer's face and head. Raffia or fabric may disguise the rest of the dancer's body to complete the costume. In all cases the body movement to music is important and fits integrally with the instrumental and vocal music.

ZOOM OUT: FLOWS OF IDEAS AND SOUNDS

Indigenous musical instruments, along with aesthetic notions such as timbral preferences or tone colors and musical forms, flow through many types of music in Africa, from the traditional to the popular. As previously mentioned, popular music bands frequently combine local instruments with those of foreign origin. Nigerian *fuji* performers integrate indigenous hourglass pressure drums with lap steel guitars, electric guitars, keyboards and drum kits. Malian *wassoulou* songs, heavily rooted in local hunters' music, feature a harp lute *(kamale ngoni)* derived from the hunter's harp lute *(donso ngoni)*. Additional strings and guitar-style tuning pegs are added to the *kamale ngoni,* which, along with acoustic guitar, violin, and iron rasp, accompanies songs sung by women in call-and-response style. In Zimbabwe, *chimurenga* musicians transfer melodic patterns from the *mbira* (plucked lamellophone) onto the electric guitar, then add bass, drums, the *mbira* itself, and call-and-response vocals to create a style that sounds like an electrified version of music from *bira* spirit possession rituals. These kinds of musical blends are facilitated by mass media and the constant movement of Africans back and forth between urban and village contexts.

Similarly, traditional musicians incorporate ideas and sounds from urban popular music styles into older forms. In Dan masked performances, master drummers quote rhythms from popular songs heard on radio and television in their drummed solos. When the dancing *ge* mask spirit matches the rhythms with ankle bells on his dancing feet, the crowd recognizes the rhythms and responds with shouts and hearty applause. In Senegal, Wolof *sabar* drummers create rhythmic passages *(bàkk)* inspired by everything from music seen on Japanese and American television programs to the sound of an electric fan.

Musical styles, and indeed even musicians themselves, flow back and forth between traditional performance contexts and performances on concert stages. In Ghana, Akom ritual practitioners perform in Akan villages, where performance spaces are formed by a crowd gathered in a circle in the village commons. Some of these same musicians will also perform Akom on stages in the capital city, Accra, often to honor the Ghanaian nation.

Just as indigenous musical instruments and ideas about music have flowed from local community contexts to concert stages, they have also made their way into Christian worship services. In many parts of Africa, early Christian missionaries stressed European-style four-part harmony to the exclusion of local musical practice. Over time, though, Africans began incorporating local instruments and even local aesthetics into church services. Every other Sunday at the Catholic church in Man, Ivory Coast, for example, a Dan chorus performs, using Dan drums and rattles and singing hymns in harmonies or parallel fourths in call-and-response manner, according to Dan custom. This pattern has been replicated in many places on the continent, as Africans, via music and dance, have crafted a form of Christian worship that more closely matches their cultural and ethnic identities than the music introduced by early missionaries. At the same time, these Christian churches have also incorporated African American religious musics. In Liberia, a typical Sunday service in a Lutheran church in Monrovia is often the occasion for the indigenous style of music from the Kpelle and Loma peoples as well as gospel songs, transplanted from the United States, and hymns from the hymnbook in four-harmony. The electronic organ is played alongside the electric guitar and the indigenous drums and gourd rattle.

At times, ideas flow through music in a covert way. In the Zimbabwean war for independence, which, like the musical style mentioned above, was called the *chimurenga* (literally, "struggle"), musicians recorded songs using metaphors in the indigenous Shona language that communicated coded messages to freedom fighters. Colonial administrators would not understand the lyrics until the *chimurenga* songs were broadcast over the radio and the message had already been communicated. Similarly, *chimurenga* artists used Shona proverbs as song texts to criticize colonial rulers:

Chiri mumusakasaka   He who is (hiding) in a grass shelter
Chinozinzwira   gets a firsthand taste of discomfort

Since the rulers were not mentioned by name, and interpretation of the proverbs required a certain level of cultural knowledge that the rulers generally lacked, the songs' meanings were lost on them, but they were clearly communicated to Shona audiences. Meanwhile, in rural gatherings, villagers drummed, danced, and sang to raise the spirits of visiting soldiers. Multiple kinds of music were thus used as resources for the ultimately successful struggle against the colonial powers, and the sounds and texts of these styles became associated with the struggle itself.

In this case, serious messages and protest were conveyed in what was on the surface entertainment music. Like the choir in Liberia who performed at a funeral shortly before the civil war, musicians in Zimbabwe carried out political struggles through music.

ZOOM IN: SOUNDS IN CIRCULATION

Sound in Africa is everywhere noticed, admired, and shaped. Bus drivers take pride in horns that play tunes. Postal workers in Ghana cancel stamps in a deliberate rhythm that not only accomplishes the task at hand but entertains the workers as they interlock their rhythms. In African musics, sound imitates many things—the sounds of nature, of birds, of spirits. Virtually everything is subject to portrayal in sound and all of these voices combine in music events.

Sound becomes a medium for other senses as well. Consider the plight of the woman in this text of a song recorded by Ruth M. Stone in Liberia:

Our fellow young women, I raised my eyes to the sky, I lowered them. My tears fell *gata-gata* like corn from an old corn farm.

Gata-gata imitates not only the audible dropping of the corn kernels but the visual glimpsing of the tears rolling down the woman's face and falling to the ground in full drops. On other occasions singers depict visual beauty. They sing about the smooth, shiny blackness of a well-carved bowl with a thin exterior wall that the hero's wife carves in a Kpelle epic. Or a singer tries to show a little boy running very fast by imitating the sound of his running: *ki-li-ki-li-ki-li.*

Timbre, or tone color, the shading of sound that makes a trumpet sound different from a flute, a metal gong from a drum, matters a great deal to many Africans. English-speakers, however, lack the basic vocabulary to describe timbre, and Western staff notation only crudely indicates anything about it. In the 1930s ethnomusicologist George Herzog made some early cylinder phonograph recordings and discovered that among the Jabo of southeastern Liberia musical sounds are conceived as "large" or "small"; the large sounds are found in the lower register of pitches, and the small sounds are found in the upper register. The Kpelle of central

Liberia talk about sound in similar ways. But when they refer to large voices and small voices, they are commenting not only about pitch but about tone color as well. They think of a large voice as resonant and hollow, "voice swallowed," while a small voice is more penetrating and less resonant, "voice coming out." Dan drummers distinguish *gbin* sounds from those that are *kpè*. *Gbin* sounds are lower in pitch but also "heavier," referring to timbral density. To create a more *gbin* sound, a drummer will add a buzzing metal resonator to his instrument and then strike the drum's head in such a way to bring out the lowest frequencies and darker tones. *Kpè* sounds, by contrast, are considered "dry," and are achieved by striking the drum head near its edge to emphasize a less resonant timbre and higher pitch.

People in Africa highly value musical "voices" in interaction, and as a result often think of performance in a transactional sense. Like two people pulling at either end of a tug-of-war rope, rather than two people simply standing alone, one part rarely exists without the other. To understand one part is to do so only by seeing how it balances with another. Two xylophone players in southeast Africa sit opposite each other and share the same instrument. One has the responsibility of starting the performance; the other responds. One player fits his notes in between the notes of the other player. Similarly, an *mbira* player of Zimbabwe designates one part he plays as *kushaura* (to lead the piece) and the other part as *kutsinhira* (to exchange parts of a song). Africans extend this same transactional tendency to popular music instrumentation as well. Fela Kuti's Afrobeat bands would feature multiple guitar lines that seemed to converse with each other throughout his lengthy songs.

In a different sense, the prevalent call-and-response form of African music is transactional. A soloist gives the call and the chorus replies. Though the parts may overlap and form a neat dovetail so that no space between the two is obvious, the solo holds license to vary while the chorus gives never-changing support. In this way the Kpelle speak of the singer "raising the song" and the chorus "agreeing underneath the song." An hourglass drummer has problems playing his part alone, even though the beats of his part cross with the second drum. The drummer complains that he cannot "hear" his part without the second drum playing, expressing the idea that drums converse much as singers do.

Performers take the notion of transaction beyond the call-and-response, for they delight in segmentation and fragmentation within a performance from which they later create a profound togetherness. While in call-and-response one part performs a phrase of music and the other part answers with another phrase of music, in hocket a number of musicians each play one or two notes that all combine to make a single melody. Each part is much shorter and the fit is much tighter than in ordinary call-and-response. The Kpelle horn ensembles mentioned earlier, groups that traditionally are attached to the chiefs, delight in this idea. Six horns combine their brief motifs to make a unit of music. The Kpelle hocket vocally in bush-clearing songs, where the voices interlock with great precision even as the slit drums are being played in the background. The Shona of Zimbabwe interlock panpipe sounds with voice and syllables and add leg- and hand-rattle accompaniment. Indeed, the hocket, in which performers depend upon split-second coordination, is one of the most highly valued music forms in Africa. A song might begin quite simply, but as the performance progresses, the performers add layer upon layer of segments and fragments with voices, instruments, and rattles. They all fit together in a complex of sound and movement and create a living, vibrating event of considerable beauty.

ZOOM OUT: CYCLES OF EXCHANGE

Call-and-response is just one of many aesthetic practices that has circulated widely as African peoples and their musics have spread globally. Africa can be understood to be a part of a trans-Atlantic region in which peoples of African descent live in great numbers, from South America to the Caribbean to North America and Europe. Africa can also be understood as part of a trans–Indian Ocean region, including Arabia, India, and other parts of Asia, where Africans now live.

A cycle of cultural and musical exchange between Africa and the Americas began with the horrific dispersal of African peoples throughout the Americas during the Atlantic slave trade, which lasted from the sixteenth to the nineteenth centuries. Another cycle of cultural and musical exchange took place between African and Arabia as another era of slave trade brought Africans from the eastern, central, and southern African regions to Arabia and the Indian subcontinent. African peoples in the Americas blended African and European musical ideas to create new musics such as jazz, African American gospel, and Afro-Cuban rumba.

Beginning in the early twentieth century, these sounds from the African diaspora began cycling back to Africa via radio broadcasts and the nascent 78 rpm record industry. These new sounds in turn influenced Africans to create yet more new styles. For instance, in the mid-twentieth century Congolese musicians adapted Afro-Cuban rumba to create *soukous,* whose infectious percussion, rhythm guitar arpeggios, and flowing lead guitar melodies spread across the continent to become one of the most influential African popular music styles of the twentieth century.

This cycle of exchange continues today through the spread of new musical forms via the mass media and increased travel between Africa and the Americas. Rap and hip-hop have taken the African continent by storm; it is mostly young Africans who use this new form, often to comment on social problems such as the HIV/AIDS epidemic. According to Alex Perullo, popular Tanzanian rapper Mwanafalsafa scored a major hit in 2002 with a song whose Swahili title translates as "He Died of AIDS," in which the song's protagonist preaches safe sex to his friends, only to himself perish from the disease because of not following his own advice. Rap competitions are common in nightclubs in cities around the continent. At one such bar in Blantyre, Malawi, scholars Lisa Gilman and John Fenn observed DJs warming up the crowd for a rap competition by spinning songs from across the

Figure 9.8. Tiken Jah Fakoly performs for an educational benefit in Abidjan, Côte d'Ivoire, on April 25, 2009.
Getty Images.

diaspora, including Malawian hits, Congolese *soukous,* South African *kwaito,* and American rap and rhythm and blues.

Reggae, first created by Jamaicans of African descent in the 1960s, remains a popular form in Africa. Like reggae pioneer Bob Marley, contemporary reggae stars Alpha Blondy and Tiken Jah Fakoly of Ivory Coast use reggae to express political dissent and call for social change. In 2001, Fakoly's song "Promesses de Caméléon" (Promises of the Chameleon) was so effective in criticizing coup leader Robert Guei that Fakoly was forced to flee the country and lived for years in exile.

Many popular musicians combine influences from across the diaspora in single songs. Angelique Kidjo's powerful song "Welcome" begins with a field recording of Muslim women in the north of her native Benin. After a verse sung in her native Fon language, Kidjo leads an African American gospel-style chorus singing (in English, though Benin is a French-speaking nation) the song's refrain, "People say 'welcome' / People say 'my house is your house.'" South Africa's Soweto Gospel Choir combines southern African vocal traditions—themselves influenced by European missionary church harmony—with African American gospel styles to create a distinctive, rousing sound. Much African popular music can today be best understood as transnational music that results from the centuries-old flow of culture around the Atlantic, a flow that has only accelerated in recent years.

The cycle of exchange with the Americas is but one of many cultural flows impacting musics in Africa. Equally influential is the history of cultural exchange with the Arab world. As was the case with the history of interaction between Europe and Africa interaction, Arab interactions with Africa included conquest, religious proselytizing, and trade, including the trafficking of slaves. The slave trade in the Indian Ocean brought East Africans to parts of the Arabian Peninsula such as Oman. Parts of the eastern coast of Africa and the island of Zanzibar were in fact, for centuries, part of the Sultanate of Oman. This cultural exchange has resulted in African-derived musical styles in Oman as well as centuries-old musical blends of Arabic and African musics on the Swahili coast. In Tanzania, large orchestras perform "classical" *taarab,* an Arabic-influenced genre of sung Swahili poetry, while smaller, amplified bands perform a popular genre derived from *taarab* for dancing crowds.

Again, trade and the spread of Islam were among the major factors linking the Arabian Peninsula, northern Africa, and Africa south of the Sahara. West Africa also bears a great deal of influence from the Arab world. In northern Nigeria, for example, Hausa states adopted titles and practices from the Muslim world for centuries. Royal musicians playing kettle-shaped drums accompany emirs on public appearances, and double-reed oboe players use circular breathing to create non-stop, highly ornamented melodic flows bearing much resemblance to melodic phrasings in northern Africa and the Middle East. Islamic communities in Africa often share certain core musical aesthetic preferences, such as melismatic singing styles in more nasalized tones, and highly ornamented melodies in monophonic styles. These shared preferences led Senegalese popular musician Youssou N'Dour to cross the continent and collaborate with an Egyptian orchestra in the creation of the hugely successful, Grammy-winning album *Egypt.* While this album exhibits the historical connections between the Arabian Peninsula and Africa, it is best understood as an inter-African cultural exchange rooted in shared history and a common religious tradition.

MOSAICS IN MOTION

Musics on the African continent today flow through a dazzling variety of events, instruments, costumes, and forms. Though from all evidence African musics have always changed, some kinds have changed more rapidly than others as peoples have mingled their musics in interesting ways. The oral history of people of Gbeyilataa in Kpelle country (though not the present practice) indicates that the harp lute of the Mande *griots* was played by some court musicians. This is not surprising given the role of many Mande traders in the Kpelle area. The Beni dance and drill teams of East Africa played European brass band instruments, adapting Western music and creatively blending local elements. These groups, flourishing from the 1890s to the 1960s, were observed in 1945 by A. M. Jones, who described how they danced four abreast, in time with the music, parodying the British army officers with extravagant airs.

On a broader scale, a number of countries today support musical performance troupes that select local dances and songs and present them on a Western-type stage. The performance is adjusted to a theater audience. When the National Dance Troupe of Guinea performs in New York at the Brooklyn Academy of Music, included in one portion of the repertoire is a modified ceremony from the Poro secret society. In many ensembles, national culture is emphasized and local differences are minimized.

This was the case for the Kendeja troupe, which was developed in Liberia. Young children were selected to live in Monrovia from the age of six, seven, or eight and grew up in a dormitory together with young performers of different ethnic groups. While they shared songs they brought from their home villages, these were often adapted to suit the sensibilities of international audiences and the requirements of the stage.

These international audiences became accustomed to learning about Africa from these traveling musical groups, whether they performed in Libya, China, or New York. Peter Adegboyega Badejo's opera *Asa Ibile Yoruba* (The Ways of the Land of the Yoruba) premiered in Schoenberg Hall on the campus of the University of California at Los Angeles before an enthusiastic Western audience.

At a local level, many schools in Africa have brought in performers to teach young children indigenous music—often with influences from other places in the context of a Western education. Zimbabwean schools are well known for their choirs or instrumental ensembles, and they compete in regional events as they exhibit their skills. At school graduations these troupes from all over Africa exhibit their skills at playing music that mingles both outside influences and local musical traditions. Thus the flow of the arts through African life continues.

In the end, the music of Africa should be conceived as something that flows not only in tight local communities but also much more broadly: to the Americas and back, to Asia and back, to Europe and back, and to Latin America and back. Such flows occur not just once in history but many times, in a continually circulating fashion. These musics are essential to the fabric of life, whether it be entertainment, a ritual such as a funeral, work, or war. The sounds of Africa represent vitality, a mosaic in motion, and a balance within everyday life. Whether struggling in war or battling HIV/AIDs, whether commemorating the birth of a child or the death of a great chief, whether clearing the bush for a rice field or planting the seed, whether relaxing after a day in the mines or socializing after laboring on the rubber plantation, music brings an essential glue to hold things together. Through these performances, people can reorder their feelings and live life with a sense of balance and renewed vigor.

SUGGESTIONS FOR FURTHER READING

Berliner, Paul. 1993 [1978]. *The Soul of Mbira: Music and Traditions of the Shona People of Zimbabwe*. Chicago: University of Chicago Press.
Brempong, Owusu. 1984. "Akan Highlife in Ghana: Songs of Cultural Transition." Manuscript. Indiana University, ProQuest, UMI Dissertations Publishing, 1986.

Charry, Eric. 2000. *Mande Music: Traditional and Modern Music of the Maninka and Mandinka of Western Africa.* Chicago: University of Chicago Press.

Chernoff, John M. 1979. *African Rhythm and African Sensibility: Aesthetics and Social Action in African Musical Idioms.* Chicago: University of Chicago Press.

Gilman, Lisa, and John Fenn. 2006. "Dance, Gender, and Popular Music in Malawi: The Case of Rap and Ragga." *Popular Music* 25(3): 369–81.

Hampton, Barbara L. 1984. "Music and Ritual Symbolism in the Ga Funeral." *Yearbook for Traditional Music* 14: 75–105.

Jones, Arthur M. 1945. "African Music: The *Mganda* Dance." *African Studies* 4, no. 4.

Perullo, Alex. 2011. *Live from Dar es Salaam: Popular Music and Tanzania's Music Economy.* Bloomington: Indiana University Press.

Pongweni, Alec J. C. 1997. "The Chimurenga Songs of the Zimbabwean War of Liberation." In *Readings in African Popular Culture,* ed. Karin Barber. Bloomington: Indiana University Press.

Reed, Daniel B. 2003. *Dan Ge Performance: Masks and Music in Contemporary Côte d'Ivoire.* Bloomington: Indiana University Press.

———. 2012. "Promises of the Chameleon: Reggae Artist Tiken Jah Fakoly's Intertextual Contestation of Power in Côte d'Ivoire." In *Hip Hop Africa and Other Stories of New African Music in a Globalized World,* ed. Eric Charry. Bloomington: Indiana University Press.

Stone, Ruth M. 1982 *Let the Inside Be Sweet: The Interpretation of Music Event among the Kpelle of Liberia.* Bloomington: Indiana University Press.

Tang, Patricia. 2007. *Masters of the Sabar: Wolof Griot Percussionists of Senegal.* Philadelphia: Temple University Press.

Thompson, Robert F. 1974. *African Art in Motion: Icon and Act.* Los Angeles: University of California Press.

DISCOGRAPHY

Fakoly, Tiken Jah. 2007. "Non à l'Excision." *L'Africain.* Wrasse Records.

———. 2008 [2000]. "Promesses de Caméléon." *Le Caméléon.* Barclay Records.

Kidjo, Angelique. 1996. "Welcome." *Fifa.* Universal/Island Records.

N'Dour, Youssou. 2004. *Egypt.* Nonesuch Records.

10 Literature in Africa

Eileen Julien

Truth depends not only on who listens but on who speaks.
—Birago Diop

When most Americans and Europeans use the expression "African literature," they are referring to the poetry, plays, and novels written by Africans that reach Western and Northern shores. These have typically been written in English, French, and, increasingly, Portuguese. If one takes the long or broad view, however, these contemporary works of international standing are but one segment of a vast array of word arts in Africa, which have a long, complex, and varied history.

We have no record of the earliest oral traditions, but we know that verbal arts in Africa, oral and written, are ancient and long preceded the modern era, characterized by European colonialism and the introduction of European languages. African literature can be said to include Egyptian texts from the second and third millennia BCE; the sixth-century Latin-language texts of Augustine of Hippo; texts produced in Ge'ez, the ancient language of the region that has become Ethiopia, such as those of the Axumite period (fourth to seventh centuries); and Arabic-language texts, such as those of fourteenth-century North Africa, seventeenth-century Timbuktu in the western Sahel, and the nineteenth-century eastern coast of Africa. And alongside the widely known contemporary traditions in imported but now Africanized languages and forms, there is ongoing written and oral production in indigenous languages such as Amharic, Kiswahili, Pulaar, Yoruba, and Zulu. Moreover, many bards, storytellers, poets, and writers in these languages have embraced contemporary genres and new media. This vast contemporary production of African-language literature and "orature" (oral traditions) is largely unknown and ignored by those outside the continent. Inside Africa, these oral and more accessible popular texts may be the best-known and most-appreciated literary forms.

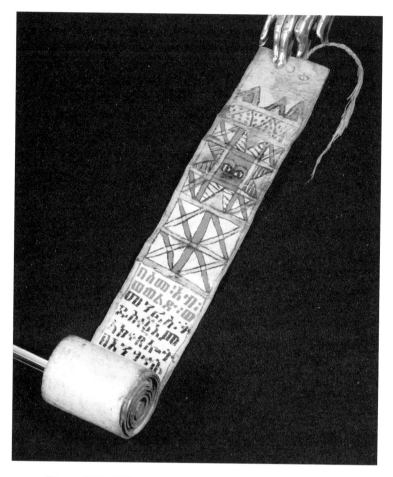

Figure 10.1. Vellum scroll in Ge'ez intended to ward off pain,
suffering, or spirits. Undated, but probably early nineteenth century.
Lilly Library, Indiana University.

Europhone writers—those using European languages—draw on these indigenous oral and literary traditions as well as those of Europe, the Americas, and Asia,
while African-language writers and practitioners of orature similarly dialogue with
or reference Europhone writers and take up the broad range of issues that are of
interest today across the world.

Africa is a vast continent, consisting of more than fifty nations and, by some
estimates, more than two thousand languages and ethnic groups. Despite cultural
similarities across the continent and a virtually ubiquitous history of imperialism
and neocolonialism, there are many African experiences and many verbal expressions of them. Literature from across the continent has never been homogeneous or

Figure 10.2. Fragment of nineteenth- or early twentieth-century copy of *Dalā'il al-khayrāt,* The Proofs of Good Deeds, a celebrated book of devotions for the Prophet Muhammad, composed in Arabic by the fifteenth-century North African Sufi saint al-Jazūlī and ornamented with Hausa, Mande, and Akan patterns and motifs.
Lilly Library, Indiana University.

coherent. Moreover, to see in proper perspective what is most often referred to as African literature is also to recognize that it has been until recently a gendered body of work.

Literary practice in Africa and understanding of it are continuously evolving. During the period of decolonization and formal declarations of independence around the continent in the mid-twentieth century, many literary texts portrayed the injustices and racism of the colonial period and the promise of independence. Beyond the 1960s, new "intra-African" themes of class, ethnicity, gender, and national identities emerged, thanks in part to the ever-increasing number of women writers, and there was greater awareness of written and oral production in mother tongues such as those mentioned above. There have also been new frameworks and vocabulary for studying cultural processes, which are themselves the subject of debate: *postcolonialism, popular culture, performance, diaspora*. Greater critical attention is being paid to the politics of local and international publishing and distribution and to multiple readerships in and beyond Africa. These developments have coincided with and have, in fact, helped produce a general shift in literary sensibility away from literature as pure *art,* a major paradigm for much of the twentieth century, to literature as *text,* an act between parties located within historical, socioeconomic, and other contexts. Of these developments, writing by women from around the continent has been especially important because it often challenges directly the meanings ascribed to the works of literary forefathers, bringing those works into sharper relief, forcing us to see their limits alongside their merits.

There are many ways to divide the terrain of literature written by Africans. These approaches reflect the fact that the continent is home to many different ethnic groups and cultural practices, political and physical geographies, local and nonlocal languages. Thus we routinely divide the literatures of Africa by *region* (West Africa, East Africa, North Africa, Central Africa, southern Africa, each of which is more or less distinctive environmentally and historically), by *ethnicity* (the Mande, for example, live across the region now divided by the states of Guinea, Mali, Côte d'Ivoire, Burkina Faso, and Senegal), or by *nationality* (a heritage of nineteenth-century European literary practice, which privileges the force of national history and identity and whose merit in the African context has been debated for many years).

Literature produced in Africa is also often categorized by *language* of expression, such as Hausa, Lingala, Xhosa, "Lusophone," "Anglophone," "Francophone" (the last term being especially vexed) and, as elsewhere, by *genre:* poetry, proverb, epic, tale, short story, novel, drama, essay. (These terms have become a universal idiom for literary genres, even as they often obscure rich local classifications of literary and oral works.) The field has also been examined in terms of "generations" of writers, that is, cohorts defined by distinctive issues and styles anchored in specific historical realities—those writing in the period of decolonizaton (*anticolonial, cultural nationalist* writers), those writing in the postindependence era (*postcolonial* writers), and those writing increasingly from abroad (*diasporic* writers)—even though there is overlap in issues and their treatment across these so-called generations. These many approaches suggest not only the diversity and complexity of life on the African continent and in its diasporas but also the stuff of which literature is made: language, aesthetic and literary traditions, culture and history, sociopolitical reality.

This chapter focuses on major themes and trends of African texts that American undergraduates routinely encounter in their classes and then goes on to describe contemporary debates and developments in this field of study as well as challenges and prospects facing African writers and readers of African texts. Some reference will be made to orature and literature in mother tongues.

THEMES AND TRENDS

Literary production in Africa is vast and varied, but there are several impulses or currents in creative works of which we will make special note. The first is the reclaiming of voice and subjectivity, especially characteristic of Europhone writing in the colonial and early postindependence periods. Other themes to which we will devote attention include the critique of power, which has been the main feature of postindependence writing, and contestations of edenic representations of a precolonial African past. There is also an ever-growing awareness and exploration of hybrid African identities.

COLONIALISM AND SELF-REPRESENTATION

In the 1950s and 1960s, as nations around the continent moved to achieve decolonization, many Africans took up the pen. There had been African creative writers, essayists, and polemicists writing in African and European languages well before this time; in fact, the printing press arrived in Africa as early as the 1820s, and it was quickly put to use by African nationals for political and cultural purposes. As early as 1926, the Senegalese Bakary Diallo produced *Force-Bonté* (Great Goodness); and by 1929 the prolific writer Félix Couchoro of Togo published *L'Esclave* (The Slave); the South African Sol Plaatje published *Mhudi* in 1930; in 1931, Thomas Mofolo published *Chaka,* translated from Sesotho; the Senegalese Ousmane Socé brought out *Karim* in 1935; and Peter Abraham published *Mine Boy* in 1946. One remarkable work of fiction, Amos Tutuola's *The Palm-Wine Drinkard,* made a singular impression when it was published in London in 1952. Tutuola's adventurous tale and hero are virtually lifted from the repertoire of Yoruba oral traditions and placed on the page in effective but non-"literary" English. The combination of rich imagination and untutored language gave the work a freshness and originality that garnered critical acclaim abroad and spawned great controversy among African writers and elites.

These works and others took up the issues of "national" history, of complex—and often conflicted—identities, and of modernity, issues that would still be critical twenty and thirty years later. But it was in the vast, concerted literary practice of mid-century that the moment of acceleration of contemporary African literature can be situated. This literature could justifiably be called "African" because it dealt with phenomena—race and racism, undoing alienation, reclaiming identity—whose reach could be felt throughout the continent. And there was by this point a wide audience for such texts, in Africa's Atlantic diasporas, throughout Europe, and among African publics themselves.

In the era immediately preceding and following formal declarations of independence, Europhone narrative and poetry were born, for the most part, in protest against history and myths constructed in conjunction with the colonial enterprise. Writers struggled to correct Eurocentric images, to rewrite fictionally and poetically the history of precolonial and colonial Africa, and to affirm African perspectives. The implicit or explicit urge to challenge the premises of colonialism was often realized in autobiography or pseudo-autobiography, describing the journey that writers themselves had made, away from home to other shores and back again. African intellectuals and writers felt keenly that "truth," as Senegalese Birago Diop had written in a neotraditional tale, depends also on *who* speaks.

In 1958, Chinua Achebe published *Things Fall Apart,* a novel that by century's end would become the world's most widely read work by an African. Characterized by a language rich in proverbs and images of agrarian life, this novel and Achebe's later *Arrow of God* (1964) portray the complex, delicately balanced social ecology of Igbo village life as it confronts the newly arrived imperial power. Achebe's protagonists are flawed but dignified men whose interactions with British emissaries are tragic and sometimes fatal. Like other writers of those years, Achebe wrote in response to denigrating mythologies and representations of Africans by nineteenth- and twentieth-century British and European writers such as Joyce Cary, James Conrad, Jules Verne, and Pierre Loti, to show, as Achebe put it, that the African past was not one long night of savagery before the coming of Europe.

Ngugi wa Thiong'o's early trilogy of novels (*Weep Not, Child,* 1964; *The River Between,* 1965; and *A Grain of Wheat,* 1967), set in the days of the Emergency, Mau Mau, and the period immediately preceding Kenyan independence in 1963, explores the many facets of individual Kenyan lives within the context of colonialism: their experiences of education, excision, religious conflict, collective struggle, and the cost of resistance. Through the interrelated stories of its characters, *A Grain of Wheat* suggests, moreover, the coalescing of lives and forces in the making of historical events.

A decade later, Nigerian poet, playwright, novelist, and essayist Wole Soyinka aspired also to reclaim African subjectivity and agency. In *Death and the King's Horseman* (1975), Soyinka represents the colonial factor as incidental, a mere catalyst in the metaphysical crisis of a flawed character, who is nonetheless the agent of his own destiny and of history. Elesin Oba, the horseman who must die in order to follow his deceased king to "the other side," sees in the intervention of the British colonial authority a chance to stay his death and indulge his passion for life and love. Through every theatrical means—drum, chant, gesture, dance, as well as wordplay drawing on Yoruba poetic traditions—Soyinka suggests the majesty, social significance, and great personal cost and honor of Elesin's task, and ultimately the magnitude of his failure.

A particular strain and manifestation of anticolonial poetry is the French-language tradition known as *négritude.* It was in Paris of the 1930s under the spell of surrealism, primitivism, and jazz that the idea of *négritude* arose. African and West Indian students, who were French colonial citizens and subjects, had come to the capital to complete their education. Products of colonial schools and assimilationist policies that sought to make them French, they had been taught to reject their African cultures of origin and to emulate the culture of the French. They had experienced an arguably deeper alienation than their counterparts schooled under British colonialism, with its more instrumental view of African cultures and languages. Now inspired by their African American brothers of the Harlem Renaissance and "New Negro" movement and the claims of German ethnographer Leo Frobenius and others, they felt the need to affirm those cultures from which they had been alienated, and they sought the means, both intellectual and literary, to rehabilitate African civilizations in Africa and the New World. The prime vehicles of this renewal were Jane and Paulette Nardal's salon and journal, *La Revue du monde noir*. The poetry of *négritude* grew out of this nexus both to reaffirm "African values" and an African identity and, according to Léopold Sédar Senghor, to be open to the world.

In 1948, Senghor published the *Anthologie de la nouvelle poésie nègre et malgache* (Anthology of New Black and Malagasy Poetry), in which he assembled work by French-speaking Caribbean and African poets, each of whom had "returned to the source," composing poems out of the matrix of African culture. The tone and themes of *négritude* poetry vary from poet to poet. Birago Diop's majestic "Souffles" (best translated perhaps as "Spirits") seems to emanate self-assuredly from West African oral traditions and village culture, as it affirms traditional beliefs in the cyclical nature of life and in the ever-abiding presence of the ancestors. David Diop, at the other end of the spectrum, vehemently and passionately denounces slavery and colonial domination.

There are two Africas in many *négritude* poems: a utopian, pastoral Africa of precolonial times and a victimized, suffering Africa of colonialism. In both instances, Africa is often represented metaphorically as female, as in Senghor's "Femme noire" (Black Woman) or David Diop's "À une danseuse noire" (To a Black Dancer). *Négritude* poems may also juxtapose an Africa characterized by the communion of humans and nature with a deadened Europe of alienation and failed humanity, as in Senghor's "Prayer to the Masks" (Prière aux masques), translated by Melvin Dixon (*Léopold Sédar Senghor: The Collected Poetry*, 1991):

> Let us answer "present" at the rebirth of the World
> As white flour cannot rise without the leaven.
> Who else will teach rhythm to the world
> Deadened by machines and cannons?
> Who will sound the shout of joy at daybreak to wake orphans and the dead?
> Tell me, who will bring back the memory of life
> To the man of gutted hopes?

"Prayer to the Masks" thus emphasizes the complementarity of "Africa" and "Europe," but in doing so it ironically lends credence to notions of their supposed essential difference, a difference that has often formed the basis of judgments of inferiority and superiority.

Another facet of the anticolonial tradition within French-language literature was its stress on the cultural dilemma of the *assimilé* or the contrast between two essentially different worlds. Camara Laye's narrative of childhood in Guinea, *L'enfant noir (The Dark Child)*, is another example. Written under difficult conditions, when Laye was an autoworker in France, the narrative nostalgically constructs home as an idyllic space in which the figure of the mother, nature, and the joys and virtues of village life are fused. Cheikh Hamidou Kane of Senegal, in a philosophical, semi-autobiographical narrative, *L'aventure ambiguë (Ambiguous Adventure)*, adds to these contrasting paradigms of "Africa" and "the West" yet another layer of opposition: the spiritual transcendence of ascetic Islam and the numbing preoccupation with material well-being that are, for him, characteristic of Africa and the West, respectively.

Other writers of the period likewise wrote scathing fictions contrasting Africa and Europe. Cameroonians Ferdinand Oyono (*Une vie de boy*, 1956 [*Houseboy*, 1966]; *Le vieux nègre et la médaille*, 1956 [*The Old Man and the Medal*, 1969]) and Mongo Béti (*Le Pauvre Christ de Bomba*, 1956 [*The Poor Christ of Bomba*, 1971]; *Mission terminée*, 1957 [*Mission to Kala*, 1964]) provided the French-language tradition with its most satirical portraits of mediocre and hypocritical French colonizers. And Ugandan Okot p'Bitek, in a celebrated satiric poem, *Song of Lawino* (1966), translated from Acoli and modeled on songs of the oral tradition, uses the persona of a scorned wife to attack indiscriminate assimilation of Western ways.

However, not all anticolonial writers stressed such oppositions. Ousmane Sembene's epic novel of the 1948 railway strike in then French West Africa, *Les bouts de bois de Dieu (God's Bits of Wood)*, is a powerful anticolonial fiction that moves beyond the opposition between static moments or sets of values ("tradition" and "modernity" or "good" authentic ways and "bad" alien ones). Sembene, a Marxist, conceives of change not as the tragic and fatal undoing of cultural identity but as a means of achieving a more just society, an inevitable process that is unquestionably difficult but transformative. In Sembene's novel, the Bambara and Wolof abandon divisive definitions of identity based on ethnic group and caste and forge a larger and more powerful identification based on the common work they do. Under Sembene's pen, urban work and technology are disentangled from debilitating ideologies of racial and ethnic identity, and the strike forces women and men to realize that the supposedly private and feminine sphere of the kitchen and the public, masculine, and political sphere of the railroad are inextricably bound in one and the same space of deprivation and injustice.

Still more violent struggles for liberation occurred in other countries around the continent that were home to white settlers. To the north, Morocco, Tunisia, and Algeria had also undergone the bitter experience of French colonialism. Algeria, France's premier settler colony on the continent, had waged a protracted, horrific anticolonial war. Among the many notable French-language North African novels of this period are *La grande maison* (1952) by Algerian Mohammed Dib; *Le passé simple* (1954) by Moroccan Driss Chraïbi; and *Nedjma* (1956) by Algerian Kateb

Yacine. Tunisian Albert Memmi also wrote a powerful essay denouncing the effects of colonialism, *The Colonizer and the Colonized* (1957). Questions of identity and culture have continued to generate incisive and powerful fictions, such as *La mémoire tatouée* (1971) and *Amour bilingue* (1983; *Love in Two Languages*) by Moroccan Abdelkebir Khatibi. The very history of French conquest in the nineteenth century and the Algerian war of resistance in the 1950s are likewise revisited and retold through the experiences of women in Assia Djebar's *L'amour la fantasia* (1985) and *Femmes d'Alger dans leur appartement* (2002).

Decades later, southern Africa was the scene of lengthy anticolonial struggles. Because of Angola's long war of liberation, the condemnation of colonial domination and the determination to bear witness are intense and urgent in the Portuguese-language poetry of Agostinho Neto (*Sagrada Esperanca*, 1974 [*Sacred Hope*]) and the fiction of José Luandino Vieira (*A Vida Verdadeira de Domingos Xavier,* 1974 [*The Real Life of Domingos Xavier,* 1978, published first in French in 1971, when Vieira was incarcerated]).

Chenjerai Hove's *Bones* (1988), winner of the 1989 Japanese-sponsored Noma Award, given each year to "the best book published in Africa," and Shimmer Chinodya's *Harvest of Thorns* (1989) were important literary testimonies to the *chimurenga,* the decade-long war of liberation in Zimbabwe.

Through the mid-1990s, protracted struggles against the brutal regime of apartheid in South Africa and its ripple effects across southern Africa were the impetus for a vast production of oral and written texts. In fact, South Africa has significant literary traditions in English, Afrikaans, Zulu, Xhosa, and other languages, with English-language literature being written by white South Africans of British and Afrikaner descent and by black South Africans and those of mixed descent. Olive Schreiner's *Story of an African Farm* (1883) is a remarkable novel, given its time, but liberal writing by white South Africans came to international attention in 1948 with Alan Paton's *Cry, the Beloved Country.* Prominent white South African writers of recent years include the prolific poet and novelist Breyten Breytenbach (*True Confessions of an Albino Terrorist,* 1984); novelist, playwright, and translator André Brink, best known in the West perhaps for *A Dry White Season,* 1979, and J. M. Coetzee, who won the Nobel Prize for Literature in 2003 and whose *Life and Times of Michael K.,* 1983, and *Disgrace,* 1999, each won the Booker Prize.

South African Nadine Gordimer, the Nobel laureate of 1991, is also a writer of fiction. She too has published many novels and collections of short stories, including *Burger's Daughter* (1979), *July's People* (1981), *A Sport of Nature* (1987), *My Son's Story* (1990), and *Jump and Other Stories* (1991). One of the unique strengths of Gordimer's fiction is its sustained probing of racial and gender identities through incidents, objects, and her characters' very own voices. In particular, she deconstructs whiteness and masculinity (and their opposites) as natural attributes.

Athol Fugard, the white South African playwright, has been a highly visible presence in New York theater circles for many years. Among his plays are *Boesman and Lena* (1969), still being performed in the United States as of this writing;

Master Harold and the Boys (1982); and *Sizwe Bansi Is Dead,* co-authored with John Kani and Winston Ntshona (1976). Fugard's plays are spare dramas of survivors, those who cope with lives entangled and nearly wasted in the snares of apartheid.

While liberal white South Africans, by and large, have expressed the guilt, fear, alienation, and general malaise of the white minority living under apartheid, black and black-identified South African writers have written of the deprivation, injustices, violence, and anger suffered by the black majority. Their narratives are often set in the cities and townships.

Among the earliest narratives of black life under apartheid are autobiographical novels set in urban South Africa, *Mine Boy* (1946) and *Tell Freedom* (1954) by Peter Abrahams, and *Down Second Avenue* (1959) by Ezekel Mphalele. The alienation of life in the slums of apartheid is also the subject of Alex LaGuma's naturalist fictions *A Walk in the Night* (1967) and *In the Fog of the Season's End* (1972). Mbulelo Mzamane's *Children of Soweto* (1981) stresses the self-awareness, determination, and resilience of black South African youth in particular.

In the category of fiction, South Africans such as Richard Rive, James Matthews, and Miriam Tlali have made particular use and developed particular talents for the short story. In addition, many well-known novelists, including Alex LaGuma, Besssie Head, and Mbulelo Mzamane, have practiced this form of short fiction to special effect.

Yet poetry was a singularly important medium for black South Africans writing under apartheid. Oswald Mtshali's *Sounds of a Cowhide Drum* (1971) and *Fire-flames* (1980), Sipho Sepamla's *Hurry Up to It!* (1975), *The Blues Is You in Me* (1976), and *The Soweto I Love* (1977), and Mongane Wally Serote's *Yakhal'inkomo* (1972) and *No Baby Must Weep* (1975) are all forged in the crucible of black urban life in South Africa—revealing not only the repression of township life but struggle, vibrancy, and humor. Of South African exiles residing in the United States, the poet Dennis Brutus, who had been imprisoned on Robben Island, was surely the best-known. Brutus's poetry (*Sirens, Knuckles and Boots,* 1963; *Stubborn Hope,* 1978) is poised between an unrelenting naturalism, in which life in prison, in urban slums, or in exile has been narrowed, caged, trivialized, and demeaned, and a painful, tenacious desire for life as it might be, that space of imagination, possibility, energy, and renewal. Albie Sachs's *The Soft Vengeance of a Freedom Fighter* (1991), a remarkable memoir of the personal costs of antiapartheid struggle, affirms, as does the poetry of Brutus, the belief in humanity that may inspire and grow in struggle.

It is worth noting in passing that memoirs of imprisonment are a veritable genre on the continent: Brutus's *Letters to Martha* (1969); *Rue du Retour* (2003; originally published in French as *Le chemin des ordalies*) by Moroccan Abdellatif Laâbi; Wole Soyinka's *The Man Died* (1971); Ngugi's *Detained* (1981); and Egyptian Nawal el Saadawi's *Memoirs from the Women's Prison* (1984).

Finally, with respect to South Africa, then, the tenor of literature has shifted since the 1990s, with the liberation of Nelson Mandela, who had been imprisoned for twenty-seven years, and the coming to power of the African National Congress in the first democratic South African elections. This shift will be taken up again below.

THE LOGIC OF POSTINDEPENDENCE POWER, WEALTH, AND CAPITAL

The critique of foreign domination under colonialism and the concomitant, urgent issue of identity are, as indicated above, often constructed as a conflict between the assimilation of "Western" ways and an African authenticity, and they are often articulated in realist narratives. With the advent of formal independence little by little throughout the continent, these issues gradually cede center stage to disillusionment and a critique of abusive power and corruption, such as Achebe unveils in his novels *No Longer at Ease* (1960) and *Man of the People* (1966).

The earliest fiction of Ghana's premier novelist, Ayi Kwei Armah, *The Beautyful Ones Are Not Yet Born* (1968) is set in the last days of the Nkrumah regime. In this novel of disillusionment and alienation, a railway clerk, "the man," makes his way in a greedy and corrupt world. In later novels, from *Two Thousand Seasons* (1973) and *The Healers* (1978) to *Osiris Rising* (1995), Armah's fiction moves from the focus on the personal experience of disillusionment to historical and allegorical analyses of African failure to resist Arab and Western conquerors.

In recent works, the critique of postindependence regimes goes hand in hand with a change in literary form that Ngugi wa Thiong'o suggests in his provocative essay *Decolonising the Mind* (1986):

> How does a writer, a novelist, shock his readers by telling them that these [heads of state who collaborate with imperialist powers] are neo-slaves when they themselves, the neo-slaves, are openly announcing the fact on the rooftops? How do you shock your readers by pointing out that these are mass murderers, looters, robbers, thieves, when they, the perpetrators of these anti-people crimes, are not even attempting to hide the fact? When in some cases they are actually and proudly celebrating their massacre of children, and the theft and robbery of the nation? How do you satirise their utterances and claims when their own words beat all fictional exaggerations?

Within the last decades of the twentieth century, as Africans grappled with the new abuses of neocolonial regimes and seemingly inexorable global processes, the literary landscape was strewn with quite stunning fictions of failure. Congolese writers Sony Labou Tansi (*La vie et demie,* 1979 *[Life and a Half]* and *L'Etat honteux,* 1981 [The Shameful State]) and Henri Lopès (*Le Pleurer-Rire,* 1982 *[The Laughing Cry,* 1987]) have given us compelling satires of dictatorship. Labou Tansi's comic and nearly delirious fables and plays expose not only the corruption and savagery of such dictators but their pathetic frailty and insecurity. Ngugi's fictions, *Petals of Blood, Devil on the Cross, Matigari,* and most recently *Wizard of the Crow* (2006), signal the greed for wealth and power unleashed by "independence" and the betrayal of Kenyan peasants and workers by leaders who collaborate with international capitalism when they do not vie with it. These fictions cross over into the absurd and turn away from the realism that characterizes many early texts focusing on the ills of colonialism. As Ngugi has suggested, writers invent forms commensurate to their perceptions and intuitions of new and troubling realities.

CONTESTATIONS

The *négritude* poets had defended the humanity of those whose humanity had been denied on the basis of "race," a step that was unquestionably necessary. But what this meant often was an affirmation of an African or racial essence and the idealization of a time before colonialism that was knowable mostly through the interpretive lenses of anthropological, literary, and perhaps oral discourses. Traits that were held to be "naturally" African—such as love of nature, rhythm, spirituality— and that had been negatively valued were now seen as positive. These particular representations of African identity and a racial or pan-African nation came and continue to come under attack by African intellectuals and writers, most notably Wole Soyinka (*Myth, Literature and the African World,* 1976), Marcien Towa (*Léopold Sédar Senghor: Négritude ou servitude?,* 1971) and Stanislas Adotévi (*Négritude et négrologues,* 1972). Likewise, literary sequels to and revisions of this perspective now abound.

Yambo Ouologuem's *Bound to Violence* (1968), set in Sahelian West Africa, is a chronicle of a fictional dynasty that is corrupt, barbarous, and politically astute—a fitting adversary, then, for the newly arrived French colonials. Ouologuem negates *négritude*'s claim of precolonial goodness and seems to assert instead an inherent African violence.

A still more important sequel to and revision of these early representations is the writing by women, which has developed rapidly since the 1980s. What was missing in the early chorus of voices denouncing the arrogance and violence of the various forms of colonialism, and what was in some cases ignored, were female voices. As recent writing by women makes clear, gender gives writing a particular cast. Anticolonial male writers critique the imperial and colonial project for its racism and oppression, but they nonetheless (and not unlike the European objects of their critique) portray these matters as they pertain to men, and they formulate a vision of independence or of utopias in which women are either "goddesses," such as muses and idealized mothers, or mere helpmates. Women writers of that era and new writers, however, introduce matters of gender explicitly, as they nonetheless critique the underpinnings of the colonial project or its aftermath.

It is in this sense that Mariama Bâ's 1981 epistolary novel *So Long a Letter* shook the literary landscape. At the death of her husband, Bâ's heroine, Ramatoulaye, writes a "long letter" to her divorced friend Aïssatou, now residing with her sons in the United States. Through the experience of writing, Rama comes to terms with her own independence, having been betrayed by her husband of many years, who took as his second wife a friend of their teenage daughter.

If Ouologuem's *Bound to Violence* had already questioned the premises of black nationalism and of a "pure" time before colonialism, Bâ's novel made clear that the nationalism and independence that these now celebrated male writers had been defending were, by and large, patriarchal: women were symbols of the nation or, at best, helpers of man, who alone would reap the full fruits of independence. In Bâ's novel, which is imbued with its own prejudices, we nonetheless see a conflation of class biases, male vanity, and female complicity in the practice of polygyny. In this novel and her posthumous *Scarlet Song,* which describes the stakes and constraints of interracial or, more precisely, cross-cultural marriage, one can infer the gender biases of these early notions of nation and identity.

As with the French-language literatures of Africa, a powerful force in English-language literature has been the emergence of women writers, who have filled what was a deep literary silence surrounding women's lives. Flora Nwapa's *Efuru* (1966) suggests the tension between women's desires and the strictures of womanhood in the same era that Achebe and other male writers seemed to portray as the nearly golden age before colonialism. She concludes her novel with this haunting passage:

> Efuru slept soundly that night. She dreamt of the woman of the lake, her beauty, her long hair and her riches. She had lived for ages at the bottom of the lake. She was as old as the lake itself. She was happy, she was wealthy. She was beautiful. She gave women beauty and wealth but she had no child. She had never experienced the joy of motherhood. Why then did the women worship her?

The passage above opens a path for Nwapa's sister novelist from Nigeria, Buchi Emecheta, who has authored many novels. The most acclaimed of these may well be *The Joys of Motherhood* (1979), which examines marriage and the family in the village and colonial city from a woman's perspective. Emecheta has now created her own publishing house in London, where she resides.

Ghanaian Ama Ata Aidoo, in her early collection of short stories and sketches *No Sweetness Here* (1971), gives voice to women's concerns as they face problems of urbanization and Westernization: standards of beauty, the absence of husbands and fathers, prostitution, clashing values and expectations. In a play, *Anowa* (1970), remarkable for its time, Aidoo boldly explores the intersection of women's oppression and transatlantic slavery. And in another novel of this early period, *Our Sister Killjoy* (1977), Aidoo stages an amorous encounter between two women, a Ghanaian and a German, in Berlin. In a more recent novel, *Changes* (1992), Aidoo examines the meaning of friendship, love, marriage, and family for young women of diverse religions, backgrounds, and cities in contemporary West Africa.

If for Sembene social transformation proceeds from the material world of the workplace and the kitchen, that is, from the outside in, for South African writer

Bessie Head this transformation proceeds from the heart and spirit, from the inside out. Head, who has been of particular interest for Western feminists, sets her fictions in rural Botswana, where she lived in exile. *When Rain Clouds Gather* (1968), *Maru* (1971), *A Question of Power* (1974), *Serowe: Village of the Rain-Wind* (1981), and a collection of short stories, *The Collector of Treasures* (1977), lay bare the mystifications of race, gender, and a patriarchal God. A particularly moving scene from *Rain Clouds* exemplifies this transformation: titular authority and might give way to the moral force of ordinary people. The mean-spirited and reactionary rural Botswanan chief is disarmed by the sheer presence of the villagers who have come purposefully to sit in his yard and wait for him to emerge and face them. They make no threats of violence, but he knows they will no longer tolerate his excesses, that he is effectively divested of power.

Another avowed feminist, well known to Western readers, is Egyptian physician Nawal el Saadawi, who has been a staunch critic of oppressive political and religious regimes. She has written innumerable Arabic-language narratives such as *Woman at Point Zero* (1975) and *The Fall of the Imam* (1987).

Nervous Conditions (1988), an account by Zimbabwean Tsitsi Dangarembga, is the story of women's resistance and resignation before the double bondage of settler colonialism and patriarchy. *Le baobab fou* (1982; The Abandoned Baobab) by Senegalese Ken Bugul is a rebellious young woman's account of coming of age, of the journey from countryside to city. This fierce and ambiguous autobiographical narrative traces the heroine's hellish road from her Senegalese village to Brussels, while Dangarembga's young Tambu struggles against the racism of colonial Rhodesia, the deprivations of her class, and the male privilege of her brother, father, and uncle. Women who survive, who provide, who circumvent patriarchy are the heroines of this story. A new poetic language and feminist voice arrived on the scene in Yvonne Vera's retelling of Zimbabwe's colonial encounter and wars of liberation, *Nehanda* (1994) and *Under the Tongue* (1996), and her bold, passionate explorations of female desire, *Butterfly Burning* (2000) and *Stone Virgins* (2002).

The Somali novelist Nuruddin Farah (*From a Crooked Rib,* 1970; *A Naked Needle,* 1976; *Sweet and Sour Milk,* 1979; *Sardines,* 1981; *Maps,* 1986) also earned a reputation for a feminist stance: his female protagonists bring into sharp focus issues of gender and nationalism. Another searing contestation of the national project in this period comes from Dambudzo Marechera of Zimbabwe, whose collection of short fiction *The House of Hunger* (1978), winner of the 1979 Guardian Fiction Prize, recounts, in near verbal delirium, the brutalization and violence of life in a Zimbabwean township.

Many of the established writers have continued to write with new perspectives or in new ways. Achebe's *Anthills of the Savannah* (1987), for example, set in the city of Lagos, is a "dialogic" narrative, interweaving several perspectives and several registers of language, the voices of women and men of professional and popular classes.

Figure 10.3. Book signing by Yvonne Vera (Zimbabwe) and Calixthe Beyala (Cameroon), Humboldt University, Berlin, spring 2002. *Eileen Julien.*

Les Soleils des indépendences (1968; *The Suns of Independence,* 1981), the first novel by Ivorian Ahmadou Kourouma, was a momentous event in the French-language tradition because of its nearly creolized, Malinke-inflected French and its exploration of the relationship between masculinity and nation, as embodied in its protagonist, the noble Fama, dispossessed by colonialism and the ensuing independence. The rhythms of spoken language also characterize Kourouma's later work, for example, *Allah n'est pas obligé* (1999; *Allah Is Not Obliged,* 2007), which has become a staple of a new genre, the child-soldier narrative.

Interesting use has been made of the detective or mystery story, or, more generally, of teleological endings, as in Ngugi's *Petals of Blood* (1977) and *Devil on the Cross,* translated from the Gikuyu (1982); in Boubacar Boris Diop's novels, from the earliest, *Le Temps de Tamango* (1981; The time of Tamango) to the more recent *Murambi: Le livre des ossements* (2000; *Murambi: The Book of Bones,* 2006); and in Sembene's *Le Dernier de l'empire* (1981; *The Last of the Empire,* 1983) and Asse Gueye's *No Woman No Cry* (1986). Some scholars have argued that teleological endings suggest the ability of the reading subject to reorder facts, to rewrite history and thereby create a sense of power to shape destiny. That interpretation would offer insight into the popularity of this genre in postindependence African nations. The increasing interest in this genre and other new forms suggests ever broadening and diverse experiences and perspectives. There has been an increase in narratives of war, of ethnic or civil violence, in which global forces, too, are at work: Ken Saro-Wiwa's *Sozaboy: A Novel in Rotten English* (1986), the aforementioned *Murambi* and *Allah n'est pas obligé* (1999), Ishmael Beah's *A Long Way Gone: Memoirs of a Boy Soldier* (2007), and Emmanuel Dongala's *Johnny chien méchant* (2002; *Johnny Mad Dog*, 2007).

Following the Rwandan genocide of 1994, in which perhaps one million people were killed, a group of French-language writers—including Senegalese Boubacar Boris Diop *(Murambi)*, Guinean Tierno Monénembo (*L'aîné des orphelins,* 2000 [*The Oldest Orphan,* 2004]), Ivorian Véronique Tadjo (*L'ombre d'Imana: Voyages jusqu'au bout du Rwanda,* 2000 [*The Shadow of Imana: Travels in the Heart of Rwanda,* 2002]), Abdourahmane Waberi (*Moisson de crânes,* 2000 [Harvest of skulls])—were invited for a several-month visit to Rwanda, after which they wrote novels to bear witness to what they had seen and learned about the massacre.

At the other end of the spectrum, the publishing house Nouvelles Editions Ivoiriennes has created the French-language romance series *Adoras.* Such "popular" fictions, like the many pamphlets from Nigeria's Onitsha market, appeal especially to urban youth, students, and workers aspiring to modern, middle class lifestyles. Written in African and European languages, such fictions, it has been argued, often offer moral and practical advice (Stephanie Newell, *Readings in African Popular Fiction,* 2002).

Likewise, a "magical" or "animist" realist vein has developed in fiction by Africans, embodied most prominently in *The Famished Road* (1991) by Nigerian Ben Okri. This Booker Award–winning novel, the story of an *abiku,* a spirit child, born to poor Nigerian parents, can be thought of as a descendant of Tutuola's narrative.

If we turn from narrative to performance and poetry, alongside Nobel laureate Wole Soyinka, the most popular playwright and director in Nigeria may well be Femi Osofisan, author of more than fifty stage and television plays, including *Esu and the Vagabond Minstrels* (1975) and *Morountodoun* (1969), about a farmers' uprising in western Nigeria and drawing on the myth of Moremi, the Ife queen who surrendered herself to an enemy camp in order to learn their secrets. Among other distinguished Nigerian writers are poet and playwright John Pepper Clark, who has also edited and transcribed the Ijaw epic *The Ozidi Saga* (1977); the syncretic modernist poet Christopher Okigbo (*Labyrinths with Paths of Thunder,* 1971); and neotraditional poet Niyi Osundare (*The Eye of the Earth,* 1986), winner of the Commonwealth Poetry Prize and the Noma Award.

Among Ghana's well-known poets whose work is marked by Ewe oral traditions are Kofi Awoonor (*This Earth, My Brother,* 1971; *Breast of the Earth,* 1975) and Kofi Anyidoho (*Earthchild,* 1985; *Ancestral Logic and Caribbean Blues,* 1992).

Malawi's most renowned poet is Jack Mapanje (*Of Chameleons and Gods*, 1981; *The Beasts of Nalunga*, 2007). It is safe to assume, of course, that there are countless poets today writing and performing in every language on the continent. If, for example, we take only the case of contemporary Nigerian English-language poets, who are ever conscious of the enormous imbalances of power in Africa today, including the abuses of an endless chain of military and postindependence dictators, a short list might include Odia Ofeimun (*The Poet Lied*, 1989; *Dreams at Work*, 2000; *Go Tell the Generals*, 2008), Ogaga Ifowodo (*Homeland and Other Poems*, 1998; *Madiba*, 2003) Toyin Adewale (*Naked Testimonies*, 1995; and *Twenty-Five Nigerian Poets*, 2000, the latter an anthology co-edited with the African American Ishmael Reed), Uche Nduka (*Flower Child*, 1998; *Bremen Poems*, 1995; *Chiaroscuro*, 1997), and Tade Ipadeola (*A Time of Signs*, 2000).

Literary traditions in Kiswahili (or Swahili) are exemplary of African-language literatures. Swahili developed through many centuries of contact with Arabic-speaking inhabitants along Africa's East Coast and has absorbed elements of Persian, German, Portuguese, English, and French. Today it is the mother tongue of approximately five million people, but thanks in part to German and British colonial governments, it is spoken by at least eighty million people from Tanzania and Kenya to Somalia in the north, the Comoros Islands to the east, and Uganda and the Democratic Republic of the Congo in the interior.

As with virtually all oral and written African-language poetic traditions, dating and authorial attribution of historical Swahili poems is difficult. While the oldest existing manuscripts from the Swahili coast bear dates from the late seventeenth and early eighteenth centuries, scholars hypothesize much earlier origins for written Swahili verse. It is often unclear whether dates on manuscripts indicate the actual date of composition of a poem, the date of its performance and scripting, or the date of copying of a manuscript. Oral texts could have been written down decades or centuries after their first composition, and written texts could have been memorized and transmitted orally for equally long periods. It is likely that many Swahili poems circulated simultaneously in writing and by word of mouth. The boundary between oral and written modes has never been rigid, and both methods of composing and preserving poems persist still today.

In addition, although the majority of Swahili manuscripts that have survived from the eighteenth and nineteenth centuries focus on themes and narratives taken straight from the Qur'an and the Arab Islamic tradition, modern readers should not assume that local secular matters were not the material of poetic expression in Swahili. Religious poems may have been preserved for devotional reasons, but the tradition always also included poems on social and political topics, perhaps even in greater abundance than the former.

One poetic genre from these centuries, the *utenzi* (or *utendi*), is often equated with the "epic" in English. Mwengo wa Athumani's *Utendi wa Tambuka* (circa 1728) offers a fictional account of battles between the forces of the Prophet Muhammad and those of the Byzantine emperor Heraclius from a Muslim perspective. Another,

Mwana Kupona binti Mshamu's 1858 *Utendi wa Mwana Kupona*, composed on the poet's deathbed for her daughter, offers motherly teachings on appropriate conduct for a woman in Swahili society; these are read by some as reinforcing patriarchal values and by others as subverting them. Still other poems in this genre narrate the life and death of Swahili poet Fumo Liyono or contemplate the ruins of the once splendid city of Pate and the ephemeral nature of life. The shorter form, the *shairi*, often treated social and political matters, such as the violent resistance of the Swahili people of Mombasa to Omani occupation, as well as more intimate and humorous poems about local disputes and personal relations within the Mombasa community.

Contemporary Swahili poetry has tended to adhere to classical structure and poetic conventions, even as it focuses on modern social themes. *Sauti ya Dhiki* (1973) by Kenyan poet Abdilatif Abdalla is a collection of poems written during his political imprisonment from 1969 to 1972 and contains scathing criticism of the government of then-president Jomo Kenyatta. Tanzanian poets Kaluta Amri Abedi and Saadan Kandoro, on the other hand, were adherents of nationalist politics who worked to promote Swahili as Tanzania's national language. Swahili also saw during this period controversial experimentation with new forms, including free verse, exemplified in the collection *Kichomi* (1974; Twinge) by Tanzanian Euphrase Kezilahabi.

The writer most often associated with both modern transformations of Swahili's classical poetic forms and the emergence of fiction in Swahili is Tanzanian Shabaan Robert. He is often credited with writing the first novel in Swahili, the utopian *Kusadikika* (1951; Believable). The late twentieth century saw many new developments in fiction, including the exploration of the inner consciousness of narrators and the rise of popular fiction, such as detective novels, sexually adventurous works, and populist novels, the last often focusing on social inequalities and failed government policies. Still newer trends in fiction can be seen in recent novels, including, for example, Said A. Mohamed's *Babu Alipofufuka* (2001; When Grandfather came back to life) and Kezilahabi's *Nagona* (1990; The insight), which are "magical," often are intertextual (referencing other texts), and abandon a realist narrative mode (that is, they do not seek to create the sense of a real, concrete world). A few female feminist novelists have also appeared: Zanzibari Zainab Burhani (*Mwisho wa Koja*, 1997; The end of the bouquet) and Kenyan Clara Momanyi (*Tumaini*, 2006).

Major playwrights in Swahili include the prolific Alamin Mazrui of Kenya (*Kilio cha Haki*, 1981 [Cry for justice], in which a female union leader awakens the political consciousness of her fellow workers) and Tanzanians Penina Muhando (*Hatia*, 1972 [Guilt], focusing on economic uncertainty and madness) and Ebrahim Hussein (*Kinjekitile*, 1969; *Kwenye Ukingo wa Thim*, 1988 [*At the Edge of Thim*, 2000], both warning against an uncritical embrace of "tradition"). Hussein is considered one of Swahili's most accomplished authors in any genre, drawing on both Western dramaturgy and Swahili mythological and oral traditions.

While the origins and history of Swahili literature are distinctive, this brief survey may suggest nonetheless the parallels and continuities with other African-language traditions and the Europhone traditions that dominate the study of literature from Africa in the American classroom. Such histories could be written for any number of African languages.

DEBATES AND CHALLENGES

A long-standing debate in African literary circles has focused on the implications and consequences of writing in "national" or now Africanized European languages. Ngugi wa Thiong'o has for many years urged writers to write in African languages. If one follows his argument in *Decolonising the Mind* (1986), this would seem to be especially a matter both of the inadequacy of non-African languages for conveying African experiences and of the audience for whom the author writes. If writers and intellectuals want to address their compatriots, most of whom are not fluent in European languages, it would make sense that writers write in the languages and aesthetic traditions of those compatriots. This shift in audience will also affect what writers say and the perspectives they offer, and it will foster the growth of African languages and literatures.

Figure 10.4. In Senegal, books can be purchased in bookstores and in open-air markets. *Djibril Sy.*

These are good arguments. It is hard to disagree with the idea of communicating with one's audience in a shared language. And there is indeed a rich and unique expressiveness of each (African) language—what translation theory conceptualizes as the *untranslatable*. Moreover, pushing the limits of written expression in recently codified languages for which there are historical oral traditions but a dearth of current written literary texts is critical to the development of those languages as flexible contemporary media. So, for example, the Senegalese journalist and novelist Boubacar Boris Diop has written his first novel in Wolof, *Doomi Golo* (2003; The monkey's kids).

But the choice of language of expression is not as clear-cut as it may at first seem. Many writers, who have been reading, learning, and writing in European languages since childhood, are as at home in European languages as they are in their maternal languages, perhaps more so. Sony Labou Tansi put it succinctly when he said that any language in which you cry, in which you love, is fully your language. Regrettably, many Europhone authors do not know how to write their mother tongues, and while they revere oral traditions, they themselves may be mediocre oral storytellers. Moreover, most writers are addressing multiple publics, not only those of their own ethnicity but other compatriots who speak different languages, other Africans on the continent and in diasporas from the United States to the Caribbean to Spain, India, and China, and still other readers who are not even especially Africa-identified. Many of the earliest Europhone texts were written precisely to "talk back" to European imperialism. For these reasons, there are many powerful forces—metropolitan publishers, foreign academies and media, paying readerships abroad, and still lower literacy rates in most "national" languages than in European ones—militating against the abandonment of Europhone texts and publishing.

At the same time, there are many thriving African-language literatures, such as those in Amharic, Yoruba, Pulaar, Zulu, and Swahili, as we have seen, and they are increasingly legitimated by school and university curricula, their use as "national" or "official" languages, and the interest of local publishers and ever-growing African readerships.

Another important debate in the field of African literary studies, as in African studies generally, has been the very meaning of the term "African." Those who define Africa either racially or culturally often look toward the past, "original" (which is to say, precolonial) Africa to locate the signs of African authenticity. They may equate certain forms, such as proverbs and tales, or types of language, such as colloquial or creolized French or English, as the true expressions of Africa and those to which writers of European language texts especially should aspire or which they should emulate.

Others such as philosophers Kwame Anthony Appiah and V. Y. Mudimbe, historian Terence Ranger, and anthropologist Johannes Fabian argue that such supposedly pure, authentic forms and the notion of static "traditional times" are largely invented on the basis of the dubious colonial archive of anthropological, missionary, and administrative documents to which Chinua Achebe refers in the last paragraph of *Things Fall Apart*. The Arabic-language writer Tayeb el Salih of Sudan (*Wedding of Zein*, 1969; *Season of Migration to the North*, 1966) has argued similarly that Africa has always been syncretic.

To champion a narrow African authenticity based on what is ultimately an arbitrarily chosen moment of the past, then, is to ignore Africa's own complex history of encounters. Depending on the criteria used, it could mean excluding the creative work of writers of Lebanese or Martinican origin in Senegal, for example, or the work of writers of Indian descent in Tanzania and Kenya such as award-winning novelist Moyez Vassanji (*The Gunny Sack*, 1989; *The Book of Secrets*, 1994; *The In-Between World of Vikram Lall*, 2003), for whom Asian African communities' experiences of colonial oppression and decolonization trouble their relationship to the nation. Similarly, it would, in all likelihood, exclude the work of white writers of British or Afrikaner descent in southern Africa, such as Nadine Gordimer or J. M. Coetzee. Doris Lessing (*The Grass Is Singing*, 1950; *The Golden Notebook*, 1962), who grew up in Zimbabwe (then Rhodesia), signals the critical, if troubled, identification of these writers with Africa when she states, "All white South African literature is the literature of exile, not from Europe, but from Africa" (Kathryn Wagner, *Rereading Nadine Gordimer*, 1994).

Narrow claims for authenticity would exclude the fiction of the prolific Egyptian Nobel laureate Naguib Mahfouz (*Zabalawi*, 1963; *Miramar*, 1967), whose Arabic-language texts reveal deep familiarity with literatures of the world. So too the innumerable plays of the innovative Egyptian playwright Tawfiq al-Hakim, who has sought to fuse Egyptian and Western dramatic traditions (*The Sultan's Dilemma*, 1960; *The Fate of a Cockroach*, 1966). It would also mean excluding much of the work of Wole Soyinka, who draws on the mythologies and poetic traditions not only of the Yoruba of Nigeria but of other countries as diverse as Britain, Greece, and Japan. Soyinka's *Death and the King's Horseman* makes this point explicitly: there is no contradiction in being African and riding and embracing the crest of world currents, be they technological or cultural. Africans too have diverse origins, "races," genders, and sexualities. Let us note, moreover, that this chapter is entitled *not* "African Literature" but simply, if nonetheless dauntingly, "Literature in Africa." The period in which "African-ness" might be defined above all by anti-imperialism and anti-racism has passed.

Thus the circumstances in which novels, plays, and poetry, many of them the legacy of imperialism, are produced and studied are as important to our understanding of the practice of literature in Africa as are the style and images on the pages we read. Many factors give African writing its character and at the same time impinge on its development. One of the terrible, ironic testimonies to the vitality of literatures across Africa, to their resolute denunciation of multiple forms of domination, is the fact that writers—Kofi Awoonor, Mongo Beti, Bessie Head, Dennis Brutus, Nuruddin Farah, Abdelatif Laâbi, Jack Mapanje, Ngugi wa Thiong'o, Nawal el Saadawi, and Wole Soyinka, to name some of the most prominent—are routinely censored or forced into exile, or even incarcerated, tortured, or executed, as was Nigerian

Ken Saro-Wiwa in 1995. African writers have often wandered, taught, and written on foreign shores because they could not do so at home. Books by writers residing in Africa are still more likely to be published and marketed in Paris and London than in Dakar or Lagos, and those published in major overseas capitals are more likely to garner international acclaim. Books written by Africans are also more plentiful in university libraries in Europe and the United States, and scholars outside of Africa are more likely to review and critique those books in the prominent and widely read periodicals, newspapers, and publications of the West. American students therefore have far greater access to texts written by Africans than do most African students, who typically cannot afford to buy books, were books available. And within Africa, Francocentric and Anglocentric educational legacies persist.

All these factors come between the reader and the lines on the page when one picks up a book of "African literature." To insist on such determinants of literature and to contextualize it in this way is also to recognize that our understanding of the field continues to shift. We are far more conscious of the ways in which the factors outlined above are present *in* texts, of the ways in which new texts revise the meaning of their antecedents, and of the fact that the literary act is a function of the reader and of institutions such as the university, publishing world, professional organizations, and newspapers, as well as of the writer and what is written.

Let us close this survey with reference to two important recent developments in literary production by Africans.

SOUTH AFRICAN LITERATURE TODAY

In 1990, Nelson Mandela, antiapartheid activist and leader of the armed wing of the African National Congress, was released by the South African government after twenty-seven years of imprisonment. South Africa proceeded to develop a new constitution and to hold the country's first democratic elections in which all South Africans, irrespective of "race," were able to exercise their right to vote. For most of the twentieth century, as we saw above, South African writers of all hues had grappled with the snares of apartheid. With the dismantling of the official policy, the culture of antiapartheid resistance that had shaped South African writing for decades began to crumble. As of the early 1980s, Njabulo Ndebele (*Fools and Other Stories,* 1983) urged South African writers to abandon the "spectacular" representation of antiapartheid struggle and to "rediscover the ordinary," to uncover, render, and mine the texture of everyday life for its pains, poignancy, and promise, as he himself does in an innovative novel, *The Cry of Winnie Mandela* (2003). Today, the South Africans we signaled above continue to write, of course, and a new generation of writers in English has arisen, many of them firmly addressing the complex tapestry of urban life, from poverty, unemployment, prostitution, HIV/AIDS, and xenophobia to hip urban lifestyles and consumer culture: Phaswane Mpe (*Welcome to Our Hillbrow,* 2001), K. Sello Duiker (*Thirteen Cents,* 2000; *The Quiet Violence of Dreams,* 2001), and Niq Mhlongo (*Dog Eat Dog,* 2004). Ivan Vladislavic mixes fantasy, historical events, recognizable places, and satire in fictions and nonfictions in the tradition of postmodernist aesthetics (*The Folly,* 1993; *The Restless Supermarket,* 2001). Imraan Coovadia (*The Wedding,* 2001; *Green-Eyed Thieves,* 2006) narrates with endless intertextual references and delightful prose the crises and adventures of Asian Africans both in Africa and in the Americas, while award-winning South African–born novelist and filmmaker Rayda Jacobs brings to this conclave a feminist voice recounting the lives of Muslim women at the intersection of multiple cultures (*The Middle Children,* 1994; *Eyes of the Sky,* 1995; *Confessions of a Gambler,* 2004). Zoë Wicomb, whose much acclaimed *You Can't Get Lost in Capetown* (1987) brought to full light the intersections of race and gender under apartheid, has published more recently *David's Story* (2000) and *Playing in the Light* (2006), and Zakes Mda, author of *Ways of Dying* (1995), a lyrical, magical realist story of possibility in mean circumstances, has brought out *The Heart of Redness* (2000), which probes historical legacies and social values in contemporary South Africa.

AFRICA DISPERSED

It may be apparent that any number of writers born in Africa no longer reside in their home countries but elsewhere on the continent or abroad. The trickle that began decades ago, due mostly to repressive governments, has become a torrent, not only because of ongoing oppressive and violent regimes but also because of woefully inadequate salaries and living conditions. Nor is it a phenomenon of a single class: while visual artists, writers, and filmmakers may go in search of greater freedom and resources to allow them to think deeply about their home countries and the continent from a distance, it is also the case that traders and a whole generation of youth who are stymied by stagnant economies, lack of education, and viable employment also dream the dream of emigration and opportunity.

Meanwhile, the metropolises of the former European colonizers, with their stringent policies on immigration, are no longer necessarily the destination of choice, but many young Africans, along the Atlantic cost in particular, still risk their lives in fragile boats to reach European shores. For those who survive the journey, life as an illegal immigrant without passport and appropriate documents is harrowing, as we see in *Bleu blanc rouge* (1998; *Blue White Red*), the award-winning first novel by Congolese Alain Mabanckou, and *I Was an Elephant Salesman* (1990; *Io, venditore di elefanti*), a memoir by Senegalese Pap Khouma. The United States, with its historically dynamic economy and thirst for innovation, has become something of a promised land for many young Africans, who are the most highly educated group of immigrants entering that country. And now China, which has an increasingly important presence on the African continent itself, is also becoming an important destination for African émigrés.

In addition to their maternal languages and other "national" languages, African immigrants speak and write English, French, Portuguese, Dutch, Italian, Japanese, and Chinese. Writers have begun to write not only in the languages of erstwhile colonizers in which they were schooled but in languages they come to choose. Thus, the Senegalese professor and novelist Gorgui Dieng, who remains in Senegal, writes, by choice, in English (*A Leap out of the Dark,* 2002); Pap Khouma, mentioned above, writes in the language of the country where he resides and works as a street vendor, Italian. The bright, talented Ibo novelist Chimamanda Ngozi Adichie, who has been educated largely in the United States, where she resides, writes in English of the Biafran war and contemporary political repression in her native Nigeria (*Purple Hibiscus,* 2003; *Half of a Yellow Sun,* 2006; *The Thing Around Your Neck,* 2009), whereas her compatriot Chikwe Unigwe, who lives in Belgium and writes in Dutch—which she translates for subsequent publication in English—has produced a remarkable novel about African sex workers in Antwerp (*On Black Sisters' Street,* 2011).

Algerian Assia Djebar resides and teaches in the United States, as do Nigerian Chinua Achebe, South African Zakes Mda, and Kenyan Ngugi wa Thiong'o. South African Zoë Wicomb has taught and written in both Scotland and South Africa. J. M. Coetzee of South Africa now resides in Australia. Nigerian Kole Omotoso, author of the historical novel *Just Before Dawn* (1988), works and resides in South Africa. For a decade or more, Somali Nuruddin Farah laid roots first in Nigeria, then in South Africa. Moyez Vassanji lives and writes in Canada. Congolese writer Alain Mabanckou teaches and writes in the United States. Calixthe Beyala of Cameroon, well known for her early strident feminist novels *C'est le soleil qui m'a brûlée* (1987 [*The Sun Hath Looked Upon Me,* 1996]) and *Tu t'appelleras Tanga* (1988 [*Your Name Shall Be Tanga,* 1996]) and Fatou Diome of Senegal, author of a novel whose heroine continually negotiates the space between home and abroad, *Le ventre de l'Atlantique* (2003 [*The Belly of the Atlantic,* 2008]), live and write in France, as do Nabile Farès of Algeria (*Un passager de l'occident,* 1971 [A traveler through the West]) and Tahar Ben Jelloun of Morocco (*L'enfant de sable,* 1985 [The sand child]). France has also been home to writers whose parents are French and African—Leïla Sebbar (*Shérazade,* 1982), Bessora (*53 cm,* 1999) and Marie Ndiaye (*Trois femmes puissantes,* 2009 [Three powerful women]). Senegalese novelist Ken Bugul lived for many years in Benin. South African Rayda Jacobs lived in Canada for twenty-seven years. Ivorian Véronique Tadjo, who lived for a number of years in Kenya, now teaches and writes in South Africa. And just a few years ago, Senegalese Boubacar Boris Diop divided his time between Mexico, Tunisia, and South Africa. Whatever its roots, this crisscrossing of the continent and the globe has created a broad range of experimentation and new trends in "African" writing that we may justifiably think of as transnational and diasporic.

ACKNOWLEDGMENTS

With thanks to Akin Adesokan and Natasha Vaubel. Special thanks to Meg Arenberg for her contribution to the Swahili literature section.

11 African Film

Akin Adesokan

It is a truism of African cinema that one cannot productively discuss the films that make up the field without keeping in mind the social and economic conditions under which they are made. Fifty years after the first feature film to be written, produced, and directed by an African, and with this cinematic tradition becoming as globally important an art form as African literature and the Afropop component of world music, economic, political, and cultural factors continue to be central to its full understanding. It is therefore not surprising that, across three generations, issues of political and cultural identity are a main topical preoccupation of African filmmakers. For various reasons younger, often foreign-based filmmakers have sharply reacted in their work against the biases of their predecessors who came from a background of anticolonial activism, thus showing the limitations of earlier practices. However, sociopolitical situations in contemporary African countries, as well as the larger economic order in the world, are so crucial to most forms of cultural production that they cannot be totally ignored. As a result, filmmakers have developed a more complex treatment of sociopolitical issues. Emphasis has shifted in their works from a simple notion of rejection as a way of asserting identity to the understanding that identity usually results from a number of different factors. They have begun to experiment with forms and genres, drawing on music, dance, youth culture, fashion, and sundry expressive forms and reflecting greater awareness of cinematic traditions from different parts of the world.

This chapter looks at African cinema as a historical phenomenon, focusing on the institutional, thematic, and technological changes that have shaped the field since its inception in the early 1960s. The discussion is organized along five thematic lines. These include an account of the broad cultural agendas aimed at countering the negative stereotypes of Africa, Africans, and the black world propagated through popular films of Hollywood; an in-depth look at the career of Ousmane Sembene, the late Senegalese director and arguably the most influential African filmmaker whose work embodies the central concerns of African cinema in its various stages; the different strategies developed by filmmakers to cope with the specific institutional problems militating against filmmaking as an economic and cultural practice; an overview of the development of national and regional cinemas across the continent; and the various thematic changes that African cinema has undergone, especially in the last two decades. In conclusion, we look at the new institutional developments in different parts of the continent as well as the rise of new perspectives among women and the young, and what these portend for the continuing relevance of this cinematic tradition.

AFRICAN CINEMA AS A "TOOL FOR REVOLUTION"

Prior to 1963, when Sembene released *Borom Sarret,* his first feature film, what passed for cinema in the African continent were mainly the propaganda films produced for the administrative purposes of the colonial governments. These were conventional documentaries highlighting "native" institutions and customs and aimed at foreign observers and researchers, instructional and educational films on the advantages of modern medical and technical innovations, and the like. A notable figure in this period in English-speaking countries was William Seller, whose career was closely tied to the bureaucratic structure called the Colonial Film Unit in Nigeria and Ghana (the latter formerly called the Gold Coast). After World War II, a major development in cinema came from Jean Rouch, the French ethnographer who, between 1948 and his death in 2004, produced more than a hundred films. Rouch was an exponent of "shared anthropology" in cinema, the process whereby a foreign director filmed a cultural event or ritual and later exhibited the film to the same people who had been filmed, with the expectation that mutual cultural understanding would result from the encounter. Among his major titles are *Les maîtres fous (The Mad Masters), Jaguar, La chasse au lion à l'arc (The Lion Hunters), Moi, un noir (I, a black),* and *Petit à petit (Little by Little).* Partly because of his position as a French intellectual working with young Africans who aspired to become filmmakers (such as Oumarou Ganda, Safi Faye, and Moustapha Alassane), Rouch was to prove very influential in the development of African cinema. His approach took for granted that technical expertise lay with the director, who, given the state of the technology of filmmaking, was quite often also the cameraman and the narrator, while his subjects, such as the Dogon of Mali and the Souk fishermen of Niger, possessed the knowledge of the ritual or custom being filmed. Rouch's influence was not a simple one. Indeed, some of the early African directors saw it as part of their duty to contest the assumptions behind "shared anthropology" because they saw parallels between ethnographic cinema and colonial cinema. It was an era when the old racist images of Africa and Africans propagated by Hollywood in the Tarzan films and the screen adaptations of the novels of Rider Haggard were being reinforced by some of the official policies of French and British colonial governments. The depiction of Africans in the ethnographic films of Rouch might not have been as negative as in the popular Hollywood films, but he was still a foreign interlocutor, and his primary audience was not African.

It was in this context that Sembene, a former soldier in World War II and a union organizer in Marseilles, France, came on the scene. Sembene had begun his career as a novelist, producing several stories and the novels *Le docker noir (The Black Docker)* and *Les bouts de bois de Dieu (God's Bits of Wood),* which deal with the complex relations between Africans and their French rulers in the late colonial period. But he was also concerned that these novels, written in French and published mainly in Paris, were not accessible to the illiterate and poor Africans to whom he wished to address his work. Therefore, he traveled to Moscow for technical training in filmmaking, returning in 1963 to set in motion a long and productive career. Before we come to a detailed discussion of Sembene's films, it is important to place his emergence in a wider historical context.

The period between the end of World War II in the mid-1940s and the fall of Soviet communism in the late 1980s is regarded as the period of decolonization. This was the time when African, Caribbean, and Asian countries formerly under the control of European powers—France, Britain, Belgium, the Netherlands, Portugal—achieved political independence and came into their own as sovereign nations. A corollary of political independence was the sense among intellectuals from these new nations that they also had to be in control of how the world saw them, and that the decades of negative images through the powerful medium of cinema had to be reversed. Thus, emerging filmmakers and critics developed the idea of cinema as a "tool for revolution." In a series of manifestos and communiqués and in the establishment of the Festival Panafricain du Cinéma de Ouagadougou (FESPACO) in Burkina Faso and the Carthage Film Festival in Tunisia, these filmmakers and scholars made an explicit point of relating their works to the nationalist ideals of Pan-Africanism. This was not an exclusively African development, but part of a global Third World agenda, coinciding with similar efforts in South Asia, the Middle East, and South America. In cinema history, these various efforts developed into an important aesthetic formation that goes by the name "Third Cinema" and was promoted by a group of South American artist-intellectuals.

OUSMANE SEMBENE: A DECISIVE FIGURE

Widely acknowledged as the pioneer of African cinema, the late Sembene (d. 2007) came to filmmaking at age forty, after publishing a number of canonical novels and stories. He made a total of thirteen films over forty years: *L'empire Sonhrai* (documentary, 1963), *Borom Sarret* (1963), *Niaye* (1964), *La noire de . . . (Black Girl,* 1965), *Mandabi* (1968), *Taaw* (1970), *Emitai* (1971), *Xala* (1974), *Ceddo* (1976 [1981]), *Camp de Thiaroye* (1989), *Guelwaar* (1992), *Faat Kine* (2000), and *Moolaadé* (2004). His best-known novel, *God's Bits of Wood,* is reportedly being prepared for cinema in collaboration with Danny Glover, the African American actor. Born in January 1923 in Ziguinchor, southern Senegal, the teenage Ousmane enrolled for a school certificate, the sure passport to a clerical job in a French colony. But he was expelled for assaulting a teacher and spent his early youth in Dakar, doing odd jobs. After he was demobilized as a soldier in World War II, he went back to France and worked as a dockworker and trade unionist, during which he wrote his first novels and stories. Sembene was aware that limited literacy and access to technology posed problems to potential audiences of African cultural productions, and so in 1961 he enrolled at the Gorki Institute in Moscow to study filmmaking. Two years later, he produced and directed *Borom Sarret* (*The Wagoner*, 1963). It narrates the story of a Dakar cart driver who is hired to take a client to an upscale neighborhood (the Plateau) and has his lowly transport confiscated for trespassing in such elite quarters. Shot in black and white and entirely in exterior (meaning filmed outdoors), the cart driver's internal monologue tracked through the synchronous sound of French, the nineteen-minute film captures the intrusive stare of passers-by, proof of the newness of the camera as a tool in the public domain. Cinema, Sembene declared at the outset and repeated throughout his career, was a kind of evening school. It was also a means of controlling the terms of discourse about the continent.

Two other films of that decade, *La noire de . . .* (*Black Girl*, 1965) and *Mandabi* (*The Money Order*, 1968), continue with the project of developing an African perspective in cinema. For Sembene, the question of political liberty was inseparable from the challenge of fusing different traditions—technological, narrative, artistic—in the service of a modern African society. This society is imagined as continental, and it is a potentially self-sufficient one; the filmmaker is on record as describing Africa as the center of his world: "Why be the sunflower and look up to the sun?" he asks in Férid Boughédir's historical documentary *Caméra d'Afrique* (1982). The context of production is important to an understanding of Sembene's work. In different ways, his career epitomized the problems faced by postcolonial African writers and artists, but especially filmmakers, cinema being a capital-intensive undertaking, in terms of both production and distribution.[1] Moreover, his thematic interests and portrayal of historical events put him in conflict with political authorities in his native Senegal (especially under the leadership of the poet-president Léopold Senghor), resulting in the censoring of some of his films. Sembene's films can be challenging both in the kind of questions they raise and in how such questions are raised. The viewer is at once exasperated and engaged by the "truthfulness" of a scene of confrontation, for example between the educated sergeant Diatta and the soldiers in *Camp de Thiaroye* (1989), dealing with the mass murder of African soldiers returning from World War II. While Diatta's liberal argument for dialogue is convincing, it is equally difficult to impeach the illiterate soldiers' point about the danger of negotiating with the French commanders. A similar clarity can be seen in the refusal of the film *Ceddo* to idealize traditional institutions, represented in the film by the Diola monarchy, the weakest of the groups in contention for power. In Sembene's films, the camera presents a polarized but dynamic spectacle, capturing the actors in a frontal frame, the better to support the moral or political weight of the argument. No other African filmmaker exhibits quite this signature; it is even rarer in contemporary cinema, where nuance is often synonymous with artistic sophistication. But this is not to say that Sembene's work lacks subtlety. There are several levels of narration in any number of his films, and the director's sharp sense of form keeps each thread well in focus. The stylistic approach sees resolution, which usually comes at the end of a given film, as a kind of empowerment outside the frame, as if the final word is a matter for debate in real life.

What makes Sembene's career important to any discussion of African cinema is the enduring way it has grappled with the historical, social, political, and personal dimensions of contemporary experiences on the continent. Most new-generation filmmakers are notable for their unwillingness to present their films as the mouthpieces of political engagement, preferring to play up issues of cultural mixing, exile, transnationalism, and cinema itself as a reflexive form. Sembene's later works do not ignore these issues, but they address them within the context of the director's familiar signature. Examples of this attitude toward new forms of identity and ways of being in society are present in his last two films, *Faat Kine* (1999) and *Moolaadé* (2004), parts of a trilogy on what he tagged as "stories of daily heroism." The eponymous heroine of the first film is a successful gas-station proprietor who as a young girl was impregnated and then abandoned by her teacher, and subsequently thrown out by her father for bringing shame to the family. But Faat Kine is now also the proud

Figure 11.1. Ousmane Sembene accepts the prize of the jury for *Moolaadé* at the Fourth International Film Festival in Marrakesh, Morocco, on December 12, 2004.
Getty Images.

mother of two dignified children, and her relationships toward them, her former boyfriends, and others she encounters in her line of work convey the sense of a woman with a deep awareness of her endless possibilities and her freedom to explore them. *Moolaadé,* which deals with the issue of female circumcision, closes with an extraordinary image of a huge pile of radios being burned in an attempt by the affronted men to destroy the source of the women's power to resist the age-old practice. The larger context for this spectacle is the phenomenon of global media, which is liberating for many people in the world, filmmakers no less. Sembene here appears to be killing two birds with one stone: addressing the futility of censoring a democratic mass medium such as radio, and underlining the importance of such a medium in forging identities that male-dominated societies can no longer control.

Indeed, the point could be made that through these kinds of confrontation between the old and the new, Sembene is also giving artistic relevance to questions of identity that take cognizance of the issues that younger filmmakers are wrestling with, whether they are based on the continent or outside it.

AFRICAN CINEMA AND THE PROBLEMS OF FILM PRODUCTION

The Tunisian filmmaker and critic Férid Boughédir once remarked: "Francophone African film exists because of France and also doesn't exist because of France" (Diawara 1992: 31). This comment goes to the heart of the problematic relationship between France and its former African colonies with regard to the development of African cinema. As a country with a reputable history of cinema, France in the postwar years was involved in an important, though understated, struggle with the United States over the control of the world market in film distribution. Thus, the government in Paris created a powerful Ministry of Cooperation as part of the official French policy of assimilation, even as the advent of African cinema coincided with the end of French empire. This ministry was critical in providing technical and financial aid to some of the earliest African filmmakers, and the birth of an institution such as FESPACO would have been difficult without the support of the French government. For a cultural formation predicated on the anti-imperial agenda of taking control of self-representation, African cinema was soon in the paradoxical position of being sustained technically, financially, and in terms of human support by the same institutions it had to confront. This is the paradox that Boughédir's statement highlights, and it is not limited to the role of the French Ministry of Cooperation (which is no longer in existence, having been absorbed into the Ministry of Foreign Affairs in the mid-1990s).

In the global scheme of things, new African nations were not in a position to take adequate advantage of cinema because they lacked the necessary technological expertise. Issues of education, industrialization, and technical and infrastructural development were considered of priority in countries that continued to supply a substantial amount of the world's raw materials, while cinema appeared no more than a luxury. The two dominant tendencies in cinema at the time seemed to confirm this prejudice: Hollywood films were seen as mere escapist entertainment, while serious, experimental films were regarded as sophisticated meditations that self-important artists were free to pursue but young nations could ill afford. If cinema was thought to serve any immediate purpose, this was understood to be in the area of documentation of official activities of national governments and the production of newsreels. In most cases, the apparatus of the old colonial film unit was considered up to that task.

However, this view of cinema was seriously mistaken. As an art, cinema pertains to both culture and industry—that is, a film is both a cultural object and a commodity. The finished product, screened in theaters or sold as cassettes or DVDs, is the end result not just of several collaborations but also of complex strategies of funding, distribution, and exhibition. The African continent could boast of brilliant filmmakers including Youssef Chahine (Egypt), Ousmane Sembene (Senegal), Med Hondo (Mauritania), Souleymane Cissé (Mali), and so on, but questions of distribution and the monopolies of Hollywood, Bollywood, and Hong Kong films in African cities constantly put the works of these world-class filmmakers out of the reach of African audiences. This was, and remains, a big problem for African cinema—the fact that for reasons of technical and economic logistics, African films are more widely known and discussed in North America and Western Europe than on the continent.

In the last decade and a half, there have been positive, if complex, changes. One interesting case is Zimbabwe's Film for Development Trust, which provides funds for filmmakers to produce films that have an immediate relevance because they directly address social issues. It has supported the works of writer-filmmaker Tsitsi Dangarembga *(Everybody's Child)* and producer Godwin Mawuru *(Neria)*. More recently, it has collaborated with the Nigerian director Tunde Kelani, who produced or directed a number of social-issue films *(Yellow Card; White Handkerchief)*. There is also the New Directions initiative from MNET, the South African cable network, which commissions upcoming directors to make small-budget films. The collaboration with Kelani was based on an important factor, one that has recently undercut the argument that African films do not appeal to African audiences: the rise of the Nigerian film industry, sometimes tagged as "Nollywood." This phenomenon developed out of economic necessity. Filmmakers such as Ola Balogun, Francis Oladele, and Eddie Ugbomah, all trained to use conventional technology of celluloid cinema and carry out postproduction abroad, soon realized that economic and social conditions in the country could no longer support that kind of filmmaking. Most of them gave up; others resorted to using basic video cameras and local studios to shoot and edit their films. It was a rough and unpretty beginning, and there is no doubt that the industry, in spite of its successes, is still light-years away from the dreams of filmmakers such as Sembene or Abderrahmane Sissako. But the films are available not just on Nigerian streets but across the continent and in many parts of the world as well, in a manner that Sembene only dreamed of. Since the technology of filmmaking has become increasingly cheaper and many more filmmakers are being trained and better exposed, it is hoped that the technical and ideological blind spots in the Nigerian films will be overcome with time. There is a similar development taking place in Ghana, a country that shared the British colonial heritage with Nigeria and whose film industry was similarly shaped by policies arising from the British establishment's understanding of the role of film. The difference here is best understood in terms of the difference between the work of Rouch and Seller, as discussed above.

NATIONAL AND REGIONAL CINEMAS: A BRIEF HISTORICAL SURVEY

The history of cinema on the African continent is inseparable from the history of European colonialism. The birth of cinema in the mid-1890s coincided with the nineteenth-century process of colonial conquest, and what we watch and study as African cinema has developed in part through the instrumentality of the administrative system known as *la francophonie,* the cultural-linguistic sphere of French influence outside Europe, as well as the British Colonial Film Unit (although the film industries of Egypt and South Africa constitute important exceptions on the continent). As the critic Roy Armes points out in his recent history of African filmmaking, the African films produced within this paradigm are industrial and cultural products of individuals and institutions that came into being under nationalism, the decisive development of the modern era. The historical process of nationalism thus ensured that films would be perceived and treated as belonging to discrete nations, and that institutions would be established (or at least conceived) to support the development of cinema. Thus although an institution such as FESPACO has continued to advance the cause of African film, its ability to do so cannot be fully understood outside of the competing (and sometimes complementary) policy goals of the government of Burkina Faso and France's Bureau of Cinema. What this reveals, more in Francophone African countries than in Anglophone or Lusophone ones, is the analogy between nation and language as it pertains to the field of literary studies. In other words, a national cinema is believed to be the form for the expression of different aspects of the culture of a given country, and it performs this role within the parameters of the language of cinema, much as literature was believed to do for a given country, such as Italian literature did for Italy and the Italian language.

However, the idea of a national cinema as embodying the artistic vision of filmmakers identified with a particular nation remained powerful even in countries that did not have the benefit of the patronage of a former colonial overlord. As the filmmaker and film theorist John Akomfrah argued some years ago, nationalist sentiments within a particular country represented a phase that independence-era Pan-African intellectuals believed would be transcended. This hope was not realized, however, and so the film industry continued to be organized discretely within individual countries, and always as part of the kind of industrialization that was expected to transform each country into a modern, self-reproducing society. It was out of this sense of national self-determination that countries such as Nigeria, Senegal, Ghana, Cameroon, and Kenya all established different institutions dedicated to the cinema industry in the 1970s and 1980s. While it is true that these corporations or cinema societies also saw to questions of distribution and exhibition of all motion pictures, including foreign imports, they certainly abetted the production of local work, such as Sembene's acclaimed film *Xala*, the first film to be co-produced with Senegal's National Society for Cinema.

Two examples are relevant in shedding light on this relationship between the nation-state and film production in the African context. In Boughédir's famous documentary *Caméra d'Afrique,* the question of the monopoly of distribution networks by powerful companies (not easily regulated by the governments) provided the basis for a rancorous discussion between filmmakers and financiers. Given the perception that distributors and financiers were influential in determining which African films were seen on the continent, it was revealed in that documentary that fourteen African countries decided to nationalize their film industries in 1980 as a way of breaking the monopoly exercised by the foreign distributors. The extent to which such actions succeeded in mobilizing film production remains uncertain, as the unavailability of African films continues to be an issue. Second, during the 1980s, the Belgian scholar Victor Bachy produced a series of monographs that offered overviews of cinema-related activities in select African countries. These monographs were commissioned by the International Catholic Organization for Cinema and Audiovisuals (OCIC) and published by the Paris-based L'Harmattan. They included volumes on Senegal (Paulin Soumanou Vieyra), Niger (Ousmane Ilbo), Cameroon (Arthur Si Bita), and Nigeria (Françoise Balogun). The rationale behind the series was national segmentation of film production, and this has to be seen in relation to Akomfrah's argument about the limitations of the Pan-African ideal in a form such as cinema, which in order to be national has to be equally about culture and industry.

The picture was different both in Lusophone countries and within that group. Each of these countries—Angola, Mozambique, Guinea-Bissau, São Tomé and Principe, and Cape Verde—came into its own through wars of liberation against Portugal in the 1960s and 1970s. Liberation went hand in hand with cinema, and in most cases as part of the process of national reconstruction that followed each successful war. The film historian Claire Andrade-Watkins speaks of this production context as that of "liberation cinema," which drew some of its ideological orientation from the notion of Third Cinema. She also notes the decisive impact of the filmmaker Ruy Guerra in the development of the film industry in Mozambique, perhaps the most successful of the experiments in liberation cinema in countries with Marxist-Leninist political sympathies. Guerra's role was more decisive than the experiments by leading French filmmakers, notably Jean Rouch and Jean-Luc Godard. In Angola, the enthusiasm for film production was not sustained following the attainment of independence, but film production remains a function largely supported by the national ministry of culture. Perhaps the career of the Bissauan filmmaker Flora Gomes best illustrates the travails of national cinema in Lusophone countries. Here was an accomplished filmmaker with a recognizable style and a sizable oeuvre, but without any kind of film industry as support base.

This picture will not be complete without an idea of the situation in North Africa. Historically, countries such as Egypt and Morocco had an earlier start on filmmaking than most of the countries to the south. In fact, cinema in Egypt ranks next to South Africa's cinema in terms of its development more as an industry and less as a practice tied to the assertion of cultural and/or historical identities. For example, the career of the late Youssef Chahine drew upon a history of modernist art specific to the history of Alexandria, putting this director in the league of world-famous filmmakers. Indeed, Chahine, from a bourgeois Coptic background, studied acting in the United States, attending the Pasadena Playhouse, and was already making films in the early 1950s. His autobiographical film, *Alexandria . . . Why* (1978), gives an idea of this director's aesthetic worldview: not only do few African directors attempt such self-analysis in their work, but it is also rare to find a trilogy of films devoted to a native city, such as we have from Chahine's oeuvre.

Chahine may have been a modernist master before the politicized era of FES-PACO and its strings of communiqués that sought to tie filmmaking to the political agenda of decolonization, but there are other North African filmmakers who did not view their work outside of the worldwide progressive ideas that caught on in the mid-1960s. Topmost in this category are Tunisian directors Férid Boughédir and Tahar Cheriaa, both of whom identified with the ideological direction followed by the independence-era filmmakers. Indeed, for them, filmmaking was a political tool, and their progressive political orientation enabled them to relate to the continent in terms of common sociopolitical issues faced by the people, irrespective of cultural or racial differences. Of course, the political optimism that informed the attitude of the Tunisian cineasts has largely faded not only on the continent but also across the world, and the works of younger directors from North Africa are developed within the national cinema industry while also participating in the global artistic network, like those of many African filmmakers. Nor is the history of filmmaking in these countries a sum of the directors' histories. In Egypt, the industrial form of cinema ensured the growth of the melodrama, and this may explain the vibrancy of this cinema relative to much of the continent.

What all this points to is the diverse ways in which cinema has found its place across the continent. Although nationalism was the driving force behind cultural development, it is worthy of note that the idea of national cinema, as culture and industry, remains highly problematic in the African context.

CHANGING FACES OF AFRICAN CINEMA

Released in 1987, both *Yeelen* (*Brightness,* dir. Souleymane Cissé) and *La vie est belle* (*Life Is Rosy,* dir. Mweze Ngangura) seem to point early to the changing aesthetics of

African cinema. As suggested earlier, some critics and practitioners have argued that political didacticism in film is the great turnoff to mass audiences. They contend that cinema is a form of entertainment, and the militancy of political cinema limits its appeal to the continent's diverse audiences. By using the popular genre of music comedy *(La vie est belle)* and allegory *(Yeelen),* the two directors suggest alternative ways of creating a self-sustaining industry based on nondidactic approaches to storytelling. Perhaps it was a coincidence that these films came out at about the same time, but a close look at films produced in the past decade and a half will reveal that a proliferation of aesthetic modes is far from accidental. Young directors such as Jean-Pierre Bekolo, Jean-Marie Teno, Fanta Régina Nacro, Abderrahmane Sissako, Moussa Sene Absa, Flora Gomes, Zola Maseko, Idrissa Ouedraogo, Mahamat Saleh-Haroun, Joseph Gaï Ramaka, and many others are taking African cinema to a level of self-awareness that puts them at par with their contemporaries in other parts of the world. The defining character of cinema in this phase is not so much its historical identity as its aesthetic openness. For these filmmakers, being African goes without saying, but cinema is a tool they choose consciously, and that choice comes with different kinds of responsibilities. There is no doubt that this generation of directors is able to take African identity for granted largely because the previous generation had labored under such a burden. It is also important to note that although most of the directors discussed here are young, the artistic innovation characteristic of the new tendency is not limited to young directors.

This new tendency in African cinema has five identifiable features. First, there is a concern with film as a distinct form with its own language. This is manifested in the ways that a given film simultaneously develops as a story and draws attention to cinema as a medium unlike any other. For example, Gomes's second film, *Udju azul di Yonta (The Blue Eyes of Yonta,* 1991), tells the story of a poor student who writes a romantic letter to a beautiful young girl, who in turn is infatuated with an older man. As this intriguing narrative unfolds, the viewer is attracted to the self-consciousness of the camera through pauses, artificial darkness or light, and low-angle shots, all occurring without compromising or overstating the importance of the narrative. This concern with the apparatus of cinema is raised to the level of an argument in Bekolo's 1996 film *Aristotle's Plot,* where we are invited to meditate on conventional storytelling originating in Aristotle's *The Poetics* and its implications for the future of cinema in an African context.

Indeed, the question of genre this film broaches is the second feature of the new African cinema. Different films demonstrate that although drama is important in cinema, it is only one of several possibilities. Thus, many new films are using different genres and forms either to supplement a film's story line or as its central motif. Ramaka's *Karmen Gei* retells the Carmen story in the context of early twenty-first-century Senegal, using music, dance, and other forms of spectacle in a way that prioritizes these forms without undermining the basic narration. A similar approach is present in Sene Absa's *Madame Brouette* (2002), which turns the cliché of a

Figure 11.2. Poster for *Karmen Gei.*
Joseph Gaï Ramaka.

wayward, dangerous beauty on its head by revealing the exploitation that under-pins gender and class relations. It is also a musical, lively with color and spectacle. In *Nha Fala* (My Voice, 2002), Gomes uses the genre of the musical to reflect on the challenges of remembering the past while seeking personal fulfillment and self-expression. Obviously, this explosion of interest in music testifies to the continent's cultural heritage and the global commercial viability of Afropop.

However, the musical is only one of the new genres. There is also a clever use of technology—especially radio—in a number of the new films. We see this in *La vie sur terre* (*Life on Earth*, 1999), Sissako's genre-defying film about the new millennium, where passages from the work of Aimé Césaire are read as an "on-air library" to counteract the effects of illiteracy and limited access to new technology. As the example of Sembene's *Moolaadé* (2004) shows above, the "small medium" of radio is held up as a liberating tool for the women and the young. Over the last decade, African filmmakers have also shown compelling interest in science fiction and futuristic themes, such as in *Pumzi* (2010), *Les saignantes* (2005), and *Afrique paradis* (2006).

A third feature of the new cinema is stylistic experimentation, a rather broad category that may apply to some aspects of the features already discussed. One film that breaks into this mode quite loudly is *Quartier Mozart* (1992), Bekolo's first full-length feature, about sexual politics in a Yaoundé neighborhood. Through jump cuts, syncopated rhythms, direct address, and still montages, the film shows a concern with cinematic language similar to *Udju azul di Yonta,* but with less interest in the latter's story-driven approach. Although *Quartier Mozart* marks the advent of a new generation, Bekolo is on record as paying homage to the work of the Senegalese director Djibril Diop Mambéty, whose *Touki-Bouki* (1973) remains a truly experimental African film, ahead of its time in many ways. Fanta Nacro's *Un certain regard* ranks with *Aristotle's Plot* in its exposure of how an African film is made—especially the relationship between a director and the social conditions of his or her location. A similar question forms the basis of Haroun's *Bye-Bye Africa* (1999), a reflexive personal essay about the viability of cinema as an industrial formation in economically destitute Chad. What is common to the films that raise experimentation to the level of discourse is that they correspondingly downplay explicit narrative. In this sense, in spite of its interests in film language as such, Gomes's *Udju azul di Yonta* will not qualify as an experimental work. But the feature is indeed broad enough to contain other kinds of approach to filmmaking. For example, the much-praised crime fiction film from the Democratic Republic of Congo, *Viva Riva* (dir. Djo Munga, 2010), departs sharply from the different tendencies that have defined African cinema up till now. This film, like most of the films coming out of Nollywood in Nigeria, consciously puts the story first, and plays with an astute sense of desires, realities, and the different cultural flows within and outside the continent to speak to the world. Without minimizing the importance of the historical background and ongoing sociopolitical orientation of African filmmaking, it is clear that the most promising advances in this cinematic tradition will come from a broad range of stylistic experimentations.

Following from this is the fourth feature, namely, that most of these directors are aware of international film styles and are not inhibited about acknowledging these styles in their work or in interviews. Not only do they acknowledge others' influences, but their aesthetic choices are also impacting on filmmaking practices in other parts of the world. Boughédir is on record as crediting Gaston Kaboré's *Wend Kuuni* (1982) as the film that influenced him while working on his *Halfaouine*. "When Gaston Kaboré films *Wend Kuuni,* holding his close-up shot of the boy longer than is normally accepted in the rules of classic montage, something magic[al] suddenly happens at that precise moment. It was a great lesson for me! He had the necessary perception to cut the shot later, and those few 'extra' seconds generate an emotion that I had never seen before" (Barlet 1998). Kaboré, who uses horses and riders in *Wend Kuuni* in a style reminiscent of Westerns, has in turn remarked of Charlie Chaplin: "He was able to make the sun correspond with the moon. By that I mean he was able to crystallize and signify meaning in a gesture or image, to make one image equal a thousand words" (Martin 2003: 165).

This attitude toward international styles and influences is not limited to directors' statements. Bekolo's 2005 film *Les saignantes (The bloody ones)* looks at different cinematic genres—sci-fi, detective, thriller, mystery—and raises questions about their relevance in ways that demonstrate his ongoing concern with the issues broached in *Aristotle's Plot*. The final scene of *Udju azul di Yonta*, where children dance around the swimming pool, has been described as a complex homage to Federico Fellini, the Italian filmmaker. Even a supposedly "traditional" story such as *Yeelen* has affinities with Stanley Kubrick's *2001: A Space Odyssey*. Sissako, who is becoming famous for the light touch and the quiet pace of his films, describes this relationship as more of a fascination with certain films than with their directors. With these examples, which are far from exhaustive, the point is not that African filmmakers are interesting when they "appropriate" or "copy" the styles of Western filmmakers—Sembene was an inspiration to a generation of filmmakers around the world—but that the earlier attitude that treated cross-cultural dialogues in cinema with suspicion no longer has much purchase.

The fifth feature, then, is a more nuanced understanding of politics. The fact that young filmmakers have tended to emphasize the aesthetic aspects of filming has encouraged the perception that African cinema is now in a "post-engagement" phase. It is true that fewer filmmakers exhibit the kind of poignant didacticism one observes in the work of Sembene, but this is not to say that new films lack politics altogether. Rather, they look at politics as part of everyday life, as one sees in Jean-Marie Teno's *Chef!* (1999) and Kelani's *Agogo Eewo* (2002), to cite two examples. Others have become preoccupied with social issues—health, women's empowerment, the debt crisis, conflict resolution—in ways that direct the questions inward. As a corrective to the frivolous treatment of the problems of war and genocide in Africa in a number of Hollywood films, Régina Nacro offers *La nuit de la verité (The Night of Truth,* 2004), which draws on indigenous practices of dialogue and restitution. Sissako's *Bamako* (2006) attempts a remorseless critique of the World Bank as part of the corporate globalization that perpetuates the impoverishment of the world's populations, with a specific interest in contemporary Africa. The last two films by Sembene (*Faat Kine* and *Moolaadé*) are memorable for their interest in the social condition of women, addressing questions of empowerment and female genital mutilation, respectively. The late Mambéty's *La petite vendeuse du soleil (The Little Girl Who Sold the Sun)* and *Le franc* also turned the searchlight on "little people." Given the continent's diversity and the increasing availability of information about different aspects of everyday life, African cinema is most likely more complex than it is at the moment in its depiction of African realities.

LOOKING FORWARD

In recent years, South Africa has been playing a prominent role in the development of African filmmaking. This is not surprising, for the country's cinema industry has always been important, although it was ill served by the claustrophobia of apartheid rule. Given its better-organized production and distribution facilities, institutional supports historically linked to Ouagadougou and Bamako are being redirected toward South Africa, according to recent reports. The government-owned but commercial South African Broadcasting Corporation (SABC) is in the forefront of the innovative packaging of African films. Its satellite channel, Africa Magic, regularly screens Nollywood and Francophone African films across the continent and in parts of the Caribbean.

Changes in information technology and the increasing availability, affordability, and portability of digital technology mean that filmmaking will become less daunting than before, and African filmmakers are set to take advantage of these changes. This is most obvious in the emergence of Nollywood, which combines the cheap technology of video with story lines that African audiences can relate to, fashioning a cinematic practice whose main strengths are its ability to proliferate and change according to socioeconomic conditions. We also observe the growth of film festivals in different parts of the continent, such as Sithengi in South Africa, the Zanzibar Film Festival, the Zuma Film Festival in Abuja, Nigeria, and the now-inclusive Cairo International Film Festival, not to forget FESPACO. Side by side with the growth of film festivals is a phenomenon that few people notice but which is in fact crucial to the sustenance of African filmmaking: the emergence of film training institutes, through either individual efforts (such as Institut Imagine in Burkina Faso, directed by the filmmaker Gaston Kaboré), governmental structures (the National Film School in Accra, Ghana), or a combination of both (the Nigerian Film Institute in Jos, and the Scriptwriting Workshop directed by the writer-producer Amaka Igwe in Nigeria).

One notable development in African filmmaking is the increasing presence of female filmmakers and the sophistication of their work. Throughout the short history of this cinematic tradition, women such as Safi Faye and Sarah Maldoror have made a serious impact, but their work has not received the kind of attention extended to their male counterparts. This is part of the big problem of the lopsidedness of access that, because of socialization processes and especially those in education, has been available to women as compared to men. However, the world has changed, and women filmmakers are becoming as visible as men. Among the more productively engaging directors across the continent are the Zimbabwean author and director Tsitsi Dangarembga *(Everyone's Child)*, the Burkinabe Régina Nacro

(The Night of Truth), and the Nigerian-born Afro-German expatriate director Branwen Okpako *(Valley of the Innocents, The Education of Auma Obama).* Nacro made a number of short films early in her career, and recently produced and directed the full-length fiction *The Night of Truth* (2004), a film that explicitly presents conflict resolution as an African responsibility. In many ways, this film (set in the aftermath of a horrific war not unlike what happened in Sierra Leone or Liberia in the 1990s) challenges the viewer to contrast the images, argumentation, characterization, and resolution with those of Hollywood films focusing on comparable themes *(Blood Diamond, Hotel Rwanda)* and made around the same time. The combination of factors such as the increasing mobility of people with talent and education, the relative affordability of the technical components of filmmaking, and progressive actions creating opportunities for women is sure to bring greater visibility to the work of these fine directors, as well as draw attention to those working in all sorts of difficult circumstances.

Related to this is the case of young directors, based outside the continent and within, whose cultural and educational backgrounds do not encourage a simple equation between political identity (as Africans) and artistic orientation. These directors are too numerous to mention, and even a brief list would be biased, but recent works by Newton Aduaka, Alain Gomis, Zola Maseko, Branwen Okpako, Nadia Labidi, Seke Somolu, and Kadiatou Konaté demonstrate extremely diverse perspectives about the nature of filmmaking and the status of political art. While some of these directors identify with specific countries and some do not, the adversarial contexts of their professional lives are likely to encourage very complex views of the world, and of Africa as a historical reality. To take a very interesting example, the Haitian-born director Raoul Peck grew up in the colonial Congo (before it became Zaire and then Democratic Republic of the Congo) and has made a few films focusing on that country and on other aspects of contemporary African experience. The fact that he may not claim an African nationality is not enough to view his work as irrelevant to any discussion of African filmmaking.

These concluding observations should be understood within an important context: the great challenge of making films available to African audiences. There is a critical shortage of cinema houses in major African cities, and where they are available, the major fare tend to be films distributed through international monopolies. It is true that the internet and other new media provide reliable means of distributing films, and that there are now new ways of being in public and attending to one's needs as a consumer, beyond what the pioneering filmmakers ever imagined. Nevertheless, if African screen media are to continue to expand the spaces of their existence, these new opportunities for individual access cannot invalidate the need for systematic structures to support diverse public exhibitions.

ACKNOWLEDGMENT

Natasha Vaubel conducted preliminary research for the writing of this chapter and her assistance is gratefully acknowledged.

NOTE

1. For example, *Guelwaar* (1993), Sembene's major film from the early 1990s, was released abroad in 1993, but was still unavailable for public viewing in Senegal as late as 2000. See Murphy 2000: 3.

SUGGESTIONS FOR FURTHER READING

Adesokan, Akin. 2011. *Postcolonial Artists and Global Aesthetics*. Bloomington: Indiana University Press.

Akomfrah, John. 2006. "On the National in African Cinema/s." In *Theorizing National Cinema*, ed. Valentina Vitali and Paul Willemen, 272–92. London: British Film Institute.

Andrade-Watkins, Claire. 1995. "Portuguese African Cinema: Historical and Contemporary Perspectives 1969–1993." *Research in African Literatures* 26(3): 134–50.

Armes, Roy. 2006. *African Filmmaking: North and South of the Sahara*. Bloomington: Indiana University Press.

Barlet, Olivier. 1998. "The Forbidden Windows of Black African Film: Interview with Férid Boughédir." www.africultures.com/php/index.php?nav=article&no=5327.

Diawara, Manthia. 1992. *African Cinema: Politics & Culture*. Bloomington: Indiana University Press.

Martin, Michael T. 2002. "'I Am a Storyteller, Drawing Water from the Well of My Culture': Gaston Kaboré, Griot of African Cinema." *Research in African Literatures* 33(4): 161–79.

Murphy, David. 2000. *Sembene: Imagining Alternatives in Film & Fiction*. Oxford: James Currey.

Pfaff, Françoise. 2004. *Focus on African Films*. Bloomington: Indiana University Press.

12 African Politics and the Future of Democracy

Amos Sawyer, Lauren M. MacLean, and Carolyn E. Holmes

African political systems have a long history that substantially predates the arrival of Europeans in the 1400s or the political boundaries of nation-states found on any current map. The peoples of Africa have organized many different types of political systems and witnessed tremendous political changes over time. And yet one of the most enduring puzzles has been whether African political systems will grow into stable democracies. During the late 1950s and early 1960s, when the majority of African countries achieved independence from colonial rule, many analysts were hopeful about the prospects for expanding citizenship in newly independent regimes. Debates in the 1960s and 1970s about the political systems most suited for African countries were driven mainly by a desire to fast-track development within the context of the Cold War. During the 1980s, many policy makers blamed Africa's economic stagnation on corrupt governments and demanded limited (and not necessarily democratic) governance capable of implementing neoliberal economic reform. By the early 1990s, these earlier debates were tempered by the disintegration of the Soviet bloc as well as the unconvincing results of structural adjustment and the hardships they imposed on African populations. Furthermore, beginning with the National Conference in Benin, which drafted a new constitution based on citizen input, and the unbanning of resistance organizations in South Africa in 1990, which constituted the first step in reforming apartheid laws, many peoples around the continent began to rise up and demand the democratization of long-standing authoritarian systems. Much like the independence era decades earlier, the initial jubilation at democratic transition in many cases then gave way to more sober assessments of fragile or hybrid democracies, where former dictators refused in a variety of ways to relinquish their power.

Now, more than two decades after the "third wave of democracy" appeared to sweep across Africa, the debate about the prospects for democracy in Africa has not abated. The emphasis, however, has clearly changed. Scholars have moved beyond a preoccupation with the short term and the formal transition to electoral democracy to focus more deeply on the long term and informal institutions of democratic governance for sustainable development. A close examination of postindependence regimes revealed that while many had constructed various formal constitutional rules, beyond the institutional facades and slogans, most of them were essentially informal, neopatrimonial regimes. In these regimes, political leaders exercised personal power, drawing upon aspects of traditional authority (real or fictive), their legitimacy as leaders of independence movements, or sometimes both. Cliques of subpatrons linked these leaders to sectors of their populations, who served as clients and subjects, and to whom benefits flowed in exchange for political loyalty.

The challenge of African politics well into the future is to transcend neopatrimonial rule and instead develop and institutionalize systems of democratic governance that will support development by unleashing and channeling the creative potential of African peoples as they participate in politics not as subjects or clients but as citizens and leaders. Attaining this goal requires developing different types of civic values as well as different types of formal and informal political rules and arrangements. It also requires patience and some fundamental understanding of the dynamics and trajectories of African political development.

This chapter highlights the state of African politics and identifies emergent trends and challenges. It frames the discussion of electoral democracy by contextualizing the alien origin and relatively recent introduction of these institutions. After reviewing the mixed success of electoral democracy thus far, we consider the everyday politics, beyond elections, that often takes place at the local level. The chapter then considers how gender, ethnicity, and indigeneity shape whether and how Africans are represented through the diversity of central and local political institutions. The next section examines how African politics continue to traverse the boundaries of the nation-state in important ways, highlighting the role of regional organizations within Africa, such as the African Union or the Economic Community of West African States; intergovernmental agencies, such as the UN World Food Program or World Bank; and international nongovernmental organizations (NGOs) and transnational advocacy networks. The chapter concludes with some reflections on the complexities of evaluating governance and consolidating democracies in Africa.

DEMOCRACY'S ALIEN ORIGIN AND RECENT INTRODUCTION IN AFRICA

An appropriate place to begin is with the history of the conception of democracy and democratic systems of governance in Africa and their implications for the future institutionalization of democracy around the continent. Most of the institutions of democracy found in Africa today share an alien origin and were only recently introduced.

Except for the existence of broadly democratic values, the artifacts of democracy crafted in Africa do not have their origins in indigenous African political culture and lack continuity with indigenous African political systems. With respect to the existence of democratic values in precolonial African political systems, Maxwell Owusu reminds us that many indigenous African systems were, indeed, committed to values of tolerance, participatory discourse, and contestation. In many systems, even inherited positions of authority were subject to transparent mechanisms of public accountability. Owusu proposes the "adaptation" of indigenous African political institutions that are built upon these values as a strategy for establishing systems of democratic governance in Africa. But this has not been the approach to the construction of democratic institutions and organizations in Africa.

This is in part because of the experience of colonialism in Africa. The colonial state was not a democratic one, and in the vast majority of cases it did not count Africans as citizens. As Crawford Young reminds us, the colonial state did not destroy traditional institutions in Africa, but instead depended on some of those institutions to carry out its goals. The aim of the state, however, was to extract revenue and labor from the Africans over whom it ruled. According to Peter Ekeh, this system served to radically reshape the political and moral landscape by creating a rift between African citizens and centralized states.

On the eve of independence in the 1950s, diverse social groups in various parts of Africa held varying expectations about the meaning and future of democracy. And yet the formal colonial powers often encouraged, or even required, blueprints of their democratic institutions to be adopted by the new nation-states. For example, the United Kingdom provided heavy-handed "tutelage" to the Gold Coast, now Ghana, on the writing of the First Republic's constitution and evaluated over a series of elections in the 1950s whether nationalist leader Kwame Nkrumah possessed an acceptably high popular mandate to guide one of the first African nations to independence.

During the Cold War, the restrictive advice tied to the economic support of either the United States or the former Soviet Union induced divisions among political leaders in the government as well as in trade unions, farmers associations, business associations, university teachers organizations, and student unions across Africa. The ideological competition between socialism and capitalism and the bitter recriminations resulting from these cleavages contributed to framing the attitudes and discourse among African leaders late into the twentieth century.

Since the end of the Cold War, external, state-based actors have been joined by a proliferation of new players, including donors, intergovernmental organizations, and NGOs, that have sustained an interest in the promotion of democratic political systems in Africa. As a result, the debate about the development of democratic systems of governance in Africa is driven largely by external actors and is quite frequently reduced to a debate about the successful implantation of Western forms of democratic political arrangements. For example, chieftaincy traditions and systems are treated as residual institutions of diminishing importance, despite the fact that they continue to command enormous legitimacy in many parts of Africa, especially to resolve conflict and/or to mediate property rights to land.

The second important point that cannot be overlooked is that democracy in Africa is only in its early stage of evolution. Formal democratic institutions were introduced for the first time relatively recently. For example, legislative assemblies empowered with decision-making prerogatives and run by Africans were only established by the colonial powers in the 1950s, on the eve of African independence. Along with these assemblies, the position of "leader of government business" was established to assign some executive powers to individuals who were likely to become founding prime ministers. Many African countries then experienced decades of authoritarianism during the 1960s, 1970s, and 1980s under personal, single-party, and/or military rule, which has been challenged again only since the early 1990s.

Thus while there are good reasons to be concerned about the pace of democratization processes in Africa, particularly when governance failures can be a prime cause of violent conflict, concern must be tempered by the realization that the system of democratic governance that is now being established in Africa was only recently introduced. Democratic governance will require time to take strong roots, as it did in the United States, Europe, and elsewhere in the world.

THE NEW POST–COLD WAR ERA OF ELECTORAL DEMOCRACY

The preoccupation with institutionalizing Western democratic arrangements in Africa, as in other parts of the world, is focused significantly on the establishment of procedural or electoral democracy. The promotion of electoral democracy is said to call critical attention to the performance of elected leaders, thus generating demands for greater accountability and the exercise of citizens' prerogatives to replace their elected leaders through further elections. The process of repeated elections, and especially the experience of alternating ruling political parties, is said to entrench democratic values and support the development of civil society organizations and networks that promote civil liberties and political rights.

By the end of the Cold War, in the late 1980s and early 1990s, most of Africa's political leaders had long ruled as military strongmen, such as Sani Abacha of Nigeria or Gnassingbé Eyadéma of Togo; personal rulers, such as Mobutu Sese Seko of Zaire (now the Democratic Republic of the Congo) or Yoweri Museveni of Uganda; or heads of de jure single-party states, such as Félix Houphouët-Boigny of Côte d'Ivoire and Daniel arap Moi of Kenya. Each of these authoritarian leaders faced collapsing economies, reduced external assistance, and rising internal demands for change. African strongmen yielded (often not without struggle) to pressures to redefine the terms and conditions of governance and were constrained to accept democratic constitutionalism as the fundamental principle of the political regime. This demand for constitutional reform that overtook Africa in the 1990s led to the convening of sovereign national conferences and other constitutional assemblies in order to craft new constitutional rules. Governance was to be conditioned by the rule of law and not by the caprices of the "big man." The new formal rules allowed opposition parties to mobilize and organize freely, often for the first time in decades; competitive elections were to take place to select leaders; and presidential term limits were imposed, among other changes. All of these political reforms were designed to undermine neopatrimonial control and lay the foundations for a new era of electoral democracy.

MIXED RESULTS OF ELECTORAL DEMOCRACY AND COMPONENTS FOR SUCCESS

African experiences with electoral democracy show mixed results (Bratton and Van de Walle 1997). There are many cases of progress, but still some backsliding. In Kenya in 2007, elections ended in violence. In Nigeria, elections since 1993 have frequently been annulled by military leaders or heavily rigged by ruling parties; former president Olusegun Obasanjo is reported to have referred to the 2007 elections there as "a matter of do or die," for with continued access to state resources at stake, to lose the elections would be to lose everything. In South Africa,

Figure 12.1. Liberian woman casts her ballot for the presidential election in Monrovia, Liberia.
Corbis.

Angola, Namibia, Botswana, and Mozambique, ruling parties associated with the founding of democratic governments in these countries continue to dominate their electoral processes. In Liberia and Sierra Leone, democratic elections have provided an exit from bloody civil wars. And then there are cases such as Ghana, Mauritius, and Benin, where competitive elections have resulted in the institutionalization of leadership alternation back and forth between opposing political parties.

While no single formula exists for ensuring the successful entrenchment of electoral democracy in African countries, certain factors are known to be associated with the holding of free and fair elections. Among these are the existence of an independent and effective electoral commission and judiciary; autonomous legislatures to check executive power; institutionalized political parties that are not based on the zero-sum politics of personal or ethnic loyalties; and above all, a civil society dedicated to electoral democracy.

Independence and Integrity of Electoral Commissions and Courts

In all African countries where elections have resulted in the alternation of political parties, the electoral commissions have been independent and of high integrity. Bodies responsible for conducting elections can exert independence if they are autonomous and not extensions of government ministries (as is the case in some francophone African countries), with officials whose tenures are secure and with budgets guaranteed under law and controlled by themselves (subject to auditing). The success of electoral democracy in Ghana, for example, has been partially attributed to the independence and integrity of the electoral commission there. Funding for the electoral commission, by law, comes from the government's consolidated account and can be ensured by court order. Commissioners' tenures are protected, and their status and salaries are pegged to those of judges.

The judiciary's role in resolving electoral disputes can also be critical to the success of elections. Prompt decisions by courts that are perceived to be independent and impartial can reduce the prospects of election losers finding recourse in street demonstrations and violence. In many African countries, courts are not independent and do not have the capacity to respond swiftly and with credibility. South Africa and Ghana are among the exceptions. The example of Nigeria reveals how the judicial role in elections can be strengthened. Since the passage of electoral reforms in 2010, electoral disputes are now fast-tracked in the courts and are resolved much more quickly than in the past.

Autonomous Legislatures to Pass Laws and Check Executive Power

Another component for strengthening democracy in Africa is the autonomous legislature, which give true meaning to the principle of checks and balances. Legislatures perform several core functions in a democratic system, including representing their constituencies by articulating their interests at the national level, serving their constituents' needs for public goods and services, creating and passing laws through processes of debate and negotiation with other legislative members and the executive, and providing oversight of other government branches, particularly the executive wing.

African legislators have always performed functions of representation and constituency service. In systems of neopatrimonial and single-party rule that were widespread in Africa before processes of democratization began in the 1990s, legislators typically articulated local concerns in single-party legislatures and laid the grievances and requests of local constituencies before executive functionaries and presidents. In the same manner, legislators also worked on national budget processes and developed strategies that enabled them to secure material support for schools, clinics, roads, and water projects for their local constituencies. The challenge for African legislatures in multiparty democratizing systems is not to diminish the roles of representing and servicing constituency needs but to go beyond these two functions. Legislatures should participate meaningfully in lawmaking and exercise oversight of executive actions. By so doing, executive leaders are held accountable.

At this point, many African legislatures appear to be improving, but some cause for concern remains (Barkan 2009). Overall, by the end of the 2000s, most African legislatures consisted of representatives from a growing number of opposition parties. Eritrea and Swaziland were among the few with no opposition representatives. However, despite the growing number of multiparty legislatures, many African legislatures remain dominated by ruling parties and manipulated by authoritarian presidents. In Cameroon, for example, President Paul Biya in 2008 pushed constitutional amendments through the parliament in order to eliminate term limits, thereby giving him the option to run for president as many times as he wishes.

Yet there are African legislatures in which the ruling parties have large majorities but do not stifle debate and are not at the beck and call of the president. Ruling parties have huge majorities in the legislatures of Tanzania and South Africa, but both bodies are characterized by robust and unfettered debate.

In order to authoritatively participate in legislating and to provide effective executive oversight, African legislatures require greater capacity in terms of both technical staff support and improvements in physical infrastructures and facilities. South Africa provides a good example of a legislature with both; much of its physical infrastructure was constructed under apartheid rule. Even more vital to stimulate legislators' substantive participation in lawmaking and successful executive oversight is scrutiny by citizens, the media, and civil society organizations. Monitoring and evaluating the performance of legislators has become an effective way for citizens to exercise oversight of legislatures in a growing number of African countries. But this trend is developing unevenly across Africa.

The Institutionalization of Political Parties

Another factor that contributes to the success of electoral democracy is the institutionalization of two or more political parties in a competitive party system. It is important to recall that in many African countries the notion of opposition political parties is relatively new. Democratization since the early 1990s has enabled the reorganization of some historically based political parties and the formation of brand-new political parties. With little time and few organizational resources, nascent and incumbent political parties have frequently relied on the strength of a particular leader's personal appeal to mobilize potential voters. Over time, as incumbent strongmen have been finally turned out or have peacefully withdrawn from elected office, some political parties have begun to institutionalize on the basis of other shared interests.

One of the other primary appeals used by political parties in Africa has been the shared bond of ethnic identity. Although many political parties in Africa still rely on the ethnic factor for their core membership, ethnic ties are fast proving insufficient to mobilize and galvanize partisan support. For example, in Zimbabwe, Tanzania, Namibia, and Mali, among others, the rural-urban cleavage is impacting partisan politics. In postconflict Liberia and in Botswana, among other African countries, generational differences are becoming a driving force defining partisan struggles for power. Thus in some parts of Africa, the strong correlation between ethnic identity and political partisanship is being gradually weakened. Yet there are cases such as Kenya in 2007–8, where, in the face of highly competitive partisan elections, ethnic solidarity was mobilized by political elites to become the most important feature of electoral politics.

Lastly, there are also strong external factors pulling African political parties away from highly personalized and/or ethnic politics. Numerous African political parties are defining themselves in ideological terms and seeking integration into larger global networks. For example, parties such as the New Patriotic Party of Ghana, the Malawi Congress Party, and the Democratic Party of Kenya have become members or affiliates of the Centrist Democrat International (CDI), a right-of-center political party network. A corresponding left-of-center consortium of African political parties that all belong to the Socialist International includes the African National Congress of South Africa, the Alliance for Democracy in Mali, the Socialist Party of Senegal, and the Mauritian Social Democratic Party. Finally, a growing number of African parties are members of the Global Green Federation, including the Mazingira Green Party of Kenya, the Ivorian Ecological Party, and the National Union for Democracy and Development of Madagascar. It remains to be seen to what extent the association of African political parties with global party ideological groups will transform the extent of personalization or ethnic character, or affect their links with various constituencies within African societies.

Civil Society as Promoter of Electoral Democracy

In the end, the best guardian and promoter of democracy in Africa is civil society, the voluntary groups and organizations outside and independent of the state and market where African peoples get together to express their common interests. Civil society groups do not necessarily share explicitly political objectives; they can also be based on a wide range of social, economic, and cultural goals. Civil society organizations also go well beyond urban-based national and local NGOs to include an array of community-based organizations in a diversity of rural and urban locations, such as trade unions, farmers associations, producer cooperatives, professional organizations, teacher unions, student unions, women's groups, sports clubs, youth associations, Bible study groups, and savings clubs.

One of the most remarkable developments of the 1980s was the growth of self-organized civil society groups and their pivotal role in collective action at local and national levels. In countries that experienced violent conflicts, civil society groups contributed greatly to the survival strategies and social welfare of local communities as well as to conflict resolution and postconflict reconstruction. For example, in Liberia and Sierra Leone, civil society organizations, especially women's groups,

Figure 12.2. News coverage and campaign posters preceding
presidential elections in Nigeria.
Corbis.

have been widely recognized as key players in achieving peace settlements. In Nigeria, the pro-democracy movement actively fought against the oppression of military rule, especially during the Abacha regime.

Many of these groups, especially those involved in advocating for democracy and human rights, are criticized for being funded by international donors and directed by donors' agendas and priorities rather than the interests of the groups they claim to serve. Some are indeed very minimalist organizations and are sometimes referred to as merely "briefcase organizations" or owe their very existence to opportunistic interactions with foreign funders. Yet a significant number of civil society organizations are homegrown organizations with deep roots in local and national causes and constituencies and have survived over time. For example, Abdoulaye Bathily has shown that pro-democracy youth and student groups have a rich tradition in Africa that predates Samuel P. Huntington's "third wave" of democracy. There are a number of encouraging developments that suggest that civil society organizations that were focused on building democracy will contribute significantly to the sustaining of electoral democracy and the deepening of democratic governance.

First, these organizations are involved in all aspects of elections and democratic governance and are acquiring the necessary skills and capacities to perform better in years to come. Pro-democracy groups are now involved in every aspect of the electoral process, including voter education, ensuring a level playing field for all political contestants before and during the polls, declaration of results, and resolution of post-balloting disputes. In Ghana and Kenya, for example, election monitoring groups used mobile phone technology and the proliferation of independent radio stations to publicize independently and immediately exit poll information from many contested or remote neighborhoods and communities.

Second, in numerous countries, umbrella civil society federations are being organized and are strengthening capacity and building synergies between the many smaller groups. In numerous cases, civil society organizations have already developed subregional and continent-wide networks and organizations. These networks facilitate civil society organizations' participation as important actors in policy formulation for their subregion and for Africa as a whole.

Finally, election monitoring groups are building synergies with broader human rights, governance, and socioeconomic empowerment groups. For example, civil society organizations that are involved in election monitoring and human rights advocacy are increasingly cooperating with groups that are concerned with accountability and transparency in public affairs and are engaged in monitoring budget performance and expenditure patterns. In this way, the focus on elections has become part of a wider concern for the quality of political, social, and economic governance.

DEMOCRACY BEYOND ELECTIONS

The exuberance sometimes associated with the strength of the relationship between electoral democracy and the entrenchment of a democratic culture occasionally leads some analysts to treat elections as if they were the only significant element of democratic governance and the only measure of successful processes of democratization. Frequently, election-centered studies of democratization processes hinge their projections of the future of democracy in any given country on an assessment of how "free and fair" that country's elections are. Such analyses often raise expectations that there should be a smooth progression on a linear course toward what is called democratic consolidation.

While we bring to this discussion a deep appreciation of the critical importance and even the indispensable role of elections in the establishment and consolidation of democracy, we caution against the impression that there is a one-way road to the consolidation of electoral democracy. Political and social processes generally are vulnerable to internal and external shocks, which often send the democratization project on a zigzag course.

The most striking example of the building and erosion of democratic institutions in Africa is Zimbabwe. Despite a strong history of democratic contestation, an independent judiciary, and a strong civil society in the 1980s and 1990s, Zimbabwe has subsequently seen the collapse of its economy, the persistence and escalation of election- and ethnic-related violence, and the violent suppression of many forms of opposition. Although multiple parties contest elections in Zimbabwe, Robert Mugabe has remained president of the country since 1980.

The decline of Zimbabwe reveals the important connections between state capacity and democracy (Bates 2008). To build and sustain a democratic regime requires substantial state strength. In the Democratic Republic of the Congo, where road infrastructure is lacking in many areas, UN helicopters were borrowed to deliver ballots and ballot boxes for the November 2011 election. Whereas Somalia is lamented as both an authoritarian regime and a failed state, the still-unrecognized de facto state of Somaliland is frequently praised for its relatively higher level of state capacity and distinctive system of democratic governance. Since Somaliland declared itself sovereign in 1993, the political system has combined "traditional" clan and Western institutions and now allows limited multiparty competition for some political offices.

These kinds of challenges to democratic consolidation in Africa demand adaptations that often result in the development of hybrid institutions blending elements of authoritarian and neopatrimonial institutions with democratic ones. Some hybrid regimes, such as in Zambia, give the president extensive powers, while others, such as Mozambique's, have had the same party in power for decades, and still others, such as in Malawi, have sought to silence opposition voices from civil society and media. Léonardo Villalón and Peter VonDoepp remind us that in the fashioning of democratic institutions and processes, hybridity can itself be a long-standing equilibrium. African democratic institutions must not be expected to turn out as facsimiles of Western democratic institutions.

It is also important to emphasize that elections are a necessary but not sufficient condition for the establishment and consolidation of democratic governance. If it were, citizens would have only a seasonal opportunity for meaningful participation in governance, and the ballot would be the only instrument for demanding account-ability of leaders. Democratic governance has to do with the conduct of public affairs by citizens of a country through an array of diverse institutional arrange-ments designed for making and implementing decisions at various levels of gover-nance, local, national, and international (Chabal and Daloz 1999). The holding of elections is a very important part of democratic governance but not the sum total of the processes of democratic governance. This chapter, therefore, has begun with the above discussion of the state of electoral democracy in Africa but now proceeds to examine the future prospects of a range of governance institutions and processes, such as decentralization, the role of local and precolonial political authorities, the politics of representation, regionalism, and globalization.

EVERYDAY PARTICIPATION AT THE LOCAL LEVEL

Elections take place only sporadically—every four to six years in most African countries—and voter registration and voter participation may require substantial effort, such as during the 2012 election in the Democratic Republic of the Congo, when voting often involved long walks to remote polling stations and extended

Figure 12.3. AIDS activists demonstrate outside South Africa's parliament. *Corbis.*

waiting times. But, this peak of participation from voters occurs on one particular day, which is designated from the top-down by the central government (often with support from external election observers). However, democratic governance also involves everyday participation in a variety of other, nonelectoral practices of citizenship.

Public opinion polling conducted by the Afrobarometer Project in eighteen African countries between 2000 and 2012 confirms that African peoples are actively engaged in various forms of political participation besides elections. The least frequent type of non-electoral participation among Africans was protesting or demonstrating. While some Africans did take their demands to the streets—for example, the repeated protests organized by the Treatment Action Campaign demanding a more aggressive response to HIV/AIDS from the South African government—the more common forms of participation involved less intensely oppositional modes of making claims and seeking accountability. For example, in 2008–9, 68 percent of Africans occasionally or frequently met with others to discuss an issue, and 27 percent contacted their local government councilors to share their views on a problem.

Much everyday political activity in Africa is focused on a variety of state and non-state actors and institutions that are closer, more familiar, and perhaps more legitimate at the local level (Boone 2009). Clearly, the central government is not the only, or even preferred, outlet for Africans to voice their views and preferences.

One recent trend in African politics that has shifted the focus of attention to the local level is the push across the continent to decentralize. Most African governments have, at least officially, adopted decentralization programs that devolve decision making from the center to more local levels of government. The implementation of decentralization, however, has varied considerably on the ground since its initiation in many places in the early 1990s. In Ghana, decentralization was significant and largely positive; administrative reform entailed the creation of new district- and even village-level institutions that were primarily elected by and for local people. In contrast, in Côte d'Ivoire, the administration of Henri Konan Bédié (1993–99) conceived of decentralization as bringing the central government down to the people instead of having it concentrated in a few centers, so local communities gained little new decision-making power. Scholars and practitioners have highlighted the contrasts between the initial, abstract allure of decentralization and its local-level realities in Africa and around the world. On one hand, decentralization offers the potential for more effective provision of services and greater local accountability. On the other, local administration does not eliminate the role of politics and inequality—corruption and domination by political, economic, and social elites can still pose a serious challenge to governance.

A second, parallel trend that reinforces the shift toward decentralization is the tremendous growth in the role played by nonstate actors in the provision of public goods. Central governments are devolving responsibilities not only to local districts and municipalities but also to an exploding number of NGOs, community-

Figure 12.4. Community meeting in rural Kenya.
Getty Images.

based organizations, and private-sector service providers. For example, the number of NGOs in Kenya is growing by four hundred per year, and by 2009, 5,929 were officially registered with the government, according to Kenya's NGO Coordination Board. At times these nonstate actors subcontract to the state, often receiving partial funding from and/or being subject to regulation and monitoring by state agencies; at others, they bypass the state completely. In many instances, however, the boundaries between state and nonstate actors are blurred. This dramatic increase in the role played by NGOs and other nonstate actors raises important questions about the effects on state capacity as well as citizens' abilities to gain access to and accountability for public goods and services.

It is crucial to note at this point that not all local actors are new. Indeed, we highlight here a third trend in African politics at the local level: the persistence of the importance of precolonial institutions of authority. Even with the ongoing processes of market liberalization and political democratization, many precolonial political institutions of decision making continue to actively mediate local conflicts over land, resources, labor, and local revenues. For example, chieftaincy institutions in South Africa have continued to play traditional roles in the adjudication of conflicts over land but also have taken on new roles in ensuring the free and fair conduct of local elections and distributing the benefits of local development projects. In some cases, such as Ghana, Lesotho, and Namibia, the roles of precolonial authorities have been formally recognized and codified in the constitution. But in many instances, the long histories of these indigenous authorities continue to evolve informally on the ground in novel ways. The Afrobarometer public opinion data also confirm the salience of precolonial or indigenous institutions. More than 55 percent of Africans report that they trust traditional leaders, with 31 percent reporting that they trust traditional authorities to settle local disputes compared with 33 percent saying that this role should go to local government.

Taken together, the above trends in local politics suggest that African peoples are supportive of the future of democracy, but that they may in fact be experiencing and thinking about democracy in distinctive ways. Analysis of survey data showed widespread support for free and fair elections held regularly as a means of choosing political leaders (Bratton, Mattes, and Gyimah-Boadi 2005). In the 2008–9 Afrobarometer survey, close to 70 percent of respondents in a survey of eighteen countries agreed that "democracy is preferable to any other kind of government." But what did these survey participants mean by democracy? On average, 57 percent of Afrobarometer respondents shared a more material view of democracy, where they emphasized their substantive rights to employment, livelihoods, and well-being whereas 43 percent highlighted a procedural conception of democracy, emphasizing the procedures fostering political competition and civil freedoms (Bratton, Mattes, and Gyimah-Boadi 2005: 88). Indeed, in the period 2008–9, 30

Figure 12.5. Nelson Mandela votes in the first democratic elections in South Africa. *Corbis.*

percent of Africans believed that the most important task of their elected officials is to deliver development or jobs.

Afrobarometer notes, however, that a substantial minority of respondents, 22 percent, indicated that they did not care or did not know what form of government was preferable for their country. Equally important is the result showing that only 11 percent of respondents indicated that in certain circumstances, nondemocratic systems (such as a military or other authoritarian regime) would be preferable.

It may not be too great a stretch to conclude from these results that democracy is becoming deeply entrenched as a political value preference within African political cultures. Still, the concept of democracy seems more tightly linked to the lived everyday experiences of authority and service provision at the local level than to an abstract ideal. The challenge for the future of democracy is for African countries to build democratic institutions and state capacity that connect the center and the local authorities.

THE POLITICS OF REPRESENTATION

The above sections of this chapter have revealed how African politics include a wide variety of political institutions and organizations from capital cities to local communities. We turn now to the diversity of African nations and populations in order to highlight the politics of representation in Africa. Most African nation-states cover large geographic areas and include very diverse populations. African governments and other political organizations are tasked with representing the interests of many different linguistic and ethnic groups, as well as people of different genders, economic backgrounds, and living situations.

Representation refers to a relationship between citizens and the people who speak for them in the political system. Borrowing from Hanna Pitkin (1967), political scientists think of four dimensions of representation: (1) the rules that allow certain people to be elected, (2) how closely the demographics of an elected body mirror those of the whole population, (3) how closely governmental officials' actions mirror the interests of their constituents, and (4) whether constituents feel that they are being represented.

The first aspect of representation has to do with the structure of government. We have already discussed elections and the diversity and vibrancy of institutions of local government in Africa. The last facet of representation, concerning how people view their government, was also discussed above in the section on public opinion in the African context. We turn our attention now to the second and third aspects of representation, sometimes called descriptive and substantive representation, which concern who is elected and how those officials represent the interests of their constituents.

Women and Politics

In many parts of Africa, women are holding more and more legislative seats. Whereas in the 1960s approximately 1 percent of parliamentarians were female, as of 2008 more than 18 percent of legislative positions in Africa are held by women. This increase is due, in part, to the adoption of gender quotas and reserves in African parliaments. Quotas in Rwanda, South Africa, Burundi, Mozambique, and Uganda have substantially increased women's participation in elected and appointed offices (Tripp and Kang 2007).

Evidence suggests that this descriptive representation of women has resulted in a corresponding increase in the substantive representation of women's interests. For example, in the 2008 parliamentary elections in Rwanda, 56 percent of seats in the legislature were won by women. These elections marked the first time anywhere in the world that a legislature had a majority of women. These legislators, despite continued gender inequality in Rwanda, have managed to pass numerous pieces of legislation that have increased penalties for sexual violence and opened up opportunities for women through banking and land reform. Similar strides have been made in Uganda and South Africa, where women legislators have been instrumental in bringing women's concerns to the forefront and creating meaningful policy change.

African politics, known sometimes for its dependence on "big men," has also been shaped by a growing number of powerful female heads of government. Since 1993, five states in Africa have had women serve as prime minister and six states have had female vice or deputy presidents. In addition, in fourteen different African countries, twenty-three women ran in nineteen elections for the office of chief executive (Adams 2008; see also the online African Elections Database). The most prominent among women leaders in Africa today, however, is Ellen Johnson-Sirleaf. The Nobel Peace Prize winner and two-term president of Liberia is the first-ever female elected head of state in Africa.

The Maghreb and North Africa present a somewhat different environment for women's participation in politics. While scholars continue to debate whether the structure of oil-based economies or the cultural influence of Islam hinders gender equality in this region, until recently, relatively authoritarian political regimes have offered few political opportunities for the descriptive or substantive representation of women in politics. It remains to be seen whether the "Arab spring" of 2011 will perhaps produce new democratic spaces for greater female political participation.

Ethnicity and Politics

In addition to representing people on the basis of gendered interests, political systems in Africa have the task of ruling over people who identify themselves as belonging to many different ethnic groups. Ethnic groups can define themselves in terms of language, region, or narratives of shared history. These groups are not the product of "natural" or biological distinctions between people. In fact, many ethnic identities were socially constructed and politically mobilized by colonial officials; the groups became significant because of the political and material conditions of colonialism, rather than because of any inherent differences between them. Calling ethnic groups social constructions does not mean that they are trivial, however. Indeed, these different groups can be very politically important in modern African states.

Some states, such as Madagascar and Lesotho, have relatively few politically salient ethnically defined groups. In these states, other kinds of divisions, such as religion or socioeconomic class, motivate political conflict. Other countries, such as the Democratic Republic of the Congo, Nigeria, and Uganda, have a number of different ethnically defined groups that define the political landscape. These ethnically defined groups are often represented by political parties that claim to speak on behalf of the entire group. When elected, these parties also claim to act in the best interests of their particular ethnic group.

Political scientists have long argued that this kind of politicization of ethnic identity undermines democracy, economic development, and the peaceful resolution of conflict (Posner 2005). The problem with ethnic voting is that it has the potential to reduce elections to a census. If people vote based on their identity, then democratic competition is reduced to a question of which group is the largest. Additionally, if ethnically defined political parties serve only the interests of their groups, then people from other, underrepresented ethnic groups are left underserved by their governments, and broad-based economic growth can be stunted. Finally, the overlap of economic inequality and ethnic identity has frequently been seen as the source of conflict in African politics. Violence between ethnically defined communities, as in the genocide in Rwanda and Burundi in 1994 or the protracted conflict in Darfur starting in 2003, are seen by observers of African politics as evidence of how destructive the politics of ethnicity can be. Since the political salience of ethnicity cannot be eliminated, and because it can devolve into violence, African leaders and communities must manage ethnicity as a factor within political systems. They can do so through creative institutional designs and informal rules to ensure inclusion and reduce the potential negative impacts of ethnic politics. Ethnic minority set-asides or allotted seats in parliament are also one way of addressing the ethnic factor through institutional design.

Indigeneity and Politics

Indigenous or autochthonous groups in Africa present another kind of diversity that the African state is tasked with representing. The very notion of indigeneity in the African context is complex and contested. Some groups in Africa define themselves as indigenous based on distinct livelihood strategies that often conflict with those of the majority and on their claims to have lived and practiced their culture in lands that they have occupied since precolonial times. Historically, these groups tend to be economically and politically marginalized in modern African nation-states but seek to preserve their language, their culture, and access to their "original" lands within those states. Conflicts arise, however, when different groups offer competing historical narratives of origination and migration.

These rival claims to indigeneity have become increasingly visible as a growing number of indigenous populations throughout Africa have begun to articulate demands and seek protections from states and intergovernmental organizations, such as the United Nations. One of the largest groups, spanning several nation-state borders in southern Africa, is a group known as the San, Basarwa, or Bushmen. With populations dispersed throughout Botswana, Namibia, South Africa, and Angola, this diverse assembly of people, who traditionally have practiced hunter-gatherer modes of subsistence, is made up of groups such as the !Kung, /Xam, and ‡Khomani (each of the symbols in these names represents a unique click-based consonant sound). It is estimated that distant relatives of these contemporary groups have lived in the area for tens of thousands of years.

In both Botswana and South Africa, high-profile cases have been brought by representatives of the San to assert ancestral rights to lands; to fight state-mandated relocation, and to seek protections for cultural practices. In Botswana, San organizations have fought since the 1970s against the government's rezoning of traditional grazing and migration areas in the Kalahari Desert. Similar court struggles in South Africa and Namibia have resulted more recently in the emergence of several transnational activism networks that lobby on behalf of these groups.

The Tuareg people in the Sahara and Sahel have also engaged in struggles with states including Algeria, Niger, and Mali to obtain greater state support for economic development, improve political representation, and safeguard their cultural heritage. Unlike the San, however, some Tuareg have chosen to defend their claims through armed rebellion and insurgency against the central state. Armed resistance to colonial and independent states has a long history among the Tuareg, with the first such unified rebellion occurring in 1916. Insurgencies in Niger and Mali during the first half of the 1990s brought concessions from those governments. Confrontations between Tuareg groups and the Malian state resumed in 2006 when Tuareg soldiers deserted after looting one of the regional army garrisons. National and international Islamist fighters also have become active in the area. The civil war in Libya and the demise of Muammar Qaddafi resulted not only in the return to Mali of Tuaregs who had served Qaddafi but also an influx of sophisticated arms. Militant Tuareg factions and their Islamist allies took advantage of their military superiority and a power vacuum created by a coup in Bamako to establish control of northern Mali, including the cities of Gao and Timbuktu, declaring it the independent state of Azawad in April 2012, but a French invasion expelled the Islamist elements that had taken control of the insurrection. Now the secular Tuareg factions are hoping to negotiate with the recently-elected, post-coup Malian government to attain regional autonomy. This case demonstrates how the grievances of a marginalized group with claims to indigeneity can lead to a complex and volatile situation that becomes difficult to resolve.

TRANSNATIONAL AND GLOBAL POLITICS AND THE FUTURE OF DEMOCRACY IN AFRICA

While transnational linkages were important sources of mobilization and support for the highly publicized battles for indigenous rights in Saharan and southern Africa, they have also played major roles in organizing women, ethnic groups, and political parties in many regions of the continent. International cooperation among groups such as the Maasai in eastern Africa, the Tuareg in the Sahel, or the San in the south has attempted to expand environmental and land protections for these groups. Consortia of academics and activists from Africa and across the world have sought to effect change in domestic and international politics in Africa. The globalization of communication and information technologies has stimulated these transnational networks, helping citizens and groups in Africa to more effectively lobby for their rights and to draw on common resources to achieve domestic and international policy outcomes. These transnational organizations have played critical roles in diffusing new norms and defining key political concepts, such as which groups can claim to be "indigenous," what rights can or should be guaranteed by states, and how key environmental resources, including wildlife and water, should be managed.

The importance of transnational and global politics is not new in Africa, however. Indeed, African politics has long crossed the boundaries of political systems, regions, and even continents. Even before the globalization of human rights advocacy, transnational and global networks shaped African elections, humanitarian relief efforts, and efforts at conflict resolution, peacekeeping, and reconstruction. What is notable, however, is that an increasing number of transnational networks are now organized within Africa rather than originating from outside the continent.

African regional and continental organizations that promote electoral democracy have experienced rather impressive growth in experience and clout. Both the Southern African Development Community (SADC) and the Economic Community of West African States (ECOWAS) have become proficient in their elections-related interventions in their regions. For example, ECOWAS has been building the capacity to monitor political activities, especially elections, in member countries. During the 2008 elections in Ghana, ECOWAS initiated constant engagement with the Ghanaian electoral commission and security officials well before the campaign season began and continued it throughout. ECOWAS called the attention of relevant actors to elections-related concerns that included the state of security and the role of security agents, the engagement of political parties by the electoral commission in a transparent elections preparation process, and the behavior of the ruling party and

Figure 12.6. ECOWAS meeting on Mali in Abidjan, Côte d'Ivoire.
Corbis.

the major opposition parties. ECOWAS's interventions with civil society went beyond technical support for local elections monitors and involved rallying together diverse groups of civil society organizations in support of a "Ghana must win" campaign.

Support for electoral democracy by African regional and continental organizations is also buttressed by external actors. The European Union (EU), the (formerly British) Commonwealth, and the U.S.-based National Democratic Institute (NDI) are among the leading non-African organizations that are very active in promoting electoral democracy in Africa. The EU, for example, has supported considerable scientific research into identifying significant constituencies and electoral zones that are bellwethers for potential conflict during elections and targeting interventions for those areas. Since its founding in 1983, NDI has developed impressive tools for building capacity in partnership with national election monitoring coalitions. Also impressive and auguring well for the future of electoral democracy in Africa is the concerted initiative by African and international partners to ensure the integrity of election results, their acceptance by candidates, and the orderly transfer of power, especially in cases of extremely close results or where the ruling party suffered a defeat. Such was the case with elections in Senegal in 2000, when the Socialist Party and its candidate, President Abdou Diouf, were narrowly defeated, and in Ghana in 2008, when the incumbent New Patriotic Party lost. In both instances, the margin of votes that separated the two contesting parties in the presidential election and the subsequent runoff were less than a percentage point.

In addition to the role played by organizations in promoting democratic elections, one particularly visible form of international influence in Africa is related to global humanitarian responses to natural disasters and conflict. In the past several decades, several natural disasters and armed conflicts in Africa have displaced millions, both internally and internationally. Aid groups such as the international NGO Oxfam, the bilateral donor USAID, and the UN's World Food Programme have sought to relieve human suffering in these crises through the provision of short-term assistance, such as the distribution of food, water, or medical supplies, or longer-term development projects. Celebrities from the United States, western Europe, and Africa have also lent their names to these causes. For example, music, television, and film stars such as Bono, Oprah, and George Clooney have sought to use their influence to attract political attention or donor money to the places or populations for which they advocate.

Charitable work is also being pursued by some multinational corporations (MNCs) through various initiatives under the rubric of "corporate social responsibility." In some cases MNCs invest directly in infrastructure projects such as schools, clinics, or roads for the communities where they work. Over the past couple of decades, Chinese MNCs have expanded and now rival Western groups in these kinds of foreign direct investments. In other cases, MNCs have sought to channel some portion of profits from mass-market consumer products toward charitable causes in Africa, such as AIDS or malaria prevention or clean water provision. One example is the Product Red campaign, involving Gap, Apple, and Nike, among others. This strategy, sometimes labeled "ethical consumerism," has been controversial because of its reliance on the global North's consumption of scarce resources and the for-profit business models of these corporations.

The third area where transnational, regional, and global linkages have been quite prominent is in the domain of peacekeeping and conflict resolution. For example, in 2011–12 the United Nations spent $5.31 billion (approximately 68 percent of that year's global peacekeeping budget) for peacekeeping missions in Africa, including in Abyei (between Sudan and South Sudan), Côte d'Ivoire, Darfur, the Democratic Republic of the Congo, Liberia, South Sudan, and Western Sahara. Between its statutory creation in 2002 and 2011, the International Criminal Court (ICC) had pursued only twenty-six cases, all of which were for war crimes, crimes against humanity, or genocide allegedly committed in African states. While some advocates have praised ICC prosecutions, others have criticized what is perceived to be a disproportionate focus on Africa.

Here again, while the United States, former colonial powers, and the United Nations continue to exert significant influence, they are not alone. China is a rising power here as well, providing financial and direct military support to some African leaders. More significant, regional and continent-wide organizations,

Figure 12.7. Opening ceremony of the African Union Executive
Council in Addis Ababa, Ethiopia.
Corbis.

such as ECOWAS, SADC, and the African Union, play increasingly important roles
in mediating civil conflicts and promoting peace on the ground. For example, Nigeria spent more than $500 million on peacekeeping in Liberia and Sierra Leone
before the UN intervened in those countries. Since its reorganization in 2002, the
African Union, which is headquartered in Addis Ababa, Ethiopia, has deployed
peacekeeping troops in Burundi (2003), Sudan (2003–8), and Somalia, to name a
few. The old principle of non-intervention that was a feature of the African Union's
predecessor organization, the Organization of African Unity (established in 1963
and frequently mocked as the "Dictators' Club"), is now being replaced with a commitment to a new principle of "non-indifference." Another example of the development within Africa of new accountability mechanisms is the establishment by the
African Union in 2002 of the African Peer Review Mechanism (APRM) process.
The APRM is a voluntary association of more than thirty African countries that
have agreed to have independent, African assessments of their country's progress
in democratic governance and sustainable economic development. Key issues for
self-assessment and peer review include the extent to which the member countries adhere to regional and international conventions and standards on a range of
rights, including the rights of women, children, and the disabled. Other issues to be
evaluated are the exercise of good corporate citizenship and the fight against corruption. The APR Panel of Eminent Persons, which consists of five to seven members

with distinguished careers and "high moral stature," was set up to oversee these peer review processes. Clearly, Africans are developing new and innovative regional institutions within the continent to continue to build and support internal capacities for democratic governance in the future.

In sum, this chapter highlights the complex and dynamic nature of democracy in Africa. We have argued that building democracy is not a strictly one-way process that can be imposed simply with the transplantation of new, formal electoral rules. Instead, informal institutions critically shape whose voice gets heard and who makes decisions at all levels of African political systems.

Our perspective thus goes beyond an exclusive focus on how elections are organized periodically in capital cities to reveal the importance of everyday politics at the local level. We acknowledge the many continued challenges to democratic governance around the continent, but we reject the pervasive tone of "Afro-pessimism" commonly found in the popular media. Rather, we call for a cautious optimism about the future of democracy in Africa. Many citizens and civil society groups in Africa are strengthening their ability to demand accountability from their political leaders.

Of course, the way democratic governance is constructed or challenged depends crucially on the particular political histories of communities and nations. We must resist the temptation to oversimplify and generalize African politics across the continent, and instead continue to study how democracy is being conceptualized and built in varied ways in different places and at specific moments in time. We can continue to learn how Africans themselves think about democracy, and how they are shaping their own democratic futures.

SUGGESTIONS FOR FURTHER READING

Adams, Melinda. 2008. "Liberia's Election of Ellen Johnson-Sirleaf and Women's Executive Leadership in Africa." *Politics & Gender* 4(3): 475–84.

Barkan, Joel D. 2009. *Legislative Politics in Emerging African Democracies*. Boulder, CO: Lynne Rienner.

Bates, Robert. 2008. *When Things Fell Apart: State Failure in Late-Century Africa*. New York: Cambridge University Press.

Bathily, Abdoulaye. 1992. "Mai 68 à Dakar. La révolte universitaire et la démocratie." Dakar: Editions Chaka.

Boone, Catherine. 2003. *Political Topographies of the African State: Territorial Authority and Institutional Choice*. New York: Cambridge University Press.

Bratton, Michael, Robert Mattes, and E. Gyimah-Boadi. 2005. *Public Opinion, Democracy and Market Reform in Africa*. New York: Cambridge University Press.

Bratton, Michael, and Nicholas Van de Walle. 1997. *Democratic Experiments in Africa: Regime Transitions in Comparative Perspective*. New York: Cambridge University Press.

Chabal, Patrick, and Jean-Pascal Daloz. 1999. *Africa Works: Disorder as Political Instrument*. Bloomington: Indiana University Press.

Ekeh, Peter P. 1975. "Colonialism and the Two Publics in Africa: A Theoretical Statement." *Comparative Studies in Society and History* 17(1): 91–112.

Hyden, Goran. 2006. *African Politics in Comparative Perspective.* New York: Cambridge University Press.

Owusu, Maxwell. 1992. "Domesticating Democracy: Culture, Civil Society, and Constitutionalism in Africa." *Comparative Studies in Society and History* 39(1): 120–52.

Pitkin, Hanna Fenichel. 1967. *The Concept of Representation.* Berkeley: University of California Press.

Posner, Daniel N. 2005. *Institutions and Ethnic Politics in Africa.* New York: Cambridge University Press.

Tripp, Aili Mari, and Alice Kang. 2007. "The Global Impact of Quotas: On the Fast Track to Increased Female Legislative Representation." *Comparative Political Studies* 41(3): 338–61.

Villalón, Leonardo Alfonso, and Peter VonDoepp. 2005. *The Fate of Africa's Democratic Experiments: Elites and Institutions.* Bloomington: Indiana University Press.

Young, Crawford. 1994. *The African Colonial State in Comparative Perspective.* New Haven, CT: Yale University Press.

13 Development in Africa
Tempered Hope

Raymond Muhula and
Stephen N. Ndegwa

Sub-Saharan Africa, home to more than eight hundred million people in more than fifty countries, is the least-developed continent in the world. It continues to have relatively low levels of industrialization and urbanization, and instead subsists on narrow economic bases, overly dependent on primary commodities and foreign aid. Livelihoods and life chances on the continent are often among the most challenged in the world, with low life expectancy (especially with the impact of HIV/AIDS), literacy rates, and access to health care and education. Moreover, governance institutions are weak, as evidenced by the fragility of democracies emerging after three decades of authoritarianism, heavily politicized bureaucracies and judiciaries, and weak policy environments that frequently respond more to patronage networks than to competitive ideas and interests. African economies have grown slowly since the early years of independence in the late 1950s and 1960s compared to those of other nations, especially in Asia, that came into independence at the same time. By 1980, real average incomes had regressed to below the levels of the 1960s. Predictably, Africa is the only continent expected not to meet any of the eight Millennium Development Goals adopted by the United Nations in 2000 to combat the most significant development challenges by 2015.

Not surprisingly, the recent global economic crisis is likely to affect growth, given the slump in demand from high-income countries for primary products from sub-Saharan African countries. In addition, declines in direct investment and remittances from nationals living abroad and a reduction in foreign direct investment (FDI) flows will dim growth prospects.

Yet there have been remarkable strides in some development and economic indicators. The investment climate for several African countries has improved due to the adoption of sound macroeconomic policies. In many countries, inflation has been reduced to single digits; at the regional level, rates of inflation are almost half what they were in the 1990s. Additional emphasis on exchange rate stabilization—important for investors' inputs and profit estimations—has bolstered

TABLE 13.1. Foreign direct investment, net inflows (% of GDP)

	1990	1995	2000	2005	2010
Kenya	0.7	0.5	0.9	0.1	0.6
Nigeria	2.1	3.8	2.5	4.4	3.1
Ethiopia	..	0.2	1.6	2.2	1.0
Senegal	1.0	0.6	1.3	0.5	1.8
South Africa	−0.1	0.8	0.7	2.6	0.3
Low- and middle-income countries	0.7	1.9	2.5	3.3	2.6
Sub-Saharan Africa (all income levels)	0.4	1.4	2.0	3.0	2.3

investor confidence, leading to an increase in regional FDI and to a rise in net inflows as a percentage of GDP from 2 percent in 1998 to about 3 percent in 2010.[1] More important, several countries in the region, such as Cape Verde, Sierra Leone, and Burundi, have initiated reforms that have made doing business easier. In fact, the World Bank's *Doing Business Report* (2012), the leading review of investment climates, declared Africa one of the fastest-reforming regions in 2009; in 2012, it indicated that a record thirty-six out of forty-six economies improved their business regulations during that year alone. The cumulative effect of these reforms— seen in growth rates especially—forces us to reconsider the crisis perspective that dominated most discussions of African development in the 1980s and 1990s, perhaps switching to one of renewal or, given uneven gains and fragile conditions, at least tempered hope.

In the service delivery realm, marked improvements are evident in several sectors. Primary school completion rates improved from about 50 percent in 2000 to 67 percent in 2009. Similarly, enrollments for both boys and girls have improved— often as a consequence of a return to universal free education, largely due to political pressure faced by democratically elected governments. In recent years, the region has also experienced increased penetration of mobile telephony and internet connectivity, which is a direct consequence of the liberalization of a sector that had almost universally been under loss-making state-owned corporations in the 1980s. The proportion of internet users increased from less than 1 percent in 2000 to about 11 percent in 2010. Similarly, by 2010 one out two Africans had a mobile cellular subscription. A number of trends in the international discourse and practice around development have helped push institutional reforms in African countries and mutual accountability between the countries and development aid donors. The Organization of African Unity transformed into the African Union (AU), with a new post–Cold War outlook that demands and, more often than not, enforces adherence to core principles of democratic government. Moreover, the introduction of the African Peer Review Mechanism (APRM) through the New Partnership for African Development (NEPAD) elevated the mutual obligations governments and leaders have over internal governance. The APRM also "encouraged . . . the sharing of experiences among participating member states on best practices across the region to ensure cross country learning for capacity building."[2] Efforts by multilateral institutions such as the World Bank, the G-8 (i.e., the eight largest economies in the world), and the European Union have helped shift attention to growth and development in Africa, promising more aid in exchange for better governance practices and, for the World Bank especially, a focus on poverty reduction. This renewed attention to the development imperative in Africa has been complemented by initiatives around improving conditions of trade, such as the United States' Africa Growth and Opportunities Act (AGOA), the EU's Everything but Arms Initiative, and the United Kingdom's Africa Commission. An overriding commonality in all of these frameworks is a focus on nationally owned development strategies instead of prescriptions and conditions from foreign governments and donors, an emphasis on sustaining institutional governance and peer review instead of a hands-off attitude toward misgovernance, and an increase in aid volumes to reverse the stubborn lack of progress in development indices on the continent.

Overall, the retreat from deep crisis has left a mixed picture—remarkable success in some countries, reversal or decline (often after a promising start) in others. In this mix of fortunes lie some important lessons for development in Africa. This chapter reviews the status of different aspects of development and the underlying transitions that seem to drive the respective outcomes. It is clear that while the global environment (e.g., the availability of aid or FDI) and regional trends (such as a decline in conflict and a rise in regional integration) continue to have a large impact, by far the most important factors are homegrown: national policies, institutional strength, and government performance in providing public goods.

FROM STRUCTURAL ADJUSTMENT TO COUNTRY OWNERSHIP

The oil crises of the 1970s and 1980s and the subsequent drying up of credit facilities from international markets led to a rise in interest rates, making it difficult for African countries to borrow. More important, these crises led to a rise in the trade deficit from $22.2 billion in 1979 to $91.6 billion in 1981. The current account deficit rose from $31.3 billion in 1979 to $118.6 billion in 1981 (Hart and Spiro 1997: 179). At the same time, it became difficult for these countries to continue servicing their debts, and debt arrears grew at a rate surpassing that of new lending. As private lenders became increasingly wary of lending to developing countries, it became clear that African countries would not be able to meet their debt obligations. Growth rates declined, inflation rose, and both industrial and agricultural sectors suffered. Africa had officially entered what is known as its "lost decade."

In subsequent years, external debt rose and the balance of payments worsened. Action to correct distortions in African economies and put the continent on a path to stabilization seemed inevitable. The World Bank and the International Monetary Fund (also known as the Bretton Woods institutions) became the continent's lenders of last resort, giving them outsized leverage over African governments. Because of the dire economic conditions, including an inability to meet their debt obligations, African countries were forced to adopt a set of policies called structural adjustment programs. In exchange for development credits from the World Bank and short-term balance-of-payments support from the International Monetary Fund (IMF), African governments adopted policy changes to limit the role of the state in the economy (especially direct investment), and to reduce expenditures, especially in social sectors and for subsidies. The IMF insisted that African governments remove government controls on prices and open up their economies to free trade. It was expected that these austerity measures would enhance economic growth and ensure macroeconomic stability over time. African countries had been reluctant to initiate structural adjustment programs, but in the mid-1980s and 1990s, thirty-six countries agreed to the conditions. Among the late entrants were Nigeria and Mozambique, beneficiaries of debt relief under the Highly Indebted Poor Countries (HIPC) initiative, a World Bank program to assist countries manage their debt burden and allocate savings and new funds to social sectors that had been deeply affected by austerity under adjustment.

With the onset of structural adjustment, the management of African economies would undergo close scrutiny by the Bretton Woods institutions, much to the resentment of Africans. Yet the structural adjustment programs did not produce quick results, and soon African citizens were criticizing their governments for ceding too much to international institutions and further impoverishing them. Politically these policies became untenable, and their economic value was open to question and sometimes even ridicule. Violent confrontations with citizens resulted in several countries, notably Zambia, Kenya, and Nigeria. Leading Africanist scholars and institutions such as the UN Economic Commission for Africa (UNECA) began to question the rationale of structural adjustment and offered alternative frameworks for achieving the same objectives. The African Alternative Framework to Structural Adjustment Programs, presented by UNECA, proposed a state-centered approach to the management of Africa's economic affairs, while also attributing Africa's problems to external forces. African leaders—for example, Kenya's Daniel arap Moi—soon began to waver on implementation of structural adjustment while some abandoned it altogether because of the political costs. Soon, even the World Bank would admit that structural adjustment might not have been good for African countries. A new approach for dealing with African development had to be devised, one that espoused country ownership and broad public participation.

The introduction of the Poverty Reduction Strategy Papers by the World Bank as the policy instrument to inform development assistance to low-income countries helped transfer the burden of designing programs to the developing countries themselves. However, for Africa specifically, the World Bank moved a step further and created the Africa Action Plan (AAP), a document reiterating the role of individual countries and of the partnership arrangements between the bank and African countries in the effort to help Africa reach the targets of the Millennium Development Goals (MDGs). The AAP identifies four key areas of partnership:

accelerating shared growth, building capable states, sharpening focus on results, and strengthening and developing partnerships.

HOPEFUL TURNS, ENDURING CHALLENGES

Africa has shown remarkable improvement in key socioeconomic indicators. Annual growth rates have improved, mortality rates for children under five have been falling; and the number of people living in poverty (defined as earning less than $1.25 a day) has declined. However, there is continued and widespread poverty and often discontent, especially where jobs do not accompany growth. By 2007, only slightly over one-half of Africa's working-age population was employed in the formal economy. Women's participation was even lower. And even employment has not guaranteed quality of life, as many of these people are "working poor," living in households where each member earns less than $1 a day. Compared with other regions, the momentum for poverty reduction in Africa has not been great. Nevertheless, there are significant cross-country variations, as some countries are already showing promising growth patterns.

Economic performance in sub-Saharan Africa has continued to improve. During the 1990s, GDP growth averaged only 2.4 percent; from 2000 to 2004, however, GDP growth averaged 4 percent, and the rate rose to 5 percent by 2010. This new surge in growth has been fueled in part by high oil prices, increased demand from China, and a booming mineral and oil market. But a temporary slump to 2.0 percent in 2009 as a result of the global financial crisis also reveals Africa's vulnerability to shocks in the global economy. Key macroeconomic indicators such as inflation, exchange rates, and fiscal deficits have stabilized remarkably. For most African countries, the main hindrances to sustainable growth have been identified as excessive regulatory reform, institutional constraints, and weak infrastructure (World Bank 2005: 19).

Once-promising countries such as Kenya, Zimbabwe, and Nigeria have been victims of weak leadership, corruption, dictatorship, and wide variations in the provision of social services. This has not only led to a significant departure of highly skilled professionals but also contributed to poor utilization of available resources,

TABLE 13.2. GDP growth (annual %)

	1990	1995	2000	2005	2010
Kenya	4.2	4.4	0.6	5.9	5.6
Nigeria	8.2	2.5	5.4	5.4	7.8
Ethiopia	2.7	6.1	6.1	11.8	9.9
Senegal	−0.7	5.4	3.2	5.6	4.1
South Africa	−0.3	3.1	4.2	5.3	2.9
Low- and middle-income countries	1.9	3.9	5.4	7.2	7.7
Sub-Saharan Africa (all income levels)	1.2	3.8	3.6	6.0	5.0

politically motivated investment decisions, and lack of transparency and account-ability. In places such as Zimbabwe, it has led to a total breakdown in the structures of governance, leading to an unprecedented near collapse of the economy. In Kenya and Nigeria, corruption has discouraged investors and contributed to low investment numbers, while inequality contributed to political discontent, resulting in conflict in Kenya in 2008. Regulatory and bureaucratic hindrances have undermined investor confidence, slowed growth, and contributed to the stereotype of Africa as a region in crisis. On the whole, the norm of good governance has taken root in Africa, as shown by the assiduous attention citizens and governments are paying to numerous indicators. In practice, however, good governance still remains elusive in many countries, as demonstrated by recent upheavals in Mali, Guinea, and Senegal.

In the last decade, violent conflict has declined significantly at the global level. Much of this decline is attributable to the reduction of conflict in Africa. Countries such as Angola and Mozambique, long marred by civil war, are now thriving. Others such as Liberia and Sierra Leone, although they have settled their internal wars, continue on a precarious path to economic recovery. Still others, such as Somalia and Eritrea, remain economically unviable due to conflict and severe declines in governance. In certain places conflict produces dual realities. For instance, both Sudan and South Sudan have thriving oil sectors and growth but are likely to be undermined by the conflict in Darfur and increasing hostilities following the independence of South Sudan in 2011.

While significant challenges remain in demobilization and reintegration, and the threat of resurgent conflict remains all too real, the reduction in violence in several countries has opened them up to new investment and participation in the region's economic development. But such peace dividends are often feeble and fragile; building trust and capacity, as well as reconstituting social and economic integrity for refugees and internally displaced persons, remain elusive. Indeed, refugees and internally displaced persons pose special challenges. At the end of 2010, there were about three million refugees in Africa, representing about 20 percent of world refugee totals; the number of internally displaced persons was about six million by the end of 2010, representing about 42 percent of the world total, according to the UNHCR Statistical Online Population Database. This undermines productive participation in the economy and perpetuates the cycle of poverty. For Africa, the voluntary repatriation of refugees in countries such as South Sudan, Liberia, Burundi, and Democratic Republic of the Congo helped reduce the number of refugees in the region. More important, it underlined the gradual reconstruction of these hitherto strife-torn countries and augured the eventual participation of the returnees in the region's economic development.

In 2010, Africa's population was estimated to be 854 million. About 43 percent of this population was under the age of fifteen. Sub-Saharan Africa's average annual population growth rate of 2.5 percent (in 2010) is the highest in the world—it is almost double the world average, and is expected to remain at that level until

2015. Countries such as Kenya and Nigeria have average annual population growth rates that are even higher, about 3 percent. It is estimated that by 2050 Africa will account for 21 percent of the world's population, according to the UNHCR Statistical Online Population Database. Still, Africa's population growth rate has declined significantly in the last half century (it was 14 percent in 1960) and now is almost on par with that of other developing countries, which averaged 1.9 percent in 2005. One of the most worrying trends in African population growth is that the majority of Africa's population is concentrated in the fifteen-to-twenty-four age bracket. The resultant "youth bulge" has serious implications for individual countries regarding opportunities for gainful employment and service delivery (especially housing, education, and health). Furthermore, the urban population accounts for 39.6 percent of total population, with about two-thirds of urban dwellers living in slums.

When the pace of economic growth is countered by the pace of population growth, durable reductions in poverty can be difficult to achieve. Nevertheless, an important outcome of population growth and the decline in median age has been an overall decrease in the dependency ratio (the ratio of the very young and very old to those of working age). In 1995, Africa had 91 dependent people for every 100 people of working age; by 2010, the proportion of the population that depends on the working-age population had declined to 85 per 100. While that ratio is still very high compared to the global average of 54 percent, it nevertheless shows a positive trend.

HIV/AIDS remains one of the biggest obstacles to economic growth in Africa. Rapidly growing economies such as South Africa and Botswana have been hobbled by high levels of HIV/AIDS infection. In 1990, about 5 percent of Botswana's adult population (ages fifteen to forty-nine) was infected. By 2010 this number had risen to about 25 percent. Similarly, in South Africa, rates of infection have grown from less than 1 percent in 1990 to about 18 percent in 2010. However, new and innovative measures to control the pandemic seem to be yielding the desired outcomes, as the proportion of adults with HIV/AIDS is dropping in some countries. For example, Uganda experienced huge rates of infection in the 1990s, with a prevalence of almost 14 percent. By 2010, HIV prevalence in that country had declined to about 7

TABLE 13.3. Population growth (annual %)

	1990	1995	2000	2005	2010
Kenya	4.2	4.4	0.6	5.9	5.6
Nigeria	8.2	2.5	5.4	5.4	7.8
Ethiopia	2.7	6.1	6.1	11.8	9.9
Senegal	−0.7	5.4	3.2	5.6	4.1
South Africa	−0.3	3.1	4.2	5.3	2.9
Low- and middle-income countries	1.9	3.9	5.4	7.2	7.7
Sub-Saharan Africa (all income levels)	1.2	3.8	3.6	6.0	5.0

percent, the result of an aggressive intervention program by the government. Similarly, Rwanda reduced its prevalence from about 9 percent in 1990 to about 3 percent in 2010, and Congo from about 5 percent in 1990 to 3 percent in 2010. Still, HIV prevalence among adults is highest in Africa, where overall about 5 percent of those fifteen to forty-nine are infected. This is a stark difference from other developing regions such as South Asia or Latin America and the Caribbean, where prevalence in this age group is still below 1 percent. Nevertheless, countries such as Ghana, Sierra Leone, and Liberia have consistently maintained prevalence rates of about 2 percent for a decade.

TRADE AND INVESTMENT

One of the most important avenues for reducing Africa's dependence on aid is through increased and fair trade. The transformations in the international system after the Cold War imposed serious setbacks in Africa's relations with countries of the North. Preferential trade agreements were replaced with the more stringent requirements of the World Trade Organization (WTO), which, while expected to have long-term benefits for free trade, impose severe disadvantages in the short term. For instance, under WTO rules, there has been a decline in the share of agricultural exports from Africa (as a share of merchandise exports) between 1995 and 2004. From a high of 6.8 percent in 1996, it dropped to about 4.4 percent in 2002, and remained there as of 2010. Given that Africa relies on agriculture as its main economic output, a skewed international agricultural market system has had adverse effects. This is even more critical given the fact that almost two-thirds of Africa's labor force is employed in agricultural sectors.

Developed countries continue to provide subsidies to their farmers. Added to existing tariff and non-tariff barriers, this creates market distortions that undermine Africa's participation in global agricultural markets. The relatively small size of most African countries has increased their vulnerability as global players in the international trade system. It is no wonder that many nongovernmental organizations as well as African leaders themselves have increasingly called for a fairer international trade system. Nevertheless, as witnessed during global trade meetings in Doha in 2010 (known as the Doha Round), African countries, alongside other developing regions, have repeatedly tried to force consideration of issues that affect them, lobbying for reduction of tariffs for primary goods imported by the wealthy nations and compensation for short-term ill effects of further trade liberalization. However, since these trade negotiations are often years in the making, the kind of regime that would induce massive poverty-reducing growth remains elusive.

In the last decade, some African countries have proved that, given a fair trade regime internationally and pro-growth economic policies at home, the continent is capable of competing in the international market. Malawi, for instance, has recently become a net exporter of agricultural products, while Kenya is increasingly carving out a niche in horticultural products globally. Overall, there has been an

TABLE 13.4. Merchandise trade (% of GDP)

	1990	1995	2000	2005	2010
Kenya	37.9	53.8	38.1	49.5	53.6
Nigeria	67.5	73.2	64.6	63.4	65.1
Ethiopia	11.4	20.6	21.4	40.6	36.8
Senegal	34.6	49.3	52.0	58.2	54.0
South Africa	37.4	38.6	44.9	46.1	48.2
Low- and middle-income countries	31.7	38.3	45.1	55.0	48.5
Sub-Saharan Africa	42.0	47.5	51.5	57.2	58.2

increase in Africa's participation in global trade. This increased trade volume supported the increased growth in GDP for many African countries. The region itself experienced a sharp rise in trade as a percentage of GDP, with that figure growing consistently from 50 percent in 1990 to about 76 percent in 2006 before succumbing to the global economic crisis and dropping to 65 percent in 2010. Most of this trade occurred between Africa and other developing regions; the proportion of merchandise exports to developing countries outside the region increased from 15 percent in 2000 to 32 percent in 2010. Within the region, exports to developing countries remained relatively flat at an average of 12 percent between 2000 and 2010 in spite of several regional agreements and trading blocs. Conversely, the proportion of merchandise exports from Africa to high-income countries peaked at 67 percent in 2005 before gradually dropping to about 54 percent in 2010.

Africa's merchandise imports from within the region have remained low, hovering between 12 and 13 percent from 2000 to 2010. But it imported more from other developing countries outside of the region, with the total almost doubling from 15 percent of merchandise imports to 30 percent in 2010. The increase in both merchandise exports and imports is partially attributable to the role of China in African markets. The low export figures are indicative of the protectionist nature of developed-country markets and the significant barriers that African countries still confront in accessing them. In addition, the 2008 financial crisis has had an ongoing effect on trade volumes, with export figures slumping in the first quarter of 2009 in developing countries as demand for commodities and agricultural raw materials slowed in developed regions.

During the last decade, the extractives industry in Africa (and elsewhere) continued to grow, fueled by huge demands by China. Consequently, oil- and mineral-producing countries have witnessed remarkable growth in the last ten years. Angola, Chad, Nigeria, and Sudan have shown growth patterns similar to those of high-income countries, each doubling its annual GDP growth rate between 1995 and 2005. This has increased sub-Saharan Africa's industrial growth rate from an average of 2.0 percent in the 1990s to 5.2 percent in the 2000s. It is conceivable that the lack of industrial infrastructure to process much of Africa's raw materials, including natural resources such as crude oil, undermines the continent's competi-

TABLE 13.5. External debt stocks (% of GNI)

	1990	1995	2000	2005	2010
Kenya	85.8	83.8	48.9	34.3	26.9
Nigeria	130.7	131.7	77.9	22.3	4.5
Ethiopia	71.9	136.8	67.7	50.6	24.1
Senegal	68.0	82.9	78.7	44.8	28.5
South Africa	..	17.1	19.2	12.8	12.7
Low- and middle-income countries	..	38.8	37.8	26.6	21.0
Sub-Saharan Africa (all income levels)	..	..	..	..

tiveness. The windfall for oil-producing countries has been a curse for the many countries in Africa that import oil, as they have been forced to spend more in buying crude and other petroleum products.

Africa is also saddled with a large amount of external debt. To be sure, the size of the total external debt has been decreasing in the last decade. Total debt service as a percentage of gross national income (GNI) has been declining in Africa at an impressive rate, from 4 percent in 2000 to 1 percent in 2010. Still, the majority of African countries continue to remit a significant portion of their national earnings to international creditors. Africa's external debt almost tripled between 1980 and 1990, from $60 billion to about $180 billion, largely as the result of the external shocks such as the oil and debt crises of the 1970s and the attendant rise in interest rates. By 2007, the total debt owed by African countries was about $195 billion, a drop from a peak of $240 billion in 1995. This reduction in external debt is largely accounted for by the debt relief arrangements under the Heavily Indebted Poor Countries' (HIPC) Initiative created by international development partners, through the World Bank, to facilitate debt forgiveness to poor countries with large debts. Countries such as Mozambique that have benefited from this program continue to show signs of accelerated growth, with the growth rate rising from 1 percent in 1990 to 3 percent in 1995 and then to about 8 percent in 2005. However, it is important to point out that debt relief by itself does not drive growth. After a protracted civil war, Mozambique has benefited from relatively stable political conditions, low corruption, and consistent pro-growth economic policies.

While a large portion of foreign direct investment targets developed countries, Africa has seen a rise in FDI flows in recent years. The majority of this flow has been from China, India, and Brazil, with China investing in resource extraction and infrastructure, Brazil in railway construction, and India in agriculture. FDI from these and other countries constitutes a significant proportion of private financing. In 1990, FDI flows accounted for only 0.4 percent of Africa's GDP. By 2005, this had risen sevenfold, to 2.8 percent. By 2009 it accounted for about 4 percent of GDP, double the world average. Much of this flow was accounted for by increased investments in commodities such as oil and minerals. Some of Africa's top recipients of increased FDI flows in recent years are those with mineral deposits and oil.

TABLE 13.6. Workers' remittances and compensation of employees, received (% of GDP)

	1990	1995	2000	2005	2010
Kenya	1.6	3.3	4.2	4.3	5.5
Nigeria	0.0	2.9	3.0	3.0	5.1
Ethiopia	0.0	0.4	0.6	1.4	0.8
Senegal	2.5	3.0	5.0	9.1	10.5
South Africa	0.1	0.1	0.3	0.3	0.3
Low- and middle-income countries	1.1	1.2	1.4	2.0	1.7
Sub-Saharan Africa (all income levels)	0.7	1.1	1.6	1.6	2.2

In Equatorial Guinea, for example, FDI flows as a proportion of GDP rose from 8 percent in 1990 to about 19 percent in 2006. Sudan, Chad, and Nigeria, with both oil and other natural resources, have seen similar increases. Africa as a whole has also recorded a rise in average rates of growth in manufacturing from 2.1 percent in the 1990 to 3.2 percent in the 2000s.

Additionally, a significant amount of Africa's foreign exchange earnings has been through remittances from migrants abroad. It has been estimated that remittances to developing countries are double the amount of foreign aid and almost two-thirds the amount of FDI (World Bank 2008: x). The emergence of migrant remittances as a significant source of external financing for African countries has led to a focus on the role of African citizens abroad in financing development in their home countries. In 2010, remittances constituted about 2.2 percent of sub-Saharan Africa's GDP, slightly above the average for low- and middle-income countries, which was about 1.7 percent. At the country level, remittances constituted 11 percent of GDP in Senegal, 8 percent of GDP in Cape Verde, and about 5 percent of GDP in Nigeria. While this is good for Africa in the short term, dependence on remittances remains a high risk given the volatility in the global economic environment.

The entry of China into Africa has raised serious implications for Western lenders and donors. While these trade, aid, and investment partners have insisted on liberal notions of good governance and democracy and limited state ownership of economic enterprises, China has tended to downplay the relevance of those ideals in its dealings with Africa. The surge in the volume of trade with China has made it possible for some countries to survive cuts in aid and in balance-of-payments support. Africa's exports to China increased at an annual rate of 48 percent between 2000 and 2005. China continues to court African countries that have been labeled "rogue states" by the West. For example, in the past decade, China increased trade with Sudan, South Sudan, Equatorial Guinea, Chad, and Zimbabwe. China's industrial expansion has fueled its demand for oil and minerals. As a result, China has encouraged its corporations, especially state-owned companies, to increase trade with African countries. It also established demonstration centers in Africa to showcase Chinese technology and agricultural techniques, and it created the China Africa Fund, a multibillion-dollar investment fund to support companies investing in Africa. China is emerging as an important partner for Africa in the region's efforts to recover from the shocks of the global economic crisis.

The recent spurt in growth in many African countries can partly be attributed to new trade with China in the last decade. Geopolitically, Chinese interest in Africa has encouraged a "looking East" strategy that has increased the prospects of African states weaning themselves politically from years of dependence on Western countries. While this still appears to be a distant prospect, its realization is not entirely improbable. More immediately, it engenders tensions with the West and Western-dominated international financial institutions, which will likely lead to new patterns of development assistance and possible outcomes. However, an important question regarding this new relationship is whether Africa has the economic capacity to exploit the Chinese market in order to forestall the trade imbalance that is characteristic of the North-South relationship.

DEMOCRACY, GOOD GOVERNANCE, AND DEVELOPMENT

State strength and ability to deliver services in an efficient and accountable manner depend on the vitality of state institutions. These, in turn, rely on good governance, which includes free and fair elections, respect for individual liberties and property rights, a free and vibrant press, an open and impartial judiciary, well-informed and strong legislative structures, and engaged citizens. Thus, the fate of Africa's economic development is intricately interwoven with the establishment of a broad system of capable political and economic governance. African countries have rapidly liberalized over the past two decades. While some countries have lost earlier gains, there has been an increase in the number of countries satisfying minimal democratic requirements. In recent years, efforts to build democratic institutions in Africa have begun to pick up momentum. New programs on democracy and good governance have concentrated on electoral systems, civil society participation, transitional justice, and human rights. Attention has also been given to civil service reform, judicial reform, and public financial management. In countries such as Rwanda, Kenya, and Ghana, attention has been given to institutional and constitutional reforms intended to establish a robust public sector capacity. Additionally, many African countries have realized that prudent management of extractive industry resources is critical for economic growth and that mismanagement of these resources is often among the causes of strife in resource-rich countries. Consequently, many have committed themselves to the Extractive Industries Transparency Initiative (EITI). For example, Liberia was the first country in Africa to be accredited by the EITI. It has since made remarkable progress in creating a system for documenting natural resource revenues.

The international development community has played an important role in setting the pace for these developments. Nevertheless, in recent years, domestic pushes for institutional reform and transformation of the region's political power—a phenomenon known as "demand-side governance"—have gained momentum as citizens, organized in groups or as individuals, have demanded a greater say in governing their communities, more scrutiny of government action, and more substantive and equitably shared outcomes from public resources. Citizens and civil society are becoming more assertive in demanding good governance in places such as Uganda, where citizen scorecards track the performance of elected officials, and in Kenya, where the introduction of performance contracts has introduced a sense of public accountability among senior civil servants. Many countries have seen the emergence of a strong and active civil society—organizations that are autonomous from the state, such as trade unions, interest groups and NGOs, and a free and vibrant press—as a counterweight to unfettered state power. These organizations have been important voices in demanding transparency and accountability from government and in pursuing specific policies that benefit groups such as farmers and industrialists, etc.), and therefore are beginning to re-shape both politics and policies.

There has been an increase in democracy and the acceptance of good governance principles in the majority of African countries since the early 1990s, according to Freedom House. In 2009, ten African countries were rated "free," twenty-three were rated "partly free," and fifteen were rated "not free." While these figures are a far cry from what the wave of democratization in the 1990s had hoped to achieve, they do suggest that Africa's march toward democracy has continued in the last three decades. In 1980, only four African countries were rated "free," and twenty-seven were rated "not free" (Freedom House 2009). Overall, there has been an improvement, if a modest one, in political and civil liberties in the last two decades. Still, improvement in democratic freedoms in some countries is offset by decline in others (Puddington 2012).

The World Bank's own review of institutional capacity, the Country Policy and Institutional Assessment, places most African countries above a 3.5 rating on a 6.0 scale with regard to performance of their public sector management institutions. However, significant variations exist between high-performing countries such as Cape Verde, Ghana, and Tanzania, on the one hand, and low performers such as Angola, Chad, and Zimbabwe, on the other hand. One of the best indicators of good governance is how successful a government is in controlling corruption. In its 2011 Corruption Perception Index, Transparency International found that only three countries (Botswana, Mauritius, and Cape Verde) scored above the midpoint of its scale. Those three ranked thirty-sixth, forty-first, and forty-sixth, respectively, out of the global total of 182 countries. An important development on the issue of governance and development in Africa was the establishment in 2003 of the African Peer Review Mechanism, mentioned earlier in this chapter. Under this mechanism, individual countries are expected to make annual reports to a panel of African leaders on the progress that each country is making regarding the management of public affairs. By June 2012, some thirty-three African countries had signed up to be part of APRM, and some among them, such as Kenya, Benin, Rwanda, and South Africa, had been subjected to review (Wikipedia 2012). In this regard, the African Union has become more assertive in ensuring adherence to democratic principles, at least in terms of a movement toward a culture of respecting the ballot as the final arbiter of political contests. It has acted to suspend errant member countries and refused to recognize leaders that obtain power through violent means. The recent suspensions of Côte d'Ivoire, Mali, Egypt, Madagascar, and Guinea point to a more assertive African Union. Nevertheless, its reluctance to intervene in Libya and increasing condemnation of the International Criminal Court over the latter's alleged bias against Africa have undermined its focus on good governance.

The continent has recently witnessed an unprecedented number of peaceful elections and transfers of power in countries such as Botswana, Ghana, Senegal, South Africa, and Zambia. However, in Kenya, Nigeria, and Zimbabwe, age-old schisms combined with proximate causes led to violence and instability. The democratic gains of the 1990s, which were fueled by changes in the international system after the end of the Cold War, have been under threat. The return of coups d'état in places such as Côte d'Ivoire, Comoros, Guinea, and Madagascar signal that the dangers posed by instability and political violence are not over. It is, however, too early to conclude that the continent is experiencing a retreat of democracy and a return to the political instability that defined the 1970s.

While the link between good governance and economic growth still remains to be definitively demonstrated in the literature, there is nevertheless a positive correlation; it is also intuitively attractive. Not surprisingly, the fastest-growing economies in Africa are also those that show the most transparency, are better managed in terms of well-regulated but open markets and stable policies, and adhere to the rule of law. Levy (2006) identifies three groups of African countries in terms of their response to structural adjustment. The "sustained adjusters" maintained their reform agenda during the adjustment period of 1988 to 1996; the "late adjusters" initially encountered some internal contentiousness but began reforms in the later part of the 1990s and continued until 2001; and finally the "polarized" countries initiated a few reforms, ignored others, and encountered domestic political problems that undermined sustained reforms. Levy and others find that growth among the first group was higher than in the rest of the countries. Cumulatively, over the 1990s, Benin, Burkina Faso, Ghana, Malawi, Mali, Mozambique, Uganda, and Zambia have experienced consistent upward growth patterns due to consistency in reforms, compared with Côte d'Ivoire, Kenya, Nigeria, Togo, and Zimbabwe, where reforms were sporadic or reversed. The result: an exacerbation of existing tensions or even convulsions in a number of countries in the latter group at the beginning of the twenty-first century, with contested elections and sporadic violence in Kenya, Zimbabwe, and Côte d'Ivoire and weak national security regimes occasioned largely by porous borders and religious fundamentalists in both Nigeria and Kenya.

DEVELOPMENT AID FOR AFRICA

While the last decade has witnessed a significant increase in the volume of aid to Africa, it has also been a decade of intense debate regarding the usefulness of aid to the region. Opinion is still divided, with one school of thought claiming that aid has undermined growth in Africa, while the other argues that rich countries have not done enough to support Africa through aid. However, it is a fact that the majority of African countries depend on official development assistance (ODA). After a temporary decline from 31 percent of gross capital formation in 1995 to 23 percent in 2000, ODA rose again to 30 percent by 2006, the result of increased global commitment to development funding by the industrialized countries. However, by 2010 it had dropped again, to 19 percent. Nevertheless, net ODA per capita has been increasing since 1995. In 1995, that figure was $32; by 2007 it was $45, and it rose to $53 by 2010. For example, in Eritrea, Liberia, and Sierra Leone, aid as a percentage of GNI has consistently averaged over 50 percent in the last half of this decade. Conversely, Mauritius, South Africa, and Gabon have consistently maintained rates below 1 percent.

Globally, ODA has been on the rise in recent years, largely due to a concerted effort by developed countries to support Africa's development. This growth is a result of a vigorous push by Northern countries to increase aid to Africa and to improve its effectiveness. During the Gleneagles summit in 2005, leaders of the G-8 countries committed themselves to increasing aid by $25 billion annually. Subsequently, there have been improvements in aid flows, and many countries are on track to meet their commitments. But there has also been a realization that for most African countries, aid has not served the purpose of lifting millions out of poverty. Within the development community itself, it has led to intense soul-searching as to whether aid actually works. Yet, for the most part, it is generally agreed that the positive growth rates, improvements in school enrollment, and reduction in child mortality rates that African countries have experienced in the last decade have largely been the result of increased aid and the significant debt relief many African countries received as a result of the HIPC. In 2005, the Paris Declaration established the principle that governments receiving development assistance

TABLE 13.7. Net ODA received (% of GDP)

	1990	1995	2000	2005	2010
Kenya	13.8	8.1	4.0	4.1	5.1
Nigeria	0.9	0.8	0.4	5.7	1.0
Ethiopia	8.4	11.5	8.4	15.7	11.9
Senegal	14.2	13.4	9.2	8.0	7.2
South Africa	..	0.3	0.4	0.3	0.3
Low- and middle-income countries	1.5	1.1	0.8	1.1	0.6
Sub-Saharan Africa (all income levels)	5.9	5.7	3.8	5.0	4.0

need to have control over how to spend donor funds. It emphasized country ownership and called for greater streamlining of how development assistance was distributed and utilized by recipient countries.

Despite a decade of impressive growth, it would not be prudent to declare that Africa has turned the corner on development; however, it is reasonable to suggest that earlier pessimism about Africa's prospects in the twenty-first century was misplaced. Yet the issues that raised those serious doubts at the turn of the century remain relevant to the fate of development success. Tasks such as improving governance, investing in people, increasing competitiveness, and reducing aid dependency still remain critical to achieving regional economic transformation.

While significant variations exist among countries, on average the continent is moving toward accepting the basic principles of good governance, adhering to globally accepted principles of public financial management, and improving its investment climate. Added to the efforts African countries are making in improving chances for young people to enroll in school, providing resources to ensure primary school completion, and enhancing women's participation in the economy, these are expected to cumulatively result in better socioeconomic standards in the future.

Within the region itself, several countries are emerging as success stories: growing at impressive rates, reforming their governance systems, improving private sector participation, and tackling social problems by improving service delivery. But challenges remain. Africa is still the region with the slowest movement toward the achievement of the UN's Millennium Development Goals, still the region where corruption remains rampant, and still the region where breakdown into violent conflict is the likeliest. The continued existence of fragile states in places such as Somalia, political instability in Madagascar and Guinea-Bissau, and conflict in Republic of the Congo, Democratic Republic of the Congo, and the Darfur region of Sudan complicate the prospects for wider economic revitalization. Ultimately, economic development on the continent will not take a uniform path, nor will every African country experience transformation instantly. However, as evidence from Mozambique, Tanzania, and Rwanda has shown, sustained economic growth is possible provided that there is a conscious decision by those in authority to institute sound macroeconomic policies, invest in people, curb corruption, and improve the investment climate. Development partners can give aid, but no amount of external assistance can supplant the domestic commitment to social, political, and economic transformation.

GLOSSARY

African Peer Review Mechanism. Instrument created by members of the African Union as an African self-monitoring mechanism.

Balance of payments. System of recording a country's economic transaction with other countries in the international system. It may be favorable or unfavorable.

Civil society. The arena of uncoerced collective action around shared interests, purposes, and values. It embraces a diversity of spaces, actors and institutional forms, varying in their degree of formality, autonomy, and power.

Country Policy and Institutional Assessment. Measures the extent to which a country's policy and institutional framework support sustainable growth and poverty reduction, and consequently the effective use of development assistance.

Current Account Deficit. Occurs when a country's total imports of goods, services, and transfers is greater than the country's total export of goods, services, and transfers.

Dependency ratio. Ratio of those of non-active age to those of active age in a given population.

Extractive Industries Transparency Initiative. Global standard that aims to strengthen governance by improving transparency and accountability in the extractives sector.

Foreign direct investment. Investments by foreign citizens in stocks and ownership of businesses.

Gross capital formation. Private and public investment in fixed assets, changes in inventories, and net acquisitions of valuables.

Gross domestic product. Total goods produced and services offered in a country for a given year. Usually an indicator of a country wealth.

Heavily Indebted Poor Countries' (HIPC) Initiative. An arrangement created by the World Bank to cover low-income countries with severe debt.

International Development Association. Aims to reduce poverty by providing interest-free credits and grants for programs that boost economic growth, reduce inequalities, and improve people's living conditions. It was established in 1960 as part of the World Bank.

International Monetary Fund (IMF). An organization of 186 countries, working to foster global monetary cooperation, secure financial stability, facilitate international trade, promote high employment and sustainable economic growth, and reduce poverty around the world.

Millennium Development Goals. A set of eight goals adopted by world leaders in September 2000 to commit nations to a new global partnership to reduce extreme poverty by 2015.

Official Development Assistance (ODA). Disbursements of loans made on concessional terms and grants by developed countries and donor agencies to promote economic development and welfare in countries and territories in developing countries.

Paris Declaration. Resulted from the decision by donor countries and development partners to undertake far-reaching and monitorable actions to reform delivery and management of aid so as to improve its effectiveness in recipient countries.

Remittances. Transfers of funds back to their home country by migrants who are employed or intend to remain employed for more than a year in another economy in which they are considered residents.

Trade deficit. Difference between imports and exports. Most African countries import more than they export.

Unemployment. The share of the labor force that is without work but available for and seeking employment.

World Bank. Institution was created in 1944 to facilitate postwar reconstruction; over the years its mission has evolved to global poverty alleviation.

NOTES

1. Unless otherwise noted, all data are drawn from the World Bank's *World Development Indicators Database* or related publications for various years.

2. Available at http://aprm-au.org/mission.

STATISTICS CITED

UNHCR Statistical Online Database. United Nations High Commissioner for Refugees. Available at www.unhcr.org/statistics/populationdatabase. Data extracted August 5, 2012.
World Bank. 2005. *Global Monitoring Report.* Washington, DC: World Bank.
———. 2008. *Migration and Remittances Factbook 2008.* Washington, DC: World Bank.
———. 2012. *Doing Business Report.* Available at www.doingbusiness.org/reports/global-reports/doing-business-2012.

SUGGESTIONS FOR FURTHER READING

Freedom House. 2009. *Freedom in Sub-Saharan Africa.* Washington, DC: Freedom House. Available at www.freedomhouse.org/uploads/special_report/77.pdf.
Hart, Jeffrey A., and Joan E. Spiro. 1997. *The Politics of International Economic Relations.* 5th ed. New York: St. Martin's.
Levy, Brian. 2006. "Governance and Economic Development in Africa: Meeting the Challenge of Capacity Building." In *Building State Capacity in Africa,* ed. Brian Levy and Sahr Kpundeh, 1–42. Washington, DC: World Bank.
Puddington, Arch. 2012. "Essay: The Arab Uprisings and Their Global Repercussions." In Freedom House, *Freedom in the World 2012.* Available at www.freedomhouse.org/report/freedom-world-2012/essay-arab-uprisings-and-their-global-repercussions.
Wikipedia. 2012. "African Peer Review Mechanism." Available at http://en.wikipedia.org/wiki/African_Peer_Review_Mechanism.

14 Human Rights in Africa

Takyiwaa Manuh

Human rights norms are critical measures of human existence and development in the contemporary period. Within the community of nations, they have become the third institutional pillar of the United Nations since the setting up of the UN Human Rights Council in 2006. This is a fairly recent development in the long span of historical time, but there is little contention about the salience of human rights to the full enjoyment of life, dignity, and development. Although disagreements exist concerning different conceptions and expressions of human rights, no one seriously questions that they are necessary. It has been argued, for instance, that human rights should be regarded not as a regional concept but as universally applicable and relevant to all peoples of the world, irrespective of ethnicity, class, or gender. Furthermore, the notion that the origins of human rights norms are exclusively Western has been rejected in favor of a position that considers the modern concept of human rights as the present expression of a long history of struggles for social justice and resistance to oppression in all human societies (An-Na'im and Hammond 2002: 1). As noted by Radhika Coomaraswamy, former UN special rapporteur on violence against women, there is an element of rights discourse and practice that extends beyond geographical location or cultural specificity. This discourse resonates in the everyday experiences of individuals and has been used by different groups throughout the world. Moreover, over the past two decades, there has been increasing recognition of poverty or debt burden as a denial of basic human rights. This redefinition of poverty is particularly relevant for Africa, where poverty and underdevelopment are most widespread, and where the right to development (RTD) as a human rights concept has long been espoused as a means to ensure equitable and fair distribution of the benefits of development.

THE NORMATIVE FRAMEWORK FOR
HUMAN RIGHTS IN AFRICA

Cultural Specificity versus Universalism

Debates about the framework for human rights in Africa usually proceed by contrasting the existing international instruments for human rights—the Universal Declaration of Human Rights and the covenants on political and civil rights—with the regional body of normative standards encapsulated in the African Charter on Human and Peoples' Rights. Such a framing leads directly to a discussion of "cultural relativism," which is the argument about the extent to which ostensibly universal standards of human rights should be qualified and modified by the local cultural situation in distinct regions of the world, as the text and formulation of the African Charter on Human and Peoples' Rights implies.

As has been noted, there is general agreement that human rights are indispensable to the full enjoyment of life, dignity, and development. However, disagreements are sharp over the conception and expression of human rights and, in particular, the role of culture in the conception of human rights. The disagreement is broadly between universalists (who understand the Universal Declaration and the instruments that operationalize it as the final word on human rights) and relativists (who deny any notion of universal norms that approximates shared human rights). According to proponents of relativism, specific spatial and cultural realities negate the possibility of a translocal and transnational body of human rights; to them, human rights is dependent on existing conditions in a given locality, culture, or state. This would suggest that culture is fixed and immutable, when in reality culture is known to be not only historic and contingent but dynamic and constructed. Most often the notion of "immutable" culture is used to shield, maintain, and legitimize unjust practices that infringe on the rights of less powerful members of society.

In the same restricting manner, advocates of universal human rights present it as context neutral, ignoring situations when paying attention to local realities could produce a more sustainable guarantee for the protection of rights. This outlook fails to recognize that human sentiments are coded and expressed through culture, and it also ignores the necessity for inclusion and dialogue, central principles of universal human rights.

The relativist-universalist divide is not just ideological but has political and economic implications. Cultural relativism appeals to, and has often been used, by dictatorial politicians to justify their dismal human rights records and practices. It is also used by defenders of patriarchy in order to sustain the subjugation of women and maintain patriarchal arrangements; in the process, it undermines gender equality at the household, societal, and national levels. Universalists purport to go beyond what they see as the impediments posed to the full enjoyment of human rights by narrow cultural perspectives. In reality, what they espouse also curtails the scope of human rights because it restricts them to the realm of civic and political engagements. Economic, social, and cultural rights and the rights to peace, development, and a sustainable environment are not covered by an exclusively civic and political conception of rights. These are major omissions, considering the numbers of Africans who lack access to food and a sustainable environment.

Economic, Social, and Cultural Rights

In addition to the universalist-relativist divide, two broad categories are also created in most discussions on human rights: that of civil and political rights, on one hand, and that of economic, social, and cultural rights, on the other hand. In general, economic, social, and cultural rights are treated as secondary to civil and political rights, which are seen as immediate. The classification is deeply entrenched to the extent that even those who insist on the pursuit of both categories of rights as a prerequisite for human well-being accept and use the division. This might be related to the fact that important players on the international human rights scene have tended to prioritize civil and political rights. However, critical voices contend that economic, social, and cultural rights must be pursued with the same vigor as civil and political rights. This is all the more so in parts of the world where chronic poverty makes it impossible to fully enjoy and exercise civil and political rights.

Africa's historic experience of poverty and underdevelopment, the denial of Africans' humanity under colonialism, and economic stagnation, marginality, and conflict make economic, social, and cultural rights equally or more immediate than civil and political rights. The wars in Liberia, Sierra Leone, and the Democratic Republic of the Congo and the genocide in Rwanda led to the death of millions, caused mass population movements and displacements, and led to deterioration in the already precarious conditions of many ordinary people. These conflagrations stalled and in most cases reversed the moderate gains that some states had made in improving the living conditions of their citizens. In situations where basic needs of food and shelter are beyond reach, many consider the right to vote irrelevant. However, the continued disenfranchisement of such persons may perpetuate their hunger and other sources of unfreedom, rather than creating conditions to transform them. This requires, therefore, that the separated categories of rights must be brought together, because full enjoyment of one is largely dependent on the presence of the other. If human rights are viewed and pursued integrally, they then become central to the achievement of the goal of human development. A determined pursuit of one at the expense of the other will create, as is the case today, a set of rights that do not resonate with the lived reality of the most vulnerable sections of society.

Notwithstanding the obvious imperative to combine the two categories of rights, there are those who maintain that economic, social, and cultural rights are not rights but abstract aspirations, the fulfillment of which is neither immediately nor progressively binding on the state. But the efforts of activists have succeeded at times in disproving that claim and holding states accountable. While many states remain adamant that they do not have the capacity to meet the economic rights of citizens, arguing that the fulfillment of economic, social, and cultural rights is contingent on the availability of resources, courts in some jurisdictions have approached these issues from the perspective of discrimination in resource allocation against certain social groups and gender. In their view, ensuring these rights, rather than necessarily requiring additional resources, depends on redistributing existing resources to ensure equity and social justice in a manner that does not benefit an advantaged class or group.

THE HUMAN RIGHTS SITUATION IN AFRICA

Human Rights in Precolonial African Societies

The recognition, nature, and reach of human rights in precolonial or so-called traditional African societies have been the subject of protracted and sometimes raging debates. A widespread view claims that traditional African social formations were communitarian and egalitarian, and the dignity and liberties of the individual were respected while social disparity between members of society was minimal. Articulate proponents of this view, such as the Ghanaian philosopher Kwame Gyekye (1992), explain that the fundamental principles governing those societies were the interdependence of persons and the communities into which they were born, as well as the recognition of the individual dimension of personhood. Individuals, they argue, are seen as possessing a rational moral sense and a capacity for virtue and judgment that the community nurtures. They may at the same time have particular attributes that are often deployed against the community, in keeping with their right to question aspects of social arrangements that they disagree with. Individuals therefore have the will for self-direction and self-determination, reflecting inherent rights that are recognized as indispensable to their dignity and being. At the same time, social values such as peace, harmony, stability, solidarity, mutuality, and reciprocity are emphasized.

A counterassessment of traditional African societies sees the above depiction as fictional and idealized. Drawing on anthropological evidence, oral histories, personal testimonies, analyses of African proverbs, and critiques (especially by African women writers and feminists), proponents of this position insist that traditional African societies were not free from patriarchy and gender-based inequalities (International Humanist and Ethical Union 2006). In addition, depending on the social and/or political structure of societies at a given point in time, levels of solidarity regularly ebbed and flowed, and many, if not all African societies, were influenced by dynamics and personalities within the family, age set, and clan, as well as by ethnic leaders and elders. And since those societies were not isolated entities but dynamic structures that had frequent and even violent intra- and interethnic political and economic contacts with other groups and societies, they were repeatedly reconfigured. The new social orders that emerged could lead to rapid stratification in interpersonal relationships with regard to the private ownership of land, status differences between royalty and commoners, between "big men" or "patrons" and their clients or social subordinates, between elders and juniors, and between men and women. All this affected the social standing of individuals and the roles they could play in community affairs. But the evolving social orders in Africa were to be violently disrupted by colonialism, which imposed a new political, economic and social system that redefined and reconstituted power and identities and allegiances.

European Colonialism and Human Rights in Africa

Despite the discourse of civilization and modernization that justified and accompanied European colonial rule in Africa, its human rights record was abysmal. Violence accompanied its imposition, and the colonized were considered to be on the lowest rung of the evolutionary scale. Accounts of the colonial era are replete with racist bigotry and the heinous abuse of the dignity and personhood of Africans in the form of forced labor, physical violence and murder, economic deprivation and hardship, and restrictions on movement, among others.

Politically, Africans were treated as subjects of the colonizers and denied the right to participate in their internal political process. Metropolitan interests were predominant, subordinating locals under capricious laws to facilitate the extraction of economic value. While the British in particular stressed their practice of "indirect rule," all European colonial powers relied on intermediaries who were willing to help create unrepresentative systems that subordinated flexible local political processes. Existing leaders who wished to retain their positions were required to impose taxes on locals, and Europeans would impose intermediaries where no centralized authority previously existed. The genocidal murder of Congolese by Belgians under the watch of Leopold II typifies the disregard for the life and the rights of Africans under colonial rule: an estimated eight million people lost their lives in the process, as graphically documented by Hochschild (1999). But the Belgians were not alone in this; similar forms of forced labor were imposed by the French, Germans, and British.

Freedom of movement was also severely controlled in accordance with the specific interests of the particular colonial power. A classic example was in apartheid South Africa, where the majority black population was confined to native reserves and could move only upon the issuance of a pass. People were forced to work under inhumane conditions in mines and on plantations. Questioning the legitimacy of the system and its brutality led to imprisonment and, in some cases, banishment to barren places such as the infamous Robben Island, to serve as a deterrent to others. The police service and other law enforcement agents were trained to clamp down on the smallest expression of dissent in the most brutal fashion, while freedom of the press was severely curtailed through harsh laws on sedition and libel.

Racial and gender-based discriminations were widely present in daily life and in employment and access to economic opportunities. The colonized population as a whole was kept at the margins of the economy, except as a laboring class, and even members of the small African middle class, such as lawyers, teachers, and middle-level personnel in the colonial administration, worked under conditions far inferior to those enjoyed by Europeans of similar standing. In the case of women, while male-controlled cultural arrangements existed in many societies prior to colonial rule, several historical and anthropological accounts demonstrate the active collusion between anxious colonial rulers and male elders to remake and invent traditions that then turned fluid or imprecise social and cultural arrangements into hard and fixed notions of "duties," "customs," and "rights" that benefited those male elders, often at the expense of women and social juniors. Women had little or no access to the narrow and restricted education on offer and to jobs in the formal economy, as an ideology of the male breadwinner came to substitute for the complementary and valued roles that women and men often had in production and in social life. In the few instances when women were employed in the formal economy toward the end of colonial rule, they had to resign on pregnancy or marriage to enable them to fully discharge the invented alien duties of a housewife, said to be the apex of a woman's achievement. For all these reasons, a rallying cry of the anticolonial movements was the need to end material poverty and the disregard for the rights of Africans under colonial rule.

Human Rights and Nation Building in Postindependence Africa

African governments were generally anxious to replace the economic, social, and physical infrastructure that they had inherited. In many countries therefore, social amenities such as schools, hospitals, and running water were expanded to remote areas for the benefit of the long-neglected populace. Literacy rates increased significantly, the pool of trained professionals including medical doctors, engineers, and academics was expanded, and attempts were made to reduce killer diseases and mortality rates. Physical infrastructure such as roads, rail lines, and electricity were also extended beyond administrative centers and ports to various parts of the independent state. This connected villages to semiurban and urban areas and facilitated internal trade and communication. Many of these developments occurred under a paradigm in which the state played an active and central role in economic planning and policy implementation. Local industries were set up under import substitution schemes to produce basic goods that would have been imported into the economy. While these schemes faced numerous challenges, they saved the economy millions in foreign exchange, delivered jobs to the citizenry, and enabled the state to directly engage in policy making. The cumulative result of these interventions was a general improvement on the social and economic fronts into the early 1970s.

On the political front, however, the majority of states faced numerous challenges as they tried to weld into nation-states the variety of ethnic groups that had been arbitrarily brought together under colonialism. Early nationalists and postcolonial leaders of various persuasions celebrated the virtues of traditional African societies and portrayed them as equitable and democratic as a way of inverting the colonial discourses on these societies. In many cases, undemocratic cultural practices and traditions that reinforced gender, regional, and ethnic discrimination were upheld in the guise of "preserving tradition and culture" or "communal rights." Over time, the leader's views often came to represent the national view and the only right approach for the country, usually resulting in curtailment of the most basic human rights. Dissenters were cast as traitors and enemies of the nation and development, leading the Burkinabe intellectual and historian Joseph Ki-Zerbo to derisively characterize the suppression of dissent allegedly in the pursuit of development thus: "Silence: development in progress!" The highlights of the era include the abolition of constitutional liberties where they existed; the imposition of one-party and no-party regimes; scant regard for the rights of minorities, workers, and peasants, and muzzling of the media. Although the charter of the Organization of African Unity (OAU, later the African Union) supported the rights of African states to self-determination from colonial rule, it did not extend similar support to individual and community rights, and its respect for the inviolability of borders and state sovereignty aided repressive states and regimes (Oloka-Onyango 2000).

Thus independence did not mark the end of human rights violations by state actors, which deployed and in some cases extended the oppressive mechanisms of control inherited from their colonial predecessors. The usurpation of power by the military in many countries shortly after independence exacerbated the poor human rights situation. Thirty-one out of the fifty-four member states of the OAU/African Union experienced military rule at some point over a period of thirty years. While the entry of the military into active politics varied from country to country, the justifications that the military advanced for usurping power have been constant: political corruption, economic mismanagement, social instability, incompetence, and dictatorship on the part of civilian regimes. Ironically, their very first actions upon seizing power were to abrogate constitutions where they existed and to curtail fundamental rights such as free speech, freedom of association (by banning political parties and other political groupings), and freedom of movement (in the form of curfews aimed at regime security), while sanctioning wanton and indiscriminate arrests.

Press freedom and the right to voice have been frontally attacked under nearly every military junta, and decrees were passed that criminalized what the junta's leadership conceived as the media's extremes in reporting "falsehoods," which in most cases were simply reportage of the regimes' excesses. Activists who spoke out against the military's numerous excesses were detained for many years without trial, and the military and their associates arrested and brutalized whoever they identified as speaking against the regime, with such persons generally unable to seek redress in national and continental courts and commissions. The proscription of political parties and other political groupings effectively denied citizens the right to participate in the political process. Women in the public sphere were seen as particularly threatening, and systematic abuse and gender-based violence against women and girls were commonplace in many countries. As economic conditions deteriorated, increased child labor, destitution, and institutional corruption became common place in many parts of the continent. Under military rule, where the source of political power and sovereignty shifted from the people to the gun, human rights abuses were not exceptions but the overwhelming norm.

Redemocratization in Africa and the Pursuit of Human Rights

The plethora of human rights abuses bequeathed by decades of military rule and a consistent decline in the fiscal condition of individual states from the mid-1970s through the 1980s reversed the significant socioeconomic achievements that were recorded in the immediate post-independence period. The crisis that resulted from a combination of steep deterioration in the prices of Africa's exports on the world market and internal mismanagement and corruption is known as the "lost decade" in Africa's social history and development. Usually as a precondition for bailout, the Bretton Woods institutions (the World Bank and the International Monetary Fund) imposed harsh austerity measures in the form of structural adjustment programs, which required countries to drastically reduce the role of the state in economic life, liberalize the economy, cut back on public spending in the social sectors of education, health care, and water provision, and introduce fees for services. While at first glance economic liberalization might appear as the key to unlock the entrepreneurial potential of ordinary people, in combination with the massive retrenchments carried out under structural adjustment it actually served to further undermine the social and economic rights of citizens by denying them access to health care, education, and food, among other things, and destroy the livelihoods of many families.

Criticisms of and mobilization against the International Monetary Fund's and World Bank's dealings with undemocratic regimes forced the two institutions to include political liberalization as one of the conditionalities for further support. As a result, they demanded that the numerous entrenched and military regimes across the continent ensure public participation in the political process and adopt codes of good governance and rule of law. Specifically this has meant holding periodic elections, reform of public administration and the judiciary, and the creation of human rights bodies to guarantee defense of the citzenry's rights. But the reforms and their ensuing monetization of politics, the absence of internal democracy within political parties, and nonproportional representation politics that have kept the majority of the populace out of the process have been criticized for being shallow, while the militarist ethos has not disappeared even in the countries that have been redemocratized (Olukoshi 2005). The continuing illiteracy of a significant proportion of Africa's population and their inability to speak the official languages (which are often the colonial languages and the languages of the law, government, and business) have meant that large numbers of people are unable to influence the dominant discourses and conceptions of human rights. Thus even where universalist human rights discourse gains acceptance, it usually excludes the majority of ordinary Africans, who may view it with suspicion and distance.

The African Charter on Human and Peoples' Rights

The African Charter on Human and Peoples' Rights is the preeminent document for the defense of human rights on the African continent. Its provisions can be grouped under five themes: civil and political rights; economic, social, and cultural rights; group or collective rights; duties of the individual; and enforcement mechanisms. Promulgated in 1981, the charter takes account of Africa's cultural experience—both historic and contemporary—and attempts to negotiate the tension between the universalist and relativist conceptions of human rights. It aims for a distinct identity as an African document, rooted in the history and peculiarities of the continent while drawing from older instruments such as the Universal Declaration of Human Rights. It endorses and incorporates the fundamental principles enshrined in the Universal Declaration, such as equality of all and abhorrence of discrimination on the grounds of race, sex, and religion, but it marks its Africanness by espousing traditional African values such as the centrality of the family and the community at the same time as it holds individuals to certain responsibilities toward state and society and affirms the rights of oppressed people to self-determination. In so doing, it attempts to make a contribution to the corpus of human rights through its recognition of economic, social, and cultural rights as a basis for full enjoyment of civil and political rights.

In spite of the aforementioned innovations, it has been observed that the charter is weakened by a number of commissions and omissions, notably its statecentric understanding of human rights, in which the state is presented as the embodiment of the rights of the people, thereby relegating individual rights to the background. A further limitation was the charter's silence on the need for judicial reforms in a context that was replete with judicial unfairness, inadequate access to justice, delays in the administration of justice, and the maintenance of repressive laws on the statute books. No single article addressed the rights of an accused person to legal assistance, the services of an interpreter, or compensation for judicial unfairness. Many of the weaknesses in the charter result from the fundamental trade-offs that were made at the time of its promulgation to accommodate the unease of the many unelected leaders who supervised the process, as well as the urgency with which the charter was prepared due to pressure from foreign donors and local human rights activists.

Although some commentators hail the African Charter as an important milestone that places economic, social, and cultural rights on the same footing as civil and political rights, the reality is that economic rights are still inaccessible to the vast majority of Africans. It was the internal and external pressures on African states to reform their abysmal human rights records, coupled with a campaign for a fair global political economy, that led to the inscription of economic, social, and cultural rights into the charter, which was adopted by African leaders who may have relished an equitable redistribution of global wealth, but not necessarily to their citizenry. Thus, although the campaign for resource redistribution was legitimized by the need to deliver basic education, health care, and potable water to poor segments of society, many African leaders treated the rights as accruing to the state, not the citizenry, under the postcolonial fiction that equated the people with the state. Under that guise, even the most despotic regimes insisted that they articulated the will of the people despite denying their fundamental rights. Unsurprisingly, the charter is imprecise in defining the scope and concrete meaning of economic, social, and cultural rights, or of civil and political rights.

WOMEN'S RIGHTS IN AFRICA

Women, like all citizens, have fundamental rights to be treated equally, to have their bodily integrity respected, to pursue meaningful economic ventures, and to engage in civil and political activities. Unfortunately, these rights are threatened daily and abused by a combination of male-controlled or -sanctioned cultural arrangements, legislative inertia, and gender-based discrimination. As many scholars have noted, African gender relations were a complex set of negotiations and compromises between men and women, but with the introduction of customary law in the European colonial era, these practices became more rigid and now stand as a representation of the oppression of women in Western depictions of Africa. While women had little or no formal powers in some societies, in many others they possessed concrete and symbolic religious, social, political, and economic powers at the level of the household and community, enabling women to participate in reproduction as well as safeguarding their rights and autonomy in many societies. It is therefore atypical and "untraditional" in an African setting for a woman to be totally dependent on a man. Women have always contributed to family and household survival and regeneration. They have played active economic and productive roles, with many heading their own households and others assuming sole control in situations of conflict and economic upheavals when men are killed, displaced, or unavailable. But the legacy of the colonially constructed dependent woman, whose labor can be appropriated under the guise of an invented duty of a wife to supplement the labor of her husband without remuneration, still lingers on among some segments of the population, to the detriment of women's full autonomy as citizens and economic beings. It impedes their political and social participation, their access to economic resources and opportunities, and career progression and autonomy.

Women have long had access to land, by far the most important economic resource in much of rural Africa, but men and women have rarely, if ever, had identical kinds of claims to land. This is largely because the genders often have differentiated positions within kinship systems that are the primary means for organizing land access; agricultural production is similarly differentiated by tasks and inputs (Whitehead and Tsikata 2003). Land tenure systems are largely governed by customary laws (including in countries such as Uganda, Ethiopia, and Tanzania, where the state owns all land), and it is permissible in many jurisdictions for men to sell land without the knowledge and consent of their wives and children (Zeleza 2006). Over time, customary systems of land tenure have become inherently discriminatory against women, and the superimposition of Western models of land tenure has further worsened women's access. This is because reforms in many countries (e.g., Uganda, Mozambique, Malawi, Côte D'Ivoire, Tanzania, and Niger) were primarily aimed at providing secure tenure and attracting foreign investments by formalizing title to land and allocating it to individuals. This ongoing process has been shaped both by contemporary cultural perceptions of men as the proper authority in land matters and by narrow, individualistic conceptions of ownership in the formal legal regime. Structural adjustment and economic liberalization further restricted women's rights to land as the commodification of land intensified and various forms of customary entitlements that had made it possible for ordinary people, including women, to utilize communal lands were loosened. Women found their access to communal lands curtailed as community leaders and male landowners sold off communal land. The inconsistency between denying women control of and access to land and their role as the primary producers in the agricultural sector in Africa has been emphasized by the growing literature produced under a framework that analyzes the role of gender in development and in reports by the Food and Agriculture Organization of the United Nations. Many of these studies have stressed the need for fundamental changes in local and national legal frameworks and in cultural prejudices against women's access to productive resources. At the same time, extension services, know-how, credit, marketing, and transportation services must be provided to support and ensure women's equal access to productive resources. These measures would considerably reduce poverty, deprivation, and malnutrition, forms of human rights abuses specifically directed against women and rural dwellers.

In the case of urban women, several other forms of discrimination exist. The majority of women living in urban areas are engaged in retail trade in the informal economy, carrying out their business in crowded markets with poor facilities. Like rural farmers, they enjoy no social security or pension rights and are completely dependent on their own efforts. The proportionately few women who work in the formal economy tend to be in administrative and support roles in gender-segmented labor markets that create few alternative opportunities for women and girls. Many employers still prefer to recruit men over women, and it is not uncommon to find female employees in nonunionized work with little labor protection.

Changes are occurring in women's political participation and decision making across Africa, but the record is still mixed. In several countries in eastern and southern Africa (such as Rwanda, Uganda, and South Africa), political activism and the benevolence of male leaders resulted in quotas and mandates for proportional

Figure 14.1. A judge outside her courthouse in Burundi.
Corbis.

representation that enabled women to increase their representation in national and local governance structures. Rwanda now holds the world record for having the highest representation of women legislators. Some countries in West Africa are also reforming their political systems to increase women's representation, albeit at a much slower pace. A large proportion of African women do not participate actively in political decision-making processes, engage in public discourse, or openly express their views on issues that affect their well-being. This is due to unequal power relations in households and communities, the continued perception that all reproductive work including domestic chores and care work is "women's work," the increasing monetization of politics, and the perception that politics is men's work, with the consequence that the political space in many parts of Africa is still largely male-dominated.

In addition to economic and political rights, respect for the bodily integrity and sexuality of women and girls remains a major challenge. Research by activists in different parts of Africa has identified several forms of gender-based violence as a routine experience for many women. The HIV/AIDS epidemic, particularly in southern and eastern Africa, has highlighted unequal gender relations and patriarchal values, practices, and sexual cultures that subjugate women's desires and pleasures to those of men. In many instances, husbands and partners routinely disregard the right of women to withhold consent to sex or to decide the number of children they will have and their spacing, because marriage and the acceptance of bridewealth have been construed as giving a husband unimpeded access to a wife whether she consents or not. Several practices aimed at enhancing male pleasure in sex and reducing possible female infidelity, including different types of genital cutting and mutilation, have attracted widespread attention. However, as feminist legal scholar Sylvia Tamale (2007) cautions, care must also be taken to respect what communities, including women, consider as pleasure-enhancing, such as the practice of labia elongation among the Baganda in Uganda. Recent debates over passing legislation on domestic and gender-based violence in many countries, including Ghana, have highlighted the contentions over women's sexuality and the supposed "right" of a husband to "chastise" a disobedient wife. Women's struggles for respect of their rights often set them against family and social networks of which they are integral parts, and the potential for strained relations can constrain their ability to challenge the status quo. Given the minimal role of the state in the provision of social welfare, the family is an important social institution that not only defines social and economic relations between men and women but also provides access to resources.

Nonetheless, the past two decades have witnessed sustained efforts by African women to claim human rights and fundamental freedoms on the basis of equality with men. This is the outcome of continued efforts of mainly African feminists and women's rights advocates and civil society groups to deepen the ongoing democratization processes across Africa to include women's citizenship and gender justice. Increasingly, many countries have passed legislation on gender- and sexually based violence alongside laws on inheritance and succession. These efforts have been propelled by important human rights instruments such as the Solemn Declaration on Gender Equality in Africa and the Protocol to the African Charter on Human and Peoples' Rights on the Rights of Women in Africa.

WOMEN'S HUMAN RIGHTS IN THE AFRICAN REGIONAL FRAMEWORK

The African Charter on Human and Peoples' Rights has a number of provisions that frown upon discrimination and proclaim equal treatment of all, but only a single provision (in Article 18) makes reference to the situation of women, as follows: "The State shall ensure the elimination of every discrimination against women and also ensure the protection of the rights of the woman and the child as stipulated in international declarations and conventions." That language, however, is undercut by another imperative in the same article: "The State shall have the duty to assist the family which is the custodian of morals and traditional values recognized by the community." Understandably, the article has attracted numerous reviews and comments, with some concluding that the charter in its entirety gives only a passing thought to the issue of women's rights. This is because the type of family and the kind of tradition that the charter promotes are capable of legitimizing the abuse of women's rights. Similar emphases on other problematic social relations are apparent in the guidelines on state reportage, which require states to report to the African Commission on Human and Peoples' Rights on their progress in achieving the goals outlined in the charter. Even then, most of the attention centers on motherhood, marriage, and child care, at the expense of equally important issues such as gender-based violence, rights to property and employment, or women's equal participation in political decision making and national life.

In recognition of the weaknesses of the charter with respect to women's rights and of the growing activism of women's movements and networks on the continent, in 2002 the African Union promulgated the Solemn Declaration on Gender Equality in Africa.[1] It is worth noting that the Constitutive Act of the African Union affirmed the principle of gender equality and the full participation of African women as equal partners in Africa's development. The election of a woman, Gertrude Mongella of Tanzania, as first president of the African Union's Pan-African Parliament in 2004, as well as the attainment of gender parity among the commissioners signaled the commission's new seriousness.

The Solemn Declaration recognized the deficits in attaining gender equality in the areas of unequal access to political space, economic resources, and the differential impact of HIV/AIDS on women and men. The African Union declared its commitment to the eradication of violence against women and trafficking in women; the enhancement of the capacity of both urban and rural women; the full participation of women in peace processes, including postconflict negotiations and reconstruction; and the promotion of the implementation of legislation that secures the rights of women to land, property, and inheritance. The declaration also commits the African Union to the pursuit of gender-specific social, economic, and legal measures to check the spread of HIV/AIDS and its impact on women. Specific measures include a campaign against the abuse of the sexual rights of girls and wives and the setting up of AIDS Watch Africa to encourage the production of antiretroviral drugs on the continent, among others.

In 2003, the African Union adopted the Protocol to the African Charter on Human and Peoples' Rights on the Rights of Women in Africa. This was after nearly a decade of pressure from African women's rights groups, spearheaded by Women in Law and Development in Africa. Unlike the original charter, which did not name and also failed to identify and address gender-based discrimination, the protocol defines discrimination against women and commits itself to combating it in all its forms through appropriate legislation, institutions, and other measures, and to integrating a gender perspective in policy decisions, legislation, development plans, programs and activities, and all other spheres of life. It is a comprehensive document that aims to restructure and transform gender relations and practice in Africa and, concomitantly, social, cultural, and political life.

The adoption of the protocol is a significant milestone for African women. Nonetheless, obstacles remain to it becoming known and used as a reference point for the advancement of women's rights on the continent. These include the processes for enacting its provisions into national legislation and addressing the poor enforcement of already existing national laws. This reflects weak political will as well as the weakness of institutions charged with implementation and enforcement, and increases the obligations on women's rights groups and advocates to ensure that the promises contained in the protocol become reality for millions of women across Africa.

Children's Rights in Africa

Children are valued in African societies as guarantors of the continuity of societies, and traditionally they attracted considerable attention and care from their immediate and extended families as well as from the community at large, all of whom shared responsibility for their well-being. Children took part in almost all community activities and were expected to learn by doing as they accompanied adults on farms and in performing household tasks. However, other cultural practices such as child betrothal, early marriage, and corporal punishment, intended to maintain social cohesion or to instill discipline, also inhibit the physical, intellectual, and emotional growth of children and infringe on their right to bodily integrity and harmonious development.

Reductions in child mortality and morbidity and universal access to basic education for both girls and boys are among the Millennium Development Goals that the United Nations hopes to see achieved by 2015, but many African countries are not expected to meet these targets.[2] African children have been disproportionately impacted by economic and social dislocations, and the increased poverty that has accompanied neoliberal interventions has meant that poor households are forced to rely more heavily on the labor of children for their sustenance. Many children continue to drop out of school to contribute to the household economy or because their parents are unable to pay for education-related charges. Social interventions such as school feeding programs that provide basic meals have swelled enrollments, but such programs are not yet universal, and they also do not address the full range of problems that children face. Millions of children who suffer from preventable disease such as malaria, respiratory infections, diarrheal diseases, or HIV/AIDS lack access to health care and proper treatment.

The phenomena of street begging, intensive physical labor, illiteracy, sexual abuse, and other forms of abuse characterize the lives of many children whose rights have become more precarious than those of the rest of the population. Many children have also been casualties of the conflicts that have beset the continent, with boys and girls forcibly recruited into armed groups and trained to commit heinous acts that alter their psychological states, self-perception, and social existence. The phenomenon of child soldiers has cut short the development cycle of many children, making them social misfits and a threat to themselves and to others, while girls are often used as sex slaves by militant factions. Although young people make up the majority of Africa's population, they have not been given space to positively engage in the political process, and the monopolization of the public sphere by older men has relegated young people to the background. When youth are called upon to take an active part in the political process, it is often as agents of violent destruction on behalf of politicians desperate to retain or win power.

In response to the many challenges facing children and young people in Africa, in 1990 the Organization of African Unity enacted the African Charter on the Rights and Welfare of the Child, the first comprehensive document on the continent to deal with the rights of children within the peculiar social, economic, political, and cultural milieu in Africa. The charter strictly prohibits the participation of children in conflicts (an acknowledgment of the wanton abuse of children as child soldiers across the continent) and also urges protection of refugee and internally displaced children. It also frowns on traditional sociocultural practices that negatively affect the welfare of children. Acknowledging the double victimization of pregnant schoolgirls, the charter firmly insists on the rights of such girls to education and against their expulsion from school. And in the interest of the well-being of children, the charter obliges states to protect imprisoned expectant mothers and those with young children. The charter is credited with contextualizing many of the provisions in the 1979 United Nations Convention on the Rights of the Child, and it also does not predicate the fulfillment of the rights of children on the availability of state resources.

Unfortunately, implementation of the charter remains poor at best, in spite of ratification by an overwhelming number of individual African states. The African Committee of Experts on the Rights and Welfare of the Child, appointed by the African Union and tasked with the implementation of the charter's provisions, is grossly handicapped by resource constraints, inadequate staffing, and overreliance on donor agencies and NGOs. At the national level, governments have failed to translate the content of the charter into practical policies, citing the lack of resources.

Notwithstanding these challenges, some positive developments in children's rights are emerging on the continent. In South Africa, for example, there is a Children's Budget Initiative, which tracks the state's expenditure and budgetary allocations for child-related issues. There is also growing academic interest in the conditions of African children, initiated by organizations such as the Council for the Development of Social Science Research in Africa, as well as activity by civil society organizations to monitor the commitments that African governments have freely assumed on the rights and conditions of children in Africa.

HIV/AIDS in Africa: Sexuality, Body, and Gay Rights

The HIV/AIDS pandemic has ravaged lives, destroyed families and livelihoods, and decimated the labor force across Africa. Prognoses in South Africa or Botswana, for example, indicate that these countries will suffer massive labor shortages if current infection rates (17.8 and 24.8 percent, respectively, in 2009) are not quickly reduced. Though other countries have comparatively lower levels of infection, the situation there is worrying, and in the absence of properly functioning health and welfare systems, women often have to act as both caregivers and sole income earners in an atmosphere of increasingly narrow economic opportunities.

The initial reaction of patriarchal elements to the carnage of HIV/AIDS was a further tightening of the policing of women's sexuality, while men were still free to have multiple sexual partners and to demand sex from their partners, even when they knew they were infected. Continental bodies and national governments are gradually realizing the ineffectiveness of this patriarchal approach to the pandemic, and both the African Union's Solemn Declaration on Gender Equality in Africa and the Protocol to the African Charter on Human and Peoples' Rights on the Rights of Women in Africa have identified the capacity of women to negotiate for safe and voluntary sex as essential to controlling the spread of HIV/AIDS.

These efforts will be enhanced if African states abandon their hostility toward homosexuals and lesbians and recognize their inherent rights to sexual choice and sexual orientation. The failure to uphold these rights has pushed many gays and lesbians underground. Recent reports in the Ghanaian media alarmingly indicate that a large number of the members of the underground gay and lesbian community are HIV positive. One route through which infection can pass from homosexuals to heterosexuals is as a result of social control mechanisms that force gay individuals to engage in heterosexual relationships in order to avoid being "outed."

In general, gay rights have become a very contentious issue, and there is rising homophobia across Africa and attacks on gays and their supporters and advocates, often with the direct or covert support of the state and its agents. Opponents of homosexuality led by traditionalists, moralists, politicians, and religious leaders (both Christians and Muslims) argue both that homosexuality is un-African and a Western imposition on African cultural arrangements and that homosexuality is a learned perversion that is opposed to the "natural" and God-given sexual design for men and women. In denying gays, lesbians, and transgendered persons their right to express alternative sexualities, African homophobes join others worldwide, including in the West, who also denounce gays as "unnatural" and as going against the laws of God. But at the heart of the hostility toward homosexuality is a commitment to defend patriarchy and gendered social orderings and power relations that are threatened by multiple and alternative sexualities and lifestyles.

THE INSTITUTIONAL FRAMEWORK FOR PROMOTING HUMAN RIGHTS IN AFRICA

The African Commission is the main institution mandated to ensure that individual states protect and respect human rights in accordance with the provisions of both the African Charter and accompanying protocols. But the consensus among analysts is that the commission has not been successful in carrying out its responsibilities. The reasons for its underperformance include conceptual weaknesses, inadequate implementation mechanisms, and the absence of political will on the part of governments.

The reluctance of states to pay their obligatory membership dues seriously hampers the work of the commission, which then has to depend on donor support. Some commentators have recommended the creation of an African Human Rights Fund to generate resources from across the continent for the commission. An additional handicap is the absence of structures for the implementation of the provisions of the charter and the protocols.[3] This is linked to the negation of provisions of the charter by certain conventions that are carefully guarded by states, such as the principle of non-interference in internal affairs. The commission is further inhibited by contradictory obligations, such as the requirement that it must alert national leaders to human rights violations within a country before it takes any action. Other internal challenges relate to the capacity of the commissioners, their attitude toward human rights, and their willingness to make the right decisions if those decisions are likely to offend the leaders who appointed them. Since 2003, a voluntary evaluation scheme known as the African Peer Review Mechanism (APRM) has been established as one of the innovative ways through which the African Union seeks to promote human rights, good governance and socio-economic development.

ENFORCEMENT OF WOMEN'S RIGHTS

There is no uniformity in the approach to gender issues and in the rates of progress toward gender equality around Africa, and the scale of compliance with international and regional human rights instruments ranges from impressive to very poor. An example in Botswana is the case of *Unity Dow v. Attorney-General* (1992), in which judges relied on the charter to rule against practices that subjugate women, even though the national constitution did not incorporate provisions of the charter. Progressive developments symbolized by the Botswanan court's ruling may be ignored by conservative judges, state policies, and retrogressive traditions. In the Botswanan case, the government followed the lead of the court by making changes to its laws. In other settings, the state and the judiciary actually discriminate against women. For example, in 1998 the Supreme Court in Zimbabwe (in *Magaya v. Magaya*) denied a woman her rights to inheritance under the guise of upholding local custom in order to maintain social harmony. It thus contributed to the economic subordination of women under a widespread practice whereby women are deprived of the resources left behind by their spouses and parents or receive smaller portions than men. It also placed discriminatory arrangements over and above international human rights instruments such as the Convention on Elimination of all Forms of Discrimination against Women (CEDAW) and the African Charter. The patriarchal comments by the judge equating a woman to a minor in need of a man's protection raises a fundamental point about the deprivation of women's civil and political rights as a result of the denial of their economic, social, and cultural rights. The failure to use international or regional instruments to advance women's human rights in the face of oppressive customary laws that promote and uphold gender-based discrimination is another indication of the gulf that exists between well-intentioned international human rights instruments and antithetical national laws.

Women's rights may be impeded in situations where fossilized interpretations of customary law are allowed to prevail over statutory law. Working toward the incorporation and enforcement of the guarantees of human rights in legislation could be self-defeating if it fails to contend with local institutions whose norms and practices have the potential to contradict the intended goals; this is particularly true of attempts to introduce reforms in the sphere of family relations.

While conflict usually arises between the norms and practices founded on particular readings of African culture and those based on human rights principles, some authors (e.g., Nyamu-Musembi 2002, Butegwa 2002) argue that it would be erroneous to view culture as the main problem in violations of women's human rights, as customary norms are dynamic, flexible, and able to adapt to changing circumstances.

In some countries, national laws have provided avenues for women to assert their rights despite the existence of customary laws that make it difficult for them to do so. For instance, the Intestate Succession Law of 1985 in Ghana fundamentally reformed aspects of customary law in order to guarantee equitable inheritance of the estate of a deceased man by his widow and children. In Uganda, the Succession Act allows widows a 15 percent share in the estate of a deceased husband, although this is rarely calculated to include any land. In these situations of intrusions of statutory law into customary law, many women have found the formal law protective of their rights. However, access to formal laws and the courts remains limited for the majority of women, especially rural dwellers. Rwanda stands out through its attempt to recognize the rights of women and the crucial role they played in the aftermath of the genocide in 1994; this has led to the mainstreaming of gender in nearly every aspect of state policy.

In general, the Protocol to the African Charter on Human and Peoples' Rights on the Rights of Women in Africa imposes a number of important obligations on states to ensure the protection of women's human rights. Apart from these specific obligations, there are other opportunities for states to intervene effectively in protecting human rights, such as opportunities to integrate human rights issues into national constitutions, but enforcement is often lacking. Moreover, the human rights of some vulnerable groups, such as migrant farmers, have been abused in many African societies, and African national constitutions as well as African human rights instruments have failed to respond to their needs (Ibrahim 2006).

States that are parties to the protocol are also committed to implementing public education, information, education, and communication strategies that counteract perceptions of the inferiority or superiority of either sex or stereotyped roles for women and men. The Convention on Elimination of All Forms of Discrimination against Women is more explicit on the role of the state in protecting the rights of women and obliges states to take all appropriate measures to modify social and cultural patterns and behaviors with a view to eliminating prejudices in customary laws and other discriminatory practices. However, the states' implementation of such international instruments leaves much to be desired.

Although the primary responsibility for protecting human rights in Africa rests with national governments, other states and nonstate actors also have a responsibility to act in accordance with international human rights norms and standards. Courts in particular have a central role to play in upholding rights, especially when the executive is unwilling to do so. As with the Botswanan court, local judiciaries should be guided by the spirit of international human rights instruments. This should not be contingent on whether national laws specifically reference or incorporate such instruments.

African civil society organizations have played important roles in the promotion and defense of human rights. This is reflected in the substantial number of human rights groups across the continent. If such groups are to continue their crucial functions of expanding human rights, it is imperative that regulations that impede activism be repealed. At the same time, African civil society groups have to move toward a unified pursuit of economic, social, and cultural rights, including the rights of children and the aged, rather than advocating only for civil and political rights. Civil society organizations working on development and those working on human rights must cooperate because their goals are inseparable.

CHALLENGES TO SUSTAINABLE HUMAN DEVELOPMENT AND OPPORTUNITIES FOR THE ADVANCEMENT OF HUMAN RIGHTS

In spite of the milestones that have been achieved, much still needs to be done to attain sustainable human development in Africa. Basic needs such as food, shelter, and health care are not guaranteed for millions of people. Human development in Africa cannot be attained if the existing global economic hierarchies and inequalities persist, and internal reforms for fair distribution of national wealth can be sustained only if the global economic architecture is simultaneously transformed. For example, transnational corporations frequently abuse the individual and communal rights of local people by alienating land for agribusiness, polluting the environment, dumping toxic waste, or selling outdated medications. And the spread of small arms and the activities of transnational mercenaries in West Africa threaten the fledgling peace in formerly war-torn countries.

Yet significant opportunities exist to counter the above challenges and to leverage a culture of respect for human rights. Ordinary people increasingly feel empowered to participate in public debates and to mobilize around shared concerns. An emergent culture of popular demand for public accountability has the potential to check corruption, hence releasing resources for important social needs such as physical infrastructure, education, and health care. Citizens constantly monitor the performance of governments through both conventional and new media. Current issues and demands are no longer restricted to houses of parliament but are being passionately discussed on radio and television and on Facebook and Twitter. Such public-spiritedness is reconfiguring the relationship between leaders and citizens. Politicians are voted out of office if voters estimate that they have become incapable of rendering the services for which they voted them into office. Such an atmosphere is fertile for the institutionalization of a culture of respect for human rights.

NOTE

This chapter has benefited from the dedicated research assistance provided by Messrs. Peter Narh and Faisal Garba, both of whom are currently PhD students in Germany.

1. These movements include continent-wide organizations such as Solidarity on African Women's Rights, Equality Now, Women in Law and Development in Africa, Femmes Africa Solidarité, and African Women's Development and Communication Network, as well as several regional and national coalitions and networks. See http://pambazuka.org for updates.

2. There are eight Millennium Development Goals. See www.un.org/millenniumgoals.

3. The term "protocol" refers to an addition to a treaty. It may be on any topic relevant to the original treaty and is used to further address something in the treaty, address a new or emerging concern, or add a procedure for the operation and enforcement of the treaty.

SUGGESTIONS FOR FURTHER READING

An-Na'im, Alhassan A., and Jeffrey Hammond. 2002. "Cultural Transformation and Human Rights in African Societies." In *Cultural Transformations and Human Rights in Africa,* ed. Alhassan A. An-Na'im. London: Zed Books.

Butegwa, Florence. 2002. "Mediating Culture and Human Rights in Favour of Land Rights for Women in Africa: A Framework for Community-Level Action." In *Cultural Transformations and Human Rights in Africa,* ed. Alhassan A. An-Na'im. London: Zed Books.

Gyekye, Kwame. 1992. "Person and Community in Akan Thought." In *Person and Community,* ed. Kwasi Wiredu and Kwame Gyekye. Washington, DC: Council for Research in Values and Philosophy.

Hochschild, Adam. 1999. *King Leopold's Ghost. A Story of Greed, Terror and Heroism in Colonial Africa.* Boston: Mariner Books.

Ibrahim, Jibrin. 2006. "Expanding the Human Rights Regime in Africa: Citizens, Indigenes and Exclusion in Nigeria." In *Human Rights, Regionalism and the Dilemmas of Democracy in Africa,* ed. Lennart Wohlgemuth and Ebrima Sall. Dakar: CODESRIA.

International Humanist and Ethical Union. 2006. *On a Communitarian Ethos: Equality and Human Rights in Africa.* Available at www.iheu.org/node/2360.

Mutua, Makau. 2000. "The African Human Rights System: A Critical Evaluation," Human Development Report Background Paper. Available at http://hdr.undp.org/en/reports/global/hdr2000/papers/MUTUA.pdf.

Nyamu-Musembi, Celestine. 2002. "Are Local Norms and Practices Fences or Pathways? The Examples of Women's Property Rights." In *Cultural Transformations and Human Rights in Africa,* ed. Alhassan A. An-Na'im. London: Zed.

Oloka-Onyango, Joseph. 2000. "Human Rights and Sustainable Development in Contemporary Africa: A New Dawn or Retreating Horizons?" Human Development Report

Background Paper. Available at http://hdr.undp.org/en/reports/global/hdr2000/papers
/joseph%20oloka-onyango1.pdf.

Olukoshi, Adebayo. 2005. "Changing Patterns of Politics in Africa." In *Politics and Social
Movements in an Hegemonic World: Lessons from Africa, Asia and Latin America,* ed.
Atilio A. Boron and Gladys Lechini. Buenos Aires: Consejo Latinoamericano de Cien-
cias Sociales.

Tamale, Sylvia. 2007. "The Right to Culture and the Culture of Rights: A Critical Perspective on Women's Sexual Rights in Africa." In *Sex Matters,* ed. Adili Zia and Billy Kahora.
Nairobi: Urgent Action Fund.

Whitehead, Ann, and Dzodzi Tsikata. 2003. "Policy Discourses on Women's Land Rights
in Sub-Saharan Africa: The Implications of the Re-turn to the Customary." *Journal of
Agrarian Change* 3(1–2): 67–112.

Zeleza, Paul T. 2006. "Human Rights and Development in Africa: New Contexts, Challenges
and Opportunities." In *Human Rights, Regionalism and the Dilemmas of Democracy in
Africa,* ed. Lennart Wohlgemuth and Ebrima Sall. Dakar: CODESRIA.

15 Print and Electronic Resources

Marion Frank-Wilson

"**D**igital technologies, in reshaping the information landscape, also have altered the relationship between recorded knowledge and the activities of research and teaching." This statement by Dan Hazen points to several developments that have shaped the way we conduct research and that are worth keeping in mind before embarking on research in African studies. Electronic information is widely available. Libraries subscribe to vast databases, which provide access to journal literature; Google continues to digitize books and to make many of them available on the web; initiatives such as HathiTrust make the full text of out-of-copyright books available; libraries digitize many of their special collections as well as other content; individual researchers digitize their materials and post them on websites. Students and researchers expect to find large amounts of information in electronic form and, in fact, prefer it to print.

On the web, the traditional barriers to publishing—for example the peer review process for scholarly publications—are removed. Everybody can participate in electronic conversations and create and disseminate content on blogs, Facebook, and Twitter as well as other sites, and authors can remain anonymous if they choose to do so. A democratization of knowledge creation has taken place.

LIBRARY RESOURCES FOR AFRICAN STUDIES: ELECTRONIC VERSUS PRINT INFORMATION

A few things to remember when searching for information on African studies topics:

- An ever-increasing amount of African studies information is available electronically—scholarly content in library databases, digitized books in Google Books, other open-access materials produced by researchers and/or organizations in the United States, Europe, and Africa.

- Despite this wealth of electronic information, a considerable amount of information relating to Africa is still only published in print format. Research for most topics in African studies requires a combination of print and electronic sources.
- The availability of print versus electronic information varies by discipline. For example, a student interested in health-related publications may find a wealth of information online, ranging from statistics to the full text of articles and reports, whereas if that same student were to conduct research for a paper on religion in Africa, he or she would in all likelihood find some information on the web, but would have to combine that information with more in-depth books as well as journal articles from library online databases or even print issues of journals.
- Success in finding relevant sources depends not only on the researcher's ability to look in the right places and use just the right combination of print and electronic resources, but also on knowledge of the discipline and its terminology as well as on the ability to evaluate the sources found.

Important

In order to effectively search for information for a paper, not only do you have to be able to navigate this complicated world of information in print and electronic formats, but you also need to be able to evaluate the sources you encounter—how reliable, credible, objective or subjective, or scholarly are they? Please also see the section "Evaluating Online Resources" at the end of this chapter. Remember that websites change frequently, and some of the URLs in this chapter may not always be active. In case of inactive URLs, use the information in the annotation for that website to conduct keyword searches that will lead to similar websites.

Keep in Mind

Even though you may not physically enter the library's building, many of the online resources you are using are made available by the library, and in all likelihood you access the library's resources every day, albeit online. Librarians are one of those resources—don't hesitate to ask your librarian for help!

How This Chapter Works

Realizing that students will work on a variety of very individualized research topics, and considering the proliferation of resources available—in print and electronic formats, on the web, in social media, and in subscription-based databases; some of them filtered and presented by librarians, others just published on the web—it is not possible to present a comprehensive list of "most important" publications a student should consult for papers on African studies topics. Instead, the focus of this chapter is on providing resources that will provide basic information for each field, suggest examples for more in-depth research, and point out where and how to find more information.

- The sections in this chapter for the most part follow the chapters of the book. However, African studies is an interdisciplinary field, and it is hard to isolate some areas of research into separate academic disciplines. Most chapters in this book connect with content discussed in other chapters, and the same is true for this section on resources. For example, if you are writing a paper on geography in Africa, you will find information in the section "Africa: A Geographic Frame," but there will also be publications related to your topic in the sections "Legacies of the Past: Themes in African History" and "Social Relations and Livelihoods"; a student researching social relationships in African societies will consult "Social Relations and Livelihoods" but may also want to take a look at the sections on African history, urban Africa, and so on.
- Many sections in this chapter begin with a list of subtopics for each discipline. These subtopics can be used as keywords for searches in library online catalogs or on the world wide web. Consider combining the subtopics with the name of an African country to conduct a more targeted keyword search, for example, Ghana and sustainable development, or Nigeria and women's rights.
- A selection of specific resources is provided for each chapter. Where available, sections begin with overviews or research guides as a good first step, which are then followed with specific titles and/or websites and additional information on how to find more in-depth materials.

GENERAL RESOURCES

As a good first step to obtain initial, general information about a topic, consult an encyclopedia or handbook:

Africa South of the Sahara. 1971–. London: Europa Publications. Annual. Good for overview information. Arranged alphabetically by country. For each country, includes information on the country's physical and social geography, its recent political and economic history, and statistical surveys, as well as a bibliography with suggested sources for further reading.

Appiah, Kwame Anthony, and Henry Louis Gates Jr., eds. 2005. *Africana: The Encyclopedia of the African and African American Experience.* Oxford: Oxford University Press. Five-volume set. Includes information about Africans in sub-Saharan Africa, the United States, the Caribbean, Latin America, and Europe. Provides biographical information as well as detailed entries on topics such as African oral tradition, the history of writing in Africa, the transatlantic slave trade, AIDS in Africa and the United States, affirmative action, African American architects, and others.

Middleton, John, and Joseph C. Miller, eds. 2008. *New Encyclopedia of Africa.* Detroit: Thomson/Gale. Five volumes. Detailed and extensive entries.

Wikipedia, www.wikipedia.org. Freely available online encyclopedia. Word of caution: While Wikipedia is a good reference source and contains a vast amount of valuable information, it is helpful to know that content may be added and edited by anyone and may not always be accurate. If in doubt, cross-check Wikipedia's information with information in another encyclopedia or web resource.

Search Engines: Africa-Specific Web Portals versus Google

Africa-specific web portals focus exclusively on Africa and are maintained by Africana librarians. They are quality-controlled and up to date and will retrieve more targeted results than Google or other search engines. A few examples:

Africa South of the Sahara: Selected Internet Resources, www-sul.stanford.edu/depts.ssrg .africa/guide.html. Developed by Karen Fung (Stanford University) for the Electronic Technology Group of the African Studies Association. Excellent gateway to Africana information. Site is searchable by topic, country, or keyword/phrase.
A-Z of African Studies on the Internet (by Peter Limb), http://staff.lib.msu.edu/limb/a-z/az .html. Extensive list, in alphabetical order, of Africa-related websites.
Columbia University Area Studies: African Studies Internet Resources (developed by Yuusuf Caruso), www.columbia.edu/cu/lweb/indiv/africa/cuvl/index.html. Provides access to online journals and newspapers from or about Africa; also includes an international directory of African studies scholars and links to Africana library collections in the United States, Europe, and southern Africa, as well as to information on a variety of topics. The site is searchable by keywords or can be browsed by subject or country.

Also of Interest

African E-Journals Project, http://africa.isp.msu.edu/AEJP/about.htm. Includes links to the full text of eleven African scholarly journals as well as a journals directory with tables of content.
H-Africa, www.h-net.org/~africa. Extensive website and listserv. Includes links to past discussions, organized by topic (e.g., slavery, development, art, environment, etc.). Good place to find out about current topics of interest in the field of African studies.

Current News about Africa

AllAfrica.com, www.allafrica.com. Aggregates and distributes daily news from more than 130 African news organizations. Good place for news and discussions on current issues.
BBC News Africa, www.bbc.co.uk/news/world/africa. Daily, up-to-date news from and about Africa.
CNN Africa, www.cnn.com/WORLD/africa/archive. CNN's daily coverage of news about Africa.

Look on the web for numerous blogs about Africa. Keep in mind the evaluation criteria at the end of this chapter as you read information posted in blogs!

Find blogs by searching Google for blogs on Africa, or on specific African countries or topics. A few examples:

African Arguments Online, http://africanarguments.org. The Royal African Society's blog, designed to reflect debates on important and current African topics.

Africa Is a Country, http://africasacountry.com. Very active blog that tries to counter the stereotypical image of Africa in the media.

The Africanist, http://theafricanist.blogspot.com. Maintained by anthropologist Richard Vokes from the University of Canterbury, New Zealand. Blog is focused on Uganda, where the author has conducted extensive research. This is also a good example of a blog that provides a long list of links to other Africa-related blogs.

Podcasts

Africa Past and Present, http://afripod.aodl.org. Podcast about history, culture, and politics in Africa and the diaspora. Includes interviews with scholars and authors about current events and other debates about Africa.

BBC Africa Today, www.bbc.co.uk/podcasts/series/africa. Contains the day's top stories from Africa.

Find more podcasts by searching Google or iTunes.

Facebook and Twitter

Good places to look for current information and debates about your favorite authors, journals, music. Search for authors' names, journal titles, and so on.

AFRICA: A GEOGRAPHIC FRAME

Geography is an interdisciplinary field and encompasses a wide range of topics:

- Physical landscapes
- Climates
- Bioregions
- Maps
- Issues surrounding the environment
- Cities

Research on geography often overlaps with that of other academic disciplines. For information on closely connected topics, such as pan-Africanism, the slave trade, the emergence of the idea of Africa as a continent, and economic livelihoods, see the sections "Legacies of the Past: Themes in African History" and "Social Relations and Livelihoods."

Use a combination of print and online sources to obtain good search results.

Print Resources

Maddox, Gregory H. 2006. *Sub-Saharan Africa: An Environmental History.* Santa Barbara, CA: ABC Clio. Good starting point. Part of the series Nature and Human Societies. Provides a narrative analysis of a region along with a body of reference material. Also gives a detailed overview of African environmental history, including such topics as the development of food production systems, the development of societies, the reorganization of space under colonial rule, and Africa in the age of conservation and development, as well as case studies. Includes glossary with definitions of geographic terms and a chronology with an overview of the development of Africa's environment from five million years ago to 2004.

Room, Adrian. 2008. *African Placenames: Origins and Meanings of the Names for Natural Features, Towns, Cities, Provinces and Countries.* 2nd ed. Jefferson, NC: McFarland. Alphabetical listing of African place names with brief explanations of their meaning and origin.

Consult the list of recommended readings at the conclusion of the chapter "Africa: A Geographic Frame."

Online Resources

MAPS

National Geographic's Map Machine, http://maps.nationalgeographic.com/maps. Includes basic printable maps for each country.

The University of Texas Perry-Castañeda Library Map Collection, www.lib.utexas.edu/maps /africa.html. Extensive listing of high-quality maps of Africa, ranging from political to topographic and reference maps; also includes links to relevant maps on other websites.

Don't forget: many university libraries provide access to GIS (Geographic Information Systems), and librarians are available to help create customized maps.

Full-Text Resources

AllAfrica.com, http://allafrica.com/environment. Look for the section "Environment News," which includes articles from African newspapers on issues related to the environment, including water and sanitation, wildlife, agriculture and food, health, sustainable development, trade, refugees and displacement, aid and assistance, et cetera.

Digital Library of the Commons, http://dlc.dlib.indiana.edu (developed collaboratively by Indiana University's Digital Library Program and Workshop in Political Theory and Policy Analysis). Provides a more scholarly and in-depth treatment of environmental issues, with access to an extensive archive of full-text articles, papers and dissertations, links to reference sources, and a comprehensive bibliography on such common-pool resources as wildlife, land tenure and use, urban spaces, forest resources, agriculture, etc. Good source for recent and up-to-date articles as well as for older publications that may serve as background reading.

Inventory of Conflict and Environment, www1.american.edu/TED/ice/ice.htm. Part of the same project as TED. Has a worldwide approach but includes several case studies on

Africa, for example, studies on the Darfur conflict and drought, or the Tuareg and civil conflict.

Trade and Environment (TED) database, www1.american.edu/TED/ted.htm, developed by Dr. James Lee from American University in Washington, DC. Includes full-text case studies and reports on various aspects of environmental and economic issues; not focused exclusively on Africa, but a list of case studies limited to the African continent can be accessed by using the site search box to search for studies relating to Africa.

Suggested keywords for searching your library's online catalog, Google Scholar, or other databases (accessed through your library's website) for more resources:

- Africa and climate
- Country name (e.g., Nigeria) and environment
- Country name (e.g., Kenya) and wildlife
- Africa and resource management
- Country name (e.g., Somalia) and refugees
- Africa and sustainable development
- Country name and sanitation
- Political ecology and urban Africa

LEGACIES OF THE PAST: THEMES IN AFRICAN HISTORY

Reflecting Africa's long and rich history, this field covers a vast area of topics and time periods:

- Studies of the precolonial and colonial periods
- Studies exploring the connections between Africa and the Indian Ocean world and between Africa and the Atlantic Ocean world
- The slave trade
- Analyses of African countries since independence
- Studies of South Africa and its apartheid and postapartheid history

Encyclopedias, while they do not reflect current scholarship, are a good place for overview information.

Cambridge History of Africa (1975–86) and UNESCO's *General History of Africa* (1981–93). Both of these are eight-volume sets that provide detailed overviews of the continent's history by following chronological timelines beginning with Africa's prehistory, and their coverage extends well into the second half of the twentieth century. Look for them in your library's reference room.

For more concise overviews, use one-volume histories:

Cooper, Frederick. 2002. *Africa Since 1940: The Past of the Present.* New York: Cambridge University Press.

Iliffe, John. 2007. *Africans: The History of a Continent,* 2nd ed. New York: Cambridge University Press. Includes revised and updated chapters on African prehistory and the Atlantic slave trade.

Another good starting point:

Falola, Toyin. 2002. *Key Events in African History: A Reference Guide.* Westport, CT: Greenwood Press. Intended for high school and college students; contains chapters on thirty-six significant events that shaped African history. Topics include the civilizations of ancient Egypt, the spread of Islam, kingdoms of West Africa, the rise of the Swahili states, the Atlantic slave trade, the colonial experience, and the fall of apartheid.

Use Falola's book in combination with other, more detailed and recent thematic studies of aspects of African history:

Chamberlain, Muriel Evelyn. 2010. *The Scramble for Africa.* 3rd ed. Harlow: Longman. Overview, including specific case histories and primary sources, of the historical period when Europe took control of Africa, known as the "scramble for Africa."

Hawley, John C., ed. 2008. *India in Africa, Africa in India: Indian Ocean Cosmopolitanisms.* Bloomington: Indiana University Press. Edited volume that offers interpretations of the historical relationship between India and Africa while also incorporating current relationships between those two world areas.

Lovejoy, Paul. 2000. *Transformations in Slavery: A History of Slavery in Africa.* 2nd ed. New York: Cambridge University Press. While more detailed studies of various aspects of slavery, including time periods or regions where slavery took place, are available, *Transformations in Slavery* presents a history of slavery for the entire continent.

Meredith, Martin. 2005. *The State of Africa: A History of Fifty Years of Independence.* London: Free Press. Traces the history of African states, beginning when they first moved toward independence and continuing through the next fifty years.

The history of South Africa is often treated separately in the scholarly literature:

Berger, Iris. 2009. *South Africa in World History.* Oxford: Oxford University Press. Concise overview that traces the country's history from prehistory to the present; provides a general survey of South African history that integrates social history and women's history as well as the connections between the United States and South Africa.

Many primary sources relating to South African history can be accessed online:

Aluka, www.aluka.org. Provides full-text access to documents relating to struggles for freedom in southern Africa, including periodicals, personal papers, nationalist publications, life histories, speeches, and so on. Unlike DISA, Aluka is a fee-based database, so access is limited to students who are affiliated with a subscribing institution.

Digital Innovation South Africa (DISA), www.disa.ukzn.ac.za. Freely available database with full-text documents, primarily periodicals; focus on sociocultural history of South Africa between the country's struggle for freedom in the 1950s and its first democratic elections in 1994.

Historical Papers Wits, www.historicalpapers.wits.ac.za/index.php?1/P/Home. Independent South African research archive; includes a link to digitized collections that are available in an open-access environment.

South African History Online (SAHO), www.sahistory.org.za. Largest independent history education and research institute in South Africa. This website includes sources related to politics, arts, culture, and society, as well as numerous biographies of South African personalities.

Also Keep in Mind

Worger, William H., Nancy L. Clark, and Edward A. Alpers. 2010. *Africa and the West: A Documentary History.* 2nd ed. Oxford: Oxford University Press. Includes two volumes: vol. 1, *From the Slave Trade to Conquest, 1441–1905,* and vol. 2, *From Colonialism to Independence, 1875 to the Present.* Excellent selection of primary sources documenting all of Africa's relationship with the West; includes first-person narratives, poetry, correspondence, political speeches, and so on.

African History on the World Wide Web

A number of websites present both primary and secondary sources in full text, documenting the continent's history from its origins to the modern day.

Africa South of the Sahara, www-sul.stanford.edu/depts/ssrg/africa/history/africanhistory electronicbooks.html. Offers one of the most comprehensive listings of links leading to the full text of electronic books. Treasures such as accounts by the explorers and travelers of the nineteenth century as well as many current-day scholarly publications can be discovered through this portal and accessed freely on the internet. A few examples:
>   *Travels and Discoveries in North and Central Africa: Being a Journal of an Expedition Undertaken* by Heinrich Barth. Published 1896, Harper and Brothers.
>   *Travels in the Interior of Africa* by Mungo Park. Published 1860, A. and C. Black.
>   *Travels in West Africa* by Mary Henrietta Kingsley, William Forsell Kirby. Published 1897, Macmillan.

Africa South of the Sahara's section on African history, www-sul.stanford.edu/depts/ssrg/africa/history.html. Further subdivided into more than thirty topics and themes, ranging from human origins, exploration between the fifteenth and nineteenth centuries, slavery, and the colonial period to Afrocentrism, pan-Africanism, and others. Each of these subcategories links to a multitude of resources and full-text documents.

SOCIAL RELATIONS AND LIVELIHOODS

The social relationships and ways of creating livelihoods described and discussed in the chapters "Social Relations: Family, Kinship, and Community" and "Making a Living: Livelihoods in Africa" touch on many issues and are, more than any other section in this overview of resources, connected and related to almost every other chapter in this book. Consequently, sources for much of what is described in those two chapters will be found throughout the various sections of this chapter, depending on your research focus and interests. Both chapters address many issues and concepts that are typically discussed in anthropological literature. A generation of anthropologists conducting research in Africa during the colonial period produced studies that became classics in the discipline:

Evans-Pritchard, E. E. 1940. *The Nuer.* Oxford: Clarendon.
Fortes, Meyer. 1953. "The Structure of Unilineal Descent Groups." *American Anthropologist* 55:17–41.
Fortes, Meyer, and E. E. Evans-Pritchard, eds. 1940. *African Political Systems.* London: Oxford University Press.
Radcliffe-Brown, Alfred R., and Daryll Forde, eds. 1950. *African Systems of Kinship and Marriage.* London: Oxford University Press.

Contemporary cultural anthropologists explore phenomena such as:

- Transformations of kinship and marriage in relation to politico-economic processes
- Transnational families and networks
- Gender and work
- Children and youth
- Religious communities
- Media, popular culture, and globalization
- Ethnicity and the state
- Witchcraft, modernity, and development
- Resource extraction and violence

For explanations and definitions of these concepts, consult an anthropological encyclopedia in your library's reference room, such as:

Barnard, Alan, and Jonathan Spencer, eds. 2010. *The Routledge Encyclopedia of Social and Cultural Anthropology.* London: Routledge.
Levinson, David, and Melvin Ember, eds. 1996. *Encyclopedia of Cultural Anthropology.* New York: Henry Holt.

How to Find Resources

Consult the bibliographies at the end of the chapters on social relations and livelihoods. The books listed there include extensive bibliographies that will refer you to other current scholarship on your topic.

Find current journal articles in databases, most notably AnthroSource, which includes full-text issues of the American Anthropological Association's journals, bulletins, and newsletters. Note the "Resources" tab, which provides access to an extensive list of links for finding information on anthropology on the web.

Anthropology Plus, JSTOR, and Google Books and Google Scholar are other databases and search engines with relevant content.

Remember that this is an interdisciplinary field and select other databases according to your research focus. For effective keyword searches, combine some of the terms/concepts discussed in the two chapters and those listed above with country or peoples' names. Some examples:

- Marriage and Bamana
- Social anthropology and Africa (or substitute with a country name)
- Bridewealth and Niger
- Funerals and Ghana
- Migration and social relations and Senegal
- Child-headed households and South Africa
- Youth and Madagascar
- Maasai and NGOs
- Kenya (or other African country name) and urban livelihood
- Microcredit and Malawi
- Agroforestry and Gambia
- Morocco and remittances
- Social transformation and Sahara (or substitute with another region or country)

Keep in mind the interdisciplinary nature of this field as you look for resources. For example:

- If you are interested in topics related to health, healing, HIV/AIDS and its impact on African societies, the role of indigenous knowledge in healing, or something related, also consult the section "Health, Illness, and Healing in African Societies."
- For information on urban spaces, see the sections "Urban Spaces, Lives, and Projects in Africa" and "Africa: A Geographic Frame."
- For more in-depth research connected to economic livelihoods, also consult the sections "Development in Africa: Tempered Hope" and "African Politics and the Future of Democracy."
- If your research interest is the study of music and social life, be sure to look at the sections "African Music Flows," "Visual Arts in Africa," and "Religions in Africa."

RELIGIONS IN AFRICA

How to Get Started: Overviews of Religion in Africa

Asante, Molefi Kete, and Ama Mazama, eds. 2009. *Encyclopedia of African Religion*. Thousand Oaks, CA: Sage Publications. Excellent introduction to concepts in "traditional" African religions. It includes a reader's guide designed to help the reader locate articles on topics such as ancestral figures, communalism and family, concepts and ideas, deities and divinities, rituals and ceremonies, sacred spaces and objects, societies, symbols, signs and sounds, taboo, and ethics. Thought and belief systems throughout the African diaspora are also included. Available in print and in electronic format.

Bongmba, Elias, ed. 2012. *The Wiley-Blackwell Companion to African Religions.* Hoboken, NJ: John Wiley and Sons. Provides essays from international scholars on topics relating to African religious experiences in indigenous, Christian, and Islamic traditions across the continent; explores diverse methodological approaches to specific religious traditions and issues such as religion and the arts, health, politics, globalization, gender relations, and the economy.

Culture and Customs series from Greenwood Press. Several volumes, each focusing on a different African country. Each volume in the series includes a chapter on religion and worldview for the specific country.

Isichei, Elizabeth Allo. 2004. *The Religious Traditions of Africa: A History.* Westport, CT: Praeger Publishers. Provides a more detailed overview by outlining the development of Islam and Christianity across Africa and discussing "traditional" religion in detail.

Combine These Overviews with More In-depth Studies

During the past decade, the study of religion in Africa has been characterized by a proliferation of cross-disciplinary studies, such as analyses of religion and women, theological studies within contexts of reconciliation and forgiveness (e.g., in the context of post-apartheid South Africa, post-genocide Rwanda, post–civil war Liberia, etc.), religious movements, Pentecostalism, health and religion, religion in connection with culture, philosophy, anthropology, history, human rights, religion and law, etc. To find these studies in a library's online catalog, combine the topics listed here in keyword searches, for example:

- Africa and religion and women
- Africa and religion and politics
- Reconciliation and South Africa
- Africa and religion and law
- Rwanda and forgiveness

Online Resources

BBC World Service, *The Story of Africa,* www.bbc.co.uk/worldservice/africa/features /storyofafrica/. Brief overview of religions in Africa, covering such topics as Islam, Christianity, missionaries, religious practices, and so on. Includes audio clips of the original radio broadcast.

Islam in Sub-Saharan Africa, www.ascleiden.nl/Library/Webdossiers/IslamInAfrica.aspx. A web dossier/bibliography on Islam in Africa, compiled by the Library, Documentation and Information Department of the African Studies Centre in Leiden, the Netherlands. Developed in connection with a multiyear research project that culminated in a conference of leading scholars on Islam in Africa. The sources included in the dossier are publications by the conference participants and include books and articles published over the last two decades.

Religiously Remapped: Mapping Religious Trends in Africa, www.religiouslyremapped .info/. Website developed by Eugene Carl Adogla in 2007, funded by a Stanford University grant. Includes twenty-two maps on topics such as the predominant religion, the main minority religion, Christianity (including Catholicism and Protestantism), Islam (Sunnis, Shiites, and other branches), traditional religions, Baha'i, Hinduism, Buddhism, Judaism, atheism, religious freedom, religion and conflict, interesting religious facts, and religious change.

URBAN SPACES, LIVES, AND PROJECTS IN AFRICA

Recent scholarship on urban spaces in Africa acknowledges the rapid growth of African cities and the fact that much of the future of African culture and society will in some way be connected to cities.

Resources with a Historical Approach

These describe the development of African cities from the earliest time to the present day:

Anderson, David M., and Richard Rathbone eds. 2000. *Africa's Urban Past*. Oxford: James Currey. Survey of cities in Africa from a historical perspective. Each chapter focuses on one city and its history; together, the chapters combine to an overview of the history of urbanism in Africa.

Falola, Toyin, and Steven J. Salm, eds. 2005. *African Urban Spaces in Historical Perspective*. Rochester, NY: University of Rochester Press. Provides an interdisciplinary approach to the study of African urban history and culture, incorporating historical methodologies with those of anthropology, geography, literature, art, and architecture.

Freund, Bill. 2007. *The African City: A History*. Cambridge: Cambridge University Press. Provides a comprehensive overview of cities in Africa from the early origins to the present.

Works with a Focus on Contemporary Aspects of African Urbanism

Demissie, Fassil. 2007. *Postcolonial African Cities: Imperial Legacies and Postcolonial Predicaments*. London: Routledge. Describes new forms of urban development through the lens of historical developments. Themes and topics include colonial legacies, cosmopolitan spaces, and urban reconfigurations.

Murray, Martin J., and Garth A. Myers, eds. 2007. *Cities in Contemporary Africa*. New York: Palgrave Macmillan. Noteworthy for its inclusion of African scholarship. Each chapter provides a glimpse into the complex dynamics of urban life in various African cities.

Simone, Abdou Maliq. 2004. *For the City Yet to Come: Changing Life in Four Cities*. Durham, NC: Duke University Press. Series of case studies that examine informal economies and social networks in four African cities (Dakar, Pretoria, Douala, Jeddah) and argues that African cities ought to be analyzed in their specific historical contexts—which would dispute the argument that they are "failed cities" when compared to those of the North.

In addition to overviews of urban life in Africa, case studies of various aspects of life in cities might be useful. In this context, women and migrants have been important foci of urban ethnography. Examples include:

Hoodfar, Homar. 1997. *Between Marriage and the Market: Intimate Politics and Survival in Cairo.* Berkeley: University of California Press.
Study of Sahelian migrants in Brazzaville.
Whitehouse, Bruce. 2012. *Migrants and Strangers in an African City: Exile, Dignity, Belonging.* Bloomington: Indiana University Press.

Helpful Keywords

- Globalizing cities and Africa
- Urban poverty
- Sustainable cities
- Urban governance
- Urban housing and infrastructure
- Urban life and name of city
- Street children
- Migration and name of country or city

HEALTH, ILLNESS, AND HEALING IN AFRICAN SOCIETIES

Research on health, illness, and healing in Africa encompasses information on:

- Statistics
- Biomedical topics
- Sociocultural analyses of illness and healing
- Analyses of traditional medicine
- Indigenous forms of knowledge in the context of healing

Keep in Mind

A considerable amount of health-related information, such as statistics by international organizations (e.g., the World Health Organization and the United Nations), is available online on detailed websites that are more up-to-date than any comparable print resource could be. These organizations, as well as many smaller NGOs, also create and publish online research reports on such topics as:

- AIDS education and prevention
- Malaria prevention
- Indigenous knowledge

Good Starting Point

AllAfrica.com: Health, http://allafrica.com/health. News service that has a section on health; features articles on topics such as HIV/AIDS, anti-malaria campaigns, and the impact of tobacco on people's health.

HighWire Press, http://highwire.stanford.edu (a division of the Stanford University Libraries). Good place to find peer-reviewed articles on health-related topics. Includes 1,270 journals (mostly from the medical fields) and provides access to full-text journal articles. A keyword search entered in the search box "Anywhere in the text"—for example "AIDS stigma in Uganda"—will retrieve relevant articles.

Where to Look for Statistical Information

Joint United Nations Programme on HIV/AIDS, UNAIDS (co-sponsored by WHO, UNICEF, UNDP, UNFPA, UNESCO, and the World Bank), www.unaids.org/en/. Provides HIV/AIDS-related information; includes up-to-date country fact sheets with statistics and, in some cases, articles about a specific country's response to the HIV/AIDS pandemic.

United Nations Development Fund for Women (UNIFEM), www.genderandaids.org. Acknowledges the complicated situation of women in relation to HIV/AIDS; includes links to full-text country-specific articles and reports, book descriptions, conferences, and so on.

The World Health Organization's home page, www.who.int, and WHOSIS, the WHO's statistical system. Extensive information on Africa. WHOSIS is an interactive database that provides access to health statistics for the 193 WHO member states. Can be searched by health topics; also has a list of countries, providing access to core health statistics for individual countries. Areas covered: chronic diseases, child malnutrition, access to water, sanitation, information on HIV/AIDS, health expenditures, et cetera. The WHO home page also includes full-text reports on health-related issues.

Many more websites with full-text articles and/or statistical information exist—too many to mention here. Stanford University's Africa South of the Sahara/African Health and Medicine, www-sul.stanford.edu/depts/ssrg/africa/health.html, is a good place to obtain access to many of them.

Looking for Information on Various Aspects of Traditional Healing, Indigenous Knowledge and Healing

Often this kind of information is discussed and analyzed in anthropological rather than medical studies. Use a combination of print and electronic sources to find relevant information. The materials suggested for further reading, as well as the bibliographies included in those materials, at the end of the chapter "Health, Illness, and Healing in African Societies" are good places to look for print resources. Also:

Konadu, Kwasi. 2008. "Medicine and Anthropology in Twentieth Century Africa: Akan Medicine and Encounters with Medical Anthropology," *African Studies Quarterly* 10(2–3). Points to the tendency in the field of medical anthropology to focus on witchcraft as the basis of African medicine; argues that many of the existing case studies apply concepts of medical anthropology to African contexts without incorporating African perspectives.
Werbner, Richard. 2011. *Holy Hustlers, Schism, and Prophecy*. Berkeley: University of California Press. Discusses Eloyi, an apostolic faith-healing church in Gaborone, Botswana.

Also of Interest

These films on faith healing were directed by Richard Werbner:

Encountering Eloyi. 2008. Media Centre, University of Manchester. Manchester, UK: International Centre for Contemporary Cultural Research.
Séance Reflections. 2005. International Centre for Contemporary Cultural Research. Manchester, UK: International Centre for Contemporary Cultural Research. Documentary about a couple who travel to the husband's village in Botswana (Moremi) to consult a diviner and healer to determine why they are childless.
Shade Seekers and the Mixer. 2007. Media Centre, University of Manchester. Manchester, UK: International Centre for Contemporary Cultural Research, University of Manchester. Documentary set in the same village (Moremi, Botswana) as the previous film; about a healing diviner.

Online

Sharp, Lesley A. 1993. "The Possessed and the Dispossessed: Spirits, Identity and Power in a Madagascar Migrant Town," http://publishing.cdlib.org/ucpressebooks/view?docId=ft6 t1nb4hz&brand=ucpress. Full text of a book published by the University of California Press; analyzes the powerful role of spirit medium healers in the specific context of a Madagascar town.
Shikanda Portal, www.shikanda.net. Includes several articles on spirit healing by Wim van Binsbergen.
"Traditional Medicine Strategy," published by the World Health Organization, www.who .int/medicines/publications/traditionalpolicy/en/index.html. Intended as a policy framework to regulate traditional and alternative medicine, make it safer, and improve access to it.

How to Look for More Information on These Topics

Search your library's databases, such as Academic Search Premier, JSTOR, and Anthroplogy Plus. Selected keywords:

- Healing and indigenous beliefs
- Traditional healers and Africa (or use a country name)
- Spiritual healers
- Shrines
- Talismans
- Indigenous knowledge
- Indigenous magic
- Medicine (or healing) and religion
- Herbalism/healing and Africa

VISUAL ARTS IN AFRICA

Scholarship related to art in Africa focuses on various aspects, for example:

- Painting
- Sculpture
- Pottery
- Metal works
- Architecture
- Exhibitions
- Photography
- Popular art
- Traditional art
- Masks and masquerades
- Body art
- Rock art

How to Find Resources

- The sources listed at the end of the chapter "Visual Arts in Africa" are a good place to find detailed overview information on art for the African continent.
- *Grove Dictionary of Art.* 2000. New York: St. Martin's Press. Thirty-four-volume set with more than forty-one thousand articles on the arts in Africa, Asia, Europe, the Americas, and the Pacific. Many libraries have its online version *(Grove Art Online),* which provides access to the full text of all articles, with new additions, updates, and image links.
- Search your library's databases to find journal articles. JSTOR, which includes major African studies journals in the humanities, arts, and social sciences, most notably the important journal *African Art,* is particularly useful to find articles on art in Africa.

Keyword Searches

Combine the topics listed above and in the chapter on the arts in Africa with the names of African countries and/or peoples, for example:

- Africa and architecture
- South Africa and rock art
- Zulu and pottery
- Maasai and body art
- Mali and photography

Where to Look for Images

AfricaFocus, http://digicoll.library.wisc.edu/AfricaFocus/subcollections/FocusAbout.html. Online collection maintained by the University of Wisconsin–Madison Libraries. Includes digitized images and sounds of Africa that have been contributed to the university's African Studies Program. Images are arranged in subject groupings, such as artisans, buildings and structures, cities and towns, landscape, drums, rites and ceremonies, and so forth.

Google *Life* Photo Archive, http://images.google.com/hosted/life. Provides access to millions of photographs from *Life*'s photo archive. Search by keyword to find images for African art.

The Humphrey Winterton Collection of East African Photographs: 1860–1960, http://repository.library.northwestern.edu/winterton/about.html. Website that provides access to the digitized version of this collection of more than seven thousand photographs depicting life in Africa.

Selections from Eliot Elisofon Photographic Archives, http://sirismm.si.edu/siris/eepatop.htm. Research center at the National Museum of African Art. Includes more than three hundred thousand photographic images on the arts, peoples, and history of Africa. Searchable by country, by cultural groups, and by subjects.

Also look for images in Wikimedia, Wikipedia, Flickr, and YouTube, as well as Google Images and Bing Images.

Keep in Mind

Exhibitions are a place to see art displayed, and exhibition catalogs often have an impact on how art is perceived and studied. Examples of important exhibitions :

Africa Explores: 20th Century African Art, organized in 1991 by the Center (now Museum) for African Art in New York. Exhibition catalog by Susan Vogel. New York: Center for African Art, 1991. Considered a turning point in its display of the wide range and variety of visual arts in Africa.

The Global Africa Project, organized in 2010 by the Museum of Arts and Design. Catalog by Lowery Stokes Sims. New York: Museum of Arts and Design, 2010. Explores contemporary African art, design, and craft worldwide. Features more than a hundred artists working in Africa, Europe, Asia, the United States, and the Caribbean.

In/Sight: African Photographers, 1940 to the Present, shown in 1996 at the Guggenheim Museum. Exhibition catalog by Clare Bell. New York: Guggenheim Museum, 1996. First major U.S. exhibition of African photography.

The Short Century: Independence and Liberation Movements in Africa, 1945–1994, displayed in Germany, New York, and Chicago. Catalog by Okwui Enwezor. Munich: Prestel, 2001. Connected the visual arts with political changes that took place during the second half of the twentieth century.

AFRICAN MUSIC FLOWS

Sources about African music include:

- Musicological studies
- Anthropological studies of music
- Combinations of both
- Discographies (i.e., bibliographies of recordings)
- Sound recordings in various forms (records, tapes, DVDs, etc.)

Good First Step

Stone, Ruth M., ed. 1998. *The Garland Encyclopedia of World Music, Volume 1.* New York: Garland. Provides detailed overview of music in Africa. Presents connections of African music to dance, drama, other visual arts, and religion. Reflects that African music cannot be studied in isolation and, rather, is an integral part of social, cultural and political contexts. Owned by many university libraries. The volume is accompanied by a CD with music samples.

Stone, Ruth M. 2008. *The Garland Handbook of African Music.* 2nd ed. New York: Routledge. Abridged version of the encyclopedia. Takes recent scholarship on music in Africa into account. Includes emerging new research on East Africa, music and video in North Africa, music and HIV/AIDS education, women's dance in the Christian church of Malawi, and so on.

Locating More Detailed Information

These are examples of book-length case studies you can consult to find up-to-date research on African music:

Askew, Kelly. 2002. *Performing the Nation: Swahili Music and Cultural Politics in Tanzania.* Chicago: University of Chicago Press. Analysis of taarab music performance in Tanzania as an expression of Tanzanian culture and cultural policies.

Charry, Eric S. 2000. *Mande Music: Traditional and Modern Music of the Maninka and Mandinka of Western Africa.* Chicago: University of Chicago Press. Detailed analysis of Mande music in its social and historical context. Includes a disc with recordings of traditional and modern pieces of Mande music.

Monson, Ingrid T. 2000. *The African Diaspora: A Musical Perspective.* New York: Garland. Includes essays about jazz, music in Mali, music in Martinique, the Yoruba folk opera, and other topics.

Moorman, Marissa. 2008. *Intonations: A Social History of Music and Nation in Luanda, Angola, from 1945 to Recent Times.* Athens: Ohio University Press. Social history of African music from Lusophone Africa. Analyzes the relationship between culture and politics during the late colonial and postindependence periods of Angola's history.

Perullo, Alex. 2011. *Live from Dar es Salaam: Popular Music and Tanzania's Music Economy.* Bloomington: Indiana University Press.

Reed, Daniel. 2003. *Dan Ge Performance: Masks and Music in Contemporary Cote d'Ivoire.* Bloomington: Indiana University Press. Explores the social and religious contexts in which Ge, a performance among the Dan people of western Côte d'Ivoire, takes place.

For a more detailed analysis of the theory of African music:

Kubik, Gerhard. 1994. *Theory of African Music.* Wilhelmshaven: F. Noetzel.

Keep in Mind

Many scholarly books on music in Africa include CDs with music samples. Additionally, there are a variety of internet sources that provide access to African music.

Africa South of the Sahara's section on music, www-sul.stanford.edu/depts/ssrg/africa/music.html. Offers an excellent list of web links providing access to articles from African news sources, links to discussions on music, blogs, links to vendors selling African music, and many audio samples.

Also of Interest

African Music Treasures, Voice of America blog by Heather Maxwell, http://blogs.voanews.com/african-music-treasures. Features interviews with African musicians.

Afropop Worldwide, www.afropop.org. Website accompanying a radio program by Georges Collinet with music from Africa, the Caribbean, and the Americas. Includes a wealth of information, ranging from program schedules, discographies, and information on how to access African radio stations to musicians' biographies, a bibliography of books, and much more.

The Pan African Space Station (PASS), www.panafricanspacestation.org.za. Internet radio station affiliated with *Chimurenga* magazine in Cape Town, South Africa. Free streaming of music twenty-four hours a day.

LITERATURE IN AFRICA

To date, Africa has produced five African Nobel laureates:

- Albert Camus (1957, Algeria)
- John Coetzee (2003, South Africa)

- Nadine Gordimer (1991, South Africa)
- Najib Mahfuz (1988, Egypt)
- Wole Soyinka (1986, Nigeria)

In addition to these well-known writers, there are many African authors who are now considered classics, as well as a vibrant scene of younger authors. Consult the chapter "Literature in Africa" for authors' names and for information about the titles of their publications. Their works—particularly those by the well-established, older generation of writers—can easily be retrieved from most college library online catalogs by doing a search for the author's name. Alternatively, do a keyword search for Heinemann African Writers Series. Works by many well-known African authors have been published in this series, which can be found in many college and university libraries. Some libraries subscribe to a selective online version of this series, titled *African Writers Series* and published by Proquest.

Also of Interest

Africa's 100 Best Books of the 20th Century, web dossier compiled by the African Studies Centre Library Leiden, www.ascleiden.nl/?q=content/webdossiers/africas-100-best-books-20th-century. The goal of this project was to compile a list of the hundred best books and to direct the world's attention to African writing published during the twentieth century. The dossier provides background information, the top 12 list, the top 100 list, and related web resources. Includes creative writing, academic writing, and children's books.

Recent Developments

In recent years, a new generation of writers has begun to adapt genres such as the novel and the short story to African realities and ways of storytelling. In addition to writing in well-established genres, these young authors also utilize social media such as Facebook and Twitter as well as personal websites to reach out to their readers. The result is a vibrant literary scene that is increasingly attracting international attention.

Some places to look for recent works:

Caine Prize anthologies. Since the Caine Prize for African Writing was first awarded at the Zimbabwe International Book Fair in 2000, eleven anthologies of stories short-listed for the prize have been published. Find the Caine Prize anthologies by conducting a keyword search in your library's online catalog, using "Caine prize" and "African writing" as keywords. The winning and short-listed stories for the current year can also be found online on the Caine Prize's official website at www.caineprize.com/.

Gray, Stephen. 2000. *The Picador Book of African Stories*. London: Picador. Presents African short fiction, including translations of works from various languages and many works that are not usually found in other anthologies. Includes an interesting introduction that outlines the development of broad themes in African literature, from the generation of writers after independence in the 1960s, whose writing was a counterdiscourse to the colonial powers, to the next generation, which was characterized by anger and disillusionment, and writers who emerged during the late 1980s and afterward and who are developing authentic African models of literature.

Spillman, Rob. 2009. *Gods and Soldiers: The Penguin Anthology of Contemporary African Writing.* New York: Penguin Books. Includes short fiction as well as passages from novels. Excellent introduction that conveys the excitement and vibrancy of the recent African literary scene.

Look for recent African literature in various places. Publishing venues for the new generation of African writers are wide and varied. For example, an author may publish a novel in the traditional book format while also maintaining a website and a blog, have a short story published in the *New Yorker*, and be included in several anthologies of recent African writing.

Websites

The Chimamanda Ngozi Adichie website, www.l3.ulg.ac.be/adichie. (*Note:* "l" before "3" in url is lowercase L.) Nigerian author who is known for her short stories and her award-winning novels *Purple Hibiscus* (2003) and *Half of a Yellow Sun* (2006). The website includes biographical information on the author, bibliographies, and interviews.

Teju Cole, www.tejucole.com. Nigerian author who now lives in Brooklyn, New York. In addition to being a writer, he is also a photographer and an art historian. His novel *Open City* (New York: Random House, 2011) received the PEN/Hemingway Award. The website includes many of Cole's photographs, biographical information, and bibliographies. Also look for Cole's tweet-sized narratives in his project "Small Fates" on Twitter.

Other authors' names to look for:

- Tanure Ojaide
- Helon Habila
- Doreen Baingana
- Binyavanga Wainaina
- Sefi Atta
- Leila Aboulela

Blogs

Africa Is a Country, http://africasacountry.com. Includes many interesting posts and discussions on African literature.

Crime Beat, http://crimebeat.bookslive.co.za/blog. Blog about the thriving genre of crime fiction in South Africa.

African Literary and Media Initiatives on the Web

Chimurenga, www.chimurenga.co.za. A pan-African publication of writing, art, and politics. The website includes links to the Chimurenga Library, an online archive of pan-African, independent periodicals; the *Chimurenga Chronic,* a one-time edition of *Chimurenga* in the form of a newspaper, with open access to parts of it; and the Pan African Space Station, with access to the latest in African music.

Kwani?, www.kwani.org/aboutus/kwani.htm. Literary network based in Kenya and dedicated to the development of creative writing in Africa. Good place to look for news about current authors and literary initiatives.

Additional Library Resources about African Literature

To become familiar with Africa's literary heritage, guides, literary encyclopedias, dictionaries, and overview volumes are a good starting point for initial information about authors and their works and guide to further reading:

Gikandi, Simon, ed. 2003. *Encyclopedia of African Literature.* London: Routledge. Designed for readers who either encounter African literature for the first time or who seek facts on topics, writers, and movements; includes all aspects relating to the study of African literature, ranging from historical and cultural issues affecting literature to theoretical and critical frameworks that influence interpretations.

For More Detailed Information

Columbia Guides to Literature since 1945 series. Each of these three volumes, edited by a well-known scholar of African literature, provides biographical information about authors, criticism, bibliographies, and suggestions for further readings; connects the literature of specific regions to their political and social contexts.

Cox, Brian, ed. 1997. *African Writers.* New York: Charles Scribner's Sons. Offers introductions to a variety of late nineteenth- and twentieth-century literature from Africa. Provides excellent signed entries that give an overview of a writer's life, work, and the social and historical context in which he or she writes, as well as extensive bibliographies and lists of further readings. Limited to well-known authors.

Gikandi, Simon, and Evan Mwangi, eds. 2007. *The Columbia Guide to East African Literature in English since 1945.* New York: Columbia University Press.

Moss, Joyce, and Lorraine Valestuk. 2000. *World Literature and Its Times/African Literature and Its Times: Profiles of Notable Literary Works and the Historical Events That Influenced Them.* Detroit: Thomson Gale. Introduces literary works, gives plot summaries, links the works to concrete political and historical events, identifies sources used by the author.

Owomoyela, Oyekan. 2008. *The Columbia Guide to West African Literature in English since 1945.* New York: Columbia University Press.

Roscoe, Adrian. 2008. *The Columbia Guide to Central African Literature in English since 1945.* New York: Columbia University Press.

In addition to overviews and works about individual authors, much scholarship exists on various aspects related to the study of African literature, as outlined in the "Literature in Africa" chapter. Use any of the themes identified in the chapter for keyword searches in your library's online catalog or databases such as MLA, for example:

- African literature and gender
- African literature and Islam
- African literature and colonialism
- African literature and transnationalism

African Literature on the Web

Websites about and by African authors abound. These websites offer a variety of information, such as the full text of short stories, sections of novels, biographic information, poetry, essays, and interviews. Find them by searching Google using the author's name.

Good for initial research:

Literary Map of Africa, http://library.osu.edu/literary-map-of-africa/, developed by Miriam Conteh-Morgan. One of the most comprehensive and up-to-date databases serving as a research guide; offers bio-bibliographic information on African literature. Intended as a starting point for more detailed research. Includes information on Anglophone as well as Francophone and Lusophone authors.

For more detailed information on Francophone African literature, consult Brown University's guide to online resources, which includes annotated descriptions of websites extending to areas such as music, dance, theater, and the visual arts: http://dl.lib.brown.edu/francophone.

AFRICAN FILM

Relatively few online resources treat the medium at a level that provides insights into interpretations and analyses. When researching African film, therefore, use a combination of print and electronic information.

Good Starting Point for Initial, Factual Information

Armes, Roy. 2006. *African Filmmaking North and South of the Sahara.* Bloomington: Indiana University Press. Describes the origins of cinema in Africa from a historical viewpoint, from the 1890s to the first years of the new millennium; provides comprehensive overviews of films and filmmakers and also discusses the influence of political and social events, such as Islam and colonialism, on film. Outlines the development of predominant themes in African films over time, ranging from concerns with social issues of postcolonial societies to a focus on more personal themes in recent times.

Armes, Roy. 2008. *Dictionary of African Filmmakers.* Bloomington: Indiana University Press. Divided into two parts: an alphabetical listing with 1,250 filmmakers, including information about date and place of birth, training and/or film industrial experience, other creative activities, and a list of feature films; and an alphabetical listing of the countries associated with the filmmakers as well as a chronology of the feature films. For more detailed research, supplement with:

Gugler, Josef. 2003. *African Film: Re-Imagining a Continent.* Bloomington: Indiana University Press. Detailed overview of film across the African continent by discussing selected films in chapters such as "Recovering the Past," "Fighting Colonialism," and "Betrayals of Independence." The detailed film discussions succinctly situate the films in their historical, political, and social contexts. Includes helpful, substantial bibliographies for further reading.

Russell, Sharon. 1998. *A Guide to African Cinema.* Westport, CT: Greenwood Press. In-depth discussions of individual films that seek to give a representative idea of the genre in Africa. Arranged as an alphabetical listing of filmmakers and films. Each entry is followed by a list of further readings and, where applicable, a filmography.

Thakway, Melissa. 2003. *Africa Shoots Back: Alternative Perspectives in Sub-Saharan Francophone African Film.* Bloomington: Indiana University Press. Similar to Gugler's book, connecting the genre to specific social, cultural, and political contexts, but with a focus on Francophone Africa; different from the dictionaries and overviews mentioned above, the author of this book is more selective in the films she discusses and pays particular attention to specific characteristics and themes that emerge in Francophone films.

More Recently

Dovey, Lindiwe. 2009. *African Film and Literature: Adapting Violence to the Screen.* New York: Columbia Press. Discusses how African films reflect social and political conflict in Africa, for example, in relation to HIV/AIDS or racial conflict.

African Film on the World Wide Web

"African Cinema," Wikipedia entry, http://en.wikipedia.org/wiki/African_cinema. Parts of the site are still under development; nevertheless, good for analyses and/or critical information about films, filmmakers, and directors. Provides a succinct overview of the development of the genre across Africa, in addition to fairly extensive, analytical discussions of the development of cinema in individual African countries (e.g., "Cinema of Senegal," "Cinema of Nigeria," etc.) ; also includes a section on women directors, a directory of film directors by country, a bibliography for further reading about film in Africa, and links to related websites on African film. (Remember to combine this information with information found in other resources.)

Africa South of the Sahara: African Films, Movies, and Videos, www-sul.stanford.edu/depts/ssrg/africa/film.html. Extensive coverage of African film; provides annotated list of links to a variety of web sources related to the genre.

H-AfrLitCine Discussion Network, www.h-net.org/~aflitweb. A listserv devoted to African literature and cinema; good place to follow current discussions about African film. An archive of past discussions can easily be accessed from the listserv's homepage.

AFRICAN POLITICS AND THE FUTURE OF DEMOCRACY

Literature about politics in Africa is concerned with, among other things:

- Governance
- Democracy
- Political recovery/democratic movements of the 1990s
- One-party politics as well as multiparty systems
- Structural adjustment programs
- Armed conflict in areas such as Darfur, the Democratic Republic of the Congo, Somalia, and the Niger Delta
- Ethnicity and politics

General Resources, Good for Overview Information

Mehler, Andreas, Henning Melber, and Klaas Walraven, eds. *Africa Yearbook: Politics, Economy, and Society South of the Sahara.* Leiden: Brill. Joint project by major European African studies centers. Good for factual information. Has been published yearly since 2004, and each volume focuses on developments during the year it was published. Includes country-specific articles that cover domestic politics, foreign affairs, and socioeconomic developments in the states of sub-Saharan Africa. Based on scholarly work, but specifically aims at a wider target audience of students, teachers, journalists, et cetera.

The Political Handbook of Africa 2007. 2007. Washington, DC: CQ Press. Good overview of individual African countries' political situations. Provides descriptions of each country's government and politics as well as information about the constitution, the country's foreign relations, descriptions of political parties, the legislature, the press, and so forth.

Combine overviews with more in-depth analyses in books and articles, many of them available online:

Council for the Development of Social Science Research in Africa (CODESRIA), www .codesria.org/?lang=en. Headquartered in Dakar, Senegal. Provides free, open access to books on politics, although its list of publications is not as extensive as that of the HSRC. Good place to find well-researched books that shed light on various political issues from an African perspective.

Human Science Research Council (HSRC), www.hsrcpress.ac.za/home.php. Nonprofit, open-access publisher based in South Africa; members of the academic community are on its editorial board. Makes publications freely available on its website. Excellent source for well-researched publications. Publications listed under the category "Politics and International Relations" include research on most of the issues outlined above, most

notably renowned scholar Mahmood Mamdani's recent book on the Darfur crisis *(Saviours and Survivors: Darfur, Politics, and the War on Terror)*.
Nordic Africa Institute, www.nai.uu.se. One of the premier research institutes on Africa in Europe, based in Uppsala, Sweden. Extensive website with free access to full-text policy papers, political studies, and development papers, all of them in PDF format.

Remember to consult the books at the end of the chapter "African Politics and the Future of Democracy."

Keep in mind that in addition to research institutes, numerous nongovernmental and international organizations also make a wealth of information available online. Among them:

The African Union, www.au.int/en/. Union of fifty-four African states established to promote and defend African common positions, to promote good governance, human rights, and democracy, and to promote peace and security in Africa. Website includes full-text documents, speeches, news, and discussion forums as well as useful links.
Sub-Saharan Governments Search Engine, www.google.com/cse/home?cx=004216246918 580239447:kzrbc4uvlna. Search engine that retrieves websites of African governments. Useful results can be obtained by using either a country's name or language(s) as search terms.
The World Bank, UNESCO, UNICEF, and UNDP all offer a vast amount of information, which can be found either by going directly to the organization's website or by searching www.unsystem.org, the official UN web site locator, which allows searches across all UN-affiliated organizations and is an efficient way to locate documents.

Raw Data and Datasets

African Elections Database, 2004–2011, http://africanelections.tripod.com/index.html. Archive of past and present election results for African countries. Also includes political profiles for each country as well as information on political parties.
Afrobarometer, www.afrobarometer.org. Survey center based at Michigan State University. Designed to measure the social, political, and economic atmosphere in Africa. Available are four rounds of public opinion data collected since 1999. Round five is currently being conducted. The site also includes full-text working papers.

Specifically of interest:

Bratton, Michael, E. Gyimah-Boadi, and Robert Mattes. *Afrobarometer 2008–2009*. 2010. East Lansing, MI: Afrobarometer.
Polity IV, www.systemicpeace.org/polity/polity4.htm. Measures democracy in every African country annually. Used as an indicator for democracy.

DEVELOPMENT IN AFRICA: TEMPERED HOPE

Development literature includes:

* Official documents of international and nongovernmental aid organizations
* Surveys
* Overviews
* Statistics
* Responses and analyses to official documents by influential organizations, such as the World Bank
* Case studies by scholars in various disciplines

Good Introduction

Joseph, Richard, and Alexandra Gillies, eds. 2009. *Smart Aid for African Development.* Boulder, CO: Lynne Rienner. Provides and analyzes perspectives on aid.
Moss, Todd J. 2007. *African Development: Making Sense of the Issues and Actors.* Boulder, CO: Lynne Rienner.

Consider these two websites as excellent starting points with links to enormous amounts of information ranging from websites of nongovernmental and international organizations to full-text research papers, reports on development projects, policy papers, and books. Focus is on economic aspects of development, but both websites include information on related issues, such as women in development, the environment, the African Virtual University, wildlife conservation, and others:

Africa South of the Sahara's section on development, www-sul.stanford.edu/depts/ssrg /africa/devel.html.
Economic Development, Education, and Environmental Affairs, on Columbia University Libraries' African Studies Internet Resources—Virtual Library, http://library.columbia .edu/locations/global/virtual-libraries/african_studies/intlorgs/economic_development .html.

Also of Interest

Human Development Report. 1990–. New York: Oxford University Press for the United Nations Development Programme. Issued annually. Also online at http://hdr.undp.org/en /reports/global/hdr2013. Takes issues such as human rights, cultural liberty, climate change, gender, and democracy into account and does not automatically assume a connection between economic and human development. For example, titles include:
New Dimensions in Human Security
Overcoming Barriers: Human Mobility and Development
People's Participation
Sustainability and Equity: A Better Future for All

UN Statistical Database, http://unstats.un.org/unsd/databases.htm. Statistical database that covers the entire UN system. Use this database to search across UN websites for information on topics such as trade statistics, census information, demographics, and others.

Many organizations make their data and reports available on the internet.

The World Bank, www.worldbank.org. Has been strongly involved with economic development in Africa for many years and has been instrumental in implementing the controversial structural adjustment programs. Website provides large amounts of full-text information. Includes statistics, reports about specific aid projects, information on business in Africa and on indigenous knowledge, and annual reports of World Bank activities in Africa. Website has a search engine and is keyword-searchable. Of particular interest:

World Bank Data by Country, http://data.worldbank.org/country. Provides country-specific data.
World Development Indicators, http://databank.worldbank.org/ddp/home.do?Step=12& id=4&CNO=2. Statistics on education, the environment, economic policy, health, infrastructure, poverty.

World Bank and International Monetary Fund (IMF) initiatives, most notably the World Bank's structural adjustment programs, have been controversial, and alternative plans and responses exist:

The Bretton Woods Project, www.brettonwoodsproject.org. Good place to find up-to-date comments on World Bank and IMF initiatives, with reports and briefings that can be searched by keyword and specific countries. Aim of the project is to work as an "information provider, media informant and watchdog to scrutinize and influence the World Bank and International Monetary Fund."
Herbert, Ross, and Steven Gruzd. 2008. *The African Peer Review Mechanism: Lessons from the Pioneers.* Johannesburg: South African Institute of International Affairs. A new approach to improving governance, applied more recently by several African countries, is the peer review process. This in-depth study analyzes the evolving peer review process in the five African countries where it was first applied (Ghana, Kenya, Rwanda, Mauritius, and South Africa).

Find more information on websites of nongovernmental and international organizations:

The New Partnership for Africa's Development (NEPAD), www.nepad.org. NEPAD is an economic development program of the African Union. The website provides access to the full text of documents on such topics as agriculture and food security, human development, climate change, natural resource management, and economic and corporate governance. It also includes a section on news and a blog.
Southern African Development Community (SADC), www.sadc.int. Includes information on the work of SADC and the full text of key documents, such as SADC's Protocol on Energy, Protocol on Wildlife Conservation and Law Enforcement, Protocol on Trade.

Keep in Mind

The sources listed here focus mostly on economic development. However, development can be measured and evaluated in various ways, depending on the perspective of one's analysis. Other aspects related to development:

• Political, social, and cultural development
• The quality of a society's environment
• Access to sanitation
• Education
• The number of women in government

These factors are addressed in more detail in the sections on geography, politics, human rights, and social relations and livelihoods.

Also of Interest

In recent years, China's involvement with Africa has steadily increased, with impacts in political, economic, and cultural areas. There is now a burgeoning literature reflecting these developments.

"China and Africa: Emerging Patterns in Globalization and Development." Special issue of *China Quarterly,* vol. 199, 2009. Provides a good introduction to this angle of research from a development perspective.

HUMAN RIGHTS IN AFRICA

Discourse about human rights extends into a wide range of areas and includes discussions and analyses of:

• Physical abuses of individuals
• State repression
• The treatment of children
• Women's rights
• Refugees
• Academic and intellectual freedom
• Issues of censorship
• Inter-African relations

The literature on human rights in Africa reflects the complexity of these frameworks.

Good for Overview Information

Akokpri, John, and Daniel Shea Zimbler, eds. 2008. *Africa's Human Rights Architecture.* Auckland Park, South Africa: Fanele. Discusses the development of human rights frameworks in Africa since the end of the Cold War. Also analyzes human rights institutions and their work in Africa.

Lawrence, James T., ed. 2004. *Human Rights in Africa.* New York: Nova Science Publishers. Provides brief one-to-two-page country surveys, and offers bibliographies for more detailed information about each country.

Human Rights Treaties and Related Documents

African Commission on Human and Peoples' Rights, African Charter on Human and Peoples' Rights (also known as the Banjul Charter). Multiple references. Search Banjul Charter. Intended to promote and protect human rights and basic freedoms on the African continent.

Protocol to the African Charter on Human and Peoples' Rights on the Rights of Women in Africa. A supplement that focuses specifically on women's rights.

United Nations Office of the High Commissioner for Human Rights, Universal Declaration of Human Rights, www.ohchr.org/EN/UDHR/Pages/Introduction.aspx. Proclaimed on December 10, 1948, this document declares fundamental human rights to be universally protected.

The University of Minnesota Human Rights Library, www1.umn.edu/humanrts. One of the largest collections on this topic, including more than sixty thousand human rights documents. Also has a section on African human rights resources: www1.umn.edu/humanrts /africa/index.html.

Sources on Different Aspects of Human Rights in Africa

CHILDREN'S RIGHTS

Children in Africa, web dossier, compiled by the Library, Documentation and Information Department of the African Studies Centre at Leiden University (September 2008). While not all sources listed here link to full text , this dossier provides information about publications on children in Africa, focusing on themes such as children and society, children and law, children's rights, children and war, children and work, street children, children and health, orphanhood, and other topics. Also includes web resources. Use this as a bibliography of sources to be looked for in your library's online catalog.

WOMEN'S RIGHTS

Femnet—African Women's Development and Communication Network, http://femnet.co /index.php/en. Includes publications, online reports, and other information related to women's rights in Africa.

Urgent Action Fund, http://urgentactionfund-africa.or.ke/. Pan-African women's human rights organization; website has reports and other publications.

SEXUAL RIGHTS

Zia, Adilili, and Billy Kahora, eds. 2007. *Sex Matters*. Nairobi: Urgent Action Fund. Available at www.urgentactionfund-africa.or.ke/pdfs/Sex%20Matters.pdf. Provides access to reports and papers on women's rights, gay and lesbian rights, the rights of commercial sex workers, et cetera. Based on a conference on sexual rights within the context of human rights that took place in Kenya.

CENSORSHIP AND FREEDOM OF SPEECH

Article 19, the International Centre Against Censorship, www.article19.org. International human rights organization dedicated to freedom of expression. Article 19 also works on African media freedom issues.

Index on Censorship, www.indexoncensorship.org. Organization that promotes freedom of expression. Extensive website providing up-to-date information on violations of free expression around the world. Also includes a blog and a magazine.

Keep in mind that many organizations focused on defending human rights publish reports and analyses, including:

African Centre for Democracy and Human Rights Studies, www.acdhrs.org. An international NGO established to support the AU's African Charter on Human and Peoples' Rights. Website includes full-text documents, posters, reports, and so forth.

Amnesty International, www.amnesty.org. Click on a country to see reports by country as well as annual reports.

Human Rights Watch Africa, www.hrw.org/en/africa. Independent organization dedicated to defending and protecting human rights. Extensive website which includes news on current human rights abuses, full-text reports and other publications, as well as a newsletter.

EVALUATING ONLINE RESOURCES

While it has always been an integral part of any research project to evaluate the sources to be considered for a paper, the growth of digital information technology has raised the need for evaluation and assessment to a new level. Considering the sheer amount of information on the internet and the ease with which it can be posted, careful evaluation of the information one encounters is essential. Many of the same criteria one would apply when assessing a print resource are relevant for online resources as well, although in many instances on a different scale.

A Few Tips

- Many college and university libraries have websites with helpful tips on how to evaluate internet resources.
- Africa South of the Sahara, www-sul.stanford.edu/depts/ssrg/africa/guide .html, includes a link to "Evaluating Web Resources," www-sul.stanford.edu

/depts/ssrg/africa/evalu.html, which provides access to online articles discussing evaluation strategies.
- Particularly helpful is "Evaluating Internet Research Sources," by Robert Harris, Nov. 22. 2010, www.virtualsalt.com/evalu8it.htm. In this article, the author discusses:
  - The differences between various forms of information (i.e., facts, opinions, stories, interpretations, statistics)
  - How to look for information on websites' authors (including title, position, organizational affiliation), date of publication/website creation, and author's contact information
  - Evidence of quality control or peer review
  - Credibility and signs of lack of credibility (anonymity, lack of quality control, bad grammar, misspelled words)
  - Accuracy and currency of a website
  - Comprehensiveness of information
  - Objectivity, fairness
  - Worldview of author
  - Source documentation

Remember:

- If you use another person's thoughts, ideas, expressions, or images, you need to credit that author for his or her original work. Failure to do so is considered plagiarism.
- As you document the sources of information you use in your papers, apply a citation style consistently. Copies of major style manuals, such as the APA (American Psychological Association) manual, the MLA (Modern Language Association) manual, or *The Chicago Manual of Style,* are available in every library. *The Chicago Manual of Style* exists in electronic format, and many libraries provide access to that version. Be sure to ask your instructor which style to use.

Contributors

John Akare Aden is a historian of Africa and executive director of the Fort Wayne African/African American History Museum and Society. He has conducted research in Mali on the history of Bamana blacksmiths and taught African history courses at several institutions.

Akin Adesokan is a novelist and associate professor of comparative literature at Indiana University, Bloomington. His research interests are in twentieth- and twenty-first-century African and African American/African diaspora literatures and cultures, global postcoloniality, African cinema and contemporary global cinemas, nonfiction prose, and cultural theory.

Gracia Clark is professor in the Department of Anthropology at Indiana University. Her work with traders in Kumasi Central Market started in 1978 and ranges from life histories through credit, women's leadership, food security, commercial policy, marriage, and religion.

James Delehanty is a geographer and associate director of the African Studies Program at the University of Wisconsin–Madison. His research has concentrated on the historical geography of the Sahel, with particular attention to agricultural expansion in twentieth-century Niger; land tenure in West Africa and Central Asia; and the social and environmental contexts of livestock disease control in East Africa, especially Kenya.

Marion Frank-Wilson is the librarian for African studies and head of the Wells Library's Area Studies Department at Indiana University, with research interests in the intersections of open access publishing, scholarly communication, and collection development.

Maria Grosz-Ngaté is an anthropologist and associate director of the African Studies Program at Indiana University. She has conducted long-term research in Mali and Senegal with a focus on rural social transformations, gender, and Islam.

Karen Tranberg Hansen is professor emerita at Northwestern University, where she taught in the Department of Anthropology and the Program of African Studies. She is an urban and economic anthropologist whose research focuses on the informal economy, markets, trade, consumption, gender, and youth.

John H. Hanson is associate professor of history at Indiana University and an editor of *History in Africa*. His research concerns the history of West African Muslim communities during the past two hundred years, with books and articles concerning Tijaniyya Sufism in late nineteenth-century Senegal and Mali, Ahmadiyya Muslim proselytism in twentieth-century Gold Coast/Ghana, Arabic texts and translation, and West African Muslim engagements with modernity.

Carolyn E. Holmes is a doctoral candidate in the Department of Political Science at Indiana University. Her research examines the creation and consolidation of national identities and sustainable democracy in postconflict societies such as South Africa.

Eileen Julien is professor of comparative literature and French and Italian at Indiana University. She studies the connections between Africa, Europe, and the Americas, including the relationship between local African resources, such as oral traditions, and contemporary global forms such as the novel.

Tracy J. Luedke is associate professor of anthropology and coordinator of the Global Studies Program at Northeastern Illinois University. She has a long-standing research project on healing, religion, and politics in Mozambique and has recently begun a new project on the work lives of Chicago taxi drivers.

Lauren M. MacLean is associate professor in the Department of Political Science at Indiana University. MacLean's research interests focus on the politics of state formation, social welfare, and citizenship in Côte d'Ivoire, Ghana, and Kenya, as well as in American Indian/Alaska Native communities in the United States.

Takyiwaa Manuh recently retired as professor of African studies at the University of Ghana, Legon, where she was also director of the Institute of African Studies. Her research interests are in the areas of African development, gender, migration, and higher education in Africa.

Patrick McNaughton is Chancellor's Professor of Art History at Indiana University. His research interests include the roles and social clout of artists, the history of metalwork in West Africa, the power of form and the nature of aesthetics, the construction of meaning in visual culture, and the mobility of art forms across geographic and cultural space.

Raymond Muhula is with the Poverty Reduction and Economic Management Unit of the World Bank, where he works on a wide range of development issues around public sector management, especially in Liberia, Nigeria, and The Gambia. He obtained his PhD in political science from Howard University.

Stephen N. Ndegwa is advisor at the World Bank's Global Center on Conflict, Security and Development, based in Nairobi, Kenya. He was previously associate professor of government at the College of William and Mary and a Rice Family Fellow at Yale University.

Patrick O'Meara is special advisor to the Indiana University president, vice president emeritus, and professor of public and environmental affairs and political science. He was the co-editor of all previous editions of *Africa*. His interests include South African politics and international development.

Diane Pelrine is the Raymond and Laura Wielgus Curator of the Arts of Africa, Oceania, and the Americas at the Indiana University Art Museum. In addition to research connected with the museum's permanent collection of African art, she is especially interested in textiles, ceramics, and issues connected with the collecting and display of African art.

Daniel B. Reed is associate professor of folklore and ethnomusicology at Indiana University. His research has centered in West Africa, especially Côte d'Ivoire, and his areas of specialty include music and identity, mask performance, music and immigration, and HIV/AIDS and popular music.

Amos Sawyer is a political scientist with a PhD from Northwestern University and a recipient of the 2011 Gusi Peace Prize. He was the President of the Interim Government of National Unity in Liberia from 1990 to 1994, is currently chair of the Governance Commission of Liberia, and was chair of the African Union's Panel of Eminent Persons.

Ruth M. Stone is the Laura Boulton Professor and associate vice provost for research at Indiana University. Her research focuses on the study of musical performance among the Kpelle in Liberia, West Africa, particularly issues of spatial and temporal conceptualization.

Katherine Wiley is a postdoctoral fellow at the Carter G. Woodson Institute for African-American and African Studies at the University of Virginia. Her research interests include economic anthropology, work, gender, Islam, social status, dress, and humor with a focus on the Islamic Republic of Mauritania.

Index